Also by Allan R. May

Mob Stories
Gangland Gotham
Welcome to the Jungle Inn
Crimetown U.S.A.

The
Sly-Fanner
Murders

The Birth of the Mayfield Road Mob; Cleveland's Most Notorious Mafia Gang

Allan R. May

ConAllan Press, Cleveland, OH

Published by ConAllan Press, LLC
Cleveland, Ohio, USA

Library of Congress Cataloging-in-Publication Data

May, Allan R.
The Sly-Fanner Murders: The Birth of the Mayfield Road Mob;
Cleveland's Most Notorious Mafia Gang / by Allan R. May. – 1st ed.
p. cm.
Includes bibliographical reference and index.
ISBN - 13: 978-0-9837037-4-7
LCCN 2013939194

1. Mafia—Ohio—Cuyahoga County—History
2. Cleveland—Ohio—Biography
3. Gangsters—Cleveland—Biography
4. Organized Crime—Cleveland—Cuyahoga County—Ohio
5. Police—Cleveland—History
6. Murders—Cleveland—Ohio—Biography

Cover art by Lynn Bycko, Commoner Company
Design work by Connie May

First published 2014

This book is dedicated to

Lynn Duchez Bycko

Cleveland State University Library – Special Collections

Your counsel, friendship, generosity, kindness, support and technical
assistance have been invaluable all these years.
I could not have gotten to this point without you!

Table of Contents

"The Cleveland Police never gave up!"

What a fitting statement to describe this book.

The story of the Sly-Fanner Murders is a departure from what I have written in the past. While it is still about organized crime, in this case the birth and early years of Cleveland's notorious Mayfield Road Mob, its focus is a single event as opposed to a chronological history like *Welcome to the Jungle Inn* and *Crimetown U.S.A.* or a strict biographical work like *Gangland Gotham*.

The story of the murders of Wilfred Sly and George Fanner, two Cleveland businessmen slaughtered during the course of a payroll robbery gone terribly wrong, has been written about as a short-story by former local writer John Stark Bellamy and touched upon by my friend and fellow organized crime writer Rick Porrello in his book *The Rise and Fall of the Cleveland Mafia*. What makes my rendition different is that it gives a graphic overall view of what was going on in the city at that time.

In this post-World War era, one year into national Prohibition, some of the most infamous crimes ever perpetrated in this city took place in this brief time-span. During this period seven Cleveland Police officers were murdered on the streets. After the Sly-Fanner murders, on New Year's Eve 1920, a vicious crime spree shook the city and lasted for months, costing the lives of other innocent residents. Most of these crimes had nothing to do with the national crime-wave of bootlegging and rum-running, which was just beginning to take hold in America.

Into this period of incredible lawlessness stepped Edward Stanton, the newly elected Cuyahoga County Prosecutor. The young prosecutor would handle more notorious murder cases in his early years than most prosecutors would handle in a career. Also coming into the lime light was another prosecuting attorney, Frank J. Merrick, whose work would shed light on a local group of Italian criminals who would become famous during the Prohibition Era in Cleveland as the Mayfield Road Mob.

Merrick singlehandedly, through his work and later his writing, traced the origins of the gang and its initial leadership, beginning as an automobile theft ring, known as the Serra Gang. While most Cleveland crime historians associate "Big Joe" Lonardo as the early Mafia boss and Frank Milano as the first leader of the Mayfield Road Mob, Merrick informs us that Dominic Benigno "might be called Cleveland's first racketeer. Gangs had existed before his time: daring holdup men had terrorized the town before he was born and sleek-looking gentry had been known in police circles as far back as the Civil War. It remained, however, for Dominic Benigno to 'incorporate' crime."

We will never know if Benigno was an initiated member of the "honored society," the Mafia; but there's no question that he was the first leader of the Mayfield Road Mob and that members who survived the Sly-Fanner prosecutions went on to participate in the gang's dominance of organized crime in the city through the Prohibition years and up to 1939 when the notorious gang finally came to a finish with the help of famed law enforcement official Eliot Ness.

The three people who made the most significant personal contributions to this project were Lynn Duchez Bycko (to whom this book is dedicated), Charles R. Molino (this goes without saying) and my wife, Connie (who designed the book). Lynn was the key person in helping me to self-publish *Welcome to the Jungle Inn* and *Crimetown U.S.A.* For more than a decade Lynn has served as an advisor, counselor and therapist to me, and has become one of my best friends.

A special thank you to Michael Rini for supplying so much background information on the characters in this book. Michael was an endless source of information and I hope I'm able to work with him on future projects. Thank you also to John Dunn, for his technical expertise and guidance on book layout and marketing, and to Steph Barnick for sharing her talent with the creation of promotional tools. Other contributors were Ryan Jaenke and Michelle Makkos, from the Cleveland Public Library; Ric Consiglio, Ashtabula Public Library; and Ellen Sol, Rodman Public Library in Alliance, Ohio.

Of course, I want to thank the following friends and supporters who helped get me through my day: Jimmy Barber, Tommy Canitia, John Chechitelli, Patrick Downey, Abby Goldberg, Robert Gross, Jerry Kovar, Tom Leahy, Frank Monastra, Biagio Morgano, John Murray, David Pastor, Robin Stekkinger, James Trueman, Jan Vaughn, Charlotte Versagi and Fred Wolking. And a special thanks to family members: "Ma" Scurec, Tammy Cabot, Maggie and Richard May, Gary May, and the Vaciks – Nelda, Bob, Melanie and Robbie.

Opening
New Year's Eve 1920

On December 31, 1920, the country was about to face its first dry New Year's Eve since the Volstead Act went into effect the previous January. Prohibition was now the law of the land. After decades of effort the 18th Amendment to the United States Constitution had finally outlawed the manufacture, sale and transportation of alcoholic beverages. It was not a popular law.

On this day in Washington D.C. certain members of Congress were stewing over the cost of the upcoming presidential inauguration of Ohioan Warren G. Harding. Dispatches out of Marion, Ohio, where Harding resided, were promoting the gala as "the most dazzling celebration within the memory of the present generation." The price tag on the festivities was expected to top $100,000. Harding seemed to carry on this "dazzling celebration" well into his presidency, rewarding friends and political supporters and creating the scandalous and corrupt "Ohio Gang."

The sports world was celebrating the doubles victory by William T. Tilden and William K. Johnson over their Australian opponents to win the Davis Lawn Tennis Cup in Auckland, New Zealand. The Davis Cup was returning to the United States for the first time since 1914. No international matches were held between the years 1914 and 1919 due to the First World War.

In entertainment news, the *New York Times* was reporting that world renowned tenor Enrico Caruso was seriously ill with pleurisy. The singer had surgery the day before for removal of an infection from his lungs, known as empyema. Caruso was removed from the hospital to a suite at the Hotel Vanderbilt in Manhattan, where he was under the care of six physicians. The most famous Metropolitan opera singer of all-time battled health issues for another seven months before passing away on August 2 at the age of 48.

In Cleveland on this Friday, New Year's Eve morning it was 30 degrees, with a slight warm-up predicted along with the threat of rain showers for the evening. The city was anxiously awaiting the verdict in the highly publicized trial of Judge William H. McGannon for the murder of automobile mechanic Harold Kagy.

On Cleveland's near-west side, the top priority of businessmen Wilfred Sly and George Fanner this morning was a trip downtown to the First National Bank to pick up the payroll of the W.W. Sly Manufacturing

Company. It was to be a short workday for Sly, as he planned to return home and help his wife Marie with the final preparations for their annual New Year's Eve masquerade ball.

Around mid-morning the two men left the Train Avenue manufacturing facility and headed downtown. At the bank, the men picked up the modest payroll of $4,200 and after wishing the payroll clerk a Happy New Year's, the men returned to Sly's automobile for the trip back to Train Avenue. Their return trip took them back over the same roads they had traveled many times before. At the corner of Lorain and West 25th Street they passed the West Side Market, where vendors were busy with shoppers preparing for the festive holiday weekend. At West 47th Street Sly guided the big car south toward the plant just minutes away.

They soon arrived at the rickety, wooden railroad bridge. It was approximately 11:00 a.m. and the plant was in view, only a block away. The old bridge crested in the middle and the vehicle was descending down the southern half when fate pulled alongside the men in the form of a Stearns automobile. The vehicle belonged to Frederick H. Goff, president of the Cleveland Trust Company. Unfortunately, it was not Goff behind the wheel. His car was stolen the night before from in front of the Cleveland Trust Company at East 9th and Euclid Avenue. False tags were wired over the real plates. Inside were two men.

The Stearns swerved wildly, cutting off Sly's automobile, forcing him to slam on his breaks and steer the car into the wooden railing of the bridge. As the vehicle hit the railing it splintered creating a terrific noise, and for a moment it looked as if the automobile might plunge over the side and onto the railroad tracks some fifteen feet below. The loud collision brought a number of bystanders – children and adults – racing to the scene. Just seconds after the crash a Jordan automobile containing four men appeared at the north end of the bridge. Three men alighted from the car and walked toward the accident, while the driver remained behind the wheel.

Sly got out of his automobile to confront the young man who had cut him off. Angry accusations flew as one blamed the other for the mishap. Fanner got out to see what he could do, but a moment later noticed one of the men had reached into the car grabbing the satchel containing the company payroll. When Fanner protested the man pulled a gun from his pocket and shot him in the face, killing him instantly. Sly, although armed, didn't have a chance to react. He was shot twice in the head and once in the abdomen and died on the rickety bridge. While the bystanders watched in horror, the gunmen raced off in the direction of the Jordan and escaped.

There would be no annual masquerade ball at the Sly residence this New Year's Eve.

Part I

Lay of the Land

1
Meet Eddie Stanton

In 1920, Cleveland, with its population of 796,841, ranked as the fifth largest city in the United States – surpassed by New York, Chicago, Philadelphia and Detroit. During the second half of the 19th Century, Cleveland was the home of opulent wealth, headed by none other than John D. Rockefeller the richest man in America and the founder of the Standard Oil Company. Cleveland was also home to a number of other wealthy businessmen, who built their beautiful spacious mansions on a stretch of Euclid Avenue, which became known as "Millionaires' Row." Neighbors and friends in life, many shared the same final resting place in Lake View Cemetery in Section 10, an area also dubbed "Millionaires' Row."

In looking back at pictures of the city's rich history one could easily be led to believe that everyone lived the good life. This truly wasn't the case. In 1996, during Cleveland's bi-centennial celebration, a time capsule one century old was opened. The ladies of Cleveland from 1896 wrote:

> "We of today reach forth our hands across the gulf of a hundred years to clasp your hands. We make you heirs to all we have, and enjoin you to improve your heritage. We bequeath to you a city of a century; prosperous and beautiful and yet far from our ideal. Some of our streets are not well lighted; some are unpaved; many are unclean. Many of the people are poor and some are vainly seeking work at living wages. Often they, who have employment, are forced to filch hours for work from the hours that should be given to rest, recreation and study. Some of our children are robbed of their childhood. Vice parades our streets and disease lurks in many places that men and women call their homes. It sometimes happens that wealth usurps the throne that worth alone should occupy. Sometimes some of the reins of government slip from the hands of the people and public honors ill fit some who wear them. We are obliged to confess that even now.
>
> "Man's inhumanity to man makes countless thousands mourn.
>
> "How are these things with you?"

"Things" weren't so well with Eddie Stanton. On his first day as the new Cuyahoga County Prosecutor, January 1, 1921, he was getting tossed into the ring amid several high profile murder cases. But, have no doubt about it, crime in Cleveland was about to get remarkably worse.

Edward Cornelius Stanton was born April 2, 1888, on Cleveland's West Side in a neighborhood called the "Angle." Growing up in the city's 8th Ward, an area known as the "Irish Eighth," he attended St. Malachi School, St. Ignatius High School and then St. Ignatius College.[1] Although small and wiry in build, he developed a reputation as an athlete during his teenage years. His first job was working as a timekeeper on the Cleveland ore docks. He did this to supplement the family's income, which consisted of his father's $1.50-a-day job pushing a wheelbarrow loaded with iron ore around the docks, and his mother's running of the family grocery store on Washington Avenue, on the west side of the Cuyahoga River, just down from the Stanton home.

At the age of fourteen Stanton attended a political meeting of Cleveland City Councilman, Bernard "Brick" Masterson, of the Eighth Ward. Held in a tent, Masterson's fiery rhetoric inspired the young man and Stanton left the meeting determined to study law and engage the world of politics. Stanton studied law three nights a week at Cleveland Law School,[2] and clerked by day in the county auditor's office.

In 1913, Stanton passed the bar exam and began work in the county prosecutor's office. Two years later he was appointed an assistant police prosecutor by then law director William S. Fitzgerald, during the first term of Harry L. Davis's mayoralty. As a young prosecutor Stanton developed a reputation for his courtroom demeanor. He moved up the ladder to become chief assistant in the Cuyahoga County Prosecutor's office under Samuel Doerfler. Then in 1920, Cuyahoga County Republican boss Maurice Maschke, sensing a Republican landslide in the county, looked around for a bright talent to run for county prosecutor. Although only 32 years old, Stanton was the man recommended to Maschke. In November 1920, Stanton defeated Elden J. Hopple* 127,000 to 93,000 at the polls and was on his way to an eight-year run as Cuyahoga County Prosecutor.

The "Boy Wonder," as he became known, had his hands full. Three prominent murder cases were dominating the news around the time Stanton was elected, In addition, a double slaying took place the day before Stanton was sworn in – the Sly-Fanner murders. The other blockbuster cases involved George "Jiggs" Losteiner, Dan Kaber and William H. McGannon:

George "Jiggs' Losteiner

Writer John Stark Bellamy II, the city's true expert on "the foulest crimes and worst disasters in Cleveland history," wrote of George "Jiggs" Losteiner, "He was the baddest man of Roaring-Twenties Cleveland, and it speaks poorly for the civic pride of our Forest City that this truly satanic criminal is virtually forgotten today. He was violent, depraved, trigger-happy, and a life-long 'career criminal' before the term was even conceived."

Losteiner was just 15 years-old when he was arrested for the first time on a charge of purse-snatching. He received a 30-day stretch in the Warrensville Workhouse and was fined $50. Between 1905 and 1915 his record showed arrests and convictions for "larceny, highway robbery, parole violations, burglary, armed robbery, concealed weapons," and various other felonies and misdemeanors.

Losteiner's criminal career took a turn for the worse on August 3, 1918. He and another notorious Cleveland hood, John Grogan, donned Cleveland police uniforms and robbed a Walker Manufacturing Company official of a payroll totaling $22,834 near Taft Avenue and East 131st Street. During their escape the two were stopped at Richmond and Mayfield Roads in Lyndhurst, a suburb located east of the city, where a shootout with local police officers occurred. Two policemen, Edgar H. Smith and Perry Smith (no relation) were both wounded, the latter taking a bullet in the left eye. Grogan and Losteiner escaped, but not before abandoning the loot in the process.

Grogan and Losteiner laid low, but rented a garage at 14905 Elm Street in the suburb of East Cleveland. The owner became suspicious when he noticed the pair only came at night to use the car they kept there and he reported this to the local police. On December 19, 1918, two East Cleveland officers, Captain Patrick Hendricks and Patrolman Patrick Gaffney, arrived to investigate. As fate would have it, Grogan and Losteiner happened by. Confronting the unsuspecting officers, Losteiner fired point blank into Gaffney's side and he dropped to the ground. An estimated seventeen bullets were fired during the exchange. All four men were wounded in the shootout – Grogan taking one in the back; Losteiner a slug in each leg; Hendricks had a flashlight in his back pocket which when hit sent a shard of glass into his leg. Gaffney was rushed to East Cleveland Hospital with a bullet lodged in his right lung. He died there Christmas Day morning from complications. The officer left behind a wife and four children.

The two gunmen made their way to Carnegie Avenue Hospital, at 8714 Carnegie Avenue, where they threatened to kill a physician if he didn't treat them. The doctor removed slugs from both men. While Grogan demanded the return of the piece of lead pulled out of his back, Losteiner unwisely left his behind.

A mere 24 days passed before the duo struck again. This time it was at the General Baking Company on East 35th Street. Leading a half-dozen gunmen, the gang blew a safe with nitroglycerine after tying up two employees. The heist earned the men $4,000 in cash and $500 in Liberty bonds before they escaped in the taxicab which brought them to the location and waited for them to leave.

On February 9, 1919, a railroad detective in Martins Ferry, Ohio (a small town along the Ohio River just across the border from Wheeling, West Virginia) notified Cleveland police of John Grogan's presence there. A flying squad of Cleveland police officers led by Chief Frank W. Smith – which included Inspector Charles Sterling, Deputy Inspector Jacob Graul and Detective Phil Mooney – arrived and found Grogan in bed with a girlfriend. Arrested and returned to Cleveland, Grogan pleaded guilty to manslaughter in the death of Gaffney and was sentenced to life in the Ohio Penitentiary. A key piece of evidence at the trial was the .38 slug recovered from Losteiner's leg.

With Grogan behind bars, Losteiner partnered up with another criminal on the rise, Albert "Killer" Johnson. It was alleged that Johnson had killed two men in his career, the details lost to history. Johnson had one claim to fame, however, that he most likely never knew about during his lifetime – he was the only man New York City underworld big shot Arnold Rothstein ever admitted to being afraid of.

On May 16, 1917, Rothstein, known as the "Big Bankroll," was in a high-stakes card game at the Hotel St. Francis in Manhattan. That spring several of these floating card games were held up and Rothstein was sure one of his fellow gamblers was setting up the players. Around 2:00 a.m. four masked gunmen entered the suite. Rothstein dropped his bankroll, estimated at between $20,000 and $60,000, on the floor and kicked it under a carpet; still, he lost $2,600 in cash, along with a gold watch and a pearl stickpin. A friend at the card game goaded Rothstein into going to the police, who arrested Johnson a few days later. In court, Rothstein testified and Johnson was convicted and sentenced to Sing Sing. The enraged killer swore revenge on Rothstein and two months later escaped.

Johnson headed back to Manhattan to make good on his threat. Rothstein, on high-alert, was able to steer clear of becoming the third notch on Johnson's gun before the fugitive left the city for the Mid-West. Years later in a book written by his widow Carolyn Rothstein, she revealed that she confronted her husband about being afraid of Johnson. "I'm afraid, all right. There are only two people who know that, though. You and me. We're the only two people in the world I trust enough to let them know it."

John Bellamy informs us, "Johnson was quite the dapper felon, known throughout the underworld for his 'nifty' wardrobe, smooth manners, and taste for polite society. His sophisticated exterior, moreover, concealed the fact that at the age of 31, he had spent half of his life in prison." In December 1919 he killed an innocent bystander during a gun battle with police in

Toledo, Ohio. While he was being held for trial in the Lucas County Jail on Christmas Day 1919, six gunmen entered and freed him, wounding a deputy sheriff in the process.

While Johnson was on the run, he teamed with Losteiner in the robbery of the Nottingham Savings & Building Company at 13627 St. Clair Avenue, getting $10,000 in cash and bonds. The Losteiner-Johnson gang was now getting bolder. On June 18, 1920 they robbed the First National Bank of Chagrin Falls at 10:00 o'clock in the morning. Two of the robbers fired shots to get the undivided attention of the cashier. Unfortunately, the shots also got the attention of Aaron R. Chance, a 70 year-old salesman who lived in an apartment above the bank. Chance went downstairs to investigate.

"What's going on here," Chance demanded, coming through the door.

"Get back there or we'll show you!" Losteiner answered.

Chance started to back away, but apparently not fast enough for the sadistic "Jiggs." Complaining, "You move too slowly, old man," Losteiner sent a bullet crashing into the man's left leg. Chance fell to the sidewalk, bleeding profusely from the wound. He died a week later in Carnegie Avenue Hospital.

Between June 23 and October 5, 1920, "Jiggs" and Albert Johnson were reputed to be involved in bank robberies in Highland Park, Michigan, Detroit, Toledo and De Pew, New York. On Thursday morning, October 21, they pulled their last and most famous bank job. On that fateful morning, six to eight men got into a stolen Cadillac in Cleveland's Public Square. With Albert Johnson at the wheel, the crew which included Orville Taylor, a 23 year-old who had already put a year in at the Mansfield Reformatory,[3] headed to the Bedford branch of the Cleveland Trust Bank. At 2:40 p.m. the gang reached the suburb of Bedford, located southeast of the city. Johnson remained outside with the car, armed with a shotgun, while the others entered the bank.

The robbery took place just minutes before the 3:00 p.m. closing time when there were few customers. While the robbers terrorized the bank manager inside, a shot was heard outside the bank. Two people had observed the men enter the bank and seeing the armed Johnson outside, they quickly figured out what was happening. The citizens of Bedford were prepared for such an event and were soon armed and on the move. Elvor Porter, the proprietor of a tire shop, had received combat training with the 135th Machine Gun Battalion of the 37th Division in France during the war. Porter grabbed a nine-shot Colt revolver, dropped to the floor of his shop, and took aim at Johnson. The "Battle of Bedford" had begun.

The first shot Porter fired hit Johnson in the side. Stung by the bullet, the startled gunman was able to return a few wild shots as he staggered back to the car and climbed into the driver's seat. As he tried to start the Cadillac, a second bullet ripped through his neck. Johnson, bleeding profusely, fell forward across the steering wheel.

Alerted by the gunfire, Losteiner and his men headed for the door. As they did the manager set off the bank's alarm. The sound of the gunshots and the alarm brought more of the citizens of Bedford on the run – armed to the teeth. As the robbers made their way to the Cadillac, pistols, rifles and shotguns blasted away at them from up and down Main Street. A quick thinking contractor parked his truck in a way that blocked any possible escape by the Cadillac. It was unlikely the gang could even get the car started with the dying Johnson sprawled across the steering wheel.

The fusillade of bullets forced the robbers to drop the $53,000 in loot they stole and run for their lives. Pinned down at an embankment near the Pennsylvania Railroad tracks, "Jiggs" surrendered. Losteiner was shot in the eye and in the abdomen and was peppered with gunshot pellets. Albert Johnson was taken to St. Alexis Hospital, where he died on the operating table. Orville Taylor was wounded in the head, cheek and knee; one bullet passing through his tongue. He was taken, unable to speak, to City Hospital.[4] Another robber, wounded in the hand, was also captured. Two identified robbers and possibly two more men escaped.

Losteiner recovered from his wounds and was tried for the murder of Patrolman Gaffney in December 1920, just weeks before Stanton took office. "Jiggs" was defended by former assistant county prosecutors P.J. Mulligan and Stephen M. Young.[5] It was the last case prosecuted by young William J. Corrigan,* who was soon sitting across the aisle at the other trial table. The famed defense attorney's career reached a peak in the 1950s when he represented Dr. Sam Sheppard in the murder of his wife Marilyn.

Despite Losteiner's rampant criminal past, the jury came back with a recommendation of mercy after finding him guilty of murder. The verdict created a public outcry, which would only be strengthened by Losteiner's later activities at the Ohio Penitentiary.

The Murder of Dan Kaber

John Bellamy wrote, "The Kaber case remains the greatest murder story in the history of Cleveland. It remains the only homicide in the history of the world in which a grandmother, mother and granddaughter were indicted for the same first-degree murder."

Dan Kaber, a 46 year-old businessman, was murdered in July 1919. The son of successful Jewish printer, Moses Kaber, Dan had taken over the family business and lived in a spacious dwelling at 12537 Lake Avenue in Lakewood, a suburb located on the western edge of Cleveland and running along Lake Erie. Also living in the home were Kaber's wife Eva, whom he had married in September 1907, and at times her mother Mary Brickel, and Eva's daughter from a previous marriage, Marion McArdle.

Beginning in November 1918, a healthy Dan Kaber began to experience bouts of sickness that by July 1919 had reduced him to a paralyzed, bed-ridden invalid. He correctly sensed that Eva, a 39 year-old with a troubled past, was poisoning him. Poison was just one of the many attempts Eva used to try to rid herself of her husband. She once asked a medium to use her powers of "supernatural intervention" to kill Dan. On another occasion she offered a man $5,000 to run him over with an automobile. Eva was not above taking matters into her own hands, having once set the house on fire with gasoline.

It was not until Eva was introduced to Erminia "Emma" Colavito that things began to take a turn for the worse for Dan Kaber. Colavito, described by Bellamy as a "mother of five, midwife, neighborhood abortionist, and general all-around hand at the black arts," provided Eva with a "potion" to solve her problem. The debilitating process, which left Kaber an invalid, did not reach a conclusion fast enough for Eva and she soon asked Colavito for a more permanent solution. The "solution" came in the form of two hoods from Little Italy – Salvatore Cala and Vittorio Pisselli. The two toughs were hired for $3, 000 or $5,000, depending on which account you read, and a plan was hatched to dispose of the death defying Dan Kaber once and for all.

Recruiting her mother and daughter into the plot, Eva left Lakewood for Cedar Point, a resort town that would one day become the roller coaster capital of the world, located about an hour west of the city on the Lake Erie shoreline. She traveled there to establish an alibi for herself. Back in Lakewood, after one failed attempt where Mary Brickel got "cold feet" and failed to perform her role, the two assassins entered the Kaber home on the night of Friday, July 18. Entering through a door that was intentionally left unlocked, the killers climbed the stairs to the Kaber bedroom. Once inside, Cala held the paralyzed victim while Pisselli commenced to stab him 24 times. During the process Kaber cried out, "Mercy. Mercy. What have I done to you?" The dying man's last defensive resort was to get hold of Cala's thumb with his teeth and nearly bite it off.

A male nurse, staying at the home to provide care for Kaber, rushed to the scene after hearing the screams, but the deed was done and the culprits had fled. Doctors were called and the dying Kaber was taken to Lakewood Hospital. For some never explained reason, eleven of the 24 stab wounds were inflicted to Kaber's scrotum. Despite the viciousness of the attack, Kaber lived another 14 hours before expiring. Before he died he uttered that his killer was a "man with a cap" and that his "wife had done this."

During the coroner's inquest Eva Kaber "wavered and wept" while questioned by County Prosecutor Samuel Doerfler. Despite the fact that during the autopsy 40 grains of arsenic were found in the victim, the inquest's conclusion was that Dan Kaber was murdered by persons unknown.

Nearly two years passed before Stanton was elected county prosecutor. After taking office in January 1921, one of his first visitors was Moses Kaber, who was hoping to obtain justice for his son. Kaber had spent a small fortune on Pinkerton detectives and the recruiting of an informant to befriend Eva and her mother in order to gather evidence. Mary Brickel told the informant that Eva "did it and did it for the money. If they try to put it on Charlie [Brickel's son] I'll tell all I know." On May 31, 1921, Kaber, Stanton and the Lakewood Police Department set a trap for Mary Brickel by faking the arrest of her son for the murder. The trick worked and Mrs. Brickel, fearing that they would charge her son for the crime, began "singing like a canary." The next day Assistant County Prosecutor James T. Cassidy announced that first-degree murder indictments were handed down for Eva Kaber, Mary Brickel and Marion McArdle.

Eva was living in New York City at the time and, after hearing she was indicted, fled to the home of a friend. Police tracked her down and she was arrested on June 4. Her daughter Marion was arrested two days later. After waiving extradition the two were brought back to Cleveland in mid-June.

A key member of the Eva Kaber defense team was former prosecutor William J. Corrigan. Eva was guilty and Corrigan knew it. His defense was focused solely on her not receiving the electric chair. His trial strategy was two pronged – keep all woman off the jury (at which he was successful) and convince the panel she was insane. After a somewhat uneventful trial, where the only excitement seemed to be waiting for Eva to faint again, Mrs. Kaber was found guilty, having never taken the stand. On July 16, 1921, she was sentenced to life at the Marysville Reformatory.[6] Incredibly, Marion McArdle was found innocent by a sympathetic jury, while the charges against Mary Brickel were dismissed due to her age and the cooperation she provided against her daughter. Salvatore Cala received a life sentence. Vittorio Pisselli fled the country for Italy, where he was soon arrested. Tried and convicted, he was sentenced to a 30-year term.

As for Emma Colavito, despite the evidence against her, and her scurrilous past, she was acquitted by a jury. Although Cala's confession implicated Colavito in the plot, his refusal to testify against her at trial led to her acquittal. This, however, was not the end of her story.

The Trials of William H. McGannon
Of all the unsolved murders in the history of Cleveland, the killing of

Harold Kagy on the night of May 7, 1920 remains one of the most famous and certainly one of the most bizarre. What made it so unique was that one of the prime suspects was the Chief Justice of the Municipal Court, Judge William H. McGannon, who was rumored to be "the man to beat" in the upcoming Cleveland mayoral election of 1921. Again John Bellamy introduces the event:

> "For sheer duration, scandal, and almost unlimited shameless perjury, true connoisseurs of Cleveland crime among the high and mighty would probably rate the McGannon-Kagy affair as the best of breed. Before it ran its course it produced three major murder trials, a record number of perjury indictments, and the ruinous disgrace of a popular and well-respected judge. The real truth about this bizarre episode may never be known – except that almost everyone involved could not have been telling the truth for any length of time."

The principals in this unusual murder were Gannon, Harold Kagy, an automobile salesman and repair shop owner, and John W. Joyce, a well-known Irish gangster. Bellamy tells us, "Joyce was no stranger to Cleveland police. Dapper to a fault, he often sported flashy diamonds, was a Cleveland pioneer in the wearing of spats, and was reputed to have introduced the double-breasted Chesterfield overcoat to the Forest City." It wasn't Joyce's sartorial splendor that made him a police character; it was his record of a dozen arrests dating back to 1895.

On the evening of the murder, according to McGannon's later statement to police, the judge drove his Cadillac to East 55th Street to be examined by Kagy. The two men took the car for a drive to Willoughby, located in Lake County to the east of Cleveland, via Lake Shore Boulevard. On the way back the men stopped at Ferguson's Café on Euclid Avenue, near Coltman Road. There they met Joyce, who was drinking heavily. Around midnight the three men left; why Joyce accompanied them was never explained. After reaching the downtown area, McGannon claimed he exited the vehicle at East Ninth Street and Euclid Avenue in order to catch a streetcar ride home. This became a key element of the murder case. First, the men had just driven past McGannon's street, East 116th, in order to get downtown. Then, the judge could have boarded a street car at East Ninth and Euclid, but chose instead to catch it in Public Square in front of the May Company. Instead of walking west down Euclid to the square, a distance of two long blocks, he walked two blocks north to Superior, before turning west toward the square.

Meanwhile, his two companions drove north on East Ninth to Hamilton Avenue[7] and parked the car. There a mysterious figure, who came to be known as the "third man at Hamilton," appeared, and after some heated words were exchanged a shot rang out. Kagy dropped to the sidewalk after being hit in the back with a .38 slug, which ripped through his right lung. Two plain-clothes policemen and some passersby quickly got Kagy into an automobile which took him to Lakeside Hospital at 1231 Lakeside Avenue. When they arrived, Kagy informed one of the officers that John Joyce had shot him.

Back at the scene of the shooting, Joyce had fled, but not before he was recognized by several bystanders. The police, however, were more interested in the abandoned automobile, since it was soon identified as belonging to Judge McGannon. Detectives went to the judge's home, arriving about 2:00 a.m. They were surprised at this hour to be greeted not only by the judge's wife, but by several of his brothers. McGannon, they were told, was asleep in his bed. When aroused, the judge, still quite intoxicated according to officers, related his version of the events that evening.

Kagy, critically wounded, stuck to the story that Joyce had shot him, and supported McGannon's tale that the judge was let out at East Ninth and Euclid. The next day, after a clandestine meeting with McGannon, Joyce "negotiated" his surrender. Once in custody he was taken by Chief Smith to Lakeside Hospital.

"That's the man who shot me," Kagy declared.

"I didn't do it, Kagy." Joyce replied. "You know who really did it. Why don't you tell them who it really was? Why don't you tell them the truth?"

When Kagy refused to change his statement, Joyce exploded.

"I'm the goat in all of this. I'm not going to be the only one to suffer, you'll see if I am. But I'm not going to tell anything till I get to court."

The police investigation centered on the identification of the "third man at Hamilton," the description of the person fit McGannon perfectly. The newspapers were quick to realize this and demand that the judge come clean.

On May 23, Harold Kagy died from an infection that developed in his wounded lung. The day before his death, his father and brothers took a statement from him in which he identified Joyce as the gunman and denied that McGannon was present. Joyce was indicted for second-degree murder on June 4. The trial began on November 9 before Judge Maurice Bernon. Joyce was represented by attorney Walter D. Meals while newly appointed County Prosecutor Roland A. Baskin[8] represented the state. By now rumors of McGannon's involvement were so widespread that he was forced to take a leave of absence from the bench.

During the trial Joyce testified that all three men were drinking heavily that evening and that Kagy and McGannon were arguing over money. McGannon had not exited the car at East Ninth and Euclid, as he claimed, but was in it when it arrived at Hamilton and East Ninth, some six blocks north. There, Joyce claimed, he staggered from the car and leaned against a telephone pole for support. He told the court he heard an angry McGannon say to Kagy, "Where is that money? Come here. I won't stand for that." This was followed by a shot, after which Joyce said he staggered off not knowing that Kagy was hit.

When McGannon took the stand he denied all of Joyce's accusations. It boiled down to which man the jury was going to believe – an honorable judge or a gangster with a long rap sheet. The statement of Harold Kagy, which alone should have sent Joyce to the electric chair, was not allowed into evidence by Bernon. The judge ruled that it could not be considered a "death bed" statement because Kagy did not know he was dying when he made it – this despite signing the statement with fingers that were turning blue and then expiring the next day.

It was here that things really got bizarre. A procession of witnesses then took the stand to render different versions of what happened at the corner that night. Some identified the judge as the third man, some didn't. One witness who did, claimed he saw McGannon fire the weapon, another claimed it was Joyce who fired. Apparently the jury was not confused with all the strange testimony, as they deliberated just five hours before finding Joyce not guilty on November 17.

The jury's decision put the wheels in motion for an indictment of McGannon. On November 26 the judge was charged with the murder of Harold Kagy. His bond, set at $10,000, was posted by Anne Kilbane, the wife of popular Cleveland prize-fighter Johnny Kilbane. The trial began on December 14, again before Judge Maurice Bernon.

McGannon was represented by William Boyd, while Alfred A. Cartwright sat as junior counsel. The trial featured a bombshell by the prosecution. Mary Neely, a middle-aged single woman who claimed she had known the judge for 16 years, testified that she was following McGannon that night and saw him shoot Kagy. She then offered that she had met with the judge and told him to claim the shooting was an accident or to let her accept the blame.

McGannon's defense countered with some 30-odd witnesses who confirmed the judge exited the car at East Ninth and Euclid and took a round-about trek to the streetcar stop on Public Square. One of the defense witnesses was dubbed the "man with X-ray eyes" by the newspapers. A close look at his testimony revealed that he would have had to have looked through a building to see the judge from the vantage point at which he claimed to be standing.

To counter Neely's testimony the defense put on James McCafferty, a cab driver. He testified he had picked up Neely as a fare that night and was driving her around other parts of the city when she claimed to be watching McGannon shoot Kagy.

On December 29, the jury received the case at 6:15 p.m. Nearly 48 hours passed before the jury came back hopelessly deadlocked at ten to two for conviction. Bernon declared a mistrial. The second trial, which began on February 7, 1921, was prosecuted by Edward Stanton, and held before Judge Homer G. Powell. By now only two witnesses positively identified McGannon as the "third man at Hamilton." When Neely was called to testify she suddenly developed amnesia – right in the middle of her testimony. After a brief recess, she returned and declared she had not seen McGannon shoot Kagy.

The air had gone out of the prosecution's case. During the defense's case they had now found even more people willing to testify in support of the judge's strange hike to the Public Square streetcar that night. On February 18, 1921, after twenty hours of deliberations, the jury acquitted McGannon.

Stanton was incensed over the matter, as were Judges Bernon and Powell. Although McGannon could not be retried for the murder, the matter was not about to go away. Within weeks, a total of 15 indictments were issued to former defense witnesses and McGannon on charges of perjury. By now McGannon had announced that he would resign from the bench, but was holding off by lying low in a sanitarium. When his indictment was announced on April 15, Judge Florence Allen ordered him arrested, "nervous breakdown or not," and placed in the county jail.

The first perjury trial was that of James McCafferty, the cab driver. A woman bailiff, obviously acquainted with McGannon, spoke to two of the female jurors and suggested they get other women on the jury to "stick to it, as was done in the McGannon case." The bailiff was suspended and later fired. McCafferty was found guilty.

After two false starts, the perjury trial of Judge McGannon began in June 1921. The prosecution's star witness was Mary Neely. She dropped her own bombshell by admitting she had met secretly with the judge at the Hotel Mecca on the eve of his second trial. In connection with this hotel rendezvous, it became known that attorney Cartwright was aware of the clandestine meeting and he too was brought up on charges due to the fact that he sat and listened during the second trial as Neely declared she had spoken to no one regarding her perjured testimony. Later, two ex-newspaper reporters claimed they were paid by the judge to testify falsely regarding Neely's testimony during the first trial. When McGannon took the stand in his own defense he explained away his actions by claiming to have been "mentally and physically sick" at the time and was drinking heavily.

On June 25, after twenty-seven hours of deliberations, the jury found McGannon guilty of perjury. Allen was deeply disturbed at having to sentence a fellow judge, one that she had practiced before as an attorney. Stating that judges were not above the law, she sentenced him to one to ten years. McGannon had the last word. As he was being escorted from the courtroom, he raised his right hand in righteous indignation and bellowed, "As there is a Jesus Christ in heaven, he will make these people suffer as I have suffered. He will torture them and punish them as I have been punished. If they don't suffer as I have suffered, then there is no God!"

It was later left to wonder if McGannon had indeed called down the wrath of God. Neely, John Joyce and one of the ex-newspaper reporters died before the decade was out. If there was a curse, however, it affected McGannon's family, too. His oldest brother John died in June 1923; Mary McGannon, his mother died in September 1924; and another brother, Dr. A.C. McGannon drowned in Canada in August 1925.

As for the judge, McGannon served 19 months in the Ohio Penitentiary. On January 5, 1924, he was given a conditional release when it was determined that the diabetes he was suffering from might lead to his death if he was kept incarcerated. McGannon sought to be reinstated to the bar and a petition was signed by some 500 attorneys and businessmen. Before it was ruled on, McGannon left for Chicago where it was reported he was representing a business firm as a house attorney.

Despite tales of infidelity during the trials, Ann McGannon stood by her man. They were living in a "dingy" boarding house in Chicago, making plans to move to permanent spot in the Windy City. On Saturday, November 17, 1928, McGannon kissed Ann goodbye and headed out the door to catch a streetcar to his Chicago office. He had only gone a few steps when he stopped and placed his hands on his chest and remarked he was having trouble breathing. He then collapsed in the street and died of a massive coronary. He was 58 years old.

The Staff of Eddie Stanton

This was the Cleveland that Edward Stanton was handed when taking office in January 1921. Things did indeed get worse but, fortunately for the young prosecutor, he had selected "a few good men."

One of the things that made Stanton successful was his selection of assistant county prosecutors, especially two who were named "chief assistant prosecutors" – James T. Cassidy and James C. Connell.

Stanton and Cassidy grew up in the same neighborhood and were childhood friends. They attended grade school together and later St. Ignatius College. A *Plain Dealer Sunday Magazine* article from July 1921 stated, "Cassidy is to Stanton what the ham is to the celebrated egg, or what Damon was to Pythias." Both men, interviewed for the article, told a humorous story showing the competitiveness of their working relationship. "Of course we differed occasionally," said Stanton. "During the McGannon and the Kaber cases we sat up here working until midnight every night. Jim was sometimes wrong. But we would have a good night's rest and a good breakfast, and by the time we met again at 8 a.m. he would be willing to concede the error of his ways." Cassidy's version, "Eddie sometimes made mistakes, but usually after a good night's sleep he would come around to my way of thinking."

James T. Cassidy and his twin brother Charles were born August 18, 1886, on Cleveland's South Side. James attended St. Thomas Aquinas school until 1900, when at the age of 14 he went to work for the W. S. Tyler Company, a wire producing concern. Cassidy later completed his education at St. Ignatius High School before attending local colleges. According to newspaper articles, in addition to St. Ignatius College (now John Carroll University), he attended Adelbert College and Western Reserve University. It was at the latter school that he graduated with a law degree in 1912. The next year he passed the state bar examination. Cassidy helped support himself while he earned his education by working as a lamplighter.

The future prosecutor and jurist grew to impressive dimensions. He was six-feet, two-inches tall and weighed 190 pounds. He became interested in politics at an early age. A Republican, he ran for the Ward 21 seat in City Council in 1911; Ohio House of Representatives in 1912; and City Council again in 1913 – losing all three times.

In 1916, Cassidy was appointed assistant city law director by Mayor Harry L. Davis.* He remained in this capacity for four years, except for six months during the First World War when he served in the naval aviation corps. On January 1, 1921, the day after the Sly-Fanner murders, Cassidy was appointed assistant county prosecutor by Stanton. Cassidy's most outstanding talent was his oratorical abilities. Time after time they helped him drive home his points to juries. Many credited these skills with helping Stanton get elected and re-elected to office.

During his four years with Stanton, Cassidy was the lead prosecutor in most of the murder and criminal cases that gained national attention. Cassidy faced off with such infamous personalities as John W. Joyce, William H. Gannon, Eva Kaber, Salvatore Cala, Emma Colavito, "Big Jim" Morton and the Sly-Fanner killers. As early as August 1924, it was clear Cassidy had aspirations for higher office. At that time he announced his intention to run for common pleas judge in November. But Cassidy* abruptly resigned, announcing he was going to open a private law practice.

James C. Connell replaced Cassidy in 1924. Connell was born in Cleveland in 1897. His father Thomas F. Connell, was a fire warden for the city. Like Cassidy, as a youngster Connell earned money as a lamplighter in his Superior Avenue – East 55th Street neighborhood. Connell graduated from John Marshall Law School and passed the state bar in 1918. In 1922, he served as assistant police prosecutor for Cleveland. Two years later Stanton hired him as an assistant prosecutor.

If Stanton was the "Boy Wonder," Connell might have been looked upon as Superman. Comparing the styles of Cassidy and Connell a reporter stated:

> "There is, first, the violent, stormy orator who argues the jury into convicting. And then there is the quiet, philosophical, argumentative type who calmly marshals fact after fact until the jury has, almost without their knowing it, been convinced into a verdict for the state."

The reporter was discussing Connell's style during the fall term of 1925 in which the new chief assistant county prosecutor had yet to lose a case. The fall term opened with Connell handling a record 300 grand jury cases in just three weeks. By late November his record of success tallied fifteen consecutive jury trials, two cases in the appellate court and two in the state supreme court. In addition, he had obtained more than twenty guilty pleas without the defendants contesting the charges. In five cases, defendants pled guilty after opening statements. Well into the opening term of 1926, Connell was still undefeated. On February 3 he won three cases in one day.

Connell[9] remained Stanton's chief assistant until Stanton left office at the end of 1928, at which time the two men entered into a law practice together.

A New Sheriff in Town

Charles B. Stannard,* like Edward Stanton, was swept into office as Cuyahoga County Sheriff on the crest of the great Republican wave that put Warren G. Harding in the White House in November 1920. Stannard, a man with Hollywood looks, had spent the past eight years as president of Cleveland City Council. During the last four of those years he doubled as chief deputy to Sheriff A.J. "Gus" Hirstius, a power second only to Maurice Maschke in Cuyahoga County Republican politics.

Also like Stanton, Stannard faced the same crime wave that enveloped the entire county in 1921. During that crime wave, Stannard at one time had in his care 16 prisoners charged with first-degree murder.

By his own admission, Stannard's most memorable case was a double murder – the brutal, senseless, savage slaying of two Parma school teachers, Mabel Foote and Louise Wolf on February 16, 1921. On March 31, Arthur Ihlenfeld, a young man described as an imbecile, confessed to the murders. He was tried in common pleas court where William J. Corrigan was appointed his public defender. An hour into deliberations the jury came back and declared him insane. He was sentenced to the Lima State Hospital for the Criminally Insane. Stannard, as well as many others, never believed the boy's story. For years Stannard continued to run down leads, many of which took him out of state. In the end, Stannard admitted, "It is the regret of my life that the crime was never cleared up to my satisfaction."

A *Cleveland Press* series on the "Sheriffs of Cuyahoga County," which ran in December 1930, reported:

> "Stannard was the first sheriff in Cuyahoga county to refuse to lock boys in knee pants up with hardened criminals. When boys were brought to him he put them in the hospital ward. If that ward was full he simply refused to accept them. He fought for improvements in the jail and was praised generally by organizations that inspected the place.
>
> "He got rid of the accumulated filth and dirt of more than 50 years, enlarged the quarters and gave up the old sheriff's office to provide an adequate ward for the less hardened prisoners who were in his care. He managed to get the hospital ward away from the jail and moved psychopathic cases to the basement of the W. Third street building."

Another crusade Stannard took on was to recover more than 1,100 special deputy badges, considered by today's standards as a kind of glorified courtesy card that were issued by his predecessor. After a collection campaign, which ran for weeks, resulted in the return of a paltry three badges he cancelled all the commissions that were issued.

Still another area in which Stannard did battle was in attempting to keep his prisoners well-fed. He insisted that he was entitled to all the money the law allowed him for feeding county prisoners and, in addition, he collected another $1,000 a month for the care of federal prisoners. Law suits were filed to get back the money, but Stannard prevailed. Ironically, after Stannard left office in 1924, the funds collected for feeding prisoners turned into a major scandal during the term of the new sheriff – Fred Kohler, a former Cleveland police chief and mayor.

Chapter Endnotes

1. St. Ignatius College was located at West 30th and Jersey Street (Carroll Avenue). In 1923 the college changed its name to John Carroll University. Classes began in its current location, University Heights, during the mid-1930s.

2. Founded in the late 1890s Cleveland Law School was the state's first evening law school and the first to accept women. In June 1946 it merged with the John Marshall Law School to form Cleveland-Marshall Law School. Today it is an under-graduate college and part of Cleveland State University.

3. Known as the Mansfield Reformatory, the official name of the prison, located in Mansfield, Ohio was the Ohio State Reformatory. The facility opened as a training center for Union soldiers in August 1861. The camp was named Mordecai Bartley in honor of Mansfield's favorite son who served as governor of the state from 1844 to 1846. After the war, a movement was afoot to turn the property into a prison. Nearly 20 years later, the state approved the request to build an "intermediate" prison that bridged the Boys Industrial School, located in Lancaster, and the Ohio Penitentiary. Mansfield was selected as the site and the cornerstone of the intermediate state prison was laid on November 4, 1886. The east cell block of the prison was home to a 6-tier, free-standing cell-block which made the *Guiness Book of World Records* as the largest of its kind. Described as a "medieval chateauesque structure," the building served as a prison until 1990. Unique in nature, the building was used in movies, most notably *The Shawshank Redemption* and *Air Force One*. – from various Internet web sites.

"Since the doors were closed on the Reformatory, there have been legends that the prison is filled with restless spirits of tormented inmates, guards, and prison officials who were never able to leave. As expected with this type of prison, there are gruesome tales of pain, violence, suicides, murders, and other "accidental" deaths. The terrible past events trap the ghosts behind the prisons stonewalls and decaying iron cell bars." – from *The Ghost Hunter's Bible*, by Trent Brandon.

4. City Hospital began as the "township poorhouse" when it was built in 1826, on property owned by Erie Street Cemetery, to provide for elderly patients and those suffering from chronic disease. In 1837 it became City Hospital and accommodated "the poor, sick, insane, and feeble-minded."

The building was razed in 1851. In 1889 construction began on a new City Hospital on Scranton Road. A staff was organized and in place by 1892.

5. Stephen Marvin Young was "a Representative and a Senator from Ohio; born on a farm near Norwalk, Huron County, Ohio, May 4, 1889; attended the public schools and Kenyon and Adelbert Colleges; graduated from the law department of Western Reserve University, Cleveland, Ohio, 1911; admitted to the bar the same year and commenced practice in Norwalk, Ohio; member, State house of representatives 1913-1917; assistant prosecuting attorney of Cuyahoga County 1917-1918; served as a private in Company F, Third Ohio Infantry, on the Mexican border in 1916, and during the First World War served in the Field Artillery; chief assistant prosecuting attorney of Cuyahoga County 1919-1920; unsuccessful candidate for attorney general in 1922; unsuccessful Democratic candidate for the gubernatorial nomination in 1930; member of the Ohio Commission on Unemployment Insurance 1931-1932; elected as a Democrat to the Seventy-third and Seventy-fourth Congresses (March 4, 1933-January 3, 1937); was not a candidate for re-nomination in 1936, but was an unsuccessful candidate for the gubernatorial nomination; special counsel to the attorney general of Ohio 1937-1939; elected to the Seventy-seventh Congress (January 3, 1941-January 3, 1943); unsuccessful candidate for reelection in 1942 to the Seventy-eighth Congress; during the Second World War was commissioned a major in the United States Army in 1943, served in North Africa and Italy, and was discharged as a lieutenant colonel in 1946; resumed the practice of law in Cleveland, Ohio, and Washington, D.C.; elected to the Eighty-first Congress (January 3, 1949-January 3, 1951); unsuccessful candidate for reelection in 1950 to the Eighty-second Congress; in 1956 was defeated for attorney general of Ohio; elected as a Democrat to the United States Senate in 1958; reelected in 1964 and served from January 3, 1959, to January 3, 1971; was not a candidate for reelection in 1970; was a resident of Washington, D.C., at the time of his death on December 1, 1984; interment in Norwalk Cemetery, Norwalk, Ohio." – *Biographical Directory of the United States Congress 1774 - Present* http://bioguide.congress.gov/biosearch/biosearch.asp

6. Simply referred to as Marysville, due to its location in that Ohio city, the prison is the Ohio State Reformatory for Women. It was opened in 1913.

7. Prior to the construction of Erie View Plaza in the mid-1960s Hamilton Avenue ran as far west as Ontario Street.

8. Roland Baskin became the Cuyahoga County Prosecutor after the resignation of Sam Doerfler in the summer of 1920. Baskin, a Democrat, wasn't the first choice of party leaders. That honor went to State Representative Elden J. Hopple, who actually wanted the position and was planning on running for it in the fall election. Hopple said, however, he would not feel justified in conducting a campaign while on the county payroll. Hopple, the Democratic candidate that November, lost to Republican Edward Stanton. Meanwhile, Baskin was appointed to the position after Hopple's decision, during a meeting of the county's common pleas judges.

Baskin, who was named an assistant county prosecutor by Doerfler in 1918, became the youngest man to hold the office of Cuyahoga County Prosecutor at the age of 33. His term in office was a brief four months. During that time, however, Baskin prosecuted two significant cases. The first was the Serra automobile theft ring which led directly to the Sly-Fanner murders. The second was the Harold Kagy murder in which Judge William H. McGannon was the defendant.

The latter trial, which began on December 14, 1920, looked as if it could present a problem if it ran over into the next year, by which time Stanton was the new county prosecutor. Stanton wanted to keep Baskin on to complete the case, while others called for a special prosecutor to try the case from the beginning. Ironically, the choice for special prosecutor was Walter D. Meals, who defended John Joyce in the same murder case and won his client an acquittal. Meals said that prosecuting McGannon was a conflict of interest and declined. Baskin went ahead and prosecuted the case and the matter became moot when on December 29 the trial ended in a hung jury.

9. James C. Connell was appointed to the Common Pleas bench in 1941 by Ohio Governor John W. Bricker. The next year he was elected to a six year term. Near the end of his second six-year term Connell was appointed to a lifetime position on the Federal Court by President Dwight D. Eisenhower in 1954. From 1960 to 1971 Connell served as Chief Justice of the US District Court of Northern Ohio. He then went into senior reserve status. Connell died on October 30, 1973 at the age of 76.

2

Crime Wave

The year 1921 got off to a bloody start in the wake of the Sly-Fanner murders. Over the last half of 1920 there was, on the average, a major robbery or holdup every five days, and eight innocent Clevelanders were murdered as a result of those crimes, with four others being wounded. During the commission of those crimes only one criminal was killed, Albert Johnson, who was shot to death by the citizens of Bedford during the ill-fated bank robbery by the "Jiggs" Losteiner Gang.

The crime problem was the number one topic of conversation in Cleveland as letters received by the newspapers revealed. One of the common complaints was that more policemen should be "walking a beat," making law enforcement more visible – an argument that remains to this day. Several letters came in demanding armed citizen patrols. These patrols, it was suggested, should be under the control of the mayor instead of the police department. One group of West Side businessmen proposed that Mayor William Fitzgerald deputize a select group of citizens and give them police powers. The function of this "select group" was not outlined, but the businessmen wanted the identities of the civilian force concealed. One advocate of this concealment stated, "If police power is conferred upon civilians, even the regular force should not know the men thus authorized. Very often an officer is off his beat and neglecting his duty and that fact could [now] be made known." This was a solemn indication of the public's indignation toward the police department. This same group also advocated the increased use of company checks to pay employees as opposed to company officials picking up and distributing cash payrolls. Others demanded that police guards accompany the payroll transfers.

One Clevelander summed up the feelings of the population with the following:

Attention Citizens of this Fifth City!

We have a community of which we justly pride in matters civic. In war, in contribution to the needy, in advancing education and promoting the finer things of life, we stand pre-eminent, yet, in common things, such as protecting the lives of our citizens, we stand like a child at the mercy of a band of rowdies and criminals, who plunder and murder in cold blood.

Are we, a city such as ours, whose aim is to attain the highest morals, to allow this bloodshed to proceed without even asking clemency from these despots of human life?

Are we, the citizens of Cleveland, going to allow a record to be laid down that we are hovering (sic) murderers and criminals in our midst without signs of protest?

Must we raise our women and children in constant fear of having them attacked and murdered as endlessly as they have been in the past?

No! Emphatically no! If we must organize, as of old, in exterminating this nuisance, we will.

Whether the fault is due to the police or to the courts, I am not prone to say at the present. These demand further investigation by the proper authorities. I must say, though, that we are lacking in proper police protection. We have plenty of police but their energy is misdirected.

As an instance, what can be more ridiculous and worthy of comment than the fact that policemen are placed on guard for twenty-four hours for the sake of watching a petty grocery store which has been suspicioned (sic) of selling liquor? Will this eliminate the evil of liquor selling? If the police think it will, it is a false reasoning and inefficiency on their part. The police know as well as anyone else how to eliminate the liquor evil in this city if they so desired. They must first eliminate the ringleaders of liquor traffic, who are responsible for whisky to be brought here and distributed.

Take heed citizens. It is up to you to demand a clean city from the men you and I have put into office. If they cannot release us from this crime wave which is sweeping our city, then it is time that they give us the task and say "We are failures and cannot cope with the situation!" In that event, we citizens shall by force of necessity do our own protecting for the sake of our future city, if it is to be one of which we can open-heartedly boast and be proud of.

This is just a sentiment from a citizen who desires for a wholesome and safe place for men, women and children to live in.

Signed: A CITIZEN OF CLEVELAND

Two common themes, which were covered in the editorial, were a concern that the Cleveland Police Department was spending too much time trying to arrest gamblers and bootleggers, and that a need for civilian policing was needed. One war veteran called for public hangings or firing squad executions. Another urged death sentences for all gun carriers. The issue of too many guns on the street and in the wrong hands was reflected on January 7 when the first grand jury of 1921 returned nine indictments on concealed weapons charges.

Plaguing the police department was a lack of patrolmen. A force of 1,200 was authorized by the city, but only 821 were actually on the payroll as of the end of 1920. Chief Smith demanded that a force of 2,000 was needed. Smith once told a gathering, "New York [City] is only six times as large as Cleveland but has ten times the number of police. Give us an adequate force and we will minimize crime in Cleveland."

East Side City Councilman William E. Potter introduced a resolution in city council to fill the nearly 400 vacancies in the department. Potter, whose killing a decade later was the most sensational murder in the city's history (until the Marilyn Sheppard murder), also urged a "systematic campaign" to recruit the best available men for both the police and fire departments. Neither department had any recruiting procedures in place.

Mayor William Fitzgerald* was facing an uphill task. Fitzgerald was not a popular mayor. Arriving from Washington D.C. in 1903, Fitzgerald passed the Ohio Bar and began the practice of law in 1905. He opened an office in the Williamson Building and practiced law until 1911. That year he was appointed special assistant attorney general by the Ohio State attorney general. He soon got the bug for elective office and campaigned for a seat on Cleveland City Council as a Republican from the 11th Ward. Once elected, he was one of the few Republicans in council. During this time he became a protégé of Harry L. Davis. Fitzgerald ran Davis' campaign for mayor in 1913 when he lost to Newton D. Baker. Re-elected to council in 1913, Fitzgerald served as the Republican floor leader. On the instructions of Cuyahoga County Republican Party leader Maurice Maschke, Fitzgerald's role was to denounce and "view with alarm" anything Baker and the Democratic council proposed. This created one embarrassment for the Republicans when Fitzgerald fought a vigorous battle against the administration when they wanted to treat the city's drinking water with chlorine. Fitzgerald argued it would poison the citizens. Davis ran again for mayor in 1915 and this time won the election. Fitzgerald was rewarded for his loyalty by being named city law director, the top cabinet position. When Davis was re-elected in 1917 and 1919, Fitzgerald was re-appointed to the position.

Harry L. Davis had aspirations for higher office and early in 1920 began campaigning for governor. During a campaign stop in Sandusky on March 11 he announced his intention to step down as mayor and devote his fulltime to the campaign. He made his resignation effective May 1. Fitzgerald, the city's law director, under the rules of the city charter became the new mayor of Cleveland.

In early 1921 Mayor Fitzgerald's crime cleanup effort was the number one priority in the city. All police officers were ordered to active duty by Chief Smith. At the request of Smith, Fitzgerald mandated the hiring of 75 civilian chauffeurs to replace the uniformed police drivers of the flying squadrons and police emergency vehicles. He purchased new squad cars and fifteen motorcycle sidecars to speed the arrival of officers to crime scenes. Vacations and sick time were suspended until further notice. Fitzgerald then issued instructions to the civil service commission to provide a list of all eligible police candidates, which came to 163, for immediate promotion to the police force. On January 31, Safety Director Anton B. Sprosty swore in 120 new police officers. He also announced that the department had received 560 applications for the next police exam, which was scheduled in three weeks.

The new additions to the police force had some problems early on in recognizing the difference between the good guys and the bad guys. One Saturday night, a man was standing alone in the detective bureau at police headquarters.

"Come on, your cell is ready for you," announced a rookie officer.

Laughing the man went along thinking it was a joke until they reached the cell. "Who do you think I am?" he questioned the officer.

"You're Albert Bush of Canton, charged with auto stealing," claimed the new recruit.

The man chuckled and stated, "Why, I'm Edward Stanton, the county prosecutor."

"That's what they all say. In you go," snapped the officer.

Fortunately for Stanton, a seasoned jailer happened along and cleared up the mistaken identity, leaving one to wonder what happened to the real Mr. Bush.

The fall-guy for the crime wave in Cleveland, and the ineffectiveness of the police department to do anything about it, was Frank Smith now in his fourth year as chief. Smith grew up on his father's farm in Pearl Creek, New York.[1] On a visit to Cleveland in 1890 he was offered a job as a cable streetcar "gripman," operating at Superior and Payne Avenue (the two streets intersected at the time). When the "panic" of 1893 came he left the "gripman" position and became a fireman for the Lake Shore Railroad, returning to the streetcar job the next year.

During the spring of 1895 he took a day off work to take the civil service examination for the Cleveland Police Department. He was accepted and on July 1 began a 27-year career on the force. Smith first served as a beat patrolman in the Euclid Avenue and East 105th Street neighborhood. After eight years as a patrolman he was promoted to sergeant in March

1903. From there Smith's rise was rapid. A shortage of lieutenants was dealt with by allowing all the sergeants to compete for the position regardless of time in as sergeant. Smith passed the examination "with points to spare" and became a lieutenant just four months after his promotion to sergeant. He reportedly "held every rank" in the department during his career. On December 1, 1912, he was promoted to captain, serving in the 11th Precinct. In 1915 he became Captain of Detectives and was named head of the detective bureau. Less than a year later, in June 1916, he was transferred to the traffic squad and placed in charge. Smith went on a tour of cities in the east and mid-west studying traffic departments and returned to rebuild the Cleveland Traffic Bureau.

On March 8, 1917, Smith was promoted to Inspector. Over the next nine months Cleveland Police Chief W.S. Rowe, an appointee of Mayor Newton D. Baker, was under fire in the administration of Harry L. Davis. On November 10, Rowe left on a two-month vacation "intimating" that he would not return. Smith, brilliant in his understanding of police mechanics, in yearly examinations usually ranking first, was named "acting chief" in Rowe's absence. Then on January 1, 1918, after Rowe's formal resignation, Mayor Davis officially named Smith chief.

In accepting the position, Smith made it clear, "I am under obligations to no one and will operate the police, detective and vice squads to suit myself, regardless of anyone." He quickly demoted 16 detectives, whose work he considered inferior, and transferred a number of patrolmen. Smith fought to increase the number of men on the police force, but with the shortage of able men in the city due to the war, he was hard pressed. As chief he was credited with establishing the department of traffic, organizing the police academy, and was one of the first police chiefs in the country to establish a "flying squad," the forerunner of the radio-equipped squad car, as a regular part of the department

The return of soldiers after the war resulted in an employment shortage. A number of jobs were taken over by Black men during the war, who migrated from the south with the announcement that workers were needed here in the factories. With the war over and war production plants unloading unneeded labor, the city had an abundance of returning unemployed soldiers and Black workers who were suddenly out of work, all of whom needed to feed themselves and their families. For the next few years this situation led to a number of crime waves throughout the area and now, in January 1921, Smith was under the gun for the problem. A January 4 editorial in the *Cleveland News* took pot shots at the chief's efforts:

"Chief of Police Smith takes thought and decides that something must be done. And what is the chief's decision as to what his department may safely undertake by way of checking the bandit gangs that steal at will and kill with pleasure:

"By drastic police measures designed to put an end to outlawry in Cleveland, young men are to be subjected to special regulations, almost military in their severity.

"All automobiles loaded with young men exclusively are to be stopped and searched for arms, day or night. Young men whom police do not know or who are not obviously on their way home are to be searched after nightfall.

"(Ranking officers) are to instruct their men to search every man at night for concealed weapons unless the patrolman is certain of the man's character, either by knowing him or by his judgment of the man. Old men, for example, will not be stopped in this way.

"No one should be offended by these restrictions in a time like this," said Chief Smith. "The orders to stop automobiles filled with young men and to search young men at night will probably be annoying to some, but they are part of extreme measures which we feel must be taken."

The editorial questioned, "How anything useful can be accomplished by such a practice is beyond imagining. It is… rubbish, but the best Chief Smith is able to produce when spurred to supreme effort."

Help from the community was offered to fight the crime wave. On January 8 an official of the Loyal American League offered the assistance of 200 members of his organization to Chief Smith. The league was an outgrowth of the American Protective League, a volunteer secret service group that helped the government track down enemy aliens and draft dodgers during the war. The Loyal American League would provide up to three automobiles in every precinct for patrol each night at no cost to the city; the patrols would be available for "as long as the crisis demanded."

Officials of the American Legion were also formulating plans to make their members available. In addition to offering their services for patrol, the Legion members were, "turning their minds to the invention of devices whereby more effective war against criminals can be waged." This branch of their organization planned to assist by establishing an unofficial espionage system, deputizing an armed force of volunteers, and equipping automobiles with "toxic gas grenades."

The next night, the volunteers were out in force. Every available police officer, 200 Loyal American Leaguers, and 50 American Legion members were on duty from early evening until after midnight. According to one report, "In automobiles and on foot they policed the city; halting machines carrying suspicious persons, visiting pool rooms, breaking up bands of corner loafers and searching for concealed weapons." The results – not a single holdup was reported during the night.

Instead of appreciating the efforts of the volunteers, Chief Smith chose to discourage them by stating that they were of little value, since most of them soon lost their enthusiasm. On January 12 the chief spoke to members of the Chamber of Industry and told them, "One reason police did not arrest bank robbers and bandits was that they are well dressed, polished and polite. He is not a tough looking character that anybody can spot on sight." The chief outlined three ways to "assist in stamping out criminals." First, was to keep the hardened criminals in prison for their full term with no time off for good behavior; second, was to deny judges the ability to parole prisoners; and third, was to hire more policemen.

Clevelanders continued to express their views on the crime problem in the newspaper's editorial write-in sections. A sampling of titles from the January 9, *Sunday News-Leader* revealed their thoughts: "Less Pity Would Make Fewer Thugs," "Disgusted With Women Who Send Criminals Flowers," "Give Police a Chance, Let Them Show Revolvers," "Hunt Bandits, Not Stills," "Would Have Criminals 'Strung Up' In Square," and "Make Criminals Work in Streets, [with] Tags on Backs." One reader commenting on the justice system wrote, "Verdict of Ten on Jury Should Stand."

In mid-January, two state senators from Cleveland introduced bills to aid in the crime war. Senator George H. Bender presented a bill that would make highway robbery, and attempted highway robbery, punishable by life in prison if the individual possessed a weapon. Senator James Reynolds offered a bill that would make the killing of a police officer on duty a first-degree murder punishable by death or life imprisonment.

If there was any concern on the part of criminals regarding the efforts to curtail their activity it certainly didn't show. On Sunday, January 30, twenty-one crimes were committed with in a 24-hour period, climaxing early Monday morning with the murder of Gretchen Brandt, who was killed by a burglar who entered her home while she slept. The killer crushed her skull with a paving brick before plunging a knife into her heart. The brutal murder took place after Chief Smith declared the crime wave was over and ordered his men, who earlier in the month had vacations and sick time cancelled by the mayor, back to normal duty.

Over a two-year period ending in April 1921, seven police officers and one railroad detective were murdered in the line of duty.[2] The decade of the 1920s proved to be a time when criminals had the least amount of respect for those who enforced the law. In addition to the murders, other attacks on police took place. On January 15, Patrolman Ralph Dryer was having his usual Friday night supper at Miller's café on Kinsman when two men entered and began an argument with him. When the argument turned physical, Dryer was beaten over the head with his own nightstick. The next weekend, as a patrolman was searching two suspects at East 34th and Scovill Avenue, one pulled a revolver and aimed it at the officer's head. The two then ran off down the street.

The police department got the message and began to fight back. At 3:00 a.m. on February 16, a police officer, perhaps for the first time in Cleveland, used a Thompson sub-machinegun in the performance of his duty. The police were called to an East Side store where three burglars were in the process of removing $2,000 worth of merchandise. Police Sergeant Harley H. Moffat and a patrolman soon arrived at the corner of East 69th Street and St. Clair Avenue. Although it was unclear if the two were under fire, both officers began shooting. Moffat, armed with the "Tommy gun," began firing from 200 feet away. Neighbors, awakened by the loud clatter, risked their lives by sticking their heads out of windows while Moffat blasted away. The bullets riddled telephone and electric poles as well as several buildings in the area. As for the fleeing robbers, police believe they may have wounded one.

The battle police waged had some effect on criminals. On March 20, Frank Zollers was spotted holding up a man on St. Clair Avenue. Three police officers showed up and gave chase. Racing through back yards, officers fired 20 shots at the fleeing man before he was brought down. Zollers, who died in City Hospital from a bullet in the lung, was the ninth criminal to be shot that month; five of them were killed. The efforts of the police were recognized in the newspaper where they finally received a positive editorial from the *Cleveland News* on March 29:

SOME GANGS CLEANED UP

In two batches, Sunday, the police captured ten young men alleged to be thieves in two raids. Other gangs have recently been rounded up. Penitentiaries and reformatories have shown a healthy increase in population as a result. Life is at least a little bit safer in Cleveland.

If that pace could be kept up for a few months it would make a change in the crime situation in this city. The number of thugs and robbers at large is never large. They do not count more than a few hundred, at most, out of 800,000 persons in Cleveland. To put a dozen of them behind the bars, every day, and keep them there, would soon break the courage and check the activities of those still at liberty.

This would be the result, especially, if entire gangs were arrested and sent to the penitentiary. Their fate would alarm and dishearten other young criminals who watched them go to jail. They would be a most effective object lesson for sobering and curbing the groups of ruffians remaining at large.

The corner "gang" is a prolific breeder of lawlessness. Every gang disposed of by the police and the courts means the end of one source of danger and one more step toward a cleaner, safer city.

Early on the morning of April 20, a call came into the 13th Precinct house. A "mysterious automobile" was reported in the East 71st Street and Superior Avenue neighborhood. Five men were in the car with the curtains drawn. Sergeant John Faragher and four officers headed out to investigate. Parking behind the suspect vehicle, Faragher crept up alongside the driver and shoved his revolver in the driver's stomach.

"Hands up or we'll shoot," Faragher yelled.

The five men were quickly frisked and five revolvers and five black jacks were confiscated.

"I say, Faragher, don't you know me?" asked one of the occupants.

Faragher shined his flashlight toward the inquiring face and gasped, "Why it's you Sergeant [Albert J.] Westphal!"

With that, both automobiles headed back to the station "with tail lights hanging low."

Later that day, acting on an informant's tip, a police squad headed by Captain Timothy Costello surprised seven Polish gangsters after they entered the Interstate Chemical Company at East 70th Street and Quincy Avenue. The robbers were after $20,000 worth of industrial alcohol that had a resale value of $80,000. As the police confronted the robbers, a gunfight began. One robber was wounded and five others captured. Police later arrested two more gang members and announced that fifteen more arrests were expected.

Unfortunately for Chief Smith, in the midst of the success his department was starting to achieve, he suffered a personal tragedy. His son, Neil J. Smith, was killed along with two other men in a freak accident in New York. The son was working on a train engine boiler when it exploded. In an incredible coincidence, the explosion occurred just as the train was passing in front of the home of Chief Smith's brother in Victor, New York.

This tragedy was followed by the cold-blooded, heartless murder of Patrolman Elmer Sprosty (discussed in Chapter 5). The Sprosty murder, instead of slowing criminal activity down, seemed to have had just the opposite effect. Another crime wave occurred that weekend with another police officer getting shot at during a drug store robbery on Prospect Avenue. In addition, another local businessman was abducted and robbed of a $1,800 payroll, and a stolen automobile was used in the robbery of four gasoline stations.

The brazen action of the criminals was beginning to wear thin on the citizens of Cleveland. On the morning of May 5, Max Silberman, a young would-be pickpocket, attempted to steal the purse of a woman. As he did, a man who witnessed the attempt slugged him between the eyes. Silberman took off with six others in pursuit. He ran across Euclid Avenue, through the Arcade to Superior, and, after shoving a police officer out of the way, headed toward East 6th Street. The pursuing crowd caught him when he slipped and fell at East 6th and Vincent. The mob began to pummel him with fists, umbrellas and anything else they held in their hands. When police finally rescued the young man, he was bloodied and missing three teeth.

If the public's indignation toward the criminals had any effect, the criminals weren't showing it. The day after the public beating, in a twelve-hour period, police were involved in five gun battles with bandits. In addition, Stoners restaurant on Superior Avenue was robbed of $300. It was the fifth time in four months the restaurant was held up. The new crime spree ended with the daylight holdup of the Miller Brother's Shoe Company on St. Clair by three youths.

On May 10, the city recorded its fourth attempted kidnapping of the year. A 22-year-old musician was abducted by three men at Prospect and East 20th Street. She escaped her drunken captors on the West Side where they were planning to take her to a roadhouse and rape her. The three other kidnap victims were also young women, one of whom was raped.

On May 6, B. Ogden Chisholm, of the New York Prison Reform Bureau, spoke to the Engineering and the Electrical League on the roof of the Statler Hotel. The topic was "Prison Reform." Chisholm told the audience that Prohibition was the cause for the huge increase in crime in Cleveland as well as the rest of the nation. "Prohibition has made more criminals than liquor ever did," he stated, "It is one of the evils of our country today and should be abolished." He followed this with some startling statistics. The year before Prohibition began, 280,000 people in New York were sentenced for criminal offenses. In 1920, the number rose to 467,000. Chisholm also claimed that Prohibition was responsible for the increase in drug addicts in America.

Booze wasn't the only item criminals were getting rich on. On May 12, police were involved in a running gun battle with three men. The chase started at East 71st Street and ended in Bedford with the three occupants abandoning their auto and fleeing on foot through a field. Two of the men were captured and police found packages containing 65,000 cigarettes in the automobile.

Many of the crimes committed during the 1921 spree seemed more vicious than at other times. On June 2, Mrs. Fayme Britt was walking to work along Ivanhoe Road on Cleveland's East Side. An automobile pulled to a stop and three men, including Britt's husband, jumped out. Robert Britt was angry because his 22-year-old wife refused to drop divorce proceedings against him. As the two men held her arms, Britt threw acid in his wife's face, blinding her and badly burning her face and arms. Later that month, sixty-year-old Minnie Harris let a man into her home on the pretext of purchasing furniture she was offering for sale. The man demanded a diamond ring she was wearing. She refused and, as she turned to run, the man beat her over the head with a blackjack and tore the ring from her finger.

During the summer of 1921, Smith, tired of getting beat up by the daily newspapers, began withholding information from them at Central Police Station. He soon found himself a defendant in a legal suit brought against him by the publishers. In court Smith argued that the newspapers were "deliberately misrepresenting police news." He lost and was ordered to stop the practice, but he refused. Judge Manuel Levine found Smith guilty of contempt, but suspended sentence on condition that he adhere to the court's order.

On July 3, an amendment to the courts indeterminate sentencing act was to take effect. The change allowed the courts in Ohio, "to impose general sentences instead of indeterminate sentences to the penitentiary." In affect, the new amendment allowed the court to assign minimum periods for sentences, except in cases of treason and first-degree murder. Cuyahoga County Prosecutor Stanton took advantage of the introduction date of the new law to induce several hundred persons charged with felonies to plead guilty in order to avoid the possibility of longer prison terms, before the new law began. When sentenced under the old law, a convicted felon could receive from one to twenty years and be paroled in fourteen months. Under the new guidelines, a prisoner would be sentenced from five to twenty years, or fifteen to twenty years, and have to serve the minimum. Stanton's plan saved the county thousands of dollars, not to mention hours, by not having to prosecute the cases.

Stanton had become the new darling of the newspapers. Editorials heralded his accomplishments. One editorial claimed he "has done more toward making the criminal law respected in Cleveland than all other officers and citizens had been able to accomplish in two or three years of special effort." In September, Stanton released statistics showing that since the beginning of the year 1,420 indictments were returned and of those 789 pleaded guilty, or were found guilty and sent to prison, 174 were discharged, and 67 were found guilty and paroled, with the balance of the indictments still pending.

The dawn of Prohibition had created new crimes and a new breed of criminal. It also was the cause of a number of alcohol related incidents in the Cleveland Police Department. One incident, indicative of the times, occurred on April 1. Police officer John Monahan was suspended by Chief Smith on charges of intoxication in uniform while off duty. While stories of drunken police officers were not unheard of, the irony was that none of Monahan's friends or fellow officers had ever seen him take a drink, and his record of almost two years on the force was spotless. Safety Director Sprosty, who decided the patrolman's fate, told reporters, "Doesn't it go to show what prohibition will do to a man?"

In September, Second Precinct Captain Frank O. Smith and Lieutenant Thomas Duffy were found intoxicated in a café run by Mrs. Theresa Andrews, the widow of former Cleveland City Councilman John Andrews. The discovery of the two was made after George Southwell of the Dry Maintenance League was tipped off that Cleveland Police Chief Frank W. Smith (no relation) was in the café. Southwell telephoned the chief and, after reaching him in his office, the two headed down to the Andrew's café and confronted the officers. Both were suspended for failing to report the selling of liquor in the café. Police arrested Mrs. Andrews. It was not her first arrest. She was arrested several times by federal agents and police for liquor violations and had recently completed a sixty-day sentence in the Canton workhouse. During a hearing before Safety Director Sprosty, both officers claimed they were "victims of a frame-up." Sprosty upheld the suspension of Duffy who was also accused of "visiting" Mrs. Andrews in her New Wright Hotel room – accusations that she denied. Sprosty reinstated Captain Smith, who was soon transferred to an undesirable precinct by Chief Smith.

The officer's suspensions were followed by a crackdown on the saloons and "blind pigs" in the Superior / Oregon Avenue neighborhood. The forty-plus establishments in the area were either closed or refrained from selling anything but soft drinks. In addition, Chief Smith began a shake-up in the second precinct, transferring several ranking officers and placing Captain Martin Horrigan, of the traffic division, in charge of the precinct.

Things just weren't getting any better for the Cleveland Police Department. In a front-page article on November 19, the headlines read "2 Policemen on Booze Rampage Shoot Woman." The two vice officers, Martin Callan and William McGonigal, were assigned to the 16th precinct on East 130th Street between Union Avenue and Kinsman Road. At 2:00 p.m. Friday when they got off work, the two men began drinking at a soft drink parlor on Webster Avenue, owned by Mayfield Road mobster Biago DePalma. When a delivery of milk arrived Callan got angry, demanding to know why the manager permitted strikebreakers to deliver it. (At the time there was a milk strike going on in Cleveland and both officers had recently been detailed out of their regular vice work for special milk strike duty.) Callan threatened to "shoot up" the place and when he drew his service revolver he caught his badge causing him to tear his shirt and drop the gun to the floor. This diversion evidently caused him to forget his threat and he and McGonigal left the parlor.

The two men, after five hours of drinking, staggered down Central Avenue encountering Harry Stone and demanded liquor from him. When Stone replied he had none, Callan grabbed him and threatened to place him under arrest. McGonigal told Callan that Stone was a friend of his and Callan released him. The pair then approached two women. After words were exchanged, Callan began slapping one of them. A passer-by stepped in and knocked Callan to the sidewalk where he pulled his revolver. The man took ran down Central Avenue followed by a hail of bullets. When another man, witnessing Callan walking down the street with his gun in hand, said something to him, the drunken officer tried to arrest him. The frightened man ran with Callan in pursuit, blasting away at him.

The sound of gunfire caught the attention of two nearby detectives, who rushed to the scene, only to draw Callan's fire. At East 14th Street and Central Avenue the detectives dived behind a telephone pole and waited for Callan to empty his gun. Before they could reach him, however, he reloaded and began blasting away again. This time one of Callan's bullets hit Mrs. Antoinette Santoro in the leg as she raced into the street in search of her son. A crowd by now had gathered and the detectives, fearful of hitting an innocent spectator, held their fire.

A patrolman also arrived on the scene and, after helping Mrs. Santoro to safety, rushed Callan and wrestled with him. As the two detectives came to help, Callan got off a few more shots, one of which grazed one of the detectives. With the help of several local firemen, Callan was finally subdued. There were shouts of "lynch him" from the angry crowd and several men threatened to kill Callan because of the wounding of Mrs. Santoro. During all the excitement, McGonigal slipped away, but was arrested after arriving home. He confessed to firing his revolver, but into the air. McGonigal had a perfect record during his 18 months on the force. The day after the incident the chief suspended both men.

This incident was one of many that incensed Chief Smith toward Safety Director Sprosty, and bad feelings he had been harboring for months exploded. The exasperated chief told reporters, "I made a personal call on Sprosty to protest the reappointment of Callan to the police force, but despite this Callan was reinstated in October, 1920."

Callan was with the police department on and off for four years. During this time he had resigned twice. Once after charges were filed against him for shooting up a café on Orange Avenue where he was drinking. In February his partner, Albert Block was killed in an accident while the two were investigating a gambling establishment. Later that month, Callan was suspended on charges of "cowardice, lack of energy and incompetence" in connection with allowing a burglar to escape. He was reinstated by Sprosty. Chief Smith continued his assault on Sprosty stating, "Callan has resigned previous to this after he had pulled his revolver in a similar scrape in the third precinct. I told Sprosty that Callan was dangerous when intoxicated and that his reappointment might lead to a tragedy. My protests did no good. If Sprosty were to remain in office for two years more, Cleveland would have the worst demoralized police force in the country. In about nineteen out of twenty cases in which I suspend a police officer, Sprosty gives him a slap on the wrist and puts him back on the force. The only trouble with the department is the presence of twenty-five or thirty irresponsible policemen who ought to be kicked out, and the other patrolmen know who these men are. What is needed is discipline and Sprosty has prevented this [from] being enforced."

Chief Smith's argument was understandable. One of the problem officers the chief was referring to was Michael J. Harwood. The sergeant was suspended by Smith after an incident outside the Hotel Morland where Harwood, while on duty, met with Ulrich Richter, a friend of Sprosty's. When Mayor Fitzgerald upheld the suspension, Sprosty wrote a note to the sergeant apologizing for the "severity" of the punishment. Harwood then appealed the case to the Civil Service Commission and won. He was not only reinstated, Harwood was promoted to lieutenant by Sprosty. In the late 1930s, Safety Director Eliot Ness personally oversaw the investigation that sent the corrupt Harwood to the Ohio Penitentiary.

Just when things seemed like they couldn't get any worse for the department, they did. Around midnight on November 25, Patrolman Frank J. Koran was killed while chasing three men committing a robbery near Orange Avenue and East 40th Street. The 45 year-old father of three was shot eight times and died within minutes. His assailants, three Black men, disappeared into the night despite the quick arrival of "every flying squad of the East End."

An editorial appeared in the *Cleveland News* titled, "Why Policemen Fall." It hit on two elements of why the Cleveland problems existed; the justice system and the police department itself:

> "The law's breakdown has made bandits and gunmen the more ready to kill policemen or other citizens at pleasure. While all crime has been encouraged by court scandals, failure to make arrests, plentiful pardons and paroles, few penitentiary sentences and executions, merciful juries and other weaknesses of the law, no special success in capturing and punishing murderers of policemen has made policemen's lives specially respected by thugs.
>
> On the contrary, admission of unfit men to membership in the police force and failure to maintain discipline among policemen not of the conscientious class has robbed the force of the respect of criminals as well as of the confidence of the public. When so many policemen are known to become drunk, shoot up neighborhoods, drive recklessly, terrorize citizens, steal whisky or commit murder, it cannot be wondered at if killers feel as little hesitancy in killing policemen as in killing other Clevelanders."

The same day Koran was killed, two robbers followed a Cedar Road furniture store owner into his shop as he opened at 8:00 a.m. When his son arrived thirty minutes later, he found his father in the basement dead, his skull completely crushed by blows from a mallet.

The situation got uglier as a newly declared war on crime by Chief Smith seemed only to net the down and out instead of the real criminals. In the five days following the Koran and store owner's murders, the "crime roundup" resulted in the arrests of 816 men on charges of vagrancy, drunkenness, suspicion, and loitering. Only thirteen of the arrests were for felonies. As fast as these men were being sent to the Warrensville Workhouse, Welfare Director Dudley Blossom was paroling them. Police Court judges were sending men to the workhouse at the rate of 30 per hour. Meanwhile, another mini-crime wave had broken out and the police were unable to arrest any of the criminals involved. The newspapers reported the crime wave consisted of 31 burglaries, 31 robberies, 6 safe break-ins, 15 reports of grand larceny, and 58 reports of petit larceny. In addition, one man, a father of eight children, was murdered during a soft drink parlor holdup. The newspapers and Blossom were enraged at Chief Smith's misguided attempts to halt the rampant crime wave. A front-page editorial in the *Cleveland News* on December 1, read:

Our Efficient Police Heads!

"They round-up, jail and terrorize men out of work, the poor, the unfortunate, and the tramps, but they fail to catch any robbers or murderers, and banditry is rampant, as usual!

"Raiding lodging houses, shanties, dumps and other resorts of the homeless, [they are] gathering in unresisting vagrants in large numbers and aiding the courts to forward to the workhouse hundreds of hungry shivering tramps."

"Honest men are being arrested without cause," says Mr. Blossom. "Men who should never see the inside of a jail are being herded into the workhouse like cattle, without a chance to vindicate themselves. The police make no attempt to separate them. The old and the young, the guilty and the innocent, are treated alike. The majority of these men have never been convicted of a crime. They are out of work, without funds, without influence, and they are made the victims of a useless police war to rid the city of crime. Surely to be without money and jobless in these days is not a crime."

"If protecting life and property by arresting criminals and discouraging crime is the primary function of a police force…the police department is a failure."

On December 1, the dragnet brought in 53 men, of which 8 were sent to the workhouse. One of the men was arrested for carrying a concealed weapon. Blossom paroled the man after it was revealed he was a carpenter and his "weapon" was a screwdriver he was taking home from work. The man told workhouse authorities he was herded out of the court to the workhouse without ever getting a chance to explain.

The next day saw a new round of arrests when 51 "vagrants, suspicious persons and inebriates" were arraigned in police court. Only two men were sent to the Warrensville Workhouse, one for intoxication, and the other for begging. Meanwhile, overnight, four additional robberies, three burglaries, and one theft were committed without any arrests made.

By December 3, the crime round up seemed to be winding down as only nine men were arrested and three sent to the workhouse. Still the three murders and dozens of thefts and burglaries remained unsolved. The crime-wave continued and on December 8, three gunmen shot down a merchant as he tried to protect his daily receipts from the robbers on the doorstep of his Othello Avenue home. He survived after being rushed to surgery at Woman's Hospital.

During such times there was always an outcry from the public for the death penalty. It seemed to be as much a hot topic in the 1920s as it is today. Edward Stanton was zealous in his defense of the death penalty as a deterrent to crime during his years as prosecutor. An example of this came after the sentencing of Jack Gray in March 1922. Gray and a companion held up Emil Hermanson and two others on Christmas Day 1921. The incident took place at Central Avenue and Ontario as Hermanson was on his way to the Union Station to catch a train to Ashtabula to spend the holiday with his three motherless children. Gray and his cohort pulled the robbery in order to "get a little money to celebrate Christmas."

Hermanson and the others were confronted by Gray and ordered to throw their hands up. When Hermanson refused Gray shot him to death , unaware that two detectives were watching as the whole scene unfolded. During his attempt to flee, Gray was wounded three times by the pursuing officers. At trial, a jury of ten men and two women found him guilty of first degree murder in the courtroom of Judge Fred H. Wolf, but made a recommendation of mercy.

As Judge Wolf sentenced the killer to life in the Ohio Penitentiary, he reminded him, "You owe these jurors a debt of gratitude. You should be grateful to them for sparing your life."

The word "grateful" was not a term Stanton used to describe the jury. "It was a weak-kneed jury," the prosecutor declared. He then proceeded to rip the panel members for their decision, "If they had any courage at all they would have sentenced Gray to die. For if ever a man deserved to expiate his crime in the death chair he did. He was and is guilty of cold-blooded murder, done while in the act of committing a felony, and death should have been the penalty. It is verdicts such as this that encourage crime and make the man with murder in his heart defiant of the law."

Throughout the 1920s the Cleveland newspapers raged about how "murder was a safe crime" in Cleveland. Time after time they pointed out that men given life sentences by the court ended up serving less than ten years. A *Cleveland News* editorial, commenting on the situations and on Stanton's efforts for justice stated:

"Yet Prosecuting Attorney Stanton's best efforts have been brought thus close to nothing through susceptible jurors, mercy verdicts, delays, appeals, legal dodges and other factors endured by the public for the benefit of its enemies.

"And even in the few cases where conviction and imprisonment result, murderers share with lesser criminals the favor of indulgent governors, clemency boards, pardons, paroles, suspended sentences, conditional releases and various practices society permits to frustrate its courts, nullify its laws and place the lives and property of its honest members at the mercy of merciless rogues."

An expose done by the *News* in mid-1925 showed that year in Cleveland there were 65 murders committed since January 1. Of those 48 had been resolved and only one man had been ordered to die, and that sentence was being appealed.

Chapter Endnotes

1. Some reports claim Frank W. Smith was from Flint, Michigan.

2. The seven police officers were Patrolman Frank M. Moranz, September 26, 1919; Sergeant William C. Isaac, December 1, 1919; Patrolman Robert Shelton, December 7, 1919; Patrolman Walter Pruehs, October 18, 1920; Patrolman Albert Block, February 11, 1921; Patrolman August Dyke, March 24, 1921; and Patrolman Elmer Sprosty, April 21, 1921. Before the year was out, Patrolman Frank J. Koran was murdered on November 26, 1921. In addition to these officers from Cleveland, Captain Edward Connolly of the Cleveland Heights Police Department was killed on September 8, 1920.

3
Cleveland Crime Survey

On January 5, 1921, the Cleveland Foundation announced that it had hired Dr. Dean Roscoe Pound of the Harvard Law School to conduct a survey into the administration of justice in the city. *The Encyclopedia of Cleveland History* reports that the far-reaching survey "analyzed the work of the police, prosecutors, coroner's office, criminal courts, and correctional system; probed legal education; weighed the role of psychiatry in criminal justice; and assessed the adequacy of crime reporting in the local press." The survey was set up to review procedures within the Cleveland Police Department, investigate the judiciary system, which had developed a reputation for handing out short and suspended sentences, and investigate operating procedures in the jails. Roscoe was described as having "practical experience as a prosecutor and a judge and is perhaps the greatest authority in the country upon the administration of justice in the modern city. He is recognized internationally as an expert in the law."

The survey's investigation centered on the systems and administrations of the various law enforcement functions and was not to focus on individuals. Raymond Moley, director of Cleveland Foundation, stated, "We are not seeking out individuals, but there is something radically wrong somewhere and we will show it up regardless of who suffers." An advisory committee was planned and made up of members of the Bar Association, the Chamber of Commerce, the Welfare Foundation, the League of Women Voters, the Federation of Women's Clubs, and the Retail Merchants Board.

On January 29, Dr. Pound appeared at the Hollenden Hotel before an audience of more than 1,000. The City Club sponsored the noon luncheon. In a speech using words befitting a Harvard professor, Dr. Pound outlined the six divisions of his probe. They were the police department, prosecutor's office, court system, penal institutions, the municipal relations, and the medical relations. Dr. Pound pointed out that Cleveland was using laws that were introduced prior to "the Civil War, when the population was only 45,000," and that the population was nearing 800,000. In addition, he stated, "the punitive laws in force in this country are shaped after 18th century English penal codes, which does not deal with organized criminality, but only the occasional criminal who violates the law more through passion than design." After the speech, Cleveland Foundation director Moley introduced the advisory committee consisting of 35 members of the community. Amos Burt Thompson, of the law firm Thompson, Hine & Flory, was appointed chairman.

One of the first people selected by the survey team was Raymond B. Fosdick, a foremost authority on American police systems and methods. Fosdick had first-hand knowledge of Cleveland from investigating local conditions for the Rockefeller Bureau of Social Hygiene. His findings, which included investigative work in 71 other cities, were published as "American Police Systems." During his previous duties, Fosdick had worked with both Dr. Pound, and Felix Frankfurter, his second-in-command here.

The probe officially got underway on February 1. Fosdick and investigators met with Mayor Fitzgerald, Safety Director Sprosty, and Police Chief Smith to discuss cooperation between the various departments and to make sure all statistical records were made available. Assisting Fosdick as the statistician for the survey was C. E. Gehrke, a Western Reserve University sociologist. Frankfurter, whose job it was to oversee the day-to-day operations of the probe, announced that no findings would be released until the entire survey was complete.

The investigative work was completed by June 1921 and for the rest of the summer the reports were written, edited and revised. During late September and early October the reports were released in a series and detailed in the local newspapers. Each report outlined a specific area of the group's investigation and listed its recommendations.

With each new release there was controversy and complaints from the area being investigated. With the release of the report on "Prosecution," which covered both the county and the municipal offices, Alfred Bettman, the former city solicitor of Cincinnati who authored the report, spoke at an open luncheon at the Hollenden Hotel. Addressing the audience, Bettman stated that due to the comparatively low salaries of prosecutors, both county and municipal, it was hard to attract men of superior ability, and that according to a survey of members of the bar the caliber of the prosecutors was inferior.

This obviously stirred the wrath of new Cuyahoga County Prosecutor Stanton, who when informed of the comment fired back, "If the gentleman from Cincinnati can supply definite proof of his statements regarding the personnel of the prosecutors, at least in my office, I shall demand resignations at once. If he cannot produce definite proof of his assertions, he owes an immediate and public apology for his statements."

The report on the Cleveland Police Department was particularly harsh calling for a reorganization of the entire force. Most of the criticism fell on the detective bureau. The recommendations called for, "Complete overhauling of detective bureau, with a view to 'getting rid of almost the entire present personnel.'" In the survey group's assessment scale the members of the detective bureau graded below the intelligence level of the average patrolman. As with the report on the prosecutors, the survey report claimed the salaries didn't attract men of high intelligence.

Other department recommendations by the survey included:

➤ Abandonment of present division of authority by chief and director of public safety

➤ Appointment of the chief of police from civilian life and not from the ranks of patrolmen, as at present. The director, also drawn from civil life, to be given full administrative powers, with authority to appoint the chief, drawing if necessary from other cities for a man qualified for the position

➤ Establishment of a more constructive system of appointment and promotion, basing selections on police ability rather on cut-and-dried qualifications required by present civil service commission.

➤ Appointment of police women in crime prevention division, to pay strict attention to social delinquency.

➤ Reduction of number of precincts, so to reduce overhead costs and minimize duplication of effort.

➤ Punishing of intoxication by immediate dismissal (a problem which seemed to increase with the dawn of Prohibition)

Other recommendations called for recruiting procedures, enhanced training school operations and the reduction of the maximum age of new officers from 35 to 30 years of age.

While it produced only limited results in terms of reform, the survey did represent the first in depth study of the justice system in a major United States city. More importantly, it laid the groundwork for future studies such as the Commission on Law Observance & Enforcement, which became known as the Wickersham Committee, created in 1929 during President Herbert Hoover's first year in office. Another important result was the creation of the Cleveland Association for Criminal Justice. The association, made up of business and civic groups, served as a crime and justice watchdog in the city for the next thirty years.

4

Murder of Officer Sprosty

In April 1921, another senseless murder became part of the crime wave. The killer in this case would later testify during the trial of one of the Sly-Fanner slayers. In addition, the incident provided a glimpse at a mysterious figure who became a Cleveland Mafia boss, and introduced the brother of another underworld chieftain.

Robert "Bobby" Hunt was a street thug who at an early age decided a career in crime was the path he was taking. Hunt walked the walk and talked the talk of an old style hoodlum, always speaking out of the side of his mouth and having no respect for authority. Another young man, Elmer Sprosty, whose career path ran in the opposite direction of Hunt's, had the tragic misfortune of encountering the young hood.

On May 4, 1918, Hunt and a companion robbed the paymaster from the Hunkin-Conkey Construction Company of $4,100 as he was about to deliver a payroll to a construction site on Warner Road in Newburgh Heights. One of the men threw pepper in the man's eyes and then struck him down with a blackjack, while the other man waited poised behind the wheel of the getaway car. Hunt was arrested and charged with the payroll robbery and then released on bail. He went to Detroit, thus jumping bond, and on August 16 was arrested with another man and charged with breaking into a garage with intent to steal an automobile. Hunt was turned over to his bondsman who brought him back to Cleveland. On October 13, he was convicted and sentenced to the Mansfield Reformatory by Judge Manuel Levine.

Hunt was paroled on November 28, 1920, and returned to Cleveland. Less than five months later, on the night of Thursday, April 21, 1921, he was drinking in a saloon owned by Philip Goldberg at the corner of Scovill Avenue and East 14th Street. Hunt was sloppy drunk, having been in the illegal saloon most of the day. Sometime that evening seven young men arrived at the saloon. Among them were William J. "Chick" Pierce,[1] James Walsh, William "Billy Murphy" Conton, Frank Shannon and Charles "Oyster House" Austerhaut. All of the men were taxi drivers, or chauffeurs as they were popularly referred to. Many in the trade at that time used their own automobiles, but they all needed to be registered under the taxicab ordinance. This group of drivers that entered Goldberg's saloon that night had two things in common, none were registered and all had criminal records.

The chain of events that occurred next was never fully explained, the participants refusing to deliver a believable account. But a disturbance took place inside the Goldberg saloon which precipitated Hunt's actions. Whether it was a gang fight, an argument over a woman, or just several drunken men letting off steam we'll never know. Whatever the case, the participants moved outside, according to one report, where Hunt punched Austerhaut in the face. He then pulled a .32 automatic and shot twice at the sidewalk, as if imitating a gunslinger from an old Western flick where the victim was ordered to "dance."

Standing across the street, observing the commotion, was 24 year-old Patrolman Elmer Sprosty. The young man was a member of the Cleveland Police Department for just a little over six months. A star football player in high school, Sprosty had served in the Navy during the World War. During his short time on the force he had already disarmed two would-be robbers after a "thrilling chase" down Woodland Avenue. His superiors expected great things from the young officer. Perhaps it was in his blood. Sprosty's father was Cleveland Police Captain Frank D. Sprosty and his uncle was Cleveland's Director of Public Safety, Anton B. Sprosty. The junior Sprosty told friends, "My ambition is to be as good a policeman as my father."

Defying all the dangers, and walking into a situation knowing that his service revolver was inoperable, Sprosty crossed the street to put an end to the horseplay before someone was seriously hurt. By now a number of the men were scattering, some getting into an automobile that was parked nearby, facing south on Scovill. Hunt jumped on the right-side running board of the car, while William Conton stood on the left one. Seeing Sprosty coming on the run, Hunt aimed his weapon and fired. Sprosty dropped to the sidewalk. Hunt then took aim and fired twice more at the prone officer, hitting him both times. The dying officer had never bothered to draw his weapon.

Hearing the shooting was Patrolman Nathan Wachs, who was walking a nearby beat. The officer raced to the scene, arriving just as the automobile started off down Scovill. Wachs took aim and fired several shots. Claiming he had developed an "excellent shot" while in the Navy, Wachs was positive he had hit one of the men on the car's running boards.

There was some confusion as to whether Officer Sprosty was dead at the scene. While some stories indicate he was, others claim that he was taken to Charity Hospital[2] in a truck and died as doctors tried to save him. The *Cleveland News* stated Sprosty's "mother and sister were notified by telephone, but just before they reached the hospital the patrolman succumbed. Both relatives fainted on hearing the news." Later, during Hunt's murder trial, the two physicians that attended to him at Charity were called to testify.

The scene changes to a house at 3456 East 116th Street; the home of Jasper Polizzi, the brother of future Mayfield Road Mob leader Alfred "Big Al" Polizzi. Jasper's wife, Carmela later told a reporter, "I awakened about 3:00 a.m. and I heard moans and groans from the front porch. I called my husband and he and my father-in-law investigated."

"I am dying," Carmela said she heard the wounded man say as he clutched his stomach. On the Polizzi porch was Bobby Hunt, bleeding from wounds in his back, abdomen and right leg. Officer Wach's bullets had indeed found their mark; the most serious wound was a bullet that hit Hunt in the back and exited through his stomach. Jasper Polizzi and his father helped Hunt into the house, where Jasper called Dr. Guiseppe Romano, a successful physician, but a man with a strange avocation; he would one day be revealed as the leader of the Cleveland Mafia. Carmela Polizzi claimed she had never seen the wounded man in her life, and that he was not known to anyone else in the home. No one believed, however, that the house Hunt wound up at was selected at random.

After Hunt was administered to, a call was placed to the police department around noon that Friday advising them of his whereabouts. The caller was a mystery. One source said it was a woman, another claimed it was Dr. Romano. More than likely it was Romano, or at least done on his orders because Hunt was so seriously wounded none thought he would survive. Police arrived and transported the wounded man, who was described as being in a comatose state, to City Hospital where he was reported to be dying.

Police quickly rounded up the men who were in the saloon that night. William Conton was the first to spill his guts to the police, implicating Hunt and Austerhaut as the ones who fired on Sprosty. He told them a bizarre tale about how Hunt was driven around the city, finally ending up at the corner of East Sixth Street and Superior. How the seriously wounded Hunt made it from there to the Polizzi residence at East 116th Street was anyone's guess. When police searched the room Conton was renting, they found two guns, a .32 automatic and a .38 revolver. Conton said he took both guns from Hunt as he lay on the floor of the car. He claimed the weapons were used by Hunt and the .32 automatic was soon determined to be the murder weapon. Police also discovered the .32 belonged to Philip Goldberg, the proprietor of the saloon. Investigators never received a satisfactory answer as to how it ended up in Hunt's possession.

At City Hospital, Hunt admitted to being at the saloon that night but claimed he did not shoot Sprosty. As for his own wounds, he offered a ridiculous story about being shot in Toledo, being driven back and dropped off in Cleveland, and then walking to the Polizzi home.

On Monday, April 25, Patrolman Elmer Sprosty was laid to rest at West Park Cemetery. A mounted police unit escorted the body from the home of Sprosty's parents on East 96th Street to the cemetery. Among the mourners was Sprosty's estranged wife, Cecelia.

As one of the first orders of business, Acting Police Chief John Rowlands (Chief Smith was attending the funeral of his son) issued orders to all precinct commanders that officers were not to leave the station houses unless the firing mechanism of their service revolvers was in working condition. This followed two more incidents of officer's weapons failing to discharge properly. In one incident the revolver "literally fell to pieces" in the officer's hand. In the other, involving Patrolman Ernest L. Ford,[3] only half of his bullets fired during a shootout with three men at the corner of Central Avenue and East 22nd Street.

The day after Sprosty's funeral, four eyewitnesses stood in front of Bobby Hunt's bed at City Hospital and identified him as the man who fired the shots that killed the young officer. Afterward, Detective Inspector Sterling and Lieutenant Emmett J. Potts* filed murder charges against Hunt. Despite the eyewitness identification, police were still skeptical about having the right man. They still had no motive for the fracas that took place outside the Goldberg saloon, and they had no idea as to how Goldberg's gun ended up in Hunt's possession. More than one experienced investigator figured the gang selected Hunt as the fall guy simply because he wasn't expected to live.

On May 18, during a hearing before Municipal Chief Justice John P. Dempsey, Hunt was ordered held without bail while the county grand jury considered the charges. Seven material witnesses were placed under a $1,000 bail. Two days later Hunt was indicted for first-degree murder. Common Pleas Judge Florence E. Allen assigned Stephen M. Young to represent him. On June 2, the grand jury indicted Conton, Walsh and Frank Shannon, charging all three with first-degree murder. The next day Conton and Shannon were arraigned before Judge Allen. Both pled not guilty and were held without bond. After Conton informed the judge that he needed legal representation, Allen appointed Mary Grossman and Herman J. Nord to represent him. The prisoners were placed in the "murderer's row" section of the Cuyahoga County Jail. Shannon, who shared a cell with the now fully recovered Hunt, soon got into a "violent quarrel" with his cell-mate and asked to be placed in another cell.

On June 10, Detectives James Toner and Joseph Jacobs arrested James Walsh after finding him at the corner of East 17th Street and Oregon

Avenue (today Rockwell Avenue). Walsh offered no resistance and readily admitted to being at Goldberg's saloon at the time of the shooting, but claimed he had nothing to do with it. A check of Walsh's record showed he frequently used the alias "James Sullivan." His first arrest came on April 21, 1915, when he was charged with a robbery at the Hudson Hardware Company, in Hudson, Ohio. Sentenced to the penitentiary, he was paroled a year later. Three years later, on April 4, 1918, he was indicted for robbing a local man. Arrested ten months later, police files showed no disposition of the case. On June 3, 1919, he was arrested for robbery and rape. Convicted, he was sent back to the penitentiary for thirteen months. His last arrest on November 12, 1920, was for smashing the window of a Superior Avenue jewelry store. The charges were later dropped. There were more arrests to come.

On Thursday, June 23, the day Hunt was to go on trial for Sprosty's murder, Clevelanders woke up to hear about, "the most sensational jail delivery[4] in the city's history." Bobby Hunt, James Walsh and Charles Gallagher – the latter a parole violator who had replaced Shannon as Hunt's cellmate – had escaped from the county jail by sawing their way through their cell bars before overpowering four guards. A fourth prisoner, in the cell with Walsh, was also part of the plot, but was too big to squeeze out though the hole.

The *Cleveland News* gave this colorful description of the escape:

> "The delivery was staged with all the dramatic frills of a moving picture play. As though carried out according to rehearsal the trio, Hunt and Gallagher in cell No. 9, tier No. 2, and Walsh in cell No. 11, adjoining, sawed through the last bar at 2 a.m., crawled through on their stomachs and made their way to the lower floor, where they hid behind the cell block until two of the guards making their rounds passed from sight.
>
> "Then with handkerchief masks covering all but their eyes, and with revolvers drawn; they dashed up the steps leading to the jail office floor, commanded a third guard to throw up his hands and dashed into the sheriff's office.
>
> "Then a fourth guard was overpowered [Deputy Sheriff John Levine], deprived of his revolver, thrown into the cell house and locked in with the rest.
>
> "A sprint across the floor, a leap though an open window leading into Frankfort ave. and the three were as free as the air."

The escape plan worked to perfection and no one was hurt. An investigation revealed the men had sawed holes in the bottom section of the cell doors, sixteen inches high and twelve inches wide. Edges around the sawed bars, which were accompanied by rust, indicated that the process had gone on for several weeks.

A watchman from the old courthouse, located next door to the jail, saw the men crawl out through the window. Sensing an escape was in progress, he rushed to the jail and shouted for the jailers to open up. When they didn't respond, he called police headquarters where he informed Inspector Stephen Murphy that "something was wrong." After Murphy's failed attempt at raising someone by phone, he sent out a general alarm and eight flying squads rushed to the jail. Murphy was forced to crawl through the same window the men escaped through to get into the jail.

Sheriff Stannard and police officials were puzzled as to how the men got the saws, as well as the weapons they used to subdue the guards. The sheriff came under a wave of criticism after the escape. Stannard argued that he was the babysitter of an old and inadequate jail. He claimed the only way he could hold the prisoners in safe keeping was to place a guard outside every cell.

Police quickly tracked down two taxi cab drivers who had transported the three men. The first said the trio approached him outside the Hotel Cleveland and ordered him to drive them "by devious routes" to Cedar and East 36th Street. A second driver picked them up there, but where they went next was not revealed in the newspapers. Both drivers were "held for investigation," and later booked as suspicious persons. Since the gang of men who were involved in the fracas at Philip Goldberg's saloon were all taxi cab drivers, it is possible police believed the men aided the prisoners in their escape.

Within hours police had the girlfriends of the escaped men in custody. Gallagher's paramour had recently left her husband, sold her rings, and "mortgaged" her piano just days before the trio broke out. Police believed she may have been responsible for smuggling the saws and weapons to the men. Gallagher's girlfriend accused one of the jail's deputies of allowing her late night visits to see all three prisoners. She also admitted that another deputy was a frequent visitor to her home. On Saturday night Detective Roy A. Allison interviewed a woman who claimed Gallagher arrived at her West Side home shortly after the prison break to inquire about his "sweetheart." The woman claimed the girlfriend's brother recently sold a gun to Gallagher, which the girlfriend gave to the prisoner after being allowed to enter his cell. Sheriff Stannard denied this allegation declaring no visitor had ever been allowed inside a cell with a prisoner. The unnamed woman also told Allison she saw the girlfriend sewing saws into the lining of some underwear she delivered to Gallagher. On another matter, in which it was unclear how she knew, the woman claimed Walsh had allowed himself to be arrested in order to smuggle saws into Bobby Hunt.

Prosecutor Stanton announced he would ask for a special investigation of the jail break, if "facts should warrant it." He claimed the escape was a sure indication of Hunt and Walsh's guilt and predicted that when brought to trial both would end up in the death chair.

On Tuesday, June 28, it was reported that an informant, living in a tent at Geauga Lake[5] with two other campers, encountered the three escapees who announced that they would be "staying with them" for a while. Captain of Detectives, Timothy J. Costello,* who was heading the investigation, reported that the informant was a "pal" of all three of the escapees and had once served time with Walsh at the Mansfield Reformatory. During the time the men were at the campsite, Hunt brandished his revolver on more than one occasion declaring, "They'll never take me unless I'm a sieve."

Late Friday, one of the campers "strongly suggested" that the men "move on."

"Are you going to get rid of us," Hunt was alleged to have demanded.

"You bet I am," the camper replied. "I know who you three birds are. You are the three that broke jail in Cleveland. I read about it in this morning's paper. If the police would come down and find you here, I'd be in good and bad, wouldn't I, for keeping you here?"

The three campers were arrested and held as "accessories" to the jailbreak. On Sunday the escaped trio was spotted again. This time at Meyer's Lake, a resort located between Canton and Massillon.

On July 7, Hunt and his fugitive companions were believed to be part of a six-man gang that robbed the Marine National Bank in Ashtabula, Ohio of $4,700. In a response similar to that of the Bedford robbery by the Losteiner gang, the citizens of Ashtabula fired at the escaping bandits; one merchant was wounded by the return fire. The men, who many believed were hiding out in Cleveland, stole an automobile on the West Side and drove to Ashtabula, located in the far northeast corner of the state along Lake Erie. After the robbery, the men abandoned the vehicle at Ninevah Beach and made a daring escape aboard a motor boat named the "Merry G." The Coast Guard and two airplanes assisted police in an unsuccessful search for the trio. When police found the abandoned boat on a beach near Euclid Village (today the suburb Euclid), they discovered revolvers and "other paraphernalia" used in the robbery. The ensuing investigation showed police suspected the wrong men.

Two more weeks passed and then on the morning of July 14, Youngstown Police Chief James Watkins received a tip that the Cleveland fugitives were holed up in a house at 1349 Quinn Street in that city. Watkins stated two men "had visited a Girard bank and had offered to 'turn up' Walsh and Hunt for a consideration." The chief "made an investigation" and found that the tip was accurate.

Watkins contacted Sheriff Stannard, who dispatched Deputy Sheriffs Conrad Dombey and Arthur J. Bolles. At 3:30 p.m. the deputies and Watkins met to discuss a plan to capture the men. Their plan established, the three officers accompanied by thirty of "Youngstown's finest," including Detective Louis Veneroso (the Youngstown Police Department's version of Cleveland Detective Charles Cavolo), surrounded the Quinn Street home. The first man nabbed was Harry Roberts, an indicted Youngstown burglar out on bond, who proved to be a poor lookout; the *Youngstown Vindicator* reported Roberts "attempted to give the alarm, but was prevented from doing so."

Roberts informed the invading officers that no one was inside except his wife. But, as police entered the home they found Hunt and Walsh seated at the supper table, a meal being served to them by Robert's wife. Police noted, "both Hunt and Walsh were well dressed…freshly shaved and had a haircut only a few days old." Despite a gun belt holding two revolvers that was slung over the chair on which Hunt was seated, the men were taken without incident. While being handcuffed Walsh remarked, "Well, we are caught. It's a good thing you birds got us with our pants down or you would have seen some fun."

A search of the home owned by William T. Chapel, a former police captain for the New York Central Railroad, uncovered three more loaded revolvers, a large cache of ammunition and three quarts of whiskey. One of the revolvers was identified as being taken by Walsh from Deputy John Levine. Chapel was later arrested and held for hiding a car in his garage that Hunt and Walsh allegedly stole in Cleveland. Police found Chapel's plates on the stolen vehicle.

The prisoners were taken to police headquarters where they were photographed and waited for Cleveland police to arrive to take them back. While there, the pair was positively identified as the "silk shirt bandits" who had robbed a Market Street filling station in Youngstown on July 3. Hunt was reported to have had several hundred dollars on him, while Walsh had $87 when searched. One report claimed that while at the Youngstown police station, "Hunt went into a wild frenzy and, cursing and swearing, declared he would never return to Cleveland alive."

Captain Costello arrived with a couple "beefy" detectives around midnight to return the escaped prisoners to Cleveland (some newspaper reports said the men were there and took part in the arrest). It was a trip Hunt and Walsh would regret. After passing through Warren, the group was about 40 miles from Cleveland when they encountered a sudden downpour. The *Cleveland News* picks up the story:

> "The heavy rain delayed them and it was 5:30am before they arrived [in Cleveland]. At one point the machine became stuck in the mud and the prisoners, protesting bitterly, were forced to assist in pushing it onto dry ground.
>
> "Hunt breaking down completely, begged the detectives to put a bullet through his brain to save him from the 'death chair.' When his request was refused, both he and Walsh went into another wild rage and despite their shackles, tried to leap from the machine."

Hunt tried to grab the revolver of one of his captors. Meanwhile, Walsh fought a spirited battle, nearly biting off the thumb of Deputy Sheriff Bolles. The *Youngstown Telegram* reported, "When Hunt and Walsh reached the county jail the faces of both were badly disfigured from the effects of the battle, and they are now in the hospital ward of the jail."

The Cleveland officers involved in the arrest were strong in their praise of the Youngstown Police Department. Costello stated, "Never in his experience in police work had he been accorded more courtesy, nor had he seen a posse of police work with such precision."

The next day the *Cleveland News* commented on the behavior of the men in an editorial titled: "What a Difference the Death Chair Makes in the Feelings of Killers!" Expounding on the virtues of the electric chair the writer also took a few potshots at taxi drivers. In describing how the men were found in the Youngstown home, the writer stated, "The fugitives were found armed and equipped in a manner befitting taxi drivers and bad men." In part, the editorial read:

> "We relate, or repeat, at this length the story of the transition from bravado to groveling, coincident with the change of prospect from a wild and free life of crime to certain imprisonment and probable execution, because we regard it as impressive testimony on a subject vital to the community's well-being. It forcibly illustrates once more the fact that the electric chair at Columbus is the one thing in Ohio capable of putting the fear of justice in the hearts of criminals.

"It is not a new lesson. Many another time, formerly and recently, Cleveland has had opportunity to serve the high efficiency of a prospective death penalty in producing curses, shrieks, tears, threats, piteous pleading, suicidal efforts, complete nervous breakdowns and other phases of emotional acting on the part of the hardened criminals who were bold and cruel enough before their own lives were in jeopardy.

But we regard the performance given by the two boy bandits on the way back to possible justice as almost a classic example of criminal psychology – of the fact that it is one thing to the gunman's mind, to go out with a gang of pals for a wild night with taxi cabs and revolvers shooting up a "former saloon" for sport and killing a policeman without provocation, and quite another thing to face the deliberate decorous and just taking of his own life in the death house. It can be no slight influence that reduces the typical young killer, toting two guns and exalting in his badness, to the crybaby act and the contemptible spoiled-child tantrum, conduct more suggestive of squirming worms than of bold, bad heroes.

The electric chair, we submit, is a constructive agency deserving even greater usefulness than Cleveland juries have yet given it. Its unique power to inspire fear of justice is obvious. Beside removing the killer from opportunity for further killing, it commands respect for law as nothing else can do, and so deters others from killing and builds up a proper regard for the sanctity of innocent human life, providing it is used consistently enough. Regret the necessity as we may, intelligence directs us to use it as freely as occasion may require, in merciful kindness to all fellow creatures deserving protection from violent death at the hands of cowardly killers.

Back in custody in Cleveland, the first question to the captured men was, "Where is Charles Gallagher?" Hunt responded that they had "ditched" him. "Gallagher was a dumb-bell," Hunt continued. "We decided we could get along better without him. So down at Geauga Lake we told him we would go the other way from which he was going." Then Hunt, obviously trying to cover for another confederate, claimed that the saws were smuggled in for a prisoner in another cell, but the inmate left before he had a chance to make use of them. The prisoner passed them on to Hunt as a parting gift. They did say they spent only three hours sawing through the bars. "We had saws that would cut through those bars like they were paper." Another report stated the prisoners were able to drown out the noise of the saw blades by greasing them with soap and singing loudly.

Once outside the jail, the men claimed they forced a taxi driver to take them to the corner of East 36th Street and Cedar Avenue, where another vehicle, driven by a friend, was waiting. The friend then drove the trio to Geauga Lake. From there they went to Youngstown where they claimed they remained for the entire time they were fugitives. Both men sat mute when asked how they got the revolvers.

Sheriff Stannard was less than impressed with the prisoners' cooperation and went as far as to inform reporters that he was going to find out who smuggled the saws and guns into the jail by giving the prisoners the "third degree." Stannard declared, "I shall ask Detective Captain Costello to help question the men. I intend to make every effort in this examination to learn just how these men escaped and how to place the responsibility for their escape."

Walsh had another surprise waiting for him. After a tip from an informant, police were eager to question him about the murder of a Woodland Avenue hotel proprietor who was shot to death in a St. Clair Avenue saloon during the commission of a robbery. Meanwhile, both men were placed in solitary confinement with a guard posted between them. Stannard wanted the men to be tried immediately so they could be removed from his jail. In a *Cleveland Press* article headlined, "Hunt Trial To Be Rushed," the newspaper stated, "Prosecutor Stanton announced… he would demand an immediate trial for Robert Hunt and James Walsh…" The article reported Stanton would ask for a "Special Judge" to hear the case. This in contrast to a *Cleveland News* article that stated Stannard's request for a quick trial was denied, "Stanton declared he would be glad to comply with the sheriff's request but that criminal court was in adjournment and members of his own staff needed a rest." In the meantime, Stanton was busy with the murder-for-hire trial of Eva Kaber, which dominated the headlines of the three major newspapers for weeks.

It was nearly three months before the trial began. Before that, Hunt's court appointed attorney, Stephen Young, wrote a note to Judge Allen stating, "Since [Hunt's escape] he has committed robbery, I am reliably informed. In view of this and the other facts in his case, I wish to withdraw." Judge Allen granted the request.

The murder trial of Bobby Hunt began with jury selection on Monday, September 26 in Common Pleas Judge Frederick P. Walther's courtroom. Hunt was represented by Martin L. Sweeney and Dennis J. Lyon, while Assistant County Prosecutor Harry E. Parsons handled the state's case. By Friday, eleven panel members were selected from a pool of 103 potential jurors. The next Monday, October 3, the panel was completed. It contained two women.

During opening statements attorney Sweeney claimed Hunt was a victim on the night of the shooting, that he was intoxicated from an all-day drinking binge, had "lurched blindly" from Philip Goldberg's saloon, and was shot while being an innocent bystander. The jury was then taken to the crime scene at the corner of Scovill Avenue and East 14th Street. Witnesses during the first day of testimony included Officer Sprosty's mother, the two doctors who attended to him at Charity Hospital, and Cuyahoga County Coroner Dr. Ardon P. Hammond.*

On Tuesday one of the state's two key witnesses took the stand. Charles Austerhaut said he was standing outside the Goldberg saloon when Hunt staggered out with a gun in his hand. When Austerhaut confronted him, Hunt punched him in the face and then fired two wild shots into the sidewalk. Austerhaut, seeing Sprosty on foot-patrol across the street, claimed he urged Hunt to dispose of the weapon. Seeing that his words were falling on deaf ears, the witness said he turned and began to walk away. He then heard six shots fired from the direction of the automobile on which Hunt was standing on the running board.

Other witnesses, Charles "Chick" Pierce and Marian Smith, claimed to be at the scene, but said they were unaware of who was doing the shooting. Smith, a girlfriend of one of the taxi drivers, was waiting in the car when the men piled into and on it. When Wachs began shooting, she stated she went into hysterics as shattered glass was flying all around her. One bullet narrowly missed her head.

One of the subpoenaed witnesses was Philip Goldberg, who operated the saloon where the men had gathered. Goldberg had "disposed" of the saloon several months after the shooting and disappeared. Two other witnesses the state planned to call also failed to appear. The next day Goldberg appeared in the courtroom claiming he was at home sick. After a brief conversation with Parsons, the prosecutor decided not to call the former saloon owner to the stand.

On Wednesday, testimony continued with other witnesses who claimed that Hunt was the man who had fired two shots into the sidewalk. William Conton and James Walsh were also called to the stand.

The state's final key witness on Thursday was Officer Nathan Wachs. He testified that he watched as Hunt, standing on the running board of the automobile, fired two bullets into Sprosty as he lay wounded on the sidewalk. Wachs said after he fired at the fleeing automobile, he saw Hunt lurch and almost fall from the car, only to be grabbed and pulled inside by one of the car's passengers.

That afternoon the state rested and the defense began its case. Their chief witness was the defendant himself. Hunt testified that he was intoxicated when the shooting occurred. Hearing a commotion outside the saloon, he walked out to investigate only to be shot by Officer Wachs. As for his escape from the county jail, Hunt claimed he had sawed his way out because he was told "others" were going to "frame" him for the murder.

The defense called Frank E. Marco, who was serving a term in the Mansfield Reformatory, to say that a witness for the state had threatened to kill Hunt. He was followed by Dr. Romano, who was questioned about treating the defendant the night he was shot. If there was some significance to the testimony of these two, the newspapers failed to make note of it.

During closing arguments the state asked the jury to find Hunt guilty of first-degree murder and send him to the electric chair. The defense demanded an acquittal, claiming the prosecution failed to show that Hunt was armed, let alone fired the shots that took the life of Officer Sprosty.

In his instructions to the jury, Judge Walther told them that being in a drunken condition was not an excuse to commit a crime. "However," the judge added, "if you find the defendant was so deadened and senseless by drink as to be unable to form intent to kill, then you will find against him not first or second-degree murder, but manslaughter or assault and battery. [But] drunken men have sense enough ordinarily to form thoughts." Walther also told the jurors that Hunt's escape from jail had "no direct bearing on his guilt or innocence. You may consider it only as determining the defendant's conscience at the time of the escape, but it must not weigh as material fact in this case."

After the jury filed out, Judge Walther called to Officer Wachs to rise. You are a brave policeman," he declared. "This community owes you a debt of gratitude.

"Is Chief Smith in the room?" Walther asked. When nobody replied, the judge continued.

"I am sorry, I wanted your chief here to hear this commendation of your conduct. However, I shall write him a letter about it. I hope that the time may come when you will receive proper reward for your gallant conduct on that night." The judge said he regretted that Officer Sprosty could not be there, for he was a brave man, too. Wachs stood motionless and "a bit red-faced" before the packed courtroom as the judge made his comments.

The jury began its deliberations at 5:00 p.m. on Friday, October 7. They retired at 10:15 p.m., returning Saturday morning at 9:00 o'clock. It was rumored that the panel stood seven for guilty of first-degree murder without mercy, to five for guilty of manslaughter. Walther questioned the jury around noon, at which time the foreman inquired as to what the sentence would be if they agreed to second-degree murder. Later that afternoon the jury returned with a verdict of murder in the second degree. The two women jurors had held out the longest before changing their decision of sending Hunt to the death chair.

Hunt was called before Walther to hear his sentence. The judge asked him if he had anything to say. In a bit of bravado, Hunt stated, "I didn't kill Sprosty. I'm innocent. There's only two places – heaven and hell. I ask that you poll each juror. Ask if they think I killed Sprosty. If they think that I did, I want to get the chair. I don't want life imprisonment. I'm innocent."

Walther responded, "You've had a fair trial." With that, the judge sentenced him to life in prison, to which Hunt responded, "Thank you, judge."

Hunt then turned on his heels to leave the courtroom. As he passed his trial table he glanced briefly at his mother who sat sobbing; he offered her no comfort. He looked straight ahead as he was led back to the county jail.

Hunt's defense team – Sweeney and Lyons – announced they would ask for a new trial, thus delaying the trial of William Conton until the motion could be considered. Two days after the verdict Sheriff Stannard, having no interest in waiting to see if Hunt would be granted a new trial, quietly had the prisoner transferred to the Ohio Penitentiary on a late night train. Four days later Judge Walther denied the motion for a new trial.

When William Conton's trial commenced on Thursday, October 13 it began on an historic note; never before in a first-degree murder trial in the county had a defendant had a woman on the defense team. Mary Grossman,[6] a future long-time judge, was breaking new ground assisting Herman Nord in defending Conton. The trial was going to be a tough one for Prosecutor Parsons. No witness had put a gun in the hand of Conton at the scene and since the bullets found in Sprosty's body were .32s, there was only one murder weapon, which Hunt had just been found guilty of using.

On Tuesday, October 18, James Walsh, taking the stand for the state, shocked the courtroom by testifying that Frank Shannon fired the fatal shots that claimed the life of Officer Sprosty. Shannon, who was indicted in the shooting, was released at the request of the prosecutor. Thomas Ruby, the driver of the getaway car that fatal night, testified that Bobby Hunt fired twice at the officer with the .38 revolver, but the weapon misfired. Neither man said Conton fired at the policeman.

Walsh was the last witness for the state, after which defense attorneys asked the judge to dismiss the charges against Conton claiming the state had failed to connect their client to the crime. With the motion denied, the defendant took the stand on Wednesday, October 19, and denied having possession of a gun on the night he walked into Goldberg's saloon. Conton admitted taking the guns from Hunt after the shooting, as the wounded man lay on the floor of the vehicle they escaped in, and then hiding them in his room. Conton claimed Hunt was responsible for killing Officer Sprosty.

The next day closing arguments were heard. Parsons asked the jury to find the defendant guilty and to send him to the electric chair. He had made the same request in the Hunt trial. During the Conton trial Parsons had declared twice that it was the defendant, not Hunt, who fired the fatal shots. The jury began deliberating at 3:15 in the afternoon. While many, including Parsons, felt the deliberations might be lengthy, the jury was back before 8:30 that night. Not only was Conton found guilty, the jury convicted him of first-degree murder, with a recommendation of mercy.

The bewildered defendant was called before Judge Walther and asked if he had anything to say before sentence was passed. Conton replied, "I don't know how the jury could have found me guilty, when there was no evidence to show I could have committed the crime."

Although Walther sentenced Conton to life in prison, he admitted his own confusion with the verdict. He commented, "Bobby Hunt has been convicted of this murder and sentenced to life imprisonment. The evidence clearly showed only one man could have killed Sprosty. So far as we know anything about the facts, there were only two guns, a 32-caliber automatic and a 38-caliber revolver.

"The bullets found in Sprosty's body were 32-caliber. The man who fired the automatic pistol killed the officer. It is not my function to assume the duties of a jury. However, in view of what occurred here tonight, I shall vacate the journal entry overruling the motion of attorneys for Hunt that he be given a new trial and will hear argument on the motion in the near future."

The *Cleveland News* commented, "The situation presents a legal problem unique in the annals of local courts. Judge Walther...has declared he will go thoroughly over the evidence in the Hunt case again to determine just who is guilty of firing the death shots."

Mary Grossman also announced she was filing a motion for a new trial. Prosecutor Stanton, who was filling in for the absent Parsons, had no comment for reporters on the chain of events.

James Walsh was due to be tried for first-degree murder next. The defendant was represented by former judge Frank S. Day, who asked for and received a two-week postponement. On October 25, claiming there was a "surplus of defendants," Parsons asked Judge Walther to dismiss the murder charge against Walsh. The judge replied, "I am not satisfied with the Hunt-Conton situation. We have two convictions now for a murder which but one man could have committed. I intend to go into the matter thoroughly and if Walsh had anything to do with the shooting of the policeman I want to know it."

On November 1, Walther agreed to dismiss the case after Parsons declared he had "neither evidence nor witnesses" to prove Walsh was a principal in the murder. Police were still holding Walsh and pressed charges against him for stealing the revolver of Deputy Sheriff Levine during the June jailbreak. Walsh still had the gun in his possession when he was captured in Youngstown. On November 7, Walsh faced Judge Homer G. Powell to receive his sentence. Telling him point blank, "This community doesn't want you around," Powell sentenced him to a minimum of 15 years in prison on the weapons charge.[7]

Robert "Bobby" Hunt would come back to Cleveland once to testify in one of the Sly-Fanner murder trials, his last appearance in the city being in December 1921. That should have been the end of the story for Bobby Hunt. It wasn't.

Hunt enjoyed the notoriety he received for breaking out of the Cuyahoga County Jail, so the young hood boasted he could escape from any prison. At the Ohio Penitentiary he soon became a member of "First K Company," a group of inmates "comprised of the most dangerous men in the penitentiary," and was kept under special guard constantly. The honorary leader of "First K Company" was George "Jiggs" Losteiner, while another member was "Big Jim" Morton.

On November 8, 1926, in what was called the most daring prison break in the history of the Ohio Penitentiary, Hunt, Losteiner and eleven other inmates[8] made a bloody dash for freedom. Around 2:00 that afternoon a group of visitors were being escorted out of the prison. Against prison rules guard George Bennett left two gates open leading from the guardroom into the prison yard. It had probably been a habit of Bennett's to do so because on this afternoon members of "First K Company" were armed and ready to go. At 2:00 p.m. members of the group, as was part of their routine, were taking their afternoon exercise march. Elmer Callahan, a guard with 16 years' experience, was checking out the visitors, letting them pass through the first gate, into a "bull pen" area that opened into the guardroom and the unauthorized second gate.

Callahan became the first casualty. Attacked by Hunt and another inmate, they used prison-made knives and bed hooks on the veteran guard. The bed hooks were used in the cells to fasten the lower berths in the double cells to the wall when not being used. Callahan was stabbed in the face, neck, head, arm and side, as well as beaten, in the opening act. Bennett, the unsuspecting collaborator, was next. A group led by "Jiggs" put the guard out of commission by bashing him in the head six times with a hammer.

The last guard in the guardhouse, a telephone operator, was knocked unconscious by a blow from a bed hook. With all the men in the guardhouse out of commission, the escaping prisoners ("Big Jim" Morton refused to join his confederates) grabbed a small arsenal of semi-automatic handguns and began shooting wildly, shattering windows and blasting holes in the wall.

Inside the guardroom there was a waiting-room connected to a corridor leading upstairs to Warden Preston E. Thomas's residence and outside to the un-walled portion of the grounds facing Spring Street, which fronted the prison. An electronically controlled door blocked this last step to freedom. One of the gunmen found the switch and the door was opened.

A former state senator from Cincinnati, serving a term stemming from a failed brokerage firm, sounded the first alarm. Warden Thomas rushed from his office to the prison armory to unlock a cache of rifles and shotguns. Joining him was his secretary, William Payne, who had suffered a stab wound to the head, and C.W. "Tacks" Latimer,[9] a former major league baseball player and policeman, who was serving time for murder. Latimer had suffered a blow to the head, which temporarily knocked him out. The two men, after seeing to the safety of the warden's daughter, joined Thomas. The three began shooting at the fleeing prisoners as they raced over the lawn, across Spring Street, and ducked between two factory buildings before disappearing along the railroad tracks.

The firing took a toll. Warden Thomas claimed, "Every time one of us fired, someone dropped, but they got up and kept on running, excepting one. The buckshot was not heavy enough to stop them." The man who didn't get up was hit in the face with a bullet, but the wound was not life threatening. Another convict was captured before making it off the prison grounds.

The remaining eleven prisoners ran en masse down the Pennsylvania Railroad tracks to West Broad Street. Here they stopped a touring car and threw the woman driver to the pavement. Nine of the escapees, including Hunt and Losteiner, jumped in the car leaving the other two – William Smith and Oliver Glasby – to fend for themselves.

As the car raced off in the direction of London, a small town due west of Columbus, a motorcycle officer, who witnessed the car-jacking, pulled alongside the vehicle and ordered the driver to pull to the curb. Instead, the officer found himself looking at four semi-automatic pistols. He quickly dropped behind the speeding auto, pulled his service revolver and emptied it at the escaping automobile. The officer was soon joined in the chase by two more motorcycle officers and a group of men from the penitentiary.

Meanwhile, another motorcycle officer made a "Paul Revere" ride through the town of London arousing members of the National Guard, businessmen, and gun club members to action. As the convicts reached the outskirts of town they found their path blocked by an automobile surrounded by a well-armed posse led by the local prosecutor, who happened to be the brother of Ohio Attorney General Charles C. Crabbe.

With the pursuers from Columbus coming up fast from the rear, the escape vehicle careened off the road and into a ditch. All but one of the escapees fled the car and headed into a nearby cornfield with the posse on their heels firing as they ran. The prisoners stopped to return fire, but it was useless. Many in the posse were crack shots, whose hobby was trapshooting. Losteiner was wounded in the leg, another in the hand, and another had several fingers shot off. Soon the prisoners, who had senselessly wasted ammunition shooting up the guardhouse, were out of bullets and desire.

The escapees threw down their weapons and raised their hands. The ill-fated run to freedom was over. They were handcuffed together, loaded on a truck and returned to the prison. As night closed in, the two prisoners abandoned on West Broad Street were still on the loose. There was soon only one as William Smith was captured northwest of Columbus. The *Plain Dealer* reported he was found "hiding behind a large rock" and captured by an armed "barbecue stand" proprietor.

Ironically, the last prisoner to be captured was described as "mentally deficient." Oliver Glasby was captured 48 hours after the escape at Groveport, near Columbus. He was recognized by a home owner when he stopped to ask for something to eat. The man then contacted police.

In Cleveland, Prosecutor Stanton denounced the escape and demanded an immediate investigation by Governor Vic Donahey. The question on everyone's mind was if the escape was made possible by laxity in the system, or did the prisoners receive inside help in their "delivery" from the penitentiary.

One day after the escape, Donahey met with Warden Thomas, who made it clear that the escape was the result of the breaking of a long-standing rule and that there was "no collusion from either inside or from the outside." The blame for the escape was placed squarely on the shoulders of guard George Bennett for allowing both doors to be open at once. Thomas promised Bennett would be disciplined as soon as he recovered from the severe beating he received from the prisoners.

In January 1928, Hunt made another escape attempt. He failed to make it out of his cell block before he was knocked unconscious by a blackjack wielding guard. This attempt was said to have left Hunt in a morose state, undoubtedly leading to his final action.

On February 21, 1928, the *Cleveland News* reported, "'Bobby' Hunt made his last break for liberty...It was successful and no policeman's bullets or prison guard's rifles will ever have him for their target again. There was no slip up in his plans this time and the method that he took to get out of the Ohio State Penitentiary precludes capture."

Bobby Hunt was free, but only in spirit. Many thought Hunt should have "fried" in the electric chair for the murder of Officer Elmer Sprosty. While Hunt escaped the chair, he didn't escape being "fried" in his own cell after turning himself and his bunk into a flaming inferno. The 32 year-old prisoner died in the prison hospital the next morning without regaining consciousness from his injuries the previous night. The Franklin County coroner called the death, "suicide by fire."

Hunt was alone in his cell in an area called the "Bird Cage," because it was enclosed with wire netting. It was in the cell block "where notorious criminals" were quartered. Prisoners were allowed to smoke in their cells and prison officials believed Hunt set fire to his bed clothing with a match or cigarette.

Despite the coroner's verdict, there were still some who believed Hunt set the fire in another attempt to escape, that he planned to rush out of his cell when the guards opened the door. But those close to him saw the act as a last sneer at the authority he genuinely despised.

Chapter Endnotes

1. William J. "Chick" Pierce had a long criminal record and was a one-time associate of George "Jiggs" Losteiner. He was the prime suspect in the April 1929 murder of Irish bootlegger and speakeasy operator Edward O'Leary. Arrested for the killing, Pierce was acquitted after two eyewitnesses failed to recall details of the shooting while testifying at his trial.

2. In order to care for the wounded soldiers returning to the city from the Civil War, money was collected and land was purchased for a new hospital. On October 10, 1865 Charity Hospital opened on Perry Street (East 22nd). Managed by the Sisters of Charity of Augustine, Charity Hospital (later St. Vincent Charity Hospital) became Cleveland's first permanent general hospital.

3. Tragically, Patrolman Ernest L. Ford made news again on September 19, 1928, exactly six days after the murder of Patrolman Anthony Wieczorek, when he was shot to death while investigating a still operation on Scovill Avenue. Although not on duty at the time, the patrolman caught wind

of the familiar odor of mash while he was driving home with his fiancée. Ford was shot after entering a back yard at 3314 Scovill Avenue. Rushed to Charity Hospital, he died a short while later. Ford was the only Cleveland police officer to be murdered by a bootlegger during the Prohibition Era.

On November 17, 1928 Samuel Costanza, a father of eight children, was sentenced to life in prison after being convicted of second-degree murder. A statement given to Detective Sergeant Charles Cavolo by Costanzo's 15 year-old son was the key evidence in the conviction. Costanzo was defended by court-appointed attorney James T. Cassidy, the former chief assistant county prosecutor for Edward Stanton.

4. The term "delivery" was widely used at this time in describing a jail or prison break.

5. Geauga Lake in the 1920s was a resort which straddled Portage and Geauga counties in the towns of Aurora and Bainbridge Township. Camps and cabins dotted the landscape. Today it is the home of a popular amusement park.

6. Mary Grossman was the first woman in the United States elected a municipal judge. Elected in 1923 she served in that capacity until her death in January 1977. After passing the Ohio Bar in 1912 she was the second woman admitted to membership in the American Bar Association. She was the first woman to serve as a defense attorney in a capital murder case (William Conton). In the years leading up to the passing of the 19th Amendment she was a zealous advocate of the suffrage movement with fellow Clevelanders Florence E. Allen, Lethia C. Fleming and Marie R. Wing.

7. James Walsh possessed one of the most extensive criminal records on file at the Cleveland Police Department. His "rap sheet" from 1915 to 1936 showed 20 arrests involving 12 different types of crimes. Before the decade was over Walsh was questioned after two bootleg murders. In the second one, that of Edward O'Leary, the prime suspect was William "Chick" Pierce. As in the Sprosty case, Walsh was sent to prison on a concealed weapons charge.

In November 1936 Walsh was on trial for stealing an automobile two months earlier from a Hough Avenue resident. He was arrested in Elkhart, Indiana. He was acquitted in common pleas court so he could be charged by the federal government for violation of the Dyer Act, transporting a stolen vehicle across state lines, the same law that bank robber and cop killer John Dillinger broke that brought about federal participation in his manhunt.

Walsh beat the federal charge after agents were unable to prove that he actually drove the car over the state line. Weeks later, on December 19, 1936, Walsh and another man were charged with cracking a safe at the Cleveland Typographical Union on East 17ᵗʰ Street just a few doors away from Central Police Station.

8. The escapees, other than "Jiggs' Losteiner and "Bobby" Hunt were:

Burton Carter, Starke County, serving 25 years for robbery
Arthur Clayton, Cleveland, serving ten years for shooting to kill
Thomas Gerak, Cleveland, serving life for first-degree murder
Oliver Glaspy, Athens, serving three years for rape
James Johnson, Cleveland, serving ten years for robbery
Frank Mills, Toledo, serving ten years for robbery
Charles Milwetfer, Columbus, serving life for first-degree murder
Harold Nierfgarten, Auglaize County, serving life for first-degree murder
Frank Proctor, Cincinnati, serving ten years for burglary
William Smith, Cleveland, serving twenty-five years for robbery
John Wierman, Columbus, serving fifteen years for shooting to wound

9. Clifford Wesley "Tacks" Latimer played in 27 major league baseball games with five different teams from 1898 to 1902. He played catcher in all but two of those games. Latimer was born in Loveland, Ohio on November 30, 1875 and died in Cincinnati on April 24, 1936. – *The Baseball Encyclopedia* – 1974 – MacMillan Publishing Company.

Part II
Murder on the Bridge

5

Introductions by Merrick

During the Prohibition Era few knew the lay of the land, as it pertained to criminals and criminal justice in Cleveland, like Frank J. Merrick. Born on December 1, 1894, Frank Joseph Merrick was the last of 12 children. He grew up on East 82nd Street, just around the corner from the No. 16 Fire House at Woodland Avenue and East 79th Street. Throughout his young life he had a consuming interest in fires and the men who fought them.

When Merrick was nine years old his father died. Although the youngest, he contributed to the support of his family by selling newspapers on Public Square. The hustle of the ambitious paperboy caught the attention of attorney Francis J. Wing,[1] who took a liking to the youngster. Wing told the child, "You can be a judge; you can be anything you want to be, with initiative like yours." The young man decided then that he was going to pursue a career in the field of law.

Merrick attended St. Ignatius High School and then enrolled at St. Ignatius College, but had to drop out due to financial reasons. Wing offered the former newsboy $1.25 a week to work in his law office. It was not the only offer the lad received. Merrick was fond of telling the story that, "John D. Rockefeller was another of my customers and he offered me a job, too. But my mother told me it was better to practice law than to sell kerosene. She was so right."

To put himself through law school Merrick worked three days a week in Wing's office and attended Cleveland Law School at night. On the other days he arose at 3:00 a.m. and went to work as a cashier at a meat stall in the Central Market. The hard work paid off and Merrick earned his law degree in 1916.

During World War I, Merrick worked for a branch of the U.S. Justice Department assigned to the Army on a homeland security detail. As he explained it, he "traveled around the country secretly in espionage service." His work took him to army bases, munitions manufacturing locations and meeting places of alleged seditionists. Merrick recalled the work as, "interesting, but not so exciting as I thought it would be. It was embarrassing too, because I couldn't tell anyone why I was leaving town. They almost read me out of the secretaryship of the Cleveland Amateur Baseball Association because I couldn't explain why I was absent from three successive meetings."

To quench his desire for excitement Merrick enlisted in the Army. After basic training he was sent to Soissons, France as a member of 2nd Division, 9th Infantry, Company K. During the early morning hours of August 18, 1918, First Sergeant Merrick left the trenches outside Verdun in charge of a detail of sixteen men in search of enemy outposts. Merrick remembered:

> "It was dark, and we stumbled along. Shell fire was light and most of it was far over our heads. I heard one whine and ducked. Two days later I woke up in a hospital in a plaster cast and heard that six of the detail were killed. I had a broken leg, a shrapnel wound in the side and one in the arm. I was out of the war for good, although I did light office duties in London."

Merrick returned to Cleveland, took a year off, and then resumed the practice of law. In September 1920, Merrick was appointed assistant county prosecutor; at the age of 26 he was one of the youngest ever to hold that office. Although it was a short stay, the young attorney was a quick study and he soon developed an understanding of the workings of a new type of criminal that was emerging in this first year of Prohibition. Sitting second chair during the trial of the "Serra Gang," an automobile theft ring, he realized a phenomenon that came to be known as organized crime. He discovered its existence by becoming aware that the stealing of automobiles was only a small part of this gang's activities.

That being said, it is only fitting to use Merrick's own words to introduce the man who was the first leader of organized crime in this city as head of a gang which became known as the Mayfield Road Mob. Merrick described him as "Cleveland's first racketeer." On Sunday, August 27, 1933, Merrick penned an article for the *Plain Dealer* Magazine Section titled, "Giving the Low-down on Cleveland Rackets."

"Business methods have changed since my day." Thus the gray-haired office executive of today comments on the trend of the times. So in crime. Methods have changed. The gangster of today is the composite of all the evil traits of the crook of yesterday without the outward appearances. No longer can you rely upon appearances or conclude that a crook has his avocation stamped upon his countenance, mode of dress, method of conversation, or even the company he keeps. Until he is finally exposed, the gangster or racketeer of today purposely surrounds himself with circumstances designed to mislead average persons to their sorrow.

Of such a type was Dominic Benigno. From his "mob" sprung almost every known gangster and racketeer existing in Cleveland today. Some have developed from members of his old gang which operated so sinisterly in Cleveland following the war. Others have received their education in crime from his more apt and surviving pupils. A large number came into being in a boyish effort to emulate his own shrewd, suave, cold-blooded dominance.

Benigno might be called Cleveland's first racketeer. Gangs had existed before his time: daring holdup men had terrorized the town before he was born and sleek-looking gentry had been known in police circles as far back as the Civil War. It remained, however, for Dominic Benigno to "incorporate" crime.

More than that. Through 1919 and 1920 he actually made it dangerous for anyone to attempt a pay roll robbery in Cleveland. He reserved all pay roll jobs for himself and organized accordingly. Older heads in the Cleveland detective bureau remember well those daring paymaster robberies of 1919 and 1920 culminating in the Sly-Fanner robbery and double-murder.

Previous to the activities of this gang, there were occasional pay roll robberies, but to the neighborhood plug-ugly and hoodlum armed pay carriers were given a wide berth or left to a few gangs which roamed from state to state, pulling a job here or there and immediately leaving town.

Benigno conceived the idea of organizing a gang of young men of steel-like bravado to monopolize the "good" holdup business of Cleveland. He likewise inaugurated a system of exacting tribute from others engaged in such business. He supplied the brains and took the profits.

In 1919 federal prohibition went into effect. The first bootleggers of that period brought liquor from Canada for sale at high prices. This was trucked into Cleveland from border towns or smuggled over Lake Erie in small speedboats. Benigno went into the high-jacking [sic] business as an adjunct to his pay roll looting activities. His inauguration of this kind of extortion in Cleveland later developed into gang murders, one-way rides, bombings and various other terrorizing means to compel persons to pay tribute for the privilege of not being "robbed," "muscled," killed or otherwise put out of the way.

So well did he perfect his organization, that in 1920 as many as four pay roll robberies were pulled on the same day. These jobs netted thousands of dollars for Benigno.

He was not a flashy fellow. Always well dressed and bearing a hearty smile, he lived in plain surroundings with his family, and had all the outward appearances of respectability. He did not frequent the haunts of rowdies or denizens of the underworld. He loved opera and the finer theatricals and could play a good hand of bridge before that game became socially popular. He seldom drank liquor and had no time for fast women or the bright lights.

He did take delight in twitting detectives and smilingly bidding them success in their efforts to solve one of his jobs.

In 1919 and 1920 he had groups of gunmen patrolling the main highways leading into Cleveland on the lookout for trucks loaded with liquor. These cargoes were taken from the driver, unloaded into a central warehouse and sold later to the illicit liquor trade. Very often they were sold back to the original owner, who was warned to "kick in" or suffer like treatment on future shipments.

Later the imported whisky became too expensive and scarce and the small distillers and cutters of liquors began to spring up. These were accorded like treatment. A tribute was drawn from every branch of the business. Sugar, bottles, fake labels and other printing, gunny sacks and tinfoil all had to be used, and the sale and distribution of these commodities were for many years controlled by members, relatives or associates of the original Benigno gang.

Benigno had two associates who worked with him. These three formed a board of directors, passing upon most of the activities of the gang and all of the important jobs. Frank Motto secured new members. Biagio DePalma gathered data necessary to the successful completion of a job and was not above taking a hand himself now and then. He was reputed to have been the one who punished obstreperous gang members.

Motto occasionally took a fling at the actual perpetration of a robbery or high-jacking job, but Benigno was never known to participate in a crime and his only breach of this long practice brought him to the electric chair.

Benigno and his two partners – Motto and DePalma – were well known to Cleveland police. Benigno had first been arrested on October 4, 1917 and charged with burglary and larceny. After several continuances, the case was dismissed on February 15, 1918. Before the year was out, Benigno was arrested again for burglary and larceny on New Year's Eve. This time it involved the theft of $3,500 worth of cigars. His partners in the theft were John LaPaglia and Dominic Scafide. LaPaglia was one of three brothers – John and Michelino were brutally murdered and Sam was sent to prison for life for a killing. Scafide didn't fare any better. He ultimately was shot to death by a detective in Philadelphia. The cigar stealing charges were dropped.

Less than a month after the New Year's Eve burglary, Benigno was arrested as a suspicious person in Pittsburgh on January 17, 1919; charges were dismissed. Finally on May 6, 1919, he was arrested on another suspicious person's charge, which also was nolled in court. As the new decade approached, he was batting 1.000.

It should be noted in the case of Frank Motto, that his name as it appears on his gravestone in Calvary Cemetery is spelled "Amata." Although I have corrected the spelling of another gang member's name – "Purpura" throughout the text – I kept with the name "Motto" because another gang member's name was "Amato" and I felt that would be too confusing to the reader to be referring to an "Amata" and an "Amato."

Motto's rap sheet showed he was first arrested on December 8, 1914, and charged with assault with intent to rob. On December 30 the charges were dropped. Motto stayed out of the clutches of the police for almost five years until October 22, 1919, when he was charged with receiving stolen property. The property, a Berlin automobile, was stolen earlier that summer. His next run-in with the law involved an automobile theft ring for which he was indicted in January 1920.

The last member of this triumvirate, Biago "Bundy" DePalma, had a more extensive record. Born Biaso Marsiglio around 1893, it was sometime during the 1910s that he took on the first name of Biago and began using his mother's maiden name, DePalma. The name change couldn't have been to protect the family name; there were three generations of criminals in the family.

The earliest entry on DePalma's rap sheet came in 1912 when he was convicted of stealing ten gallons of whiskey. On September 28 he was sentenced to the Ohio Penitentiary. In the spring of 1917, he was indicted for robbery. Convicted, he served 20 months in the Mansfield Reformatory. This was followed by the most serious charge against him – first-degree murder.

Robert "Bobby White" Bianca was a bantamweight boxer who won the city's amateur title in the 110 pound division. Bianca was a popular figure in the Big Italy[2] section and a hero to many of the neighborhood youngsters. The *Plain Dealer* wrote, "Bobby White was the boy whom young Italians sought to follow. They knew exactly the date when he went as a 13 year-old boy to Sol Laurie, instructor in the Central Athletic Club, to train for the ring. He was their only Cleveland fighter." While Bianca collected sporadic paychecks from his boxing career, he supplemented his income by working in the office of a neighborhood physician – Dr. Guiseppe Romano, the Mafia-boss-to-be who treated the wounds of cop-killer Bobby Hunt.

On February 17, 1919, three men watched as Bianca and another man walked down Woodland Avenue. Bianca had just left Dr. Romano's office at 921 Woodland Avenue and was headed home when the second man joined him. No one was close enough to hear what the two men were discussing, but it was obviously not a friendly conversation. At 1215 Woodland Avenue the man suddenly grabbed Bianca by the shoulder and swung him around. The young boxer's quick reactions weren't enough to save him from the bullets of a revolver. Word of the murder spread quickly through the Big Italy neighborhood. Detectives were quick to round up suspects including three eyewitnesses, who were held for investigation. By midnight, eleven men were in custody, two of whom were found with concealed weapons in their possession.

Heading the investigation were Detectives Phil Mooney* and Antonio "Tony" Page* who formed the "Italian" or "Black Hand" squad.[3] Mooney became a Cleveland police officer in 1898. Born in Pittsburgh, on November 16, 1868, he was of Irish decent, sometimes being referred to as the "Irish dick." His real value to the Cleveland Police Department was his ability to speak fluent Italian. Articles throughout the 1920s, 1930s and 1940s referred to former detective Mooney as one of the greatest detectives in the history of the Cleveland Police Department. Louis B. Seltzer, editor of the *Cleveland Press*, once said of Mooney, "I know of no one in the Police Department in all of the years of my newspaper experience who was at once as able and honest as [Mooney]."

Mooney's reputation blossomed in 1906 when he was credited with almost single-handedly driving Black Hand extortionists to cover during a bloody crime spree in the city. Shortly after this, Mooney fell out of favor with then Police Chief Fred Kohler. Mooney was ordered back to uniform duty and banished to an outlying district. After Kohler was removed as police chief after a sex scandal in 1916, Mooney came back and became the ace detective of the "Italian squad" just as another wave of Black Hand violence was gripping Cleveland.

On Friday, February 21, 1919, Detectives Page, Edward Conroy and Martin Horrigan arrested Biago DePalma after hearing that he had threatened Bianca at Fire Engine House No. 18, at Orange Avenue and East 31st Street. How the two men met at the fire station was never revealed, but a captain of the fire department and one fireman admitted to hearing the two argue. Witnesses picked DePalma out of a 15-man police line-up. The next morning Detective Inspector Charles N. Sterling identified DePalma as the murder suspect and introduced a new motive for the slaying.

In May 1917, when DePalma was facing a prison term for robbery, he went to Bianca and asked if he could borrow money to finance his appeal. The two men were neighbors, DePalma living across the street at 2478 East 14th Street. Bianca refused and DePalma spent the next 20 months in the Mansfield Reformatory. Released around Christmas 1918, DePalma arrived home to find his mother was arrested on federal charges of receiving stolen property from the American Railroad Express Company. She was found guilty and was scheduled to be sentenced the week of February 24, 1919. Having been out of prison less than two months, DePalma had no money and on February 17 met Bianca at the Engine Company where he pleaded with the boxer to lend him money for an attorney to appeal his mother's case. When Bianca refused this second request, DePalma told him, "You'll be sorry." Five hours later Bianca was dead. One week after the killing, DePalma was charged with first-degree murder.

On Monday, May 5, 1919, jury selection began in the trial of DePalma, who was represented by Blasé Buonpane. The state's case was presented by Assistant Prosecutor David R. Rothkopf[4] in Judge Dan B. Cull's courtroom. It took almost three days to fill the jury box as most of the excused venire men did not wish to serve on a case that involved the death penalty. After completion of the panel on Wednesday afternoon, the jury was transported to the scene of the murder on Woodland Avenue. By Thursday several states' witnesses had identified DePalma as the killer.

The state rested its case on Thursday afternoon and the next morning DePalma took the stand. For two hours he related his movements on the day of the killing. He claimed he had gone alone to a movie house on Woodland Avenue that afternoon and was on his way home when he arrived at the murder scene, just as Bianca's body was being removed.

Prosecutors and attorneys spent five hours on closing arguments, which went well into Friday evening. Jury members began their deliberations on Saturday, but by noon Sunday, after nearly 24 hours of talks, they informed Judge Cull that they were deadlocked. It was later reported that the jurors stood at seven for conviction and five for acquittal. Rothkopf announced DePalma would be tried on the same charge within the next 30 days. A second trial would never take place and DePalma was eventually released.

On September 25, 1920, DePalma was sent to prison again, this time for carrying a concealed weapon. The incarceration separated DePalma from Benigno and Motto at a time when they needed him most. During the years after this sentence, DePalma became a "one-man crime wave," carrying on illegal activities well into the 1920s, but no longer as a member of the Mayfield Road Mob.

Introductions also need to include the two Cleveland police officers who would have the largest roles in events to come – George Matowitz and Charles Cavolo.

Few men in the Cleveland Police Department ever fit the image of the John Wayne type of law enforcement officer like George J. Matowitz, fewer were as intelligent. Matowitz was born on April 24, 1882, in what was then the country of Austria-Hungary. He was brought to Cleveland as an infant by his parents and raised in the old Haymarket District. He began his education at Brownell School, but was forced to quit while in the sixth grade due to the death of his father. He needed to find work to help support his mother and five younger siblings. After a brief stint as an upholsterer, he found work as street car conductor. But the young man wanted more out of his life's work and saw the Cleveland Police Department as a place to achieve it.

At six-feet, three-inches tall and tipping the scale at 235 pounds, Matowitz was an imposing figure when he joined the police force on May 8, 1905, at the age of 23. He spent his first five years of duty patrolling the "Roaring Third" District on foot, before briefly serving as Police Chief Fred Kohler's personal secretary. On July 1, 1910, Matowitz was promoted to sergeant and placed in charge of the city's first mounted unit. Matowitz became a proficient horseman, but his time in charge of the new unit lasted just three years. On April 26, 1913 Matowitz was promoted to lieutenant and, according to a *Cleveland News* article, "his scope of experience was broadened to include every phase of police duty covering every corner of the city. He organized the Detroit ave. – W. 39th st. station and, on three occasions, was placed in charge of the detective bureau to straighten out affairs that had become badly tangled."

Matowitz's understanding of police affairs was so in depth that shortly after he was promoted to captain, on February 21, 1918, he was placed in command of the new police training school and taught the fundamentals to prospective police officers for the next twelve months. In 1919, Matowitz was placed in charge of the detective bureau, a position he held until he was appointed Chief Inspector of Police on June 1, 1923.

In addition to keeping his body in shape with daily regiments of boxing and gymnastics, Matowitz kept his mind in condition, too. He attended night school for 19 years earning a law degree in 1930. That same year he was appointed Police Chief, a position he held longer than anyone before or after him.

Charles Cavolo* began his career with the Cleveland Police Department on February 1, 1917, as a beat patrolman in the Little Italy neighborhood where he once resided. His days as a "flat-foot" were short-lived as he was soon made a member of the vice squad. It was while Cavolo was a member of this unit that he first exhibited his knack of clever police work, which remained his trademark throughout his career. When vice squad members were having a hard time closing two "clubs" that operated openly due to efficient lookouts that were employed, Cavolo circumvented them by dressing as a tramp and making his way inside. Once Cavolo sized up the situation, he signaled to squad members outside who then crashed the club and made arrests. Like Matowitz, Cavolo was an imposing figure, near six feet tall and weighing over 200 pounds, yet both men were fleet afoot and could outrun younger, lighter men, as would soon be witnessed.

His stint on the vice squad was relatively brief, but Cavolo made quite an impression on his superiors. He was involved in 800 arrests and was soon recommended for promotion to detective. In May 1918, during his probation period within the department, Cavolo made 50 arrests, thus assuring himself of a position in the bureau. Between 1918 and 1926, Detective Cavolo helped solve 105 murder cases. Because of his Italian heritage and his knowledge of not only the criminal element in his former country, but also his own neighborhood, Cavolo was placed in charge of the department's "Black Hand squad." The squad, which included John Corso and brothers Carl and George Zicarelli, was placed in charge of all crimes committed in the Italian districts.

Chapter Endnotes

1. Francis J. Wing was the son and grandson of pioneers of Trumbull County. With the legal profession a tradition in the Wing family, Francis attended Harvard University after the Civil War. After graduation he came to Cleveland. Wing held the positions of Assistant US District Attorney for the Northern District of Ohio, Cuyahoga County Common Pleas Judge and US District Judge – the latter as an appointee of President William McKinley. Wing died on February 1, 1918. His daughter, Marie Remington Wing was one of the first two women to serve on Cleveland City Council when she was elected in 1923. She worked to establish a women's bureau in the Cleveland Police Department.

2. Big Italy became the first great population center of Sicilian and Italian immigrants in Cleveland. This settlement originally began in the old Haymarket District, the site of the Terminal Tower complex today, and contained the city's first produce markets. Later it moved further south and east. Although the description of the boundaries varied, this ethnic neighborhood was bordered by Ontario Street, Orange Avenue and Woodland Avenue on the west; Central Avenue to the east; East 40th Street to the south; while the northern border was the central city and Carnegie Avenue, where St Anthony's Church was located. Big Italy was in existence from the 1890s until about 1930, by which time the area declined into "social and moral" decay and the residents relocated to other areas of the city.

3. Legendary *Cleveland Press* editor Louis B Seltzer, who cut his teeth as a cub police reporter, was often the recipient of a tip from the duo of Mooney-Page. Many times he tagged along with them, even helping out the pair on occasion. In a 1956 editorial Seltzer wrote, "In their time the 'Mooney-Page" combination struck fear into the Cleveland underworld. On many occasions the simple fact that it became known they were 'on a case' resulted in the quarries giving up."

4. David R. Rothkopf could be considered a tragic figure. An assistant county prosecutor in 1919, he later became a defense attorney and represented some of the Mayfield Road Mob members.

Rothkopf was the brother of Louis Rothkopf, who rose to prominence as a member of what came to be known as the Cleveland Syndicate, a powerful and successful Jewish gang which included mobsters Mo Dalitz, Morris Kleinman and Sammy Tucker.

In 1931 Louis Rothkopf was wanted for questioning in the murder of former Cleveland City Councilman William E. Potter. The murder caused a media frenzy in the city which was not equaled until the murder of Marilyn Sheppard in July 1954. A fugitive for more than a year, the pressure and humiliation may have been too much to bear for the Rothkopf family. On December 8, 1931 Jack Rothkopf, a brother of Louis and David, committed suicide by hanging himself inside his garage at his home at 1843 Alvason Road in East Cleveland. The newspaper reported "ill health" may have been the reason the 36 year-old took his life.

Less than six months later, David Rothkopf, who had changed his name to David Rhodes, was found dead in a garage at the rear of his apartment at 1383 East Boulevard in Cleveland. David, who was living with a sister, went into the garage on May 13, 1932, shut the doors and turned on the ignition to his automobile. He died of carbon monoxide poisoning at the age of 40.

Ironically, both Louis Rothkopf and his wife also left this world in the same manner.

6
Serra Gang – Auto Theft Ring

The Mayfield Road Mob's involvement in one of Cleveland's most notorious murders, a payroll robbery gone terribly wrong, had its roots in an automobile theft ring, which in 1919 was stealing cars in Cleveland and transporting them to western New York State to be sold. Mayfield Road Mob members known to be participating in the ring were Nicholas Angelotta, Frank "Frankie Burns" Milazzo and Frank Motto.

Angelotta and Milazzo were arrested in Dunkirk, New York on January 5, 1920, by Cleveland Police Detective George Francke. The pair had stolen five automobiles in Cleveland and had driven them to Dunkirk for disposition. Later, Motto and Angelo Serra were arrested in Cleveland for the theft of four automobiles stolen between August 10 and September 23, 1919. The cars were Buicks and Hudsons. On January 23 all four men were arraigned. The next day each defendant pled not guilty and the judge fixed their bonds at $1,000 for each of the four counts. Motto was also charged with receiving stolen property. His bond totaled $5,000.

Police believed that Angelo Serra was the brains of the ring, which the newspapers dubbed the "Serra Gang." Serra operated a drug store at Woodland Avenue and East 28th Street. In the store, members of the gang sat and planned their crimes. Serra kept stencils there for changing license plate numbers, as well as a set of duplicate keys that could fit any automobile. In addition, Serra was a notary public and made out false bills of sales for the stolen automobiles and advised ring members when it came to legal matters.

The *Plain Dealer* described how the ring worked:

> "Operations of the alleged ring are said to have run into the hundreds of thousands of dollars, with scores of victims. Its members are said to have maintained a school on Woodland avenue near Luna Park, where classes were conducted in automobile stealing. A clearing house was conducted in Dunkirk, N.Y., it is alleged, in charges of Thomas W. Scavone, who later turned state's evidence."

Thomas W. Scavone, the self-described sales manager of the ring, was a key member of the gang working the Dunkirk end, selling the stolen automobiles to friends. Wanting out, he absconded with $1,000 of the gang's money and selected as his hiding place the U.S. Navy. Through his family, the gang got a letter to him stating he could keep the money as long as he didn't disclose the activities of the ring. Assuming he was clear of gang retaliation, Scavone went AWOL and returned home. He soon found the gang was vindictive and instead of taking a chance they might find him, he turned himself in as a deserter. Scavone was placed in a military prison at Paris Island, South Carolina.

Detectives Franke and William Brenner were assigned to the case. They interviewed Scavone and he gave up his former partners in the ring. In addition, he provided the names of five Clevelanders whose automobiles were stolen. Franke's investigation revealed at least 25 other vehicles stolen by the ring. "We have found it impossible to get some of these persons to testify," Franke said. "Some have been intimidated and threatened if they appeared in court." What followed was a series of court continuances, at least 15, until action was demanded by the Cleveland Automobile Club.

The Cleveland Automobile Club, according to *Cleveland: The Making of A City*, was founded on January 8, 1900[1] with the purpose of maintaining "a social club devoted to the sport of motoring throughout the country and to secure national legislation for the protection of motorist and their vehicles." The club was the second of its kind to be formed (New York was first) and today is the oldest in the United States.

In the late 1910s the Cleveland Automobile Club was focusing more and more of its efforts on combating auto theft and crimes committed using automobiles. Club officials saw to it that auto thieves were sentenced to long terms and participated in leniency hearings when they became eligible for parole. The efforts of the Cleveland Automobile Club were applauded by the Automobile Underwriters Association of Cleveland. Insurance companies reported that Cleveland was one of the four worst cities in the country for automobile thefts. The others were Detroit, Chicago and Kansas City.

What insurance underwriters found most troubling was the apathetic attitude of the general public toward the thefts. During this period of increased auto theft activity after the World War, insurance companies paid back the full value of the automobile despite the age of the vehicle. One insurance operator complained, "Among a certain class of car owners who carry insurance, professional car thieves operate as 'hired men' to steal cars in order that the holder of the policy may collect when he is through with his automobile, or wishes to get a new one."

In addition, the theft of automobile parts – lamps and accessories, much easier targets of thieves during that time – was also increasing. Records showed that in 1920 the public lost $1,250,000 in stolen cars and parts. One executive stated, "They leave their cars standing unlocked or locked insecurely. They leave various car parts entirely at the mercy of the sneak thief or the professional automobile parts robber. The recovery of these smaller objects is a hopeless task, of course. We have a modern profession of automobile parts thieves, who are thriving only because the owners don't care whether their parts are stolen – they know they can 'collect' from the insurance companies."

What was more alarming was the drop in recoveries of the stolen vehicles. The reason given for the drop was that, "the average car owner has little or no desire to have his stolen car brought back," since he will be reimbursed the full balance. Records from 1916 showed that 90 percent of the cars stolen in Cuyahoga County were recovered by insurance companies, police departments and by other means. In 1920, only 70 percent were being recovered and mainly due to the efforts of the insurance companies. In the end the cost was passed onto the consumer. Automobile insurance rates in Cleveland were said to be fifteen times higher than those of smaller cities. In addition to higher rates, the insurance industry pushed for reimbursement amounts significantly less than the original value of the car.

One of the most notable figures in the history of the Cleveland Automobile Club was Fred H. Caley.* As secretary of the club he represented the association in matters of theft and crimes from theft. Frank J. Merrick soon joined him. In prosecuting the "Serra Gang," Merrick, on his own initiative, went to Dunkirk to obtain evidence against the participants and spoke to witnesses, even arranging to have them brought to Cleveland to testify – all at his own expense.

On Monday, December 6, 1920 the Cuyahoga County Grand Jury began an investigation into the theft ring and why the arrested gang members had yet to be tried. Up until now the prosecutor's office claimed that its hands were tied in the case because law enforcement simply didn't have the funds to transport and house key witnesses, who resided out of state. The Cleveland Automobile Club, which was providing the impetus for the hearing, also provided the financing to bring Scavone and a marine guard to Cleveland, as well as the other Dunkirk witnesses. The club hired their own investigator, who was expected to play an important role during the inquiry. The newspapers predicted "startling disclosures – the possible uncovering of the identity of higher-ups." Assistant County Prosecutor Joseph Dembe*[2] declared "the lid will be taken off."

The grand jury investigation caused a lot of excitement and judges were already responding to the increased publicity involving automobile theft. On Monday, Judge Maurice Bernon sentenced two men, one a teenager, to indeterminate sentences at the Mansfield Reformatory. Bernon told the court, "Automobile stealing must cease. The law may have seemed lax in such cases, but the offense is a serious one. Criminal records show stolen autos have aided continually in the perpetration of crime in the past. In spite of the good past records of these boys, I would have sent them to the penitentiary had the law permitted it."

Running concurrently with the grand jury investigation were the trials of the four ring members in common pleas court. On Tuesday morning, December 7 the criminal trials of the Mayfield Road Mob members began with a whimper, not a bang. In the courtroom of Common Pleas Judge Frank S. Day, prosecutors, potential jurors and witnesses, including the ones whose appearances were financed by the auto club, were ready to go. Defense counsel and the four defendants, however, were nowhere to be found. The men's attorney Alfred A. Cartwright, was involved as junior counsel in the trial of former judge William H. McGannon. New County Prosecutor Roland Baskin* told the court he had received a phone call from Cartwright on Monday. "He said," recounted Baskin, "I have a little case coming up tomorrow, the Motto case. We're both busy getting ready for the McGannon case and I'd like to have it go over."

Baskin told Day, "The automobile cases came up long before I was prosecutor, and I was not familiar with them. I did not suspect that he referred to the automobile cases until five minutes later. Then my office made every possible effort to find Cartwright, and I notified Judge Bernon, presiding in criminal court, that we would not consent to delay, but would insist that they be tried, even if necessary to appoint special counsel if Cartwright was not present."

Cartwright and the defendants had a good reason for the delay. The *Plain Dealer* reported, "Under the statutes, persons indicted and not tried within four terms of court are automatically released from the charge. The cases are now on the fourth court term and unless tried by Jan. 1, would have to be nolled."

Day ordered that all the witnesses remain in court and directed County Detective James W. Doran[3] to locate Cartwright. The "busy" attorney, when contacted, was still at his home. He arrived in court at 10:45. As a defense attorney he immediately began by defending himself and contradicting statements made by the prosecutor.

"I called Mr. Baskin by telephone before noon Monday and asked that the Motto trial be deferred by reason of my engagement in other matters. He assented. He knew what the nature of the cases was."

Detective Francke asked Cartwright if his goal was to have the cases thrown out of court under the statute of limitations.

"Sure, I would. If I had the opportunity," Cartwright responded.

Judge Day then chastised both Baskin and Cartwright. "The handling of these cases is a monstrous disregard of official duty," Day declared, "The fact that these cases have been passed fifteen or twenty times is unbelievable in the administration of justice.

"The prosecutor's office and the previous prosecutor [Samuel Doerfler] are to be severely criticized. Why Mr. Baskin passed those cases is beyond the conception of this court. His conduct in this matter is very blamable."

Day then ordered Cartwright to find his clients and bring them to court. Cartwright balked, claiming he was not prepared to go to trial on such short notice in view of the fact that he had made arrangements for a continuance. He stated that he was "very busy" with the McGannon case.

Day declared, "You are engaged in this room uninterruptedly until these cases are disposed."

Detective Francke and attorney Cartwright left and went directly to the home of Frank Milazzo, found him in bed, and delivered him to the courtroom to be tried first. Shortly after the jury was sworn, a bailiff discovered Frank Motto sitting among the spectators in the gallery. He was taken into custody. Before court adjourned for the day, Judge Day increased the bonds of both men by $1,000 per count, doubling the total. Unable to satisfy the new amount they were taken to the county jail to spend the night. The next morning when Nick Angelotta and Angelo Serra appeared in court they, like their ring partners before them, had their bonds doubled and were placed in the county jail.

Milazzo was indicted on a separate count with Julius Pettinatto in February 1920 for stealing an automobile belonging to Charles Hubbell, president of the Yankee Tire Company. Milazzo pled guilty before Judge Thomas M. Kennedy back on May 17, but had not been sentenced. Pettinatto pleaded not guilty, was tried and convicted. On November 22, his appeal for a new trial was denied, but he remained free on bond and had not been sentenced.

Judge Kennedy, who had come under a lot of pressure, claimed he would sentence Milazzo as soon as he was brought before him. "I issued a capias [warrant] for him, but the sheriff's office has been unable to find him," the judge claimed. "I advised attorney Cartwright, who defended him, to bring him into court. He has not brought him before me." The deputy county clerk said his office records showed that the warrant was ordered withdrawn by Kennedy, something the judge denied doing. Assistant County Prosecutor Merrick informed the court he would deliver Milazzo to Judge Kennedy's courtroom the next morning for sentencing.

The next morning when Milazzo appeared in Judge Day's courtroom he was whisked away and taken before Judge Kennedy, who promptly sentenced him to an indeterminate term in the Mansfield Reformatory for the Hubbell auto theft. His indictment with the Serra ring was held up until he finished his sentence. A warrant was immediately issued for the arrest of Julius Pettinatto to have him sentenced and taken to prison.

Angelotta was to be tried next for stealing the automobile of a White Avenue man on August 27, 1919. Representing Angelotta was former prosecutor David R. Rothkopf. Attorney Cartwright informed the judge that he had to turn over the reins because of the McGannon case. He remained in the courtroom, however, for most of the trial.

Frank Merrick handled the prosecution for the state. The assistant prosecutor figured he had four shots to gain a conviction on each defendant, as the counts were to be tried one at a time. If the jury acquitted, or deadlocked on any of the charges, the state would move onto the next count. Merrick announced that a "representative" of the four defendants approached him before the sentencing of Milazzo with a "suggestion" that two of the men would plead guilty if the charges against the other two were nolled. Merrick didn't disclose which two were to receive the free pass and it didn't matter anyway because he refused the offer. Two police officers were stationed in Day's courtroom to search witnesses and spectators for weapons. The extra security was due to death threats being issued against the state's star witness, Thomas Scavone.

The state produced a Dunkirk witness who testified he saw the defendant inside the car in that city, before it was sold to another resident there. When Scavone took the stand to testify the first thing he did was point out to the judge several men in the gallery who he claimed had threatened him. The men were escorted out of the courtroom, searched for weapons and then ordered to leave.

The next day Scavone finished his testimony. He explained how the thefts were planned in the Serra drugstore and carried out by the members of the ring. He talked about one theft where he and Angelotta obtained a license plate through the Cleveland Automobile Club, placed it on a stolen auto and drove it to Buffalo, where they sold it for $800. On Friday, December 10, the case was handed to the jury. Shortly after deliberations began, Merrick was approached by a man outside Judge Day's courtroom.

"You better not go too far with this stuff – something might happen to you," threatened the man.

"Go chase yourself," replied Merrick.

In addition to this confrontation, Merrick received several death threats by telephone, a tactic Mayfield Road Mob members used frequently over the years to intimidate.

Late on Friday afternoon the jury returned with a verdict of guilty. Day immediately sentenced Angelotta to a term in the Mansfield Reformatory.

The convicted man asked if he could be sent to the Ohio Penitentiary instead, giving as his reason that smoking was permitted there. The request was denied.

Judge Day announced that court would be held on Saturday in order to move the cases along. Frank Motto was the next defendant to be tried. The auto theft represented Motto's fourth arrest. His record showed no convictions for the prior three – assault to rob in December 1914, receiving stolen property in October 1919 and an arrest for suspicion in January 1920.

During Scavone's testimony he described Motto as one of the ring's leaders. He told the jury that he and Motto opened an automobile livery business (similar to today's rental agencies) in August 1919. Shortly thereafter, he said Motto introduced him to Angelotta and Serra. He claimed the three men "induced" him to join their gang, which began with the unloading of the stolen automobile in Buffalo. After Scavone deserted the Navy, he claimed Motto made threats on his life.

On Monday morning, December 13 Motto took the stand in his own defense. He denied introducing Scavone to the other defendants and that he had ever threatened him. The jury didn't take long to return a verdict of guilty. Motto advised Judge Day he wanted to appeal the case. Angered at this decision, Merrick threatened to try him immediately on one of the other charges. The judge gave Motto some time to reconsider.

On Tuesday morning the trial for Angelo Serra began. Scavone, again the key witness, said that Serra's drug store was used as the gang's headquarters. He testified that in Serra's capacity as a notary public he helped the gang dispose of $500,000 worth of automobiles it had stolen. It was announced during the trial that the Cleveland Bar Association would act immediately to strip Serra of his notary public certificate.

The jury received the case Wednesday afternoon and deliberated late into the night without reaching a verdict. The judge ordered them sequestered for the night in the Hotel Cleveland,[4] where the two women on the jury were given a separate room. On Thursday morning the jury returned a guilty verdict. Serra's attorney requested that the court defer sentencing until Saturday so that he might have time to collect evidence on which to file an appeal. On Friday, Rothkopf announced he was going to appeal the conviction on the grounds that once a jury begins its deliberations the panel is not to be separated, obviously alluding to the fact that the two women were moved to another room. Merrick scoffed at the contention.

Meanwhile, Thursday morning, after the guilty verdict for Serra was announced, Frank Motto asked Judge Day if he could have time to settle his personal affairs before being sent to prison. The judge wanted to know if Motto was going to file an appeal, which would give him that time. Motto was given until 4:00 p.m. to decide.

Why Frank Motto decided to appeal his case instead of sucking it up and heading off to prison, like Angelotta and Milazzo, to serve his term will never be known. What is known is that before representing him in his appeal the attorney wanted $1,500 to handle the work and Motto was desperate for money. His plan to get it put the wheels in motion for one of Cleveland's most notorious crimes and, in the end, instead of a short prison term, Motto would pay with his life – along the way eight others would also die.

Chapter Endnotes

1. The first board of trustees of the Cleveland Automobile Club was a "Who's Who" of the local automobile manufacturing scene, which was second only to Detroit – Walter C. Baker, George L. Weiss, Alexander Winton, E.L. Strong, Fred R. White, Windsor T. White, L.H. Rogers, F.B. Stearns and R.A. Rainey. Strong served as its first president.

Fueled by its steel industry, Cleveland became the early leader in automobile manufacturing in the country. The Cleveland Automobile Club announced a year after its founding that the city had six automobile factories in operation, despite reporting a mere 150 cars in the city. In 1902 the Cleveland Automobile Club joined with nine other automobile clubs in the country to form the American Automobile Association (AAA). The Cleveland chapter provided numerous amenities for its members, including emergency roadside maintenance and bail bond services. In 1978 the Cleveland Automobile Club became the Ohio Motorists Association.

2. The term of the grand jury ended on December 31, 1920 and the panel was dismissed before all the evidence was presented by Joseph Dembe. The assistant prosecutor was out of work with the new Stanton administration coming in, but vowed that "in the capacity of a private attorney" he would present the evidence to the new grand jury. With all the major cases Stanton was handed the auto theft ring seemed to take a back seat.

3. James W. Doran was one of Cleveland's greatest police officers from a by-gone era. He began his police career in 1884 and finished as a detective sergeant in charge of the department's first detective bureau in 1909. He then began a career as a county detective serving every prosecutor from John A. Kline through the career of Edward Stanton. Among the famous

cases Doran worked were the Cassie Chadwick swindling case, the murder of Cleveland Heights millionaire William L. Rice, and the killing of Dan Kaber. Doran spent 45 years in police work. He died in the Cleveland Clinic after complications from surgery on February 1, 1932 at the age of 72.

4. The Hotel Cleveland opened on the south-west corner of Public Square on December 16, 1918. The site had operated as a hotel since 1815 under thirteen different names. It became an important part of the Union Terminal complex built by the Van Swerigen brothers during the latter half of the 1920s. Today the hotel is still operating as the Renaissance Cleveland Hotel.

7
Sly-Fanner Payroll Robbery

The W.W. Sly Manufacturing Company was founded by William W. Sly in 1874. The company produced equipment for foundries – tumbling barrels, cupolas and sand blasting machinery. It was located at 4700 Train Avenue on Cleveland's near-West Side, an area that once carried the nickname, "Clogsville" due to the bottlenecking of the trains that passed through.

William Sly was born on a farm in Walled Lake, Michigan in 1834. In his late twenties he helped organize Company I, of the 22nd Michigan Infantry and fought in a number of Civil War battles. In 1869, bucking the "Go west, young man" attitude, Sly moved east settling in Cleveland with his wife Mary and two children, Wilfred Colfax, born in 1862, and Maude Mildred, born in 1881. He began work with the Cleveland Nickel Company. When that company suffered a financial setback, Sly left to start his own business.

After the completion of his son's education, Sly took Wilfred into the business, where he quickly rose through the ranks. Wilfred was born in Oakland County, Michigan and moved to Cleveland as a child. In his youth he was considered a "great athlete." His specialty was bicycle riding, the old high-wheel type. He participated in a number of local competitions involving distance riding. Sly won several state and sectional championships as a bike rider. He was also an avid yachtsman, a member of the Cleveland Yacht Club. In addition, Sly also enjoyed hunting and fishing. His fishing excursions to Canada during the summers sometimes lasted up to two months.

Sly married Marie M. Kurtz in April 1894. The couple resided at 13474 Lake Avenue in Lakewood, a home noted for its gardens and "the hospitality showed to guests." Every year the Slys hosted a masquerade ball on New Year's Eve. The couple had no children.

In the business world Wilfred was a student of industrial relations. He served as the director of the Industrial Association of Cleveland for a number of years. One of Sly's close friends at the firm was George K. Fanner, whose father, George J., was vice president of the company. There was more than a 20-year age difference between the men. Fanner and his wife, Ethyl, also resided in Lakewood, at 1285 Virginia Avenue.

On May 23, 1911, William W. Sly died at his Crawford Road home from "complications of diseases," at the age of 77. He was buried in Lake View Cemetery, where veterans of the Grand Army of the Republic (GAR) conducted the burial service.

At the time of his father's death, Wilfred held the position of Secretary of the manufacturing company. Leadership passed into his hands and he became president before he was 50 years old. His friend George K. Fanner rose too in the organization, reaching the rank of plant superintendent.

During the war years the company employed as many as 300 men. In slack times in the foundry business the plant operated with a reduced force of 70 to 80 men working a four to five day workweek. Sly and Fanner both had stellar reputations with their employees. One opinion about them, on which most employees agreed, was summed up by one worker: "You couldn't find better folks to work for. When I was on the shop committee Mr. Sly and Mr. Fanner heard every complaint we had and fixed up all the troubles. A man could come into Mr. Sly's office in his overalls and talk to him about his job. He was one of the most easily approached men in Cleveland. Every man in the shop would say that."

As with practically all manufacturing businesses at the time, or any other company with a large workforce for that matter, employees were paid in cash. It was a period before the business community had the safe guards of bank wire transfers and commercial armored car use. At the time many business payrolls were handled by company officials who went to the bank on a weekly, bi-monthly, or monthly schedule to pick up the cash to pay their employees. If companies didn't hire or provide armed escorts, if they didn't alter their travel procedures by taking different routes to and from the bank, or they didn't schedule different pick-up times, they could easily become targets for payroll bandits. During the late teens and early 1920s, Cleveland experienced a multitude of payroll robberies. The robberies were becoming a regular feature on the front pages of the three daily newspapers. In late December 1920, Sly read a newspaper report about an attempted payroll robbery in Chicago in which the intended victim fought with a robber who tried to make off with the money. The intended victim had "routed" the would-be bandit. Telling a friend of the account, Sly declared, "That's the kind of man I admire." On the last day of 1920, Cleveland experienced its most sensational payroll robbery.

As Wilfred Sly and George Fanner left the Train Avenue manufacturing facility this morning both were armed with handguns. As they headed downtown their most likely route into the city was north on West 47th Street, over the wooden Nickel Plate Railroad bridge, to Lorain Avenue and then east on Lorain to West 25th Street. North on West 25th to Detroit Avenue and then east over the Detroit-Superior Bridge entering Public Square from the west. At the bank, the men picked up the payroll of $4,200 from William. R. Mesker. They followed the same route back to Train Avenue in their return.

The men soon arrived at the rickety, wooden railroad bridge and began crossing. All of a sudden two men in a Stearns automobile sped past them and then cut them off. Sly slammed on the breaks and in attempting to avoid the Stearns the car careened into the side of the wooden bridge, coming to a halt just avoiding a plunge to the railroad tracks below. The loud noise created by the crash was heard by a number of nearby residents which brought both children and adults rushing to the scene. Moments after the crash a third automobile appeared at the north end of the bridge; a Jordan from which three men alighted and moved toward the accident scene, while a fourth remained behind the wheel.

What happened next was horrific. The story is now told by the witnesses[1] who were on or near the bridge that morning:

Otto Walter, proprietor of a florist shop at 5112 Clark Avenue. "I was driving north in W. 47th street and had just got to the bridge when I saw the two automobiles coming across the bridge toward me. I thought at first they were racing, and, because it didn't look good to me, I stopped my Ford coupe until they should get across.

"The Stearns car deliberately swerved in front of the other one, and when I heard the wood breaking, I thought they had both gone over the edge. When they stopped I ran up to them.

"Mr. Sly had gotten out of his car and was running up toward the other one. As I came up, a man with a brown suit and cap came out of the car which had swerved, and Sly said to him. 'What are you trying to do? Wreck me? I never heard of such a thing.' The other man swore at him, and started the argument over whose fault it was.

"I said I had seen what happened, and Mr. Sly said, 'Will you give me your name and address on a piece of paper.' Then it all happened like a flash.

"The man in brown, I think said: 'There you ___ __ _____,' and shot Sly down in front of me. Sly's body turned over once, and the man shot him again through the head. Then he jammed the same gun into my ribs, and said, 'You put 'em up.'

"I turned and ran, and he fired at me and missed. I yelled for help, and ran to the first house I could find, where I telephoned to the police. When I came out, they had driven away. I helped another man take Mr. Fanner, who was lying on the bridge, to the hospital in my automobile. We found a gun in his pocket at the hospital."

Mrs. Maude Toohey, 2137 West 47th Street. "I had left my home to go up to one of the stores on Lorain avenue, and had just started across the bridge when the two automobiles came running across side by side. I just chanced to look up the minute the car crashed into the railing, and I screamed so that my daughter back in our home heard me and ran out to see if I were hurt.

"Mr. Sly came out of his car, looking very mad, and I went up to him, saw that he was unhurt, and said, 'You had a narrow escape. What made that car drive in front of you?' He said, 'I am going to find out. Those men must be crazy.'

"A tall man, who wore a cap, had climbed out of the first car and was arguing with Mr. Sly. Then another from the first car came over and reached into Mr. Sly's car for a satchel. Mr. Fanner grabbed at him, and the man pulled out a pistol and fired. Mr. Fanner said, 'My God. Oh, my God,' and fell over. Then more shots came and I saw Mr. Sly fall, too. The man who had reached for the suit case put his gun back in his pocket, and then he turned to me, and said, 'Keep your _____ mouth shut, you ___ ___ _____, or I'll shoot you too.'

"Another car, which they say was waiting with its engine running on the north side of the bridge, came up. All of the men but one got into it. He was the one who had spoken to me, and he pulled his gun out again and threw it into the car in which the bandits rode away. Then he ran south in W. 47th street"

Miss Irene Walker, 2092 West 47th Street. "I heard the crash as the Sly car hit the side of the bridge. I know that Mr. Sly didn't think then that it was a holdup. He got on the running board of his car and started to argue with the men, who had left the Stearns car and returned, as if to view the damage.

"I heard Mr. Sly say: 'It is absolutely your fault. You shouldn't have driven in front of us this way.'

"The two bandits were denying their responsibility when the third car pulled up and three men descended. They joined in the argument.

"Then I saw guns flash and heard bullets sing. A little short man, dressed in brown, with a brown cap started the shooting. This man, I think, did all the shooting.

Mrs. Mary Blaich, 2092 West 47th Street. "I was working in my house when I heard the crash of the automobiles coming together. My son, H.J. Blaich, who was looking out of the window at the time, told me to run downstairs and see the auto accident. I went down and found the two machines standing close together fifteen feet from the corner of my house. The men in the two machines were arguing. Sly and Fanner had gotten out of their automobile and all five of the bandits, who were all slight young men, were arguing very close to them.

"Sly said, 'You had no chains on your machine.'

"One of the bandits said, 'You'll have to get witnesses.'

"Sly then took my name and my son's name and wrote them in a notebook. He was standing close to his machine.

"Then I heard what I took to be an explosion in the muffler of one of the machines. I saw Sly fall. His face was blown partly off. He was shot by a man standing very close to him, not a yard away. The man fired five shots at him.

"Then he pointed the gun directly at me and said, 'Run, you ____,' I ran back to my house. I saw the bandits jump into their machine on the other side of the bridge and drive north. Thinking the affair was all over, I started out to where the men were lying shot. But the man who had shot Sly ran through our yard westward and met me going in the opposite direction. He was left behind. He had his gun pointed at me and would have shot me, I am sure, if he had had any bullets left.

"He yelled, 'get back in the house, you ____. Don't you phone. Damn you, don't you phone.'

"I ran back into the house and the man went ahead till he came to the alley back of our house. Then he ran south in the opposite direction from the bandits.

Miss Edith Marklew, 2159 West 45th Street. "I was about to cross the Nickel Plate bridge from the north side when I saw the two automobiles pass. They came together on the other side of the bridge. I walked over and stopped to hear the argument. The man who killed Sly was tall and slim, wore a dark suit, a brown cap and tan shoes. He was saying to Mr. Sly that he couldn't have prevented the accident because he skidded. Mr. Sly said the man had no chains on his auto. Then Sly put his hand into his pocket to get some paper and before he could draw out his hand he was killed. Then the man who shot him put his gun against me and yelled, 'Get away from here.'"[2]

One article claimed that "more than a score" of children ran to the scene. Two of them were quoted in the *Plain Dealer* report:

Elmer Walker, 12, Detroit Junior High School student. "I saw Sly pull his gun from his pocket and put it back in when he started to take the names of people who saw the accident. Sly had a nickel plated revolver. All five of the bandits had gotten out of their automobile and were standing around. All five of them had guns. They started shooting and we started running."

Herbert Barnes, 11, 2100 West 47th Street, a pupil at Orchard School. "Elmer Walker and I got there soon after we heard the autos hit and the bridge break. I saw Mr. Sly take a revolver out of his pocket and put it back again. Mr. Sly must have thought they were going to hold him up and then changed his mind."

There were other accounts printed, but the reader was left to wonder if all the people were witnessing the same incident. It's no wonder police and prosecutors are skeptical about "eyewitness" testimony.

While there was little doubt that the two men died instantly, they were both transported to Fairview Hospital,[3] then located at 3305 Franklin Circle. Sly was found to have two bullet wounds to the head and one in the abdomen. Fanner was killed by a single shot that entered beneath his right eye and pierced his brain. Both men were killed with .38 slugs.

Cleveland police arrived in minutes and scoured the neighborhood looking for the Jordan automobile and the bandit who escaped on foot. They came up empty. After interviewing witnesses they quickly put out this description of the robbers:

No. 1 – Leader of the gang and Sly's alleged murderer: wore a brown suit, cap and brown shoes; about 26, 5 feet 5 inches tall, 140 pounds; had an overhanging upper lip.
No. 2 – About 30, 5 feet 7 inches tall, 150 pounds, dark suit and hat.
No. 3 – About 22, 5 feet 6 inches tall, 140 pounds, light complexion; wore green knitted tassel cap and green sweater.
No. 4 – About 22, 5 feet 6 inches tall, 130 pounds; dark suit and cap, muddy shoes.
No. 5 – About 24, 5 feet 9 inches tall, 145 pounds, slender, dark complexion; wore long coat with high fur collar and dark hat and suit.
No. 6 – Driver of the car in which the bandits escaped: dark cap; about 23.
CAR in which bandits escaped identified by the witnesses variously as black, closed type Marmon, Mercer or Jordan.

At the Sly home, Marie was prostrated with grief and placed under the care of a doctor. Ethyl Fanner collapsed, but quickly regained her composure, feeling she needed to be strong for her ten-year-old daughter Marion. After sending the child to a neighbor's home, she talked to reporters. In tears she said, I can't understand why they shot him. Why didn't they take the money and go? They need not have shot him in cold blood."

Ethyl Fanner then alluded to the recent verdict in the trial of George "Jiggs" Losteiner. "It is no wonder," she stated, "that thieves do not hesitate to kill, after the "Jiggs" Losteiner trial. The courts are too easy."

At the W.W. Sly Manufacturing Company, a sign on the door where the men went to get paid read: "No Pay Today." Another sign stated: "Owing to the death of Mr. Sly and Mr. Fanner, factory will be closed Monday." There was a somber mood throughout the plant, as many of the workers, most long-time employees, were saddened by the loss and wondered about the future of the firm.

In assessing the crime and the description of the robbers as being youths, Police Chief Smith stated in a *Plain Dealer* interview that "veteran criminals resorted to killing only when they were hard pressed for escape, while most of the shootings committed in the activities of a crime have been found to originate with scared novices."

In contrast, the *Cleveland News* reported, "The killings in the Sly payroll robbery was clearly the work of men of much experience, men who kill when they shoot and who do that shooting without a second of warning if they think there is a danger of capture or the balking of their plans."

Police brought the eyewitnesses from the bridge to police headquarters to view photos from the "rogue's gallery." Meanwhile, all three newspapers ran front-page articles on the current crime wave and what needed to be done to bring it under control. The editorials were most critical of the weaknesses in the court system. Leading the crusade was E. Arthur Roberts of the *Plain Dealer*. In a series which ran several days, Roberts pointed out flaws in the justice system. One of the examples he cited was the recent auto theft ring. Little did he know that this case was directly responsible for the double murder which was causing the current furor.

Of the three Cleveland dailies the *Cleveland News* was by far the most critical. Claiming that the police were "accomplishing practically nothing," a front page editorial on January 2 began:

Bandit Bullets Stir Ultimatum "Crime Must Go"

Whole City, Stung by Challenge of Double Murder, Car Station Holdup, Rises in Demand Police or City Hall Do Something to Make Life Safe.

"Does Cleveland today belong to the gunman and the killer?

"Or does it belong to the law-abiding citizens of this community?

"Lawlessness stalks the streets, contemptuous of what is called police protection.

"Death, bloody and awful, at the beck of the bandit-killer's whim, walks at the shoulder of every man and woman whose tasks take him or her where there may be gain for the seizing for the thug.

"No longer is it a fear of mere robbery that confronts the decent citizen – it is the chill horror of being struck down by the outlaws' bullet or his bludgeon."

The next day the *Cleveland Press* took its shot:

"Make Cleveland Safe!

"Many causes are given for this increase in violent crime, but at the bottom of it all lies the fact that for five years past Cleveland has had a reputation of being an "easy" town, as this newspaper has so often pointed out. Crooks everywhere came to regard Cleveland as a place of refuge. Now that New York and Chicago are driving out their thugs, what more natural than that they should stop off at the half-way place – Cleveland, the "easy" town!

"All crookdom knew about the infamous Order 73 which forbade the police from making vice arrests or raids on gambling houses or similar resorts without permission from City Hall. Crooks knew that towns that tolerated vice dens were "safe" towns for their kinds of operations."

On Monday afternoon, January 3, funeral services were held for George Fanner from his Virginia Avenue home. The services were followed by his burial in Riverside Cemetery on the city's West Side. The next afternoon the funeral for Wilfred Sly was held. After the services at the Lake Avenue home, Sly was buried in Lake View Cemetery next to his father. The W.W. Sly Manufacturing Company remained closed until Wednesday morning as many of the employees attended both funerals.

Today W.W. Sly Manufacturing Company operates as Sly, Inc., a manufacturer of industrial dust collectors and air cleaners in Strongsville, Ohio. The old Train Avenue factory is the present site of GRG Trucking Company, Inc. The structure, situated between the I-90 freeway and railroad tracks to the north and a mixed ethnic neighborhood to the south, lies across the street from several dilapidated brick buildings.

The tragic double-slaying did nothing to deter Cleveland hoodlums over the New Year's weekend as several more crimes were committed. Prominent among them was the hold up of a Standard Oil gas station at the corner of Superior and West Sixth Street, the robbery of the Miles Theatre[4] located at the corner of East Ninth Street and Prospect Avenue, and the robbery of Clark's No. 5 restaurant at 1325 Euclid Avenue. In this last robbery, two gunmen entered the eatery about 2:30 in the morning and forced 40 customers into the kitchen, taking a pot shot at one woman who didn't move fast enough.

In charge of the Sly-Fanner investigation was Detective Inspector Charles N. Sterling. The 25-year veteran had joined the Cleveland Police Department on New Year's Day 1896. His early years on the force were served on the West Side, where he was assigned to the West 28th Street / Detroit Avenue Precinct. Sterling rose steadily up the ranks – 1906 sergeant, 1911 lieutenant, 1917 captain, and 1918 deputy inspector. In this last promotion he was placed in charge of the detective bureau, of which he was a member since 1914. The *Plain Dealer* said of Sterling, "Payroll robberies, which came with the regularity of pay day itself, murders, shootings, burglaries and a host of smaller crimes made this period [after the World War] a trying one for the detective bureau and its head." Throughout it all, Sterling remained a tireless officer. Sterling was once described by a supervisor as being "known to go without sleep for two days at a time when he was 'hot on the trail' of a criminal. Police work was not only employment, but a hobby as well."

Sterling was involved in a number of notable cases involving such big name criminals of the day as George "Jiggs" Losteiner, John Grogan, and "Big Jim" Morton. In the latter case he brought Morton back from Toledo after his arrest there to answer for the robbery of the West Cleveland Bank in 1919. Sterling prepared the case against Grogan that sent the bank robber / cop killer to jail for the rest of his life.

The inspector was liked and respected throughout the city. The *Cleveland Press* wrote, "During his career he was stationed in almost every section of the city and his popularity was city-wide. His ruddy face, always on the verge of a smile, his vice-like handshake, his leniency toward young first-offenders, were known to thousands."

The police were under a lot of pressure to make arrests and a new cleanup campaign was on in the city. On January 2, Detective Inspector Sterling and Detective Captain George J. Matowitz received a tip that the men they were looking for in the Sly-Fanner murders were holed up in the Graystone Hotel at 2118 Prospect Avenue. The tip came from a taxi cab driver who overheard some men discussing a plan to rob a bank. A raid was staged for 5:00 Monday morning. Breaking into the room police found five young men[5] sound asleep. The *Cleveland News* reported:

"Five revolvers, two shot guns and a high-powered rifle were found in the dingy back room where the bandits made their headquarters. One of the revolvers is said to have had two discharged cartridges in the cylinder of the same caliber that killed Sly and Fanner.

"Half burned cigarettes were strewn about the dingy room, playing cards were thrown in a heap in one corner and clothing of every kind was scattered about the floor. A table, two chairs and a cot was the only furniture.

"Hats, coats and shoes found there offered no clew to the identity of the occupants, for every label had been removed. The six taken at the hotel were all well-dressed youths, but every mark of identification had been cut from the clothing they wore.

"The names they gave at police headquarters are believed to be fictitious. Police are endeavoring to learn their identity through fingerprints and Bertillon measurements.

"A detail of police was stationed at the hotel to watch for the appearance of other members of the band and shortly before noon the sixth youth was taken in custody when he appeared at the entrance of the room."

Due to the cab driver's tip, police had six suspects in custody and they were sure at least one of these men was tied to the Sly-Fanner murders. They were about to catch another big break, also reported to them by an alert citizen. A short time after the killings a Jordan automobile parked at the Hotel Winton[6] garage at 1002 Prospect. As the driver was leaving, he said to the parking lot attendant that if anyone asked about the time he came in, to say it was a half-hour earlier. A short while later the attendant heard about the murders, became suspicious and notified police.

The *Cleveland News* reported on the day of the murders that, "The car, which the bandits abandoned at the scene of the crime, is listed as belonging to D. Galletti, 1909 Scovill ave." The *News* was mistaken about the automobile. The abandoned car was Goff's stolen Stearns. The next morning the *Plain Dealer* correctly reported, "The reports of the license numbers of the car in which the escape was made were at variance as they were made by the spectators of the crime, but one certain number which was reported by more than one witness is that of a car which late yesterday police traced to a Scovill avenue S.E. home." It was later reported that the discrepancies in the eyewitness reporting of the license plate number was due to the fact that the corner was bent back to obscure one of the numbers. The interesting part here is that Galletti was the maiden name of Dominic Benigno's wife, and the Mayfield Road Mob leader lived at 1909 Scovill Avenue.

While there was never any mention in the newspapers of a police inquiry at the Scovill Avenue address, detectives staked out the garage to see if anyone would come and claim the automobile. The plan worked to perfection as not one, but three underworld characters showed up at different intervals to remove the automobile. After each arrest the police made no effort to confiscate the vehicle. They just left it there to see who came after it next. Each man was arrested after trying to drive the car away that Monday. The order in which the men came in was not revealed, but two of the men were Mayfield Road Mob members, Dominic Benigno and Charles Coletto, while the third, John Lonardo, was the younger brother of Cleveland Mafia boss "Big Joe" Lonardo. When arrested, the three gave their occupations as clerk, bookkeeper and laborer respectively.

One of the unanswered mysteries of the Sly-Fanner murders was why did the three men show up at three different times and try to remove the automobile. After the first man tried and disappeared into police custody, what prompted the second effort and then the third?

During the recent cleanup campaign, one of the men brought in was Mayfield Road Mob member John Angersola. He was charged with carrying a concealed weapon. John and his brothers Fred and George were all members of the Mayfield Road Mob. All three adopted the last name of King. John "Johnny King" Angersola was the most prominent of the brothers and always ranked near the top of the gang.

Perhaps due to his gang affiliation, the police lumped John Angersola with the other three men picked up at the Hotel Winton garage and said only that three of the four were arrested there, failing to differentiate who hadn't. Later police positively identified Benigno and Lonardo as being arrested at the garage, but again refused to reveal who the third man was. After they were arraigned it became obvious that the third man was Coletto, but the purpose for the police deception was never explained.

Another Mayfield Road Mob member caught in the police dragnet was Frank Motto the desperate car thief. Motto, however, was one of the nearly 40 prisoners police paraded before eyewitness, who couldn't identify any of them. Motto was released, abandoned the plan to appeal his conviction, and went off to serve his sentence in the Mansfield Reformatory

Between the Graystone Hotel raid and the Hotel Winton garage arrests, police believed they had three of the five gunmen from the Sly-Fanner murders. On January 3, it was falsely reported that the three were positively identified by eyewitnesses, according to a statement allegedly released by Inspector Sterling. The next day another statement attributed to Sterling claimed, "although no identifications to warrant placing a murder charge could be obtained, one suspect was declared by a witness of Sly's killing to be the 'man who did the shooting.'" This man, it was reported, was one of the six arrested in the Graystone Hotel raid. Whoever the man was that police apprehended at the hotel, he was never identified by name in the newspapers as having been a member of the Sly-Fanner murder crew.

The days following the hotel raid and the garage arrests were discouraging for the police. Despite their initial success after the 48-hour weekend crime spree, they were unable to get a break in any of the cases. With all the witnesses brought in from the Sly-Fanner killings, the restaurant robbery and the theatre holdup, only three of them recognized a single suspect, but none was positive in their identification.

One day after Sterling announced he had three of the Sly-Fanner murderers under lock and key, the embarrassed inspector sadly announced, "I am not satisfied with any of the identification. I do not feel that I could place a murder charge against a man because three witnesses have said he looked like one of the men in the murder or robbery."

Prosecutor Stanton asked the county to offer a $500 reward for the arrest and conviction of the murder participants. After the funerals of Sly and Fanner, one of the first orders of business by friends of the pair was to establish a substantial reward fund. Ben D. Weller, a friend of both victims, made the initial donation of $100 towards a projected fund of $5,000. Weller explained, "We are heartily in sympathy with the suggestion of County Prosecutor Edward C. Stanton in asking for a reward of $500, but the amount involved in the robbery was so much greater that we believe at least $5,000 should be raised for the reward." The reward eventually totaled $8,500.

By January 5, police had still not removed the Jordan from the Hotel Winton garage. They brought a number of witnesses there to view it. Investigators were skeptical up to this point because several of the witnesses from the bridge claimed the automobile was a Mercer. By Thursday, eight people had positively identified the automobile as the escape vehicle and police brought in its owner Luminato "Louis" Galletti, an aged East End baker and the father-in-law of Benigno. Police had still not made public the names of the men arrested at the garage, but said that the baker's son-in-law was one of the men being held. Asked by a reporter who the prisoner was, Matowitz replied, "You will know him when we book him for the murder."

Perhaps one of the reasons the suspects couldn't be identified came to light on Friday, January 7. Twenty witnesses were brought before the grand jury to present evidence on the double slaying. One of the women told a detective that a "suspicious looking man had called at her home Thursday," and threatened to kill her if she told what she knew about the killings to the grand jury.

The remainder of the witnesses were quickly questioned by police who found that more than half of them had received threatening telephone calls and letters, or were "paid a visit." Most were reluctant to reveal the threats fearing retaliation. The newspapers called it a "Black Hand plot" and reported that hoods had begun canvassing the neighborhood immediately after the shooting, seeking out residents who had witnessed the murders. The visits continued over the next few days and on Thursday, the day before the grand jury hearings, death threats were issued. Police were dispatched to the West 47th Street neighborhood to see if the hoodlums returned, while a detective squad visited the "foreign district" in hopes of spotting some of the known Mayfield Road Mob associates who were still out on the street.

Despite the lack of success police were having up to this point, Inspector Sterling still believed indictments might be returned against several of the jailed suspects. Sterling had already given up hope of any of the Graystone Hotel suspects being tied to the Sly-Fanner killings, every effort to connect these men with the slayings failed.

While the grand jury was hearing evidence, police were advised that lawyers for the Mayfield Road Mob members were going to file habeas corpus motions for their clients. The police had no choice but to charge them as suspicious persons in order to hold them. On Friday evening the four were arraigned before Police Judge George A. Howells. The judge set bond at $40,000 apiece, a record amount for a suspicious person's charge. Angersola, Benigno and Coletto made the trek back to the county jail, while the 23 year-old John Lonardo, the Mafia boss's brother, was bailed out less than two hours after he was booked.

Meanwhile, things weren't going well with the grand jury. The panel met again Saturday morning to hear more witness testimony, but by the end of the day it was reported there was only one identification made by one witness and it was only "partial." Even employees at the Hotel Winton garage didn't tell the same story as to when the Jordan arrived. Two claimed the car was driven in between 11:30 a.m. and noon; while a third attendant stated the driver came in at 11:00, just prior to the time the murders were committed. By Wednesday, January 12, the grand jury had questioned 15 of the 21 witnesses to the Sly-Fanner murders and no one could put John Lonardo[7] or Charles Coletto at the scene; only one had said Benigno was there.

The police were clearly frustrated. On Tuesday night, members of the vice squad were at the Princess Dance Hall[8] at 1826 East 13th near Euclid Avenue where they spotted two girls who they believed had "some acquaintance" with the Mayfield Road Mob members in custody. The girls were seen talking with four young men.[9] The vice squad members "roughly parted" the men from their dance partners, shoved them into a corner, and kept them there for more than an hour with the other dancers looking on. The men, said to have clean records, were "held for investigation," refused food, and prevented from contacting relatives, some of whom thought the worst had happened when the young men did not return home. The next day the four were released with Inspector Sterling's apologies after 18 hours in the hands of police.

On Tuesday, January 24 the grand jury returned "no bills" on the three Sly-Fanner murder suspects, meaning they would not be indicted. Prosecutor Stanton said, "Every particle of evidence gathered by the police had been submitted to the jury, which was unable to vote indictments on the few facts offered."

While the police couldn't charge the men with murder, they continued to hold Angersola, Benigno and Coletto on the suspicious person charges. On February 18, on the recommendation of police prosecutors and city detectives, Judge Howells dismissed the cases.[10] The *Cleveland News* reported, "The final chapter in the history of the collapse of the police department's efforts to ferret out the murderers of Wilfred C. Sly and George Fanner...was written."

The Cleveland Police Department had not given up. The efforts to apprehend the slayers of the two local businessmen in one of the city's most dastardly crimes continued for the next 15 years. The dismissal of charges for the three Mayfield Road Mob members in mid-February 1921 was not the "final chapter" in the Sly-Fanner murder saga. Instead, it was simply the beginning.

Chapter Endnotes

1. Compiled from accounts given in the *Cleveland News* on December 31, 1920 and the *Plain Dealer* on January 1, 1921.

2. I would be remiss if I didn't show the account of the shootings from the last two witnesses, Mrs. B.B. Blaich (listed as Mary Blake) and Miss Edith Marklew (listed as Mrs. Marley), as it appeared a day earlier in the *Cleveland News*:

> Mrs. Mary Blake, who lives at 2092 W. 47th st., only a few feet from the scene of the murders, was at her front gate talking with Mrs. Edith Markley, 2159 W. 45th st., a visitor, [when] Sly's automobile crashed into the bridge railing.

Mrs. Blake tells this story, which is corroborated by Mrs. Markley:
"I was talking to Mrs. Markley when Mr. Sly's car crashed into the bridge railing after the other machine cut over in front of it.

"Two men got out and argued with Sly and Fanner. Then for some reason Sly pulled a gun. Before he could shoot one of the two bandits shot both Sly and Fanner.

"Then he turned toward Mrs. Markley and me, waving the revolver, I ran to the rear of the house. Mrs. Markley ran down the street. The bandit followed me and ran into an alley back of the house going south."

This emphasizes my previous comment regarding "eyewitness" testimony.

3. Today known as Fairview General Hospital and located at 18101 Lorain Avenue. The hospital began "as a training school for religious sisters to provide care and religious instruction to the community. It was originally established as the Society for Christian Care of the Sick & Needy (also known as the Bethesda Deaconess House)." – *The Encyclopedia of Cleveland History*.

It was also known as "German Hospital" because it served the large German population that settled on the city's near-west side. During World War I the hospital changed its identity from German Hospital, for obvious reasons, to Fairview Park Hospital, taking its new name from a nearby park, not the suburb of the same name. From 1896 to 1955 the hospital remained at the Franklin Circle address, and then moved to its present location.

4. When it opened on October 26, 1913 the Miles Theatre was called "America's Most Beautiful Vaudeville Palace." Located at 2071 East Ninth Street, at the corner of Prospect, the opulent theatre, "a heaven of rosy velour and damask, of gold fringe and green velvet," cost nearly a half-million dollars to build. Big name entertainers who performed there included Bert Lahr and a young Mickey Rooney. Over the years the theatre changed names – Miles, Columbia, Great Lakes and Carter – and format – vaudeville, movies and burlesque – as it was opened, closed and remodeled in a battle to survive financially. The theatre was torn down during the fall of 1959.

5. Four of the five young men were later identified as James Adams, James Albondante, Samuel Gaglione and "Roxie" Laurie. Gaglione and

Laurie quickly ratted out the others for their involvement in the robbery of the Ukrainian American Building & Loan Company.

6. The Winton Hotel went through several transformations and ownerships. Erected in 1917 at 1012 Prospect Avenue near East Ninth, the hotel was named in honor of Cleveland automobile pioneer, Alexander Winton. In 1931, under new ownership, it was renamed the Carter Hotel in honor of early Cleveland settler, Lorenzo Carter, who established the city's first tavern. In later years it was purchased and renamed the Pick-Carter Hotel. By the 1960s the hotel began to deteriorate and it eventually became government subsidized housing for the poor. It is still in existence.

7. There was never any proof that John Lonardo had any part in the Sly-Fanner murders. The fact that the youngest brother of the city's Mafia boss was arrested trying to help Dominic Benigno reveals, however, the power that the first leader of the Mayfield Road Mob wielded.

8. The Cleveland City Directory lists the Princess Dance Hall at the same address as the Dreamland Dance Hall, both at 1826 East 13th Street near Chester.
Dancing became one of the most popular recreational activities in Cleveland, as well as in other major cities, between 1910 and 1950. In Cleveland during this period more than 150 dance halls were in operation. This number did not include dance floors operating in hotels, night clubs or privately held halls. Just prior to this period dance pavilions operated at places like Edgewater Park and Gordon Park. They later were popular at area amusement parks, like Luna Park and Euclid Beach.
Unfortunately many of these places drew the attention of an undesirable element of Cleveland society – prostitutes and young hoods. Prostitutes began to infiltrate the downtown dance halls after being pushed out of the "Hamilton – Red Light" district in the spring of 1915. The prostitutes propositioned young men at the dance halls and headed off to the nearest hotel. Many hotel managers, who didn't want their establishments to get a bad name, refused rooms to women who did not have a suitcase or overnight bag when checking in. Dance hall personnel soon began to notice a number of women attending the dances with small suitcases. One enterprising businessman began renting suitcases for a quarter a night out of his Chester Avenue office.

9. The four men were Robert Coghill, Morris Cohn, Alvin Dragin and G.E. Langdon.

10. As for John Angersola, he appeared before Judge Florence Allen on March 14 on a charge of forfeiting his bond on March 7 when he failed to appear in court on a concealed weapons charge. Police believed he was involved in the murders, but weren't sure how. Assistant County Prosecutor James T. Cassidy asked Allen to set Angersola's bond as high as possible as they regarded him as a material witness to the killings. The judge obliged, setting his bond at $50,000 and sending him to the county jail. The next month, on April 15, Judge Allen sentenced him to one to three years in the Ohio Penitentiary on the concealed weapons charge. It had not been a good week for the Mayfield Road Mob heavy. Two days earlier he was sentenced to one to fifteen years in prison by Judge Bernon for taking $300 from Harry Yarnish during a robbery in December 1920. Angersola was allowed to remain free on bond while the filing of petitions took place. On October 14, 1921, James Sancetta, a fellow Mayfield Road Mob member and an alibi witness for Angersola, was sentenced to a term of eight years in the penitentiary after being convicted of perjury. He claimed the defendant was in his car at a time when Angersola was actually in police custody.

8

Arrest of Sam Purpura

As in all investigations, police did not reveal everything they knew to the public. Three hours after the murders the main shooter was fingered – Sam Purpura. The reader should be aware that while all the newspapers spelled his name "Purpera," his headstone reveals the spelling as "Purpura." I have used both names throughout the text, using "Purpera" only where he is referred to by the newspapers, which is quite frequent.

Ignatius "Sam" Purpura was born on March 27, 1904 in Pittsburgh, Pennsylvania, to Mary and Charles Purpura; both parents were from Sicily. Purpura had three brothers and two sisters. Only Sam and one sister were born in America. The family moved to Cleveland around 1912. Sam quit school after the seventh grade and went to work as a barber. Some believed Sam might have made an honest living as a barber if he hadn't been attracted to gambling and other vices.

Purpura had black wavy hair and a large nose. One report claimed, "His eyes are the most noticeable feature. They are shifty and blink continually. His nerves are not well controlled." Purpura was six-feet, two inches tall and had a slender, but athletic build. It is interesting to note that while many of the witnesses described the man who first encountered and argued with Wilfred Sly as being "tall," the written descriptions had the man listed at various times as being between five-feet, five-inches tall and five-feet, seven-inches tall. The tallest that any of the bandits was listed was five-feet, nine-inches tall.

It was clear at an early age Purpura was heading toward a life of crime. Perhaps he was hurried along this path after meeting Mayfield Road Mob leader Dominic Benigno. Where and how the two met is not certain. Some reports claimed that they were relatives. While not blood relatives, Purpura's sister Josephine was married to Frank Galletti, whose sister Mary was the wife of Dominic Benigno. On December 17, 1920, Purpura was sent to the Boys' Detention Home at 2905 Franklin Avenue on the city's near-West Side. The next day, when an attendant opened a window near the fire escape so the boys could get some fresh air, Purpura knocked the man down and escaped. Two weeks later the teenager committed the most dastardly deed of his short life.

It was Detective Charles Cavolo who was given Purpura's name as being one of the killers by a street informant. Cavolo had a unique relationship with the Italian community that only someone of his ethnic background could obtain and cultivate. Although Cavolo knew Purpura was one of the shooters, other detectives were skeptical. By late January, Cavolo received further evidence of Purpura's involvement and was able to obtain a photograph of the youth. The previous October, Purpura was arrested in Pittsburgh and charged with receiving a stolen automobile; released on a $1,000 bond, he jumped bail and headed back to Cleveland. It was from this arrest in Pittsburgh that police were able to get the picture of Purpura, which was now part of a wanted flyer sent to police departments around the country.

Throughout February and early March police pursued the investigation. Their big break came when they received a telegram from the Los Angeles Police Department that Sam Purpura and another youth were arrested there for stealing an automobile. Purpura was arrested on the afternoon of Friday, March 11, by three Los Angeles detectives, whom the *Los Angeles Times* described as officers of the theft bureau of the Automobile Club of Southern California.[1] With Purpura at the time of his arrest was James Reynolds, a 17 year-old from San Francisco. The two youths were in a 1921 Buick, which was stolen from a San Francisco resident. The detectives, who had information on the stolen vehicle, spotted it parked at Fourth and Main Streets in downtown Los Angeles. Reynolds was behind the wheel and Purpura had gone into a nearby store to place a phone call. The two men were arrested without incident. Purpura gave his name as George Palmer.

One of the arresting detectives had in his possession a wanted circular from the Cleveland Police Department with Purpura's picture. It indicated there was a reward of $8,500 for his arrest.[2] The two men were to taken the police station, where Purpura was charged with the Cleveland murders. Believing that other suspects might have come with Purpura to the city, Los Angeles police began an immediate search for them. Meanwhile, Purpura gave the police this statement:

> "I live with my father Charles Purpera and my mother Mary Purpera at 2514 Central avenue, Cleveland. I was arrested by the Cleveland police on December 17 and charged with suspicion of automobile stealing. I was locked in a juvenile detention home. I escaped from the home by ripping away a screen window on the Sunday before Christmas and fled the city. I went to the home of my aunt, Angela Svia at 37 Mount Pleasant street, Milford, Mass. I remained with my

aunt for about a week and then went to Boston for a few days and then to Chicago, where I visited with a barber friend of mine. From Chicago I went to San Francisco and remained there three weeks. In San Francisco I met James Reynolds and we stole an automobile and came to Los Angeles about fifteen days ago. I have not been living in any one place since I came here and have been looking for work most of the time. Reynolds has also been attempting to get work. He knew me as Palmer. I don't know anything about the murders in Cleveland and was not in the city at the time. I never even saw an account of the affair in the papers. The picture on the circular is mine and they also have my name but I didn't have anything to do with the killing and have no idea how they have connected me with it."

Once notified of Purpura's arrest, Cleveland detectives raced to the homes of the other suspects only to find that they had already disappeared. It was reported that word of Purpura's arrest reached the Cleveland underworld before the police department was even aware. The *Plain Dealer* reported, "The information came to Purpera's alleged confederates through an underground channel…and enabled them to escape from this city." In the days after the arrest, Detective Captain Costello and Detective Cavolo received a number of death threat calls. They were believed to have come from Purpura's accomplices and their family members.

Prosecutor Stanton swung into action. He called for the grand jury to meet in special session on Saturday morning, March 12. Stanton asked for the cooperation of city and county officials to roundup grand jury members and eyewitnesses. The hearing was delayed because the grand jury foreman could not be located. By the time he arrived eight witnesses were present and prepared to testify. Seven of the witnesses identified Purpura from the picture Cavolo had obtained.

In addition to the eyewitnesses from the bridge, Stanton also obtained information from a prisoner in the Mansfield Reformatory. The prisoner told Stanton he was part of a gang that made plans in late November to rob the Sly-Fanner payroll. A second gang heard about the plan, however, and arrived just minutes before the first gang was ready to pull the robbery.[3] The prisoner was one of the men arrested during the raid on the Graystone Hotel on Prospect Avenue. He was sent to Mansfield after being found guilty of another crime. He told Stanton that his motivation for squealing was due to a "slight to his sweetheart" by one of the murder gang's members.

When questioned by reporters, who caught wind of the hurried grand jury hearings, the witnesses refused to give their names, and what they were questioned about, out of fear of the threats already issued. Stanton arranged for protection for all of the witnesses until other gang members could be arrested.

Late on Saturday afternoon, Common Pleas Judge Florence E. Allen received indictments from the grand jury charging Purpura and a "John Doe" with the first-degree murders of Sly and Fanner. The "John Doe" indictment was to "take care of the arrest of any suspect, wherever found, and to facilitate the extradition or other necessary legal process." The indictment was actually issued in case Purpura's West Coast accomplice, James Reynolds, actually turned out to be one of the men wanted for the murders.

Purpura and Reynolds met in San Francisco where it was believed they pulled a number of robberies.[4] In Los Angeles, just days before their arrest, they were seen trying to sell several gold watches at a jewelry store. At first, Bertillon officers from the bureau of identification in Cleveland were sure Reynolds was one of the other slaying suspects, based on Bertillon measurements received from Los Angeles detectives. Los Angeles investigators, however, soon determined Reynolds had not participated in the killings and he was turned over to San Francisco police who had a warrant charging him with automobile theft.

On Saturday night, Detective Inspector Sterling and Prosecutor Stanton boarded a west-bound train that got them into Los Angeles on Wednesday. On Monday morning Detectives Clarence E. Banks and Max C. Mettel were dispatched to Columbus, the state capital, to obtain the extradition request from former Cleveland mayor, now Ohio Governor, Harry L. Davis.

Stanton and Sterling arrived in Los Angeles, after the four day train ride, on Wednesday afternoon, March 16. They wasted no in time questioning Purpura. After introductions and formalities, the two were led to a cell where Purpura awaited them. A small crowd of law enforcement officers gathered around. Sterling spoke first, opening up to the prisoner he said, "Sam, you're a young man, with all your life before you. You are in trouble, but it is your old, gray-haired mother who is going to be really hurt in this. I think you owe it to her to tell it all."

At first the prisoner sat smug and refused to cooperate "steadfastly maintaining his innocence." Purpura was clearly intimidated by all the attention. Sterling then asked, "If I come in the cell with you, away from this crowd of men, will you talk?" When Purpura promised he would, Sterling entered. The inspector told the young man, "Sam, you are in a sad predicament. I do not know how to begin to talk to you. You realize we must have had some evidence when we sent circulars broadcast throughout the country."

In Purpura's response it was clear to the inspector what his concern was. "Do you think I will get the chair?" he asked.

"I cannot tell you anything about that," Sterling answered. "That's the court's job. You can tell the story, however, in a manner that won't look as bad as if you allowed someone else to do the telling."

Purpura agreed to talk and Sterling called for Stanton to join them. The prosecutor began going through the evidence they had gathered, concluding that they had enough to convict him of first-degree murder. At this point Purpura's arrogance vanished. He soon acknowledged, "I did it!" Purpura then began relating details of the crime:

> "We talked this over for a long while. On the day of the blowoff, we went out to the bridge in two machines. We stalled until the car with the goods in came our way, and then the auto I was in drove alongside the other machine as close as we could.
>
> "It was not long until we had 'em huggin' the rail of the bridge and they had to cut their speed. Sly tumbled to the fact that something was wrong and pulled a gun, pointing it straight at me.
>
> "We convinced them that it was a mistake and that our steering gear was out of whack. Sly put up his gun, and all six of us began to shoot up the other car.
>
> "Some of the others got the money and beat it. I never showed for my cut and never got any of the coin."

Several times throughout his confession Purpura made self-serving comments:

> ➤ I guess it's the chair for me now. They've got the goods on me, and I couldn't do anything but confess.
> ➤ I'm afraid there's not a chance for me – I'm just as good as dead now.
> ➤ It's funny, too. Here I am about to get the chair. And for what? I didn't get a cent of the $4,200.
> ➤ My parents aren't wealthy, but they'll pawn everything they have to keep me from the chair. So will my friends.

His confession completed, Purpura resumed the "air of indifference" he had maintained since his arrest. Not once throughout his barrage of self-serving statements did Purpura express any remorse for what he had done. Instead, he questioned whether his former colleagues had caused his demise. "Here I was chasing all over the country to avoid arrest," he declared. "But they got me. Something tells me I have been double-crossed. I am almost certain those who I thought my friends squealed." At the end of the day's interrogation Purpura pondered, "I don't think they can land me in the chair for this job – I'm too young."

When word of the confession reached Cleveland, reporters scurried to the home of Purpura's parents, Mary and Charles, at 2514 Central Avenue. Charles Purpura was a laborer in a commission house. At the time of his son's arrest he was out of work for five months. Through her tears Mary inquired when they were bringing her "boy" home. Calling her son by his birth name, Ignatius, the distraught mother stated through an interpreter, "He was a good boy until about three years ago. Then he got sick, and has been nervous. He got into some trouble because other boys prompted him to help them steal an automobile. But I know he wouldn't do anything as bad as this crime he is charged with. I think the police made him say he did it."

Purpura was only able to name two of his accomplices, claiming not to know the names of the other three. He gave Stanton the names of "three large eastern cities" where they might be found. He also revealed that one of the men was currently serving a sentence for a concealed weapons conviction. Purpura stated that of the six gang members, four were Italian and two American. The member already incarcerated was an American. This proved to be false, as was a tip that one of his accomplices was hiding just across the border in Mexico. The prosecutor along with Sterling and Banks (after he arrived) made a trip to Mexico, but returned empty handed.

Even though they had a verbal confession from the prisoner, Stanton and Sterling had to wait for the extradition papers to be signed. Detective Banks was still aboard a train headed for the state capitol in Sacramento, where California Governor William D. Stephens signed the documents before Banks headed to Los Angeles. Once police had the names of Purpura's confederates confirmed they wired authorities throughout the country, as well as all ocean ports, to be on the lookout for the suspects.

On St. Patrick's Day 1921, the grilling by Stanton continued and Purpura disclosed more. The prisoner stated that he was constantly apprised of police actions and was provided with a passport that allowed him to escape to Mexico. He told the prosecutor that at first it was his intention to flee to Italy, but when he arrived in Philadelphia he found that police there were warned to be on the lookout for him. He then headed for the West Coast and Los Angeles, stopping at a number of western cities in between.

Purpura next confirmed the admission of the Mansfield Reformatory prisoner who claimed two gangs were actually present on the bridge that day. Purpura told Stanton, "We didn't mean to kill either of those fellows, but when we saw an automobile with five or six men in it all watching us, we became excited and shot in our hurry to make our 'get away.'" Purpura said the men in the second car revealed their identity and forced the youths in the murder car to "share the loot."

Purpura admitted that he was the gang member who fled the bridge on foot, making his way through a yard and into an alley, while his companions, and the money, took off in the opposite direction. This kept him from receiving his cut of the money. He claimed he left Cleveland immediately. Despite the confession, the story changed a number of times over the next two weeks. The key points being whether or not he was the driver of the Stearns or the passenger; if he escaped the bridge by foot or in the Jordan automobile; and at what point he fled the city.

On Friday afternoon, Martin Dwyer, a prisoner at the Mansfield Reformatory, was brought to the Cuyahoga County Jail where he was grilled by Assistant County Prosecutor Cassidy regarding details of the murders he was said to possess. Dwyer denied any knowledge of the murders. He was serving time for robbery until being paroled. Arrested as a parole violator, he was returned to the prison in January. At the end of the interrogation, Cassidy ordered Dwyer held there with instructions that he was not permitted to speak to anyone.

After the newspaper reporting of Purpura's confession and subsequent statements, the business community in Cleveland was quick to respond. An effort was underway to make sure Purpura paid the ultimate price for his crimes, despite his young age. Civic organizations – the Cleveland Industrial Association (of which Sly was an executive committee member), the Cleveland Chamber of Commerce, the Cleveland Automobile Club, the West Side Chamber of Industry and the Lakewood Chamber of Commerce – asserted "that unless the extreme penalty of the law is given Purpura there will be other payroll robberies and other murdered men."

Alexander C. Brown,[5] president of the Cleveland Industrial Association, according to a *News* report, "is taking a leading part in the plan to bring Purpura to speedy trial and to see to it [there is] no 'slip-up' in the prosecution of the case, whereby the youthful slayer might obtain less than the punishment prescribed for first-degree murder." Brown asked E.J. Moore of the W.W. Sly Manufacturing Company to act as chairman of an action committee to see that "there is no delay in calling Purpera for trial."

Marie Sly was sought out by reporters for comment. Claiming there was no vengeance in her heart against Purpura, she lamented, "No other woman in Cleveland must be made to suffer what has been my lot. They say that this man who confessed to the murder is hoping to escape [punishment] because of his youth. This must not be. He must be punished by death or such tragedies will become common. If Purpera is allowed to go with a sentence of from one to twenty years, he soon will be out and doing the same thing again. I am pleading for others when I say he must suffer the death penalty."

As the train left Los Angeles, on the way to Chicago and then on to Cleveland, Purpura sat wearing handcuffs and leg irons, under the watchful eyes of Inspector Sterling and Detective Banks, locked between two murder suspects wanted in Akron, Ohio.[6] Several reporters had boarded the train to get a story and the young prisoner spoke freely. At times he appeared teary-eyed and concerned about his fate. He stated that after escaping from the bridge he leapt out of the Jordan, leaving the others behind, and took a taxi to East Ninth Street. He related that, "An hour or two after the murder I walked into a poolroom downtown and the first man I met there was Detective Captain Timothy Costello. The captain shook hands with me and asked me if I was working. I told him, 'No' and the captain said, 'I must be going, I've got to look out for the payroll bandits who killed Sly and Fanner this morning.'"

Purpura chuckled as he told this story to Detectives Banks and two reporters, "leaving me in the poolroom while he went to look for the bandits. But I felt safe enough because the other fellows had gone away in the machine." Still, Purpura felt it best to stay away from his home. The next day when he saw Detective Banks entering a downtown restaurant through the front door, Purpura slipped out the back door. When the arrests were made in the garage, Purpura stated, "I knew one of the men pulled in and I figured that was my time for pulling out. I had about $200 on me and I took a train for Boston."

Purpura claimed his escape route took him from Cleveland to Boston, then to Philadelphia, Chicago, El Paso and Juarez, Mexico. In El Paso he said he saw a wanted poster for his arrest. "I beat it for Juarez [just across the border from El Paso] so fast they didn't even know I had called there," he boasted. In Juarez the young man paid a visit to a gambling den where he had a winning night. "I won $120 and they paid me in silver dollars. If I'd have fallen in the river, I'd sure have been drowned with all that weight in my pockets"

The prisoner talked about pretty girls on the beach in Los Angeles and at one point broke into song:

"I'm on my way for a long, long stay
Behind those cold steel bars, I want to say.

> Oh, bail me out and set me free,
> For the penitentiary's no place for me.
> We're nearing home, oh my, oh my;
> I've come to say my last goodbye."

When asked by Stanton why he didn't stay in Mexico, Purpura answered, "Stay in Mexico? Say, you don't know how tough that place is. They'd just as soon kill a man as look at him. A boy of 17 might get bumped off in a country where you never know what anyone is going to do.

"I don't want to be killed. Say, you don't know how thankful I was to find I wasn't shot the day of the crime."

During one reflective mood Purpura offered, "Mother knew when I started to go wrong. Mothers always do. I have an uncle in a very good position in Sicily and she wanted me to go back to him for a couple of years or so. Look what I would have saved if I had done as she wished.

"I suppose my mother will be at the station to meet me – give her some comfort, Mr. Sterling. The only one I'm sorry for is my mother."

Perhaps his most profound statement was, "Poolrooms are the places where young fellows meet bad companions and start to go wrong."

A reporter asked, "Have you no regrets about the murders?"

Purpura replied, "It was a hell of a thing to shoot up those two decent fellows like that. Sure, I felt sorry for them and for their families. But they ain't going to make any goat out of me on this job, though I won't talk and go back on the others. I don't know all of them, anyhow." It was unclear just who Purpura meant by "they," whether he was referring to the police or other gang members.

Always conniving and making self-serving comments, Purpura continued, "I had a .32 automatic which I threw into the back of the car I drove. If the police have that gun – and I'm sure they must have found it – they will see that it was never fired. That lets me out of the shooting, doesn't it?"

As the train was crossing the California line into Nevada, Purpura asked Stanton for a pencil and paper, stating he was going to write down his confession so he would not have to be questioned again. Stanton handed him three blank Western Union telegraph forms and he wrote out this confession:

> "On 30 Dec. 1920 I was in Dreamland dance hall. I met a man
> and he told me he needed a machine for Dec.31. I said, 'All right.' At 1
> o'clock the morning of the crime I met _____. I said 'I need a machine.'
> He gave me the key and I said I'd fix him up. I then brought the Stearns

on E. 9th and some fellow jump on and we went to W. 47th and waited for a while. Then we went down the Federal Reserve bank. We waited for a while and then we followed Sly's Machine to W. 47th. When we got to the brigh (sic) we cut them short. They came out with pointed guns. When we were through arguing I walk away a little and the fellows from the Jordan came out and start shooting. They jump on the Jordan and when we went a few blocks I jump off.

"One of them had the money and he jump on the machine. _____ was at the wheel. Down W. 47th and Brigh st. we turn West to 65th and then turn north and I jump off and lelf (sic) them in there."

(signed) Sam Purpera

On Friday, March 25 the train, on the final leg of the trip home, was between Chicago and Cleveland. With time to think about his confession and the result it might cause, Purpura began to change his story. Kenneth R. Watson, of the *Cleveland Press* was one of several reporters who talked to the prisoner.

"Why did you take part in planning such a hold up?" the reporter asked.

"Oh, I just needed the money, that's all," Purpura replied.

"Didn't you feel sorry for the widows of the two murdered men?"

"I'm thinking only of myself and how I'm going to get out of this."

The prisoner had mood swings between cockiness – due to his belief that he was too young to be put to death – and terror at the thought of being strapped into the chair. During the trip Purpura stated at least a half dozen times, to anyone who listened, "They don't give anybody under 21 the chair, do they?"

By the time the train was near Cleveland, no one was sure which statements Purpura made were true – if any. His tales all seemed designed to cast the shadow of suspicion on anyone other than himself. It was obvious that even his statements during police interrogations in Cleveland and during the trials were laced with lies and inconsistencies. For a youth his age he must be given some credit for those attempts. In saying he disposed of his weapon, he made sure to say that it was a .32, knowing that the newspapers reported that both men were killed with .38s (a fact that changed during trial).

After researching dozens of articles and reading witness accounts it seems to this writer that Purpura's immaturity alone may have been the sole purpose for the senseless murders. If so, then other gang members must be held responsible for allowing him to play such a significant role in the robbery. With the publicity after the recent number of payroll robberies in the city, the bandits had to know there was an excellent chance that Sly and Fanner were armed. When the accident was perpetrated the first effort of the robbers should have been to defuse the situation and gain the victims confidence, not incite them by arguing that it was their fault, as the witnesses claimed Purpura did. This also suggests that the only reason Purpura ran in the opposite direction of the getaway car was because he already knew the other gang members were incensed with what he had done. The simple, but not well executed plan, for robbing the Sly company payroll, had turned into a cold-blooded double-murder putting all the participants' lives in jeopardy due to the inane actions of a teenaged thug who had neither the experience nor the maturity to handle himself. If the reader develops some level of sympathy for Purpura over the next few chapters, keep in mind that his actions alone accounted for the double-slaying and seven other lives – including his own – in the aftermath.

There is no question that the man in the Stearns automobile who argued with and then shot Wilfred Sly was Sam Purpura. There was no eyewitness statement that pointed to anyone else. One witness claimed Purpura actually killed both men. The autopsy information, however, given during the trials claimed the dead men were killed with different caliber weapons. In the upcoming trials, none of the men arrested were actually charged with shooting either of the victims. They were simply tried for participating in the robbery/murder of Wilfred Sly.

Friday evening the train rolled into Union Station in Cleveland. As Purpura was escorted off the train, he eyed the crowd hoping to see the friendly face of a family member to greet him. None were present. Instead, he was swarmed on by members of the police department, including Police Chief Smith and County Detective James Doran. From there Purpura was taken to the jail at the Central Station.

Purpura was quizzed and shown Bertillon photographs. The *News* reported, "Purpera was kept at city prison all night. From the moment of his arrival until midnight he was questioned and cross questioned, his story was attacked and his word disputed, but through it all he maintained a calm front, showing little nervousness and no remorse." Although claiming to know only two of his accomplices by name, Purpura identified photographs of Angelo Amato, Dominic Benigno, Frank Motto and Dominic Lonardo, the latter another brother of Mafia chieftain "Big Joe" Lonardo, actually naming three of the men as his accomplices. This identification came as vindication for Charles Cavolo. Through his network of friends and informants in the Italian community, Cavolo knew within hours who was involved. Amato and Motto were picked up in the group of suspicious persons grabbed in the days following the murders, while Benigno was arrested in the Winton Hotel garage. Other detectives, however, didn't believe Cavolo's information and with no evidence with which to charge the men all were soon released.

Police immediately put the wheels in motion to retrieve Motto, who was serving his auto theft sentence in the Mansfield Reformatory. Purpura was also brought face to face with Martin Dwyer. Purpura failed to identify him as one of the participants and he was returned to Mansfield to complete his sentence. In addition, another individual, who was held by authorities since they received a letter from his wife accusing him of being a member of the killer gang, was released after Purpura said he had never seen the man before.

On Saturday morning, after being measured by the Bertillon department, Purpura faced arraignment in the courtroom of Judge Alvin J. Pearson. The prisoner was brought into the courtroom by Inspector Sterling and Captain Matowitz, shackled to the latter. A *News* article stated, "His voice quivered and shook, the smile that had lightened his face was gone, while his sagging shoulders sharply registered dejection as he stood before a hostile audience" including many women.

For the second time Purpura was disappointed that family members were not present. He fully expected that not only would his family be there, but they would have an attorney prepared to represent him. Stanton remarked it was the most "downcast" he had seen the prisoner since his arrest. The family hadn't been totally negligent. Mary Purpura and Josephine Ratina, a cousin of the prisoner, appeared at the jail, but were denied permission to see him before arraignment. The *Sunday News Leader* reported:

> "Mrs. Mary Purpera waited all morning to see her son and then stayed into the afternoon. She appeared dejected and confused by the police station clamor, but when she saw Sam she walked up to him and began what appeared to be a scolding in their native tongue that he should be caught in such a net.
>
> "No tears fell from the mother's eyes, but the boy's lips quivered as the sharp words struck into his heart."

Afterward, Mary Purpura told reporters she expected to get an attorney for her son soon. "Attorneys are awfully expensive," she stated. She then told the media, "Sammy was always a good boy when he was small, and he is not so wicked now, perhaps. I don't believe he has done all those things that they say." When asked why she didn't meet her son at the train station, she replied she couldn't bear to see him in handcuffs.

At the hearing Judge Pearson stated, "You are arraigned here on two charges of murder. How do you plead?"

Despite the signed confession, Purpura answered in a shaky voice, "Not guilty."

"In both cases?"

"Yes, sir."

"Have you an attorney?"

"No."

"Whom do you intend to retain?"

"I don't know."

The dejection was apparent in Purpura's voice as he believed his family would do everything possible to have an attorney on hand. Pearson informed him that he should get one immediately and then remanded him to the county jail without bail. Stanton asked the judge for permission to keep the prisoner in the city jail while he was still being questioned. Pearson answered that this was a matter to be taken up with the sheriff.

Matowitz, who had taken the manacles off the prisoner while he faced the judge, placed them back on inquiring, "Do they hurt?" As Purpura was led from the courtroom the crowd surged after them until they reached the elevators. Once there, only the officers were allowed to board with their prisoner. Purpura was taken to the county jail for a short while until Stanton made arrangements with Sheriff Stannard to relocate Purpura at the city jail.

On Saturday afternoon six witnesses identified Purpura as one of the gang members on the bridge; one woman claimed he did the shooting. After this identification Purpura met with attorney Joseph Vincent Zottarelli, whom the family had asked to represent their son. The consultation lasted an hour and at the end of the session the lawyer said he would make his decision known on Monday. Zottarelli was a well-known attorney in the city. He attended Oberlin Theological School where he became a minister. He returned to Cleveland and opened a church, which later failed. Zottarelli then began his second career as a lawyer. On Monday attorney Zottarelli agreed to represent Purpura. He announced that he and his client were seeking the assistance of John J. Sullivan[7] as co-counsel. When questioned, Sullivan said no direct offer was made to him.

Later that Saturday afternoon Frank Motto arrived in Cleveland from the Mansfield Reformatory. The prisoner gave his age as 26 and his residence as 2524 East 33rd Street. He was married about six years. Under heavy questioning, Motto refused to yield any other information, but instead maintained that he had played no role in the robbery and murders. On Sunday morning the interrogation resumed. When the officials were sure they couldn't break Motto they brought in Purpura.

"You ditched me," Purpura barked at his former companion. "When we wrecked the pay car and got out of our machine you walked away and left me to face the men alone."

Inspector Sterling ordered Purpura to go over Motto's connection with the crime. Purpura began by talking about the night before the killings and a meeting with another prisoner from the Mansfield Reformatory, also in for auto theft, who had provided the Stearns automobile that was stolen from Goff and used in the robbery. The man was arrested in the Graystone Hotel raid.

Purpura stated, "When we told the man that we wanted a car for the job to be pulled the next day, he took us to one standing on Marian Avenue and turned over the keys to me. I drove it to a lot on East 35th Street near Scovill Avenue and left it there for the balance of the night.

"Early the next morning I got the car and drove down to Orange Avenue and East Ninth Street, where I met Motto. Motto and I then drove to the scene of the shooting on West 47th Street, waited about an hour and then returned downtown to the federal building. There we met the four men in the Jordan car.

"Soon one of the men pointed out a car coming from the Federal Reserve Bank [near] the Williamson Building.[8] This, he said, was the payroll car. We followed it, and as we reached the bridge Motto, who was driving, swerved to one side so as to drive the pay roll car off the road. We did not do any of the shooting. The men in the Jordan car did that."

"As the shooting ended, Motto reached into the payroll car and grabbed the bag containing the money. He ran with this to the Jordan car, where he placed it. Motto is the man who got the money."

When Purpura was finished he left the room and Motto sat silent.

"You heard what Purpura said," Sterling stated, "What have you to say about it?"

"I have nothing to say," answered Motto. "I am slated for the electric chair if I talk, and I am slated for it if I don't talk, so what's the use of me saying anything?"

With Purpura's identification, Sterling formally booked Motto on two charges of murder. On Monday morning, March 28, Motto was arraigned in police court, where he was again represented by David Rothkopf. Now the attorney claimed he was "acting by request of Motto's relatives and was not sure he would take further action." During the arraignment, the packed courtroom was infiltrated by detectives on the lookout for friends of Motto.

Prosecutors had little more than Purpura's word on which to hold Motto, but Stanton revealed that the state had "secret information on the prisoner's connection with the crime," which they did not desire to make public now. He vowed all the facts would be presented to the April-term grand jury, which would meet in one week.

Shortly after the arraignment of Motto, the *News* announced that "a nation-wide alarm" calling for the arrests of Angelo Amato, Dominic Benigno and Dominic Lonardo was sounded. The police were aggressively trying to cover all the angles, as was indicated in the *Plain Dealer* reporting of the public alert from the department:

> "Inspector Sterling…issued an appeal to the unknown driver of a green Stearns automobile which was on the scene of the shooting at the time the murders occurred. This driver stopped his machine close to the Jordan car used by the robbers in their getaway after the holdup. He had a good chance to observe the occupants of the Jordan machine. When the shooting started he drove away, and his identity has not been learned."

With Motto charged with the murders, police were now concerned about the witnesses. It was reported that residents in the West 53rd Precinct, where the murders took place, were being watched to make sure "friends" of the murder band didn't try to intimidate them.

On March 29 Sam Purpura made his boldest move yet to exploit his plight as a teenaged boy facing the electric chair. Speaking to a *Cleveland News* reporter, the prisoner claimed he had turned 17 on February 28 and therefore was only 16 at the time of the murders. Up until now Purpura had inquired incessantly as to the likelihood that a killer under the age of 21 could or would be put to death. Changing tactics, he now made his new pitch. "Both Stanton and Sterling promised me they would not send me to the electric chair," he told the reporter from his cell.

"They are not going back on that now are they?

"I'm only a boy. The other fellows were older, thirty or forty years of age. I hope they save me for my mother's sake. I am not guilty of any murder.

"Sterling told me that I would get the chair if I didn't talk. So I gave in, believing that by telling all I knew it would save me from the chair.

"I was sick at the time of the robbery and out of work, and didn't expect any shooting.

"I'm just a kid – they ought not send me up. Look at my hands – they're not a murderer's hands."

In a front-page article the *News* editorialized:

> "Is Sam Purpera, confessed member of a gang of youthful bandits which shot down two West Side citizens in one of the city's most cold-blooded crimes, to escape the death chair through pledges made by officials of immunity from the supreme penalty in exchange for 'squealing' on his associates in the crime?
>
> "This question became of paramount interest Tuesday and especially so to those who have helped in raising the $10,000 [sic] reward fund and to the families of Wilfred C. Sly and George K. Fanner, who were killed by the bandits without a show for their lives.
>
> "For Purpera, cringing and moaning in his cell, cries out to anyone who will listen to his continuous whine that he has been promised escape from electrocution by both Prosecutor Stanton and Detective Inspector Sterling."

Stanton and Sterling were quick to respond. Sterling stated, "No promises whatever, of any kind, were made Purpura to obtain his confession. He talked without urging. My hands are not tied with any pledge, either actual or implied. And Prosecutor Stanton's hands are just as free as mine. He made no promises."

Stanton echoed the police inspector's comments. "Purpera asked us countless times in Los Angeles and on the train coming east whether he would 'get the chair.' I promised him I would be fair and I think that death in the electric chair is the only thing that would be fair to him and fair to his victims. No promises of any kind, outside of that, were made to Purpera. I'll try to get the death penalty for Purpera and for every other member of the gang who is captured. They showed no mercy that last day of December and they need expect none when they go on trial," Stanton declared.

The plan that the prosecutor employed was to try each of the indicted men for the murder of Wilfred Sly only. That way if they should run into a sympathetic jury – that found the defendant not guilty or recommended mercy in their guilty verdict – they could try them on a second indictment before another jury for the murder of George Fanner.

On March 30, Inspector Sterling revealed that the sixth and last suspect in the murders was identified as Louis Komer. Known as "The Toledo Kid," the nickname was never explained by the news media. There was never any mention of his having been from Toledo or just how the title was bestowed on him. There was a rumor for years that Komer at one time was actually an employee at the W.W. Sly Manufacturing Company, but there was never anything to substantiate the story. Sterling said Komer was identified through a "secret source," whom he would not name. The inspector told reporters he was "almost positive the man whose picture appears on [prepared circulars] was connected to the double killing."

Just how the Cleveland Police Department discovered Komer was a part of the robbery team remained a mystery for several years. On the day before Stanton left the prosecutor's office on December 31, 1928, the eighth anniversary of the Sly-Fanner murders, the retiring prosecutor told a *Plain Dealer* reporter the story:

> "Stanton revealed for the first time yesterday the method by which Komer was identified. The prosecutor and his informant had been in the police Bertillon room alone, thumbing through pages of a Bertillon book when the informant, startled by a certain page that happened to have Komer's picture on it, relieved his nerves by turning back a page and pointing to another picture back to back with Komer's.
>
> "'That's the guy-you-want's brother-in-law,' he told Stanton.
>
> On a mysterious hunch Stanton went back and studied, finally concluding that it was Komer his informant meant to signify. On his next visit, Stanton told the Mansfield prisoner he knew it was Komer and the man confirmed his hunch."

Adding to the intrigue of the day, Sterling announced he was looking forward to a "startling development" in the search for Dominic Benigno. The police were on the trail on an intimate of the suspect. The next day, however, Sterling said his "startling development" had failed to materialize in the search for Benigno. It turned out that the "intimate" was Setimo Gaetano "Thomas" Benigno, brother of the suspect. He was followed to Chicago, where it was hoped he would lead police to Dominic, but police lost track of him in the Windy City.

The next day Sterling reported that two more witnesses had identified Motto as being in the Stearns automobile when it ran Sly off the road. He said a third witness could also have identified him, but was scared of retaliation. The inspector, who seemed to be making daily announcements, said that he was planning a surprise for Purpura. One which was "calculated to fasten the death penalty more securely to the young prisoner." He said it would be introduced after the trial was underway.

Meanwhile, Assistant County Prosecutor Cassidy told reporters that in the upcoming trial of Frank Motto, he was confidant of a first-degree murder conviction, without a recommendation of mercy. "I don't see how any sane jury could save [Motto] from the electric chair," he declared. Stanton was thinking the same thoughts. Stating that he was declaring war on criminals in Cleveland, the busy county prosecutor was currently seeking the death penalty for eight men who were to be tried during the April term of the common pleas court.[9] Stanton stated, "We will make Cleveland unsafe of criminals. If mothers, wives and sweethearts want mercy for their boys, let them keep them out of trouble."

Chapter Endnotes

1. A *Los Angeles Times* article claimed J.E. Erven, Harry Raymond and Harry Hickok were officers of the theft bureau of the Automobile Club of Southern California. Another story claimed Erven and Raymond were LAPD detectives and Hickok was with the ACSC.

2. The $8,500 reward (nearly $90,000 by today's standard) was to be divided by Detectives Harry Raymond and J.E. Erven, of the Los Angeles Police Department, and Harry Hickok of the theft bureau of the Automobile Club of Southern California. A legal battle was underway, however, after L.C. Larsen of Paso Robles, California hired attorneys to block the payment. Larson claimed he notified police after Purpera, using the name George Palmer, left an automobile at his garage and later told Larsen to sell it. Purpera's statement to *Cleveland Press* reporter Kenneth Watson helped support this. "I had helped to steal a machine in San Francisco and was driving to Los Angeles when the bearings on the car burned out and we put it in a garage in San Miguel," he said.

Larsen hired the law firm of White, Johnson, Cannon & Spieth to make a formal demand for the reward. Cuyahoga County Commissioners reviewed the law firm's request and announced that if Larsen was a public official on a salary he was ineligible for the reward.

As late as November 1922 there was still haggling over who was to get shares of the reward money. Also putting in claims were Thomas C. Barrow, the owner of the Bolivar garage where Benigno parked his car, Edith Marklew and members of the Blaich family, witnesses on the bridge the day of the murders, and two Mexican police officers who helped in the capture of Benigno. At that time Federal Judge D.C. Westenhaver ruled that the Cleveland people were not entitled to a share as no reward had been offered at the time of their involvement.

3. With all the excitement over the arrest of Sam Purpera, followed by the ensuing trials, this story of the alleged second gang didn't surface again until 1925. On August 16 during the search for Angelo Amato the *Sunday News Leader* reported:

> "In committing the robbery the Benigno gang had outwitted another gang that had originally planned the crime…
>
> "Word of the plans having reached Komer, he informed Benigno and his confederates, who waylaid Sly and Fanner on the Clark ave. bridge while the other bandits were waiting for them on the Abbey ave. bridge."

It was never proven if the story of a second gang of robbers was factual.

4. Another story, in the *Los Angeles Examiner*, claimed they met in Los Angeles, where Purpera found him on the street penniless and fed him.

5. A member of a prominent Cleveland family, Alexander Cushing Brown was the son of inventor Alexander Ephraim Brown who revolutionized the unloading of ore carriers on the Great Lakes with his invention – the Brown Hoisting Machine. A civic and industrial leader, Alexander C. Brown served as president of the Cleveland Chamber of Commerce in 1924. In 1947 he was named president of the Cleveland-Cliffs Iron Company. He served on the board of directors of that company until his death. Brown was pronounced dead at St. Vincent's Charity Hospital after collapsing at the Union Club on April 10, 1964. He is buried in Lake View Cemetery.

6. The two prisoners, and a woman, were under indictment for the October 8, 1920 murder of Peter Schure. In the custody of Akron Detective Edward McDonnell were Charles W. Smith, his son Charles P. Smith and Olive Montinez, a 19 year-old who was said to be posing as the elder Smith's wife. The father and son were accused of killing Schure in an outhouse at the rear of a rooming house at 421 South Main Street in Akron. One of the men knocked Schure unconscious, before both strangled him. Detective McDonnell reported that Purpera had encouraged the younger Smith to confess his crime – advising him to tell the truth as he had done. Once in Cleveland the prisoners were removed to Akron by automobile. Before the trial commenced both accused the other of the killing. On June 9 the senior Smith was acquitted of the murder by a jury.

7. In *Cleveland: The Making of a City*, noted historian William Ganson Rose described John J. Sullivan as "one of Cleveland's most distinguished lawyers during the first three decades of the century." A one-time "school teacher, reporter, city editor, and prosecuting attorney" from Trumbull County, Sullivan was appointed United States District Attorney for Northern Ohio by President William McKinley in 1900. His most famous case was the successful prosecution of famed Cleveland swindler Cassie L. Chadwick, who duped local bankers by claiming to be the daughter of multi-millionaire Andrew Carnegie. On August 30, 1930, Sullivan was returning to Cleveland from Duluth, Minnesota when he was stricken with a heart attack aboard a passenger steamer *Octorara* on Lake Michigan. He was 70 years old.

8. The Williamson Building was located in Public Square, between Euclid and Superior Avenues. The 16-story structure, opened in 1900, was torn down in 1982 to make way for the Sohio Building, today known as the BP Building.

9. In addition to Frank Motto and Sam Purpera, trials were coming up for Merton Herendon, Charles W. Habig and Chris Lonchar, charged for the murder of Cleveland Police Officer August Dyke; and Joseph Azzarello, Joseph Cassaro and Sam LaPaglia for the murder of Samuel Marano. Of these eight only Motto and Purpera found themselves in the "hot seat."

9

Trial of Frank Motto

Frank Motto was indicted[1] for the murders of Wilfred Sly and George Fanner on April 4. After hearing just one witness, Inspector Sterling, the grand jury returned the murder indictments in less than two hours. The next day Motto, without the services of an attorney, entered a plea of not guilty when arraigned before Judge Allen, who was presiding over the case.

Florence Ellinwood Allen* was born in Salt Lake City, Utah in 1884. Both parents came from academic backgrounds; her father once worked as a professor at Western Reserve University, from where Florence graduated in 1904. A music major, Allen studied in Berlin, Germany and served as a correspondent and music editor for a couple of magazine publishers. When a nerve injury cut short her dream of a career in music, she returned to Cleveland and became a music critic for the *Plain Dealer* and taught music at Laurel School.

Allen soon returned to college in pursuit of a new career – law. After obtaining a master's degree in political science and constitutional law from Western Reserve University, she was refused acceptance into the university's school of law because she was a woman. Undaunted, Allen enrolled at the law school at the University of Chicago in 1910 and two years later transferred to New York University, where she received her law degree in 1913. She returned to Cleveland and passed the Ohio bar exam the next year. A staunch supporter of the suffragette movement, Allen began work as the attorney for the Ohio Suffrage Party. In January 1917, residents of the city of East Cleveland elected to allow women the right to vote in municipal elections, making them the only city east of Chicago to do so. When this was challenged, Allen successfully defended the case before the Ohio Supreme Court.

As Allen made her way up the career ladder each step designated a first for women in the field of law. A Democrat, in 1919 Allen was appointed assistant county prosecutor. The next year, when the 19th Amendment gave women the right to vote, she became the first woman in the United States to be elected to a judgeship – the common pleas bench. Now, in May 1921, she was the first woman jurist to preside over a first-degree murder case.

On April 18, Judge Allen called Motto into court to review his trial preparations. The prisoner said he "thought" attorney Alfred A. Cartwright[2] was retained to defend him. The lawyer confirmed this and informed the court that his co-counsel was Zottarelli, who was also representing Purpura. Judge Allen told the defendant it would be difficult for him to secure a continuance beyond the trial date set for May 2 and that he had better be ready when the case begins.

Days before the Motto trial was scheduled to start, Stanton announced he would "probably" not call Purpura as a witness. The prosecutor declared he "could win the case against Motto without Purpera's testimony." Stanton was concerned about Purpura's claims of "promised immunity" and if he testified, "it's probable effect on public sentiment." But who was to be the key witness for the state if Purpura didn't testify? That question was quickly answered.

On April 28, the Detroit Police Department raided a home on Pine Street in that city. They were looking for suspects in the robbery of Morton & Company, a local brokerage firm, in which two detectives were killed and a third wounded several months earlier. Inside the house police arrested Walter and Maude Foote and Louis Komer.

As Komer was being questioned by Motor City detectives, police checked their latest wanted notices and found his fingerprints matched a circular sent out by the Cleveland Police Department. They then confirmed his identity through Bertillon records and a photograph. Inspector Sterling and George Koestle immediately departed for Detroit. On the boat ride to Detroit, Sterling suffered a heart attack. The grizzled veteran refused to be hospitalized and for the rest of his life he was plagued with heart problems. On Saturday, April 30, Cleveland police got their second break in the case when Komer confessed. Sterling sent a brief telegram to Detective Captain Costello stating that the prisoner had confessed to being present when Sly and Fanner were murdered, and that he would not fight extradition.

Once back in Cleveland, the stricken Sterling was too weak to climb the stairs at the station house and directed the questioning of Komer from a downstairs office. During the questioning Komer "turned informer" giving detectives his version of how the murders went down. He confessed his role in the plot but, as Purpura had earlier, denied he had any part in the murders. The *News* reported that Komer gave his story to George Koestle. The circumstances as to why Komer confessed to Koestle were not clear at the time, but nine months later an article about the Bertillon expert stated, "Koestle's nickname around police headquarters is 'Sympathy.' He earned it by a sympathetic manner of speech, which he uses to 'draw out' prisoners being held at police headquarters and getting them to tell things they would otherwise withhold." In his story, Komer related to Koestle that Dominic Lonardo and Angelo Amato did the killing; Dominic Benigno drove the Jordan; and Motto drove the Stearns. Komer said that Motto was the mastermind of the robbery and planned the entire thing.

After learning of his arrest, reporters interviewed the prisoner's mother, Mary Komer, who claimed her son's "downfall is due to an estrangement that arose between her husband and herself when Louis was four. Since then, she was too busy to pay much attention to him before he was ten." Komer was sent to the "city farm school" as an incorrigible in 1903 at the age of 9. His rap sheet showed arrests for armed robbery, grand larceny and pocket-picking. He served time in the Boy's Industrial School and in the penitentiary.

What caused Komer to flip and spill his guts to the police? One suggestion comes from the fact that Komer told authorities that after the robbery / murder, Angelo Amato suggested that "in the interest of safety" the gang should kill Komer. As the only non-Italian member of the gang, Komer felt a bit outnumbered. He also knew that jail wasn't necessarily a safe haven for a man in his position.

On Monday morning, Komer was arraigned before Police Judge David J. Moylan and charged with two counts of murder in the first degree. Held without bail he was bound over to the grand jury.

On Sunday night, May 1, the eve of the Motto trial, a gang of men walked up and down West 47th Street and banged on the doors of the Blaich family home shouting threats. The Blaichs were eyewitnesses to the events on the bridge. The terror tactic took place despite the promise of increased police security by prosecutors.

The next morning the case got off to an exciting start. Motto was seated at the trial table beside Deputy Sheriff Charles Weidenmann waiting for jury selection to begin. In the back of the courtroom was the defendant's mother, Mary Motto. All of a sudden she collapsed to the floor "in a swoon." Motto got up from his seat and raced to her side. As he did a number of friends closed in and began to surround him. The quick thinking Weidenmann, gun in hand, forced his way through the crowd, grabbed Motto and brought him back to the trial table.

Just moments before this scene took place in the courtroom, a man called the county jail, claimed he was Assistant County Prosecutor James T. Cassidy, and requested that Purpura be brought to the courtroom immediately. Deputies were suspicious and refused to move the prisoner. Cassidy had never placed the call. "It looks like to me," he stated, "as though someone had planned to get both men in the courtroom, take advantage of any confusion that might develop, and spirit both Purpera and Motto out of the building before we knew what was going on." The plot was defused.

The trial then ran into another problem as defense counsel, Cartwright and Zottarelli, asked for and received a four-day continuance after a "typographical error"[3] was discovered in the list of venire men called for duty. Just what this "typographical error" was, and why they needed four days to correct it was never explained.

On Thursday, May 5, Louis Komer led Stanton and deputy sheriffs to the Baker, Rauch & Lang Company, a lumberyard at West 80th Street and Edgewater Drive. He directed them to an area of the plant where he pointed out a cross-tie holding up one of the lumber piles. Komer claimed he and Motto had disposed of their weapons there after the murders. The deputies found the area they needed to search was inaccessible. Stanton solved that problem after spotting a young boy and asking him to squeeze into the area and look. The lad found the guns right where Komer said they were. The weapons, both revolvers, a .32 and a .38, were rusted from exposure. They were still loaded. Two caps, which Komer said were left with the weapons, could not be found.

The recovery of the weapons nearly didn't take place. A watchman at the lumberyard reported earlier that morning he chased away two men who were looking for something in the same area. A little detective work by Stanton uncovered that Motto had received a lady visitor the day before. He surmised that Motto had given her the location of the weapons with instructions to have someone retrieve them post-haste.

The next day, Friday, May 6, the four-day continuance was up and the trial began with jury selection. Inside the courtroom deputies and detectives were scattered about keeping an eye open for trouble makers and anticipating that another attempt might be made to rescue Motto. Inspector Sterling climbed out of his sick bed in order to be present. Deputy sheriffs outside were on the alert, too. Seeing more than 100 people gathered in front of the courthouse waiting for Motto to be brought in, they chose an alternative route taking their prisoner to the jail via the Cleveland version of the "Bridge of Sighs."[4]

As soon as all parties were present, Cartwright and Zottarelli presented Judge Allen with a barrage of motions. First they moved to have the indictment quashed, claiming that the signature of the grand jury foreman did not appear on the document. While it was absent from defense counsel's copy, Allen secured a copy of the original indictment and found that the signature was properly affixed and overruled the motion. The lawyers then filed a demurrer[5] to the indictment on the ground that it was vague. Allen quickly overruled this.

The defense team then requested a change of venue to another county. They supported this with 16 newspaper articles from local dailies, along with seven affidavits from citizens claiming news coverage had created a prejudice against Motto. Allen responded first by scolding the attorneys, stating the affidavits should have been filed weeks ago. She then questioned one of the affidavit signers, who happened to be present in the courtroom as a spectator. Responding to the judge, the man said he had not talked to anyone who believed Motto was guilty. That wasn't the answer the defense needed to support them. Allen overruled the motion; but stated if "definite evidence could be introduced" to prove prejudice she might reconsider.

After several hours were wasted on the frivolous motions the jury selection process began. The venire, consisting of 138 persons, had attorneys and prosecutors busy for the rest of the day trying to select the jurors they felt might best serve their case. The selection work continued Saturday morning. At 9:15 a.m. Zottarelli requested a continuance because co-counsel Cartwright was called to another courtroom to answer a contempt summons. Allen refused the request and ordered the selection to continue. Just before noon, Zottarelli was informed that Cartwright had withdrawn from the case after he was charged with conspiracy to obstruct justice during the second murder trial of William H. McGannon.[6] After Zottarelli informed Allen of the situation, she told him he had until Monday to select an associate attorney or she would appoint one for him. By the end of the day Saturday, a half-dozen jurors were selected. The judge sequestered the six over Sunday due to the "importance of the case."

On Monday morning there was more drama at the courthouse. Lieutenant Emmett Potts arrested Thomas Graci, after he was "aroused by the man's furtive actions." In his coat pocket Potts found a rather peculiar weapon – a combination .22 revolver and knife with a six-inch blade.[7] Graci was taken to the Central Station where he was booked on a charge of carrying concealed weapons. The wheels of justice moved fast for Graci. The next day he was indicted by the grand jury. On Wednesday he pled guilty before Judge Bernon, telling the court he found the weapon on the way to the courthouse where he was going to spend the day. Bernon immediately sentenced him to a term in the Ohio Penitentiary.

The theatrics that Monday were not over. At lunchtime one of the women witnesses told Lieutenant Potts that a man was following her around all morning. Detectives arrested an "Italian" and took him to the Central Station.

Despite the distractions, the business of the court continued. Judge Allen began the day by assigning former county prosecutor Samuel Doerfler* to assist Zottarelli. Doerfler was considered the senior member of the defense team.

While jury selection continued on Tuesday, the grand jury indicted Louis Komer on two counts of first degree murder. Komer's statement, given to George Koestle, read:

> "I was in a poolroom on Superior Avenue and East Ninth Street when Frank Motto came in. He said he was out under heavy bail and needed money. I told him about the Sly-Fanner payroll and we decided to get it. With some other fellows we went out and pulled off the job."

After Komer's indictment, it was announced he would take the stand and testify against Motto.

At the close of court Wednesday the jury was completed. Both sides had examined 119 potential jurors over five days. Two women, who were selected early in the process, were removed by peremptory challenges. The jury consisted of eleven men and one woman, Mrs. Lillian E. Markell, whom panel members selected as the jury foreman. The 45 year-old widow proved to be Motto's Waterloo.

At 9:40 Thursday morning, the jury was about to be sworn in by Assistant County Prosecutor Harold Parsons. He asked if they knew of any reason why they could not return a fair verdict. At this point juror Fred Gensler stood up and stated, "I think the defense ought to know that I, as an accountant, handle all the company's payroll. Though that wouldn't prejudice me against this defendant." Attorney Doerfler let the court know that he was willing to accept the juror at his word.

It must be kept in mind that Motto was being tried solely for the murder of Wilfred Sly. In his opening statement James Cassidy told the jurors that the robbery was planned in a Superior Avenue pool hall and how each phase of it was carried out up to the murders. He made it clear that there would be no effort to show that Motto fired any of the shots. Cassidy demanded that the defendant be given the death penalty for his participation.

In a brief opening statement, Zottarelli told the jury that his client was one of the planners of the robbery, but backed out that morning and did not participate in the actual holdup or the slayings.

The next order of business was to take the panel to the murder scene at West 47th Street, where it crossed over the Nickel Plate tracks. Motto was given the option of accompanying the panel, but declined; staying behind under heavy guard. Also remaining at the courthouse was Ethel Fanner and her mother. It was a horrendous time in the life of the woman who was left alone to raise her 10 year-old daughter. Fearing for the young girl's safety, the widow walked her to and from school every day. The morning the trial opened a *Cleveland News* reporter recorded her thoughts:

"I believe they have selected a jury that will do justice in this case.

"I believe that the men who were implicated in this affair should get the death chair the same as the men who actually fired the shots. Since the opening of this trial I have sat here and watched Motto constantly. He seems to be the very image of the men who have always been in my mind's eye as the murderers of my husband.

"Motto has viewed all of the proceedings so far with an air of the most cold-blooded nonchalance. From his demeanor in court one might imagine him at a theater or banquet. The fact that he is on trial for his life does not seem to worry him.

And sitting here, I have often thought of the justice I would like to mete out to him. There have been times when I could have taken him by the throat and killed him with my own hands."

Once the jury returned to the courtroom, the state called Marie Sly, the widow of the victim, as its first witness. This brought about the vigorous objections of defense counsel. Marie Sly, "clad in heavy mourning" wear and sobbing through most of her testimony, told the jury about the last morning she shared with her husband. That evening his body was returned to the home, she said, "Riddled with bandit's bullets."

Speaking to reporters afterward she stated, "I demand that justice be done in this case. The electric chair is far too good for the men who shot my husband. If these men are not convicted it will be an outrage on the courts of Cuyahoga County."

After Marie Sly's brief testimony, new County Coroner A.P. Hammond and former coroner P.A. Jacobs were called. Hammond was called to tell how Sly was killed and Jacobs to describe the wounds. The defense was willing to stipulate to the evidence regarding the wounds, but Cassidy insisted that the jurors hear the graphic details. The next witness, the payroll teller at the Union Trust Company (formerly First National Bank), didn't have to testify after the defense stipulated to the transaction taking place between the teller and Sly and Fanner.

Next came a procession of eyewitnesses from the bridge. Abbie Barnes, Elizabeth Kronavet, Mary, Benjamin, and Harry Blaich, each stepped down from the witness stand, walked to the defense table and tapped Motto on the shoulder to indicate identification. They all named him as the man who drove the Stearns automobile and the person who grabbed the payroll satchel before running to the Jordan. A sixth man called to the stand said he couldn't identify Motto. Each witness claimed they were drawn to the scene by the sound of the crash as Motto forced the Sly automobile into the side of the bridge.

Benjamin Blaich told the court that just prior to the gunfire, Fanner handed him a piece of paper to write his name as a witness to the accident. Blaich signed and returned the paper, which Fanner clung to in death.

"I hand you state's exhibit No. 5 and ask you whether your name is on it," inquired Assistant Prosecutor Harry Parsons, handing Blaich a bloodstained piece of paper.

"It is. That's where I signed it," answered Blaich. "He still had it in his hand when I turned him over after he had been shot."

On the stand Benjamin's wife Elizabeth Blaich testified, "I started to run at the sound of the shots, and Purpera ran through the alley into our yard after me. He caught me at the end of the alley and put one of his legs over me and held the gun up against my chest. He told me, 'Don't you phone, you bitch,' and that's all I remember. I fainted and came to after being taken upstairs in my house."

During the cross-examination of these witnesses, each was questioned about their inability to identify Motto as a member of the murder crew when brought to view suspects in a line-up at Central Police Station just days after the killings. Each of the witnesses agreed that they were unable to do so, but the newspapers elaborated no further on this part of their testimony.

The most damaging witness the state put on the first day was Lieutenant Emmett Potts. He described the interrogation of Motto. "At the meeting were Prosecutor Cassidy, Purpera, Motto, Inspector Sterling and myself," Potts related. "Motto was in custody, but he had not been charged with this crime at that time." Potts then repeated the details given in Purpura's confession. By Potts reading this the state avoided having to put Purpura on the stand, thus thwarting any chances of him claiming to the jury that he was offered immunity.

When Purpura and Motto confronted each other, Potts continued, "Inspector Sterling asked, 'Purpera, do you know Frank Motto? And Purpera answered 'yes' and pointed to Motto." Later, Potts stated, "Frank Motto sat in the room while Sam Purpera made his statement and remained silent. When Inspector Sterling asked him, "Frank, what do you say now?" Motto declined to answer.

At the close of Thursday's testimony, Judge Allen ordered Purpura brought before her. She asked if he had secured co-counsel to Zottarelli. When he answered, no, she told him if he didn't do so by morning, she would appoint counsel herself. Before trial got underway Friday morning, Purpura requested that one of the following attorneys be appointed co-counsel – William P. Corrigan, P.L.A. Leighley, Walter D. Meals or John J. Sullivan. (By the end of the day Judge Allen said she would continue

Purpura's trial until after Motto's was completed and assigned William Corrigan to assist with the defense.)

The first witness on May 13 was Inspector Sterling, who confirmed the testimony of Lieutenant Potts from the previous day. He stated that Motto refused to answer questions about the murder. County Detective James Doran then followed and told the court how Louis Komer had given them information about the hidden guns at the Baker, Rauch & Lang Company lumberyard. Next a gunsmith testified as to the caliber bullets, a .32 and a .38, that killed the two businessmen.

Described as the "last important state witness," Louis Komer took the stand and testified for an hour. He confirmed all the points that were made in Purpura's confession. Responding to the prosecution's questions about his movements after the shooting, he stated, "Motto and I went down towards the lake along West 70th Street after we had driven away from the shooting with the others. We left them at West 74th Street and Clifton Avenue.[8] Reaching a lumberyard at the edge of the boulevard, we hid our guns and separated."

Of Komer's appearance and testimony, the *Cleveland News* wrote:

> "Dressed neatly in a brown suit, Komer looked more like a student or a young man of leisure than a confessed murderer as he sat in the witness chair. He spoke clearly and directly, using excellent English, and met the gaze of attorneys and spectators squarely.
>
> "Court attaches and onlookers declared he was the best state witness that had been heard in a murder trial here in years."

Throughout the trial Marie Sly sat in the courtroom staring at Motto with a look of "undying hatred." As she left the courtroom after testimony that Thursday she encountered the defendant, hand-cuffed to a deputy, as he was being led back to the county jail. As their eyes met, Marie Sly let him know what she thought of him.

"You dirty dog!" she yelled.

"What do you mean?" he demanded

"You're one of the dirty dogs who took my husband's life, and you know it. I should like to be the one who gives your case the judgment it merits," she declared.

Motto bowed his head and pleaded with the deputy, "Come take me out of this."

Marie Sly turned to a friend and despaired, "I just wish that young gangster knew what the bullets fired by his gang meant to my life. My hope is gone, and I feel as if there is no one to whom I can turn for help. My life is desolate – I am alone. I have felt as if these bandits took my life when they shot my husband."

One day during the trial a note was delivered to Judge Allen. The note was a list beginning with her name at the top followed by the names of every juror. The note stated, "The day Motto dies, you die." In her autobiography, *To Do Justice*, Allen wrote:

> "On the smudgy paper were printed several black outlines of a hand. I was too young to be scared. It amused me. I showed the letter, more as a matter of curiosity than anything else, to one of my friends on the police force. He was not a bit amused. He said, 'Now you have to have protection.' This seemed to me unnecessary, but the police insisted, and assigned men to guard the houses where the forewoman and I lived. Now and then I woke up at night and went to the window to look out. Sitting on the stoop below me I would see the figure of a policeman watching all night long."

When the state rested their case Friday morning, defense counsel announced they had only one witness to call – Frank Motto. The defendant surprised many with his admission that he helped plan the robbery "in every detail" with two accomplices. "Komer, Benigno and I talked the entire affair over on the night before the robbery. We agreed to meet at 8 o'clock the next morning, and Benigno promised to get some other men to go with us."

Motto told the court that the next day he and Komer went to East Ninth Street and Orange Avenue. There they met Benigno and the others who had driven there in the stolen Stearns and the Jordan automobiles. "Sam Purpera and I got in the Stearns car," Motto stated. "I took the wheel and I went out to West 47th Street and the bridge over the Nickel Plate tracks, where we had agreed to lay for Sly and Fanner. The others followed in the Jordan. We waited there for half an hour, but no one showed up. So we drove back downtown to find them." Motto said he parked the Stearns on the south side of Public Square, but was ordered to move it by a detective. He then parked it on the north side of the square, but was again told by a detective to move it.

"Then the boys got ready to start out again," he said. "But meeting the detective scared me. I knew he would recognize me and would connect me with the robbery when he learned of it, so I refused to go. I got out and the two machines went off without me. I don't know what they did, who fired the shots nor who got the money. I wasn't there," Motto related. He admitted that he was arrested two days later, held for a short time, and then released. Motto said he was then sent to the reformatory to begin serving his sentence on the auto theft conviction.

At the completion of Motto's testimony, around 2:00 p.m., Prosecutor Stanton began the closing for the state. The courtroom took on an ominous appearance this Friday the 13th afternoon as lighting flashes illuminated the room during the prosecutor's emotional statement. "This man is on trial charged with one of the most heinous crimes ever committed in this county. We have shown that he is the master bandit behind the plotting of this crime. We are asking the death penalty for this man that other youthful bandits may be warned not to commit crimes so callously," Stanton said.

While Stanton raged on, Motto sat nervously with his hands clasped, avoiding the eyes of the fiery prosecutor:

"Marked across his forehead now you may read the word 'guilty.' Did you notice the quivering of his lips on the witness stand, his shaking in his chair? He was afraid he might utter a word that might show how he lied.

"If any of you were accused of murder, and the person who [implicates you] said, 'Yes, you were there and I was with you,' wouldn't you jump from your chair and say, 'That is a lie, I never was there.'

"Frank Motto sat quiet when Purpera said that to him. On the stand he said he denied it. But is Inspector Sterling and Lieutenant Potts going to lie to convict an innocent man? Before you this week has sat the arch conspirator, the mastermind of the conspiracy.

"We have proven to you that as much as a week before the crime, Motto, and he admits it by his own words, went out to steal an automobile to use in this job. Komer tells you he is guilty of this crime and says Motto was there. He does not say Motto did any of the shooting. But Komer took us to where he and Motto hid their guns. One of them, a 38-caliber gun, is Motto's. I do not know whether he fired the shot, but a 38-caliber bullet killed Sly.

"Cleveland has wondered for some time whether Motto could come before a jury such as you and tell a story such as he told on the stand and whether or not you would believe it.

"We are asking the maximum penalty in this case so that we may prevent such fiendish individuals from perpetrating murder and robbery, that we may implant a lesson in the minds of the youths of America that crimes such as this will not be tolerated in American cities."

After completion of Stanton's closing, Zottarelli took to the floor to offer a stirring closing of his own. The attorney focused on the original indictment, which claimed that Motto had fired the shot that killed Wilfred Sly:

> "I ask you Mr. Prosecutor, whether there is one scintilla of evidence that Motto committed this crime? You call in here a volume of people, realizing your inability to convict this man of murder in the first degree.
>
> "They seek to work on your sympathy and passion so they call the dead man's widow. What does Mrs. Sly testify to? Mrs. Sly does not know who committed this crime. She is a fine woman to be robbed of her husband, but she does not know who is guilty of this crime.
>
> "Then they bring in the coroner, and Mr. Goff, whose car was stolen, and a lot of other people. When they saw the weak case, they sought to inflame your hearts against this poor Italian boy with no one behind him.
>
> "Motto was in the line up at Central station two days afterward, yet these same people who identify him here, could not identify him then. And he was in Cleveland until January 11. If he were guilty of this crime, he would have flown to points where neither you nor your police ever could have found him.
>
> "When Motto drove downtown and parked the car at the square, he was waiting to go to the reformatory. And when the man told him he could not park, he became alarmed. In his mind, he thought, 'I'm in enough trouble now. I will not go through with this,' and he did not."

Due to the late hour, the defense's closing was continued to the next day. On Saturday morning the courtroom was filled to capacity. The crowd occupied "every inch" of the courtroom and spilled out into the corridors. Police, detectives and deputies were interspersed with the spectators. The *Plain Dealer* reported:

> "The officers were forced to clear a passage to permit Motto's being brought into court. As the defendant appeared, handcuffed to a deputy sheriff, he bore evidence of a sleepless night.
>
> "Deep rings appeared beneath each of his eyes, and his face was ashen. He looked neither to the right nor to the left as he was led to his seat at the trial table, and stood dejectedly as a deputy fumbled with the key to the handcuffs."

Sam Doerfler finished the defense team's argument focusing again on the failure of witnesses to identify Motto after the murders. "But months later," the attorney claimed, "those same witnesses come into court and without hesitation point him out as one of the bandits. We must have something more certain than the testimony of witnesses who can't remember a face on one occasion, but do it unhesitatingly a long time afterward."

After Doerfler's closing a slight look of confidence crept over the defendant's face until Cassidy delivered the closing rebuttal for the state. It was every bit as intense as Stanton's. The widows of both victims sobbed silently as Cassidy made an impassioned plea for the death penalty. Jabbing an accusing finger in the direction of the defendant throughout, Cassidy stated:

> "Ladies and gentlemen of the jury, Motto may cringe and cry and beg for mercy. You say to him, as I say to him now, as Mr. Sly would say if he could come into this courtroom from his cold grave: 'Be just as merciful to him as he was to me. Let your sympathies be extended to those I left behind, at the hands of this man.'
>
> "Mercy! What right has Motto to claim mercy? There is no such thing as mercy for a fiend such as he. He is entitled to just as much mercy as he gave measured by the same yardstick. He knew no mercy then, so you should show it not with him.
>
> "The only time there was a place for mercy was on the morning of December 31. Since then the only mercy and sympathy in this case should be for the widows and orphans of the two men Motto and his gang killed. I say to Motto: 'There is no mercy. He gave none, and for him there is none.'"

As Cassidy concluded, Motto sat slumped in his seat, his face white and his lips quivering. Whatever hope he had after Doerfler's closing seemed to disappear in Cassidy's fiery oratory.

Judge Allen's instructions to the jury lasted a mere 30 minutes. The *Plain Dealer* reported:

> "She reviewed the statute applicable to the charge of first degree murder, and explained to the jury that, even if it were not shown that Motto actually fired any of the shots which killed Sly, the fact that he participated in the robbery, if proved, should be sufficient to convict him of murder in the first degree.

"The law, she said, held that one who is a party to a robbery in which murder is committed is equally guilty with those who actually do the slaying."

The judge explained that the penalty for conviction of first degree murder was death in the electric chair, unless there was a recommendation of mercy from the jury. If this was the recommendation then the penalty was life in prison. She also gave the jury the option of considering second degree murder, manslaughter and robbery, explaining the penalty for each offense.

Allen completed her charge shortly after the noon hour and the jury left the courtroom to begin its deliberations. As Motto was being led out of the courtroom, Marie Sly extended her hand to James Cassidy. "I want to thank you. You've done everything you could. I'm sure justice will be done."

The jurors were out a total of six hours, four in deliberations, before they reached a verdict. Judge Allen was contacted and ordered Motto brought back to the courtroom. The prisoner entered, handcuffed to a deputy sheriff. He quickly looked toward the jury box, sweeping the member's faces, looking for some hint of a hopeful decision. The jurors stared back. No one from the defendant's family was present. Motto shifted nervously in his seat until the judge arrived.

It was 7:10 p.m. when Allen asked, "Ladies and gentlemen of the jury, have you agreed upon a verdict?"

"We have," answered foreman Lillian Markell. She handed the verdict to the bailiff.

Judge Allen read aloud, "We, the jury, do find the defendant guilty of murder in the first-degree as charged in the indictment."

The next seconds were excruciating ones for Motto as he listened for the jury's recommendation of mercy. It did not come. Zottarelli demanded that the jurors be polled. Each replied that it was their verdict when called to answer.

Judge Allen asked Motto if he had anything to say before she passed sentence.

"I have not had a fair trial," Motto complained. "I did not have all the questions asked me that I wanted by the prosecutor or by my own lawyers."

"You've had a fair trial, Motto," scolded the judge. "You have had one of the very finest criminal lawyers in the state. He had the able assistance of Mr. Zottarelli. It is the opinion of the court that you have had a fair trial.

"The court, hereby, sentences you, Frank Motto, on the 29th day of August, before the hour of sunrise, within the walls of the penitentiary, to be electrocuted by causing a current of electricity of sufficient intensity to cause death to be passed through your body; that within thirty days the sheriff deliver you to the custody of the warden of the penitentiary, and that he cause the application of the electricity. You are sentenced to pay the costs in the case and the cost of the execution, and may God have mercy on your soul."

As the judge read the sentence, juror Fred Gensler wept without shame while the other members of the panel stared coldly at the condemned man.[9]

The case produced a couple of firsts for Ohio. It was the first time in the history of the state that a woman judge sentenced a convicted killer to death. In addition, the *Plain Dealer* noted, "It was the first time in the history of the courts that a woman foreman (obviously the term forewoman or foreperson had not yet been introduced) of a jury concurred in the death verdict." Lillian Markell did more than just "concur" in the verdict; she dictated it.

While the guilt of Motto was never in question, the jury took ten ballots before agreeing on the death penalty. The first ballot stood seven for the death penalty and five for life in prison. Later it stood ten to two. At this point Markell spoke up. The widow, who had lost her only son just four months earlier, began an impassioned argument that changed the minds of the two holdouts, one of which was Gensler. Later she told reporters, "There may be some who believe in life imprisonment for murderers who show no mercy to their victims, but I am not one of them."

In an exclusive interview with the *Cleveland News*, she defended her first-degree murder without mercy decision:

> "I say this as one who has been a mother, and with a mother-love as deep and true as any woman is capable of experiencing. I have no consideration for this sloppy and soft hearted sentimentality which declares we must use 'kid-glove' methods in dealing with criminals
>
> "Take the case of Frank Motto. There was not an extenuating circumstance in his favor. It was shown that he had led a criminal career for the past fourteen years and he is now only twenty-six. He had no regard for life or property and would not avail himself of the opportunity to lead an honorable life, when given his freedom, after serving time for previous offenses.
>
> "He was capable of earning an honest living and becoming a useful citizen. He conducted a garage and was also the proprietor of a roadhouse, the latter probably questionable, but he gave evidence of business ability. But he was not content with making an honest living

and leading a useful life. He chose a career of crime and now realizes, when too late, that it does not pay.

"A life sentence does not necessarily mean that the criminal will be confined to the penitentiary for his remaining days. The power of the pardon remains with the governor and the convict is liable to be turned loose to prey upon society at any time. And he comes out more vindictive than ever, and is even more dangerous in my opinion.

"On the other hand, I honestly believe that it is more humane to inflict the death penalty than to render a life verdict, even when certain that the victim will serve for life. This applies both to the individual and the family. I so argued with my fellow jurors.

"I pointed out during the taking of the ten ballots that we, as jurors, had some conception of what confinement meant and that the family would always be thinking of what Frank was enduring. Now, when he is electrocuted and placed under the sod, the end will come. Time will heal the hurt that comes to those of his family who are left behind, at this moment, and the anxiety and fear of never knowing what he is doing and how he may be brought home will have passed.

"I know that if it had been my boy, and he had led the life that Motto has I would much rather know that the death penalty had been inflicted upon him and an end put to his criminal career than for him to be sentenced for life."

After the sentencing and the publicity of Markell's role in it, the widow received a number of Black Hand death threats. On one, which stated, "When Frank Motto dies, then his brothers will take revenge," Judge Allen, the female witnesses and the widows were also threatened. At the bottom of the page was the imprint of a life size human hand made from black tar. Bertillon Expert George Koestle tried unsuccessfully to match the print to those on record. Not all the mail Markell received was negative. She received letters of congratulation from all over the country. One letter, from a "Law Abiding Citizen," stated, "There is nothing but words of praise on the lips of all who respect law and order. God give us tens of thousands more like Judge Allen and Mrs. Markell." The threats, however, continued and in early June she applied to the police department for permission to carry a revolver. Despite the publicity, her popularity, and the very real threat of reprisal, the request was denied.

Missing from the courthouse at the time the verdict was read were the widows of the slain men. Tracked down by reporters shortly after the sentence was announced, Marie Sly stated, "Oh, I am very glad of it. I think he got just what he deserves, and I hope all the others to be tried for the same crime get the same thing."

Ethyl Fanner's response was much the same, "Of course everyone knows I'm glad it turned out that way. I hope the others receive the same penalty, for they are all equally guilty, whether all fired the shots which killed or not."

Two people who were not "glad" with the sentence were Purpura and Komer. Purpura reportedly "crept to a corner of his cell and huddled against the bars." Komer declared, "I'm sick and disgusted with the whole thing. I haven't anything to say." This response seemed highly peculiar due to the fact it was Komer's testimony that helped seal a guilty verdict and a scheduled trip to the chair for his former companion.

On Sunday evening, a jailed cabaret singer, occupying a cell four tiers below where Motto and Purpura were housed, began singing. Motto requested through a deputy that the man sing "Mother Machree."[10] Motto and Purpura wept openly as the words floated up to their cells. A deputy, on special duty, overseeing the three prisoners reported that Motto told him several times, "It's all over. Only a miracle can save me, and I know it." On Monday, Zottarelli's motion for a new trial, which claimed the court had erred in not allowing a change of venue, and on certain objections, was overruled by Judge Allen. Later that day Motto was delivered to the Ohio Penitentiary. He was placed on "death row," the cell block reserved for condemned prisoners to await their fate.

In a later interview, Motto claimed Judge Allen and jury foreman Lillian Markell were responsible for his fate. "Never talk to me again about how merciful women are," he said. "If I were ever on trial again I'd insist on having a *regular* judge and jury. I thought women had soft hearts, but that's a lot of bunk!"

Chapter Endnotes

1. Due to a legal technicality at the time, Governor Harry L. Davis had to grant Motto a pardon on his auto theft conviction before he could be tried on murder charges. The pardon became void if Motto were acquitted of the capital charges.

2. Alfred A. Cartwright died on April 17, 1947, at the age of 63 in Columbus, Ohio.

3. The *Plain Dealer* referred to it as "irregularities in the drawing of the venire men."

4. The name "Bridge of Sighs," claims several origins. Venice, Italy's *Ponte de Sospiri*, or "Bridge of Sighs," may have been the inspiration for such architectural fantasies" Antonio Contino's bridge over the Rio di Palazzo was erected in the year 1600 to connect the Doge's prisons, or *Prigioni*, with the inquisitor's rooms in the main palace.   Another   claim is the name "Bridge of Sighs" was invented in the 19th Century, when Lord Byron helped to popularize the belief that the bridge's name was inspired by the sighs of condemned prisoners as they were led through it to the executioner. (In reality, the days of inquisitions and summary executions were over by the time the bridge was built, and the cells under the palace roof were occupied mostly by small time criminals.)

Still another claims the "Bridge of Sighs" received its name in the 17th century, because the prisoners who passed through it on their way to the prison cells on the other side most likely saw the beautiful sight of the lagoon and the island of S. Georgio and freedom for the last time.

5. A demurrer is defined as, "A plea to dismiss a lawsuit on the grounds that although the opposition's statements may be true, they are insufficient to sustain the claim." – *The American Heritage Dictionary*.

6. During his trial, William McGannon met secretly with Mary E. Neely, a witness for the state. McGannon claimed his meeting was "for the purpose of seeing that the truth be established." After a mistrial, McGannon was brought up on contempt charges for having obtained perjured testimony from Neely. Attorney A.A. Cartwright was charged too. On October 6, 1921, Common Pleas Judge Robert H. Day found McGannon guilty, but released Cartwright stating that although he knew the former judge and Miss Neely had met, and that her testimony was perjured, there was no evidence to show he had conspired with McGannon.

7. "More gimmick than serious weaponry," according to small arms aficionado Gary E. May. Revolvers of this type were manufactured by Colt, Smith & Wesson, Iver Johnson, and Harrington & Richardson. The production period of these items were mostly from 1880 to the end of World War I. These guns today can cost collectors upwards of $1,000.

8. Although the *Cleveland News* printed Clifton Avenue, this is most likely a mistake as Clifton is a boulevard and doesn't intersect with West 74th Street. It's more probable that they were referring to Clinton Avenue which does intersect with West 74th Street.

9. After the jury was dismissed, Fred Gensler approached Judge Allen and asked if he could give his jury fee to some charity, claiming he could not accept the money. Allen informed him he was free to do whatever he wanted with the money.

10. "Mother Macree" and "When Irish Eyes are Smiling" were written by Clevelander Ernest R. Ball, who is buried in Lake View Cemetery.

10

Trial of Sam Purpura

The trial of Ignatius "Sam" Purpura for the first-degree murder of Wilfred Sly was held in the courtroom of Common Pleas Judge Maurice Bernon* on May 15, 1921. The judge was one of the most respected jurists in the city. A year after graduating from Western Reserve Law School in 1906, Bernon was elected to his first public office at the age of 21, becoming a Cleveland City Councilman. As a Democrat on City Council he came under the wing of Mayor Tom L. Johnson and quickly became known as "one of the boys." But it was Johnson's protégé, Newton D. Baker, who became Bernon's mentor.

After two years in council he was appointed assistant city solicitor under Baker and held that position until 1911. Baker put Bernon on the Democratic legislative slate and he served as a member of the state senate in 1913 and 1914. The next year Bernon was appointed municipal judge by Governor James M. Cox and elected to the position the next year. In 1917, Bernon resigned from the bench to go into private practice, but a year later he found himself serving as special counsel to the state attorney general.

In April 1920, Governor Cox again appointed Bernon to fill an open position on the bench, this time in the Common Pleas Court. In November of that year he was elected to a two-year un-expired term. Two years later Bernon led the judicial ticket, winning a full six-year term. When he resigned from the bench in 1924, Bernon claimed, "I had to get out and make some money for my family. The bench is a good place to starve."

On this May 15, Monday morning, jury selection for Purpura got underway and was surprisingly rapid. By the end of the second day the jury was selected from 45 potential candidates. The selection of four women to the jury, and the two-day completion of the jury panel in a first-degree murder trial, set a precedent in the county. Prosecutor Stanton was confident of a victory stating, "We have more direct evidence against Purpera than we had against Motto." The evidence consisting of Purpura's and Komer's confessions.

William J. Corrigan, chief counsel for Purpura, seemed unaffected by the fact that it was a woman who drove the jury to deciding on the death penalty in the Motto case. After that decision there were a number of newspaper articles, which pointed out that around the country courts were finding that women, just introduced to the jury pool, were not reluctant to put a convicted criminal to death.[1] Corrigan asked jurors if they believed "each member of the band which participated in the murders and robberies should be given the same punishment," regardless of their role. The young attorney was able to keep to five the number of jurors with this opinion. Meanwhile, the principal reason prosecutors used for disqualification was anyone who had an aversion to the death penalty.

Testimony in the Purpura trial began the same way it did in Motto's, with the jurors visiting the crime scene before hearing Marie Sly as the state's first witness. She was followed by bank and company officials, Fred Goff[2], former County Coroner Jacobs and two eyewitnesses who claimed they saw Purpura on the bridge.

Then came the state's key witness, Edith Marklew who divulged this evidence:

> "When the Sly-Fanner car was jammed against the railing, the second car came up alongside, and Purpera and his companion began to talk to Sly and Fanner.
>
> "Purpera jumped out of the car, which had stopped, and tried to convince Fanner that the accident was not his fault. Fanner stood on the running board of his car, with a gun in his hand.
>
> "Then Purpera turned to go back to his own car. When he got back, he suddenly whirled about and dashed back towards Fanner and Sly.
>
> "He reached in his pocket, drew a revolver, and fired two shots, hitting one man in the face and the other in the body. Both men fell to the ground.
>
> "I ran across the bridge and went into Mrs. Blaich's house. I don't know where Purpera went."

The testimony was a broadside to Corrigan and caused a sensation in the courtroom. It was the first time Purpura was actually named as one of the shooters. Despite a lengthy cross-examination, Corrigan could not shake the witness from the key point – that she had seen Purpura fire bullets into both businessmen.

It didn't get any easier for defense counsel when Irene Walker took the stand. She testified, "Sam Purpera shot Sly, and he fell. I was stunned and I ran into the house." On cross-examination Walker readily admitted she wasn't able to identify any of the suspects from the photographs shown to her by police. But, she claimed correctly that Purpura's picture was not among the ones police showed her. The first time she saw Purpura's face, Walker said, was in a newspaper article and she recognized him immediately as the man who shot Sly.

Mary Blaich then took the stand and repeated her testimony from the Motto trial in which she stated Purpura chased her down and ordered her not to phone the police.

During the afternoon session a large crowd came to hear the testimony of Inspector Sterling. The *Plain Dealer* reported, "Every available inch of space in the court room was crowded. A score of police cadets, seated in rows back of the trial table, added to the special detail of police and the squad of deputy sheriffs assigned to the room, and presented a strange spectacle."

While the inspector recalled the confession and the conversations that took place with the defendant in Los Angeles, Purpura maintained a "stolid silence." The exuberance he displayed on his return to Cleveland was long gone. The hope the young man possessed of avoiding execution disappeared with the sentencing of Frank Motto to the electric chair. Now with testimony introduced that he was actually one of the shooters, a fact which he adamantly denied since his capture, his mood was further dampened. The presence of his mother in the courtroom did little to lift his spirits.

On Friday morning, May 20, Sterling ended his testimony under cross-examination by Corrigan. The defense gained one important admission from the police inspector. Sterling said he believed Purpura was telling the truth about not being involved in the shooting. How the jury weighed this in the face of eyewitness testimony to the contrary remained to be seen. Detective Banks was then called to the stand to corroborate the testimony of Sterling regarding the hand written confession Purpura made.

To the surprise of many, the state rested its case without calling Louis Komer. Corrigan announced the defense might call Komer as a witness if the state didn't. Whatever Corrigan thought he could extract from Komer to help his case is lost to history – the "Toledo Kid" refused to take the stand, declaring that if he didn't appear for the state he wouldn't appear at all.

Sam Purpura took the stand as the defense opened its case. He recited the events of December 30 and 31 to the jury, beginning with meeting Dominic Benigno in the Dreamland Dance Hall late in the evening. Purpura said he had known Benigno for years. He related how Benigno had told him to get an automobile from a man named Clarence Brown. Purpura then left the dance hall, went to a Prospect Avenue garage and got the vehicle.

The next morning he drove the Stearns to East Ninth Street and Orange Avenue where he said he met Frank Motto for the first time. He claimed that even at this point he didn't know a robbery was planned. Next he was asked about the events on the bridge that morning. Purpura gave this account after the accident, "The Jordan car passed us, turned and came back, with Benigno at the wheel. The rest had gotten out, and were coming up on foot. I went over to the Jordan car, and just as I reached it I heard shooting. I leaped in and in a moment the rest came on the run and the car sped away." Purpura said he exited the car at West 56th Street and went home.

On cross-examination Cassidy had a field day with the youth as the experienced prosecutor caught the defendant in a multitude of lies. Purpura shifted nervously in the witness chair as he wilted under the barrage of questions.

He admitted, "When I took the car to East Ninth and Orange Avenue...I knew the job was to be a payroll stickup." During the ride to the bridge, Purpura was told by Motto that the car they were following contained Sly, Fanner and the company payroll. At one point during the torrid cross-examination attorney Zottarelli jumped to his feet, objecting to "the manner in which this poor boy is being hounded by the prosecutor."

Judge Bernon overruled the objection stating that Cassidy's questioning was "perfectly proper." He reprimanded the defense lawyer and instructed the jury to disregard the objection.

The only statement Purpura stuck to was his adamant declaration that he had left the revolver in the automobile and did not have it on him when he exited the Stearns to confront the two businessmen about the accident.

Purpura was followed on the stand by his frail mother. Mary Purpura was called to confirm only her son's claim that he was 17 years-old. There was some suggestion that he was actually older. An objection by the prosecution prevented her answer and with that the defense's case was over.

At 2:00 p.m. Assistant Prosecutor Harry Parsons delivered the closing argument for the state. Then Zottarelli went first as counsel split the defense's closing statement for Purpura. When he was finished, attorney Corrigan began a dramatic dialogue with jurors, emphasizing Purpura's youth and crafting his statement into a plea for a recommendation of mercy. For nearly an hour Corrigan hammered away with an argument that brought many of the spectators to tears, as well as two women jurors:

"Justice in this case is not the chair, unless you decide it is the chair. Justice can be a recommendation of mercy if you decide that is justice. If you think it is justice, send him to the chair, but be satisfied that when you hear the newsboys crying out that verdict there is no qualm in your heart.

"Judge this boy as he should be judged. I say the evidence is not convincing that he fired any shot or killed Sly or Fanner. I am holding no brief for murders. I have no desire that crime should wend its way freely in this city.

"This child – and he is a child – was not the perpetrator of the deed. He does not deserve the same punishment as Motto and the rest. They used him as a tool in this matter, and that's all he was.

Inspector Sterling does not believe the two women who identified Purpera, because he told you on the witness stand that he believed Purpera told the truth in his confession.

"Mr. Prosecutor, you used Louis Komer in the Motto case. If Purpera is not telling the truth, why did you not bring Komer up from his cell in county jail and have him say it is a lie? Two bullets, a 32 and a 38 caliber, killed Sly and Fanner. No one man did that killing.

"Go over the conditions of this boy's youth. You have a son, Mrs. Garrett [addressing one of the women jurors]. You have exerted every good influence over that son of yours. This boy was raised in the slums. At the age of six, as you heard it from the stand, he went to work in a barbershop. He was raised in the gutters. He has not brains enough to realize the predicament he is in.

"Sending a 17 year-old to the chair is not going to stop crime in this city. Eradicate the slums in the congested districts and you will have eliminated the cause of crime. The boy's life is ahead of him. There is some good in him yet. Perhaps, through a life of penitence, he may redeem himself."

The tears that flowed throughout the courtroom were the first sign of sympathy that were directed at Purpura since the trial began. Mary Purpura sat sobbing throughout, her head resting on the shoulder of a teenaged niece. Two women who weren't teary-eyed were Marie Sly and Ethyl Fanner, who were seated just a few feet behind Mary Purpura. The two widows, still adorned in black, sat with grim looks on their faces as they stared at the jurors. If the women had lost any hope due to Corrigan's impassioned plea, they soon regained it when Cassidy stood to return volley.

The prosecutor, reminding the jurors of their oaths that "no influence of sympathy would sway them from arriving at a just and impartial verdict," gave his closing rebuttal:

"The testimony is conclusive. Sam Purpera is identified by two women as the man who killed two men in cold blood. What reason would either of those women have for testifying as they did if it were not the truth? Would it not have been far easier for them to fail to identify him? But Sam Purpera's face remains fixed in their minds forever. They could not be mistaken.

"There is nothing before you but a plea for mercy, except the suggestion that the state did not prove that Purpera fired the shot. The court will tell you it is not necessary, that it makes no difference who fired the shot as far as the guilt or innocence of Purpera is concerned.

"Sam claims he did not know of the plan of the robbery. It was he who procured the car to use in the job. Counsel says he is not old enough to vote. He is old enough to tote a gun and shoot down two citizens in cold blood, if he is old enough for anything.

"Purpera's raising in the slums is not responsible for his being here. He is here because he is a criminal at heart and chose the lines of least resistance.

"They would ask you to place him in the penitentiary now. He escaped from the detention home just a month before this murder was committed. He would not stay there. Purpera knew right from wrong when he was six years old. Purpera knew the night before exactly what the robbery would entail.

"He was to play the role of the betrayer. He was to allay the suspicions of these two citizens when their car was purposely ditched by him and Motto.

"With more treachery than I can conceive in the heart of any beast, he then whipped out a gun and shot them down in cold blood; without a chance to say to their Maker, 'God, have mercy.' And he asks you for mercy.

"Sam Purpera, on that morning when you [fired] your gun, you knew that you were the murderer of Sly and Fanner, and from that time on you deserved the maximum penalty at the hands of this jury.

"Purpera gave death to two men. He only can get death for one. As he was merciful to Sly and Fanner, so you be merciful to him."

Judge Bernon's charge to the jury lasted less than 20 minutes. He did not offer them as many options as Judge Allen had allowed the Motto jury. He told the panel they could find Purpura guilty of first-degree murder – with or without a recommendation of mercy – or acquit him.

The jurors began their deliberations around 5:00 p.m. Thursday evening. At 9:45, after not reaching a verdict, they were locked up for the night. The next morning it took the jurors a little over an hour to reach a unanimous decision. Purpura was brought to the courtroom, like Motto handcuffed to a deputy sheriff, to hear his fate. As he sat next to attorney Zottarelli, he scanned the faces of the jurors for some sign of hope. He didn't find one.

Judge Bernon entered the courtroom and was handed the jury's decision. The judge read out loud, "We, the jury in this case, being duly impaneled and sworn, do find the defendant, Sam Purpera, guilty in the first-degree, as charged in the indictment."

The guilty verdict came as a surprise to no one. The case had boiled down to whether the jury was going to send him to the electric chair or show him mercy. Everyone in the courtroom, except the judge and jurors, held their collective breaths to hear if the words, "And we recommend that mercy be shown him," were forthcoming. As in the case of Motto, they never came.

Judge Bernon called the defendant to the bench for sentencing. Purpura, his face white with fear and using his hand to steady himself on the judge's table, faced the jurist. "Have you anything to say before sentence is pronounced?" asked the judge.

"I am innocent," answered Purpura in a voice almost inaudible.

"You are not innocent," responded Bernon. "The verdict of the jury is a just one and according to the evidence. This admission you made on the stand of your connection with the crime supports the verdict."

Bernon then stated firmly, "It is the sentence of this court that within the next thirty days you be taken to the state penitentiary in Columbus and that you be kept there until August 29, 1921, that sometime between midnight and dawn on August 29 you be placed in the electric chair and that a current of electricity of sufficient intensity to cause death be passed through your body, the application of said current to continue until you are dead.

"And may God have mercy on your soul!"

If indeed Purpura was 17, he was the youngest person ever to be sentenced to the electric chair in Cuyahoga County. Zottarelli announced immediately that he would file a motion for a new trial, "contending that the court erred in not instructing the jury that it could return a verdict of a lesser degree of homicide if members saw fit."[3]

No sooner had the sentence been given that three deputies stepped forward to surround the convicted youth. Purpura turned around, offering his arms for the handcuffs. Sheriff Stannard was on hand to lead the deputies, who "half dragged" the prisoner back to his cell. Purpura, who was up pacing his cell all night, was returned to it to await transfer to the

Ohio Penitentiary. The once talkative teen repeated only three words on his way back, "They got me!" After learning of the guilty verdict, a crowd of morbid curious gathered at the county jail, in hopes of getting a glimpse of the condemned man as he was being brought back. A squad of mounted police quickly dispersed them, many of them re-gathering in Public Square.

After Purpura was led away, Judge Bernon addressed the jury. "I have spent a sleepless night, and I know that yours also has been very restless," he said. "But I hope you may be consoled by the consciousness that you have done your duty. The verdict you returned was the only one possible under the circumstances."

The jurors had taken a total of thirteen[4] ballots. On the first ballot the panel had found Purpura guilty, but was split nine to three for the death penalty, with all four women in favor of the defendant getting the chair. After ten ballots that night the jury was still split. On Friday morning, three more ballots were taken and on the last one the two hold-out jurors gave in.

Edith Garrett, the mother of a 21 year-old son, said she had much sympathy for Mary Purpura, but felt that only the death penalty could bring real justice. "We felt in giving him the chair we were treating him better than we would have by giving him a life sentence in the penitentiary. There he would learn nothing but the worst of life, and he might later be released by pardon and commit more crimes."

Few people were in the courtroom at the time the verdict and sentence was announced. As during the reading of the Motto verdict, the widows of Sly and Fanner were not present, but this time the newspapers didn't send reporters to get comments. Mrs. Mary Pope, the mother of Ethyl Fanner, was present along with her son.

Mary Purpura had not been notified of the verdict. Shortly after 10:00 a.m. she appeared alone at the jail. She was escorted to her son's cell where she heard the decision from him, after which the distraught mother cried uncontrollably. After she left the jail her condemned son flew into a rage. He threw himself on his cot and screamed curses at both the judge and the jury. Jumping to his feet he scattered all of his tin dishes about the cell, before tearing the mattress from the cot. Several deputies were called to restrain him.

Stannard wanted to get Purpura to Columbus immediately after the sentence, but the crowd of people who gathered made this a dangerous task. Instead, plans were made to move him Saturday afternoon. The next morning he had one final visit with his mother. The *Plain Dealer* described Mary Purpura as a "crushed, foreign-speaking little woman, who cried disconsolately throughout her brief visit at her condemned son's cell."

During his last moments before leaving the County Jail Purpura was a calm man. The *Sunday News-Leader* reported, "He shook hands with deputies at the jail in apparent good humor, and exhibited no trace of the wrath he has vented in his solitary cell in murderers' row. He smiled cheerfully when he was taken through the offices in the jail and placed in an automobile."

Around mid-afternoon Purpura, handcuffed to Deputy Sheriff Charles Weidenmann, was removed to the Union Depot. His guards walked him through the baggage room to avoid notice and placed him on the 4:00 p.m. Big Four train to Columbus without incident. Once in Columbus he was placed in a cell at the Ohio Penitentiary not far from Frank Motto. Interviewed just days after arriving, Purpura blamed the Cleveland newspapers for his downfall, most notably the *Cleveland News*. He complained. "The newspapers killed me, and I'll say so to my dying day. The *News* was the worst of the lot. It was the public sentiment they stirred up that brought me here." By now Purpura was spending his time reading the bible and a prayer book. "If I'd spent more time with those books," he stated, "maybe I wouldn't be here now."

With Motto and Purpura tucked safely away in the condemned prisoners' wing of the penitentiary, the focus shifted to the remaining four suspects. Circulars were already sent with photographs to cities throughout the United States. Prosecutor Stanton and Police Chief Smith were confident, however, that Dominic Benigno and Dominic Lonardo had fled to Italy or Sicily; as early as May 4 the prosecutor had confirmed that Angelo Amato was in Italy. The authorities were prepared to seek the cooperation of police in all the major Italian cities in capturing all three. They knew that if the men were arrested in Italy they would be tried there since no extradition treaty existed between the two countries. Stanton was already preparing for such a contingency by taking depositions from all the witnesses so they could be used in an Italian court of law.

Meanwhile, Louis Komer was still behind bars in the county jail facing a trial date of June 13. There was speculation that the trial might be continued until the September term of court so that Komer could be used as a state's witness in the trials of the three others, proving that prosecutors were confident they might all be in custody shortly.

Komer lived in mortal fear that friends of the condemned men or friends and relatives of the hunted suspects might try to kill him. In a letter to Chief Deputy C.M. Dombey on May 24, Komer pleaded that he be permitted to remain in his "murderers' row" cell at all times and that he not have to exercise with the other inmates in an open area known as the "bull pen." Komer told Dombey in the letter, "It isn't safe for me in the bull pen because many would like to see me out of the way." Dombey granted the request.

During the last week of May 1921, a police frenzy was on when it was believed that one or two of the suspects had re-entered the city. The excitement began on May 26 when it was reported that a "secret indictment" was issued for a fourth suspect. It was reported that Angelo Amato was back in the city. Detective Phillip Mooney was leading the search for Amato throughout "Little Italy." The entire neighborhood was turned upside down in an effort to locate him. Dominic Benigno was also rumored to have returned to the city. The *Cleveland News* reported:

> "An intensive search through all parts of town has been carried on for twenty-four hours without a moment's let up.
>
> Midnight conferences in police headquarters resulted in squads being sent through the city on fruitless 'tips,' city detectives filtering through resorts known to have been haunts of the gangsters, marked the activities since Wednesday morning.
>
> All through the night the search continued, and as one by one detectives and squads returned empty-handed, efforts to find the slayer were redoubled."

It is interesting to note that in the reporting of this renewed manhunt, that the *News* titled its article, "Police Rake City In New Hunt For Purpera's Gang." How the killing combine had suddenly taken on the name of the gang's youngest and weakest member seems absurd. With three of the members tied to the Mayfield Road Mob and another, Dominic Lonardo, a younger brother of the city's Mafia boss, it seems ludicrous that the newspaper associated leadership of the gang to Purpura. For years following the incident, the newspapers invariably referred to any person connected to the Mayfield Road Mob, or any person connected to the murderers, as members of the Sly-Fanner gang.

Chapter Endnotes

1. An article on the front-page of the *Cleveland News* on June 3, 1921 reported on a case in Cincinnati, Ohio where a man was on trial for first-degree murder. The man's attorney peremptorily challenged five prospective women jurors. When asked why, the attorney stated, "Women are merciless, much more so than men. The record in criminal cases shows that they are invariably for conviction. I will not have a woman on this jury if I can help it."

2. Frederick H. Goff (December 15, 1858 – March 14, 1923) "was a lawyer, banker, and civic leader who developed the ideas for both the living trust and the community trust, using the latter idea to establish the Cleveland Foundation in 1914." Goff served as president of the Cleveland Trust Company from June 1908 until his death in March 1923. After the Sly-Fanner murders, the city reacted to the alarming number of high-profile criminal cases by conducting the Cleveland Survey of Criminal Justice, the first comprehensive analysis of the law-enforcement system and related departments in a major United States city. Funded by the Cleveland Foundation the result of the study was the Cleveland Association for Criminal Justice, of which Goff served as first director.

3. There seemed to be some confusion from the reporting as to whether both members of defense counsel were present. Two newspapers mentioned only the presence of Zottarelli, while the *Cleveland Press* mentioned Corrigan alone. The *Press* claimed Corrigan filed the motion for a new trial, the *News* reported it was Zottarelli who filed the motion.

4. The *Cleveland News* did a sidebar about the role Friday and the number "13" had played so far:

> "Hoodoo numbers and days have played a strange part in the state's efforts to mete out punishment for the murders of Wilfred C. Sly and George K. Fanner.
>
> Sam Purpera was found guilty of first degree murder on the jury's thirteenth ballot. The verdict was returned on a Friday. The motion for a re-trial, which will be filed by his attorneys, contains thirteen separate counts.
>
> Louis Komer, now in county jail charged with the murders, is to go to trial on the thirteenth of June. And he has spent thirteen years in penal institutions.
>
> The defense in the trial of Frank Motto convicted and sentenced to death, rested its case on Friday, the thirteenth, on which day Motto took the stand to tell his story."

11

Arrest of Dominic Benigno

There were conflicting stories as to when Dominic Benigno vacated Cleveland. One had it that he "went peacefully about his business" until word reached him of Purpura's Los Angeles arrest on March 11. Another story states he left Cleveland on February 28, ten days after police released him due to lack of evidence after his arrest in the Hotel Winton garage on January 3. By most accounts he went to Chicago and then to El Paso where he was able to purchase a fake passport, for one dollar, and cross over into Mexico, making his way to Guadalajara and then to Mexico City.

After Purpura's arrest, police went to the Benigno home only to find he was gone. When he was positively identified by Purpura as a member of the robbery team, the driver of the Jordan automobile, police stepped up their efforts to locate him. Suspecting he had fled the city, and probably the country as well, Detectives Mooney and Cavolo went to the United States Post Office and spoke to inspectors about keeping an eye on the incoming mail for the Benigno family. Around mid-May they got a break when a letter arrived showing a Guadalajara return address.

Cavolo went to Chief Smith and informed him of Benigno's whereabouts. Smith met with Prosecutor Stanton to discuss a plan of action. The problem was that neither the county nor the police department had the funds to send officers in pursuit of the suspect. This was resolved when the Cleveland Automobile Club agreed to "advance" $2,000 to send detectives to Mexico and bring Benigno back. Smith took the club's proposal to Stanton, who agreed that "no efforts should be spared in trying to run down the rest of the Sly-Fanner murder gang." Fred Caley, of the automobile club, at one point during the ordeal wired the detectives informing them, "We don't care what it costs. Follow them to the end of the world if necessary." Smith assigned Detective Captain George Matowitz and Cavolo to make the trip. Smith was determined to make sure this was no wild goose chase; he called Cavolo to his office.

"I don't want you to tip your secrets," Smith told the detective, "but how sure are you that Benigno is in Mexico?"

"I'm absolutely certain that he is in Guadalajara. I even know the name of the hotel where he is staying, [and] where he was a few days ago," Cavolo assured him.

It should be noted here that over the years there have been different versions of the story of how Benigno was discovered. While it was initially reported that Detectives Cavolo and Mooney found him through a letter at the post office addressed to Benigno's family, another report claims the information first came to the attention of the Cleveland Automobile Club. Later on, it was reported that the detectives "intercepted a letter" from Charles Coletto, who was traveling with Benigno, that he had mailed to his family on Paul Avenue. Coletto told his family he was in Mexico in the company of Benigno. If this latter report was true the information didn't get shared with Matowitz or Stanton. It is very possible that due to Cavolo's influence in the Italian community that someone simply told him the whereabouts of the fugitive.

Smith decided to act quickly. That evening Matowitz called in sick. Word circulated through the bureau that he would be incapacitated for a while. Next, word came that Cavolo received a telegram informing him of an uncle's death in Buffalo, which, to the casual observer, seemed like the longest funeral in history. Matowitz and Cavolo's historic ordeal began on May 23 when they departed by train for Washington D.C. Both were instructed not to tell a soul of their mission, not even family members. While police brass and Cleveland Automobile Club officials thought the absence of the two would be temporary, Matowitz and Cavolo would not step foot in Cleveland again until July 19.

A few days went by without a word from Matowitz – a practice the captain continued almost the entire time he was gone – and then on Thursday, May 26, Smith was awakened when an early morning telegram arrived. Matowitz wrote:

> "Fletcher [assistant Secretary of State] too busy. Explained case to undersecretary and extradition solicitor. Extradition solicitor advises requests be made through Gov. Davis by letter. Then they will consider requesting the Mexican government to bring Benigno to the border after we get him."

Matowitz later recalled (Matowitz's personal recollections will appear italicized), *"Before going to Mexico and after the fugitives...we had gone to Washington to get papers authorizing us to bring our man back. Such papers we were told would not be possible. We asked for letters of introduction to Mexican authorities. These too were refused. I told the Washington officials that I would then proceed on my own hook and trust to luck."*

Chief Smith and Assistant Prosecutor Cassidy met later that morning and were soon aboard a train for Columbus, Ohio to consult with Governor

Davis. Before leaving, Smith wired Matowitz telling him to meet him in Pittsburgh later that night. In Columbus, Smith provided Davis with all the pertinent facts of the case. The governor wrote a letter to Secretary of State Charles Evans Hughes and handed it to the chief. At 10:30 that night, Smith met Matowitz in Pittsburgh and gave him the letter. Matowitz then returned to Washington D.C. on a midnight train. The next day the chief received a wire from Matowitz:

> "…everything was fixed up and too much credit cannot be given Congressman Harry C. Gahn[1] for his efforts and interest in the affair. He just about broke his neck getting me an interview."

In signing off, Matowitz said he and Cavolo were off to Mexico to get their man and would cable as soon as they had him in custody.

Matowitz continues, *"The trip to Texas and thence into Mexico was uneventful. We reached Mexico City on June 2 and went to the Regis Hotel, where we were registered. We went to see the United States charge d'affaires, but he said he would be unable to assist us in our search at Guadalajara because of the uncertainty of relations between the United States and Mexico. He also charged us to be careful lest we precipitate trouble by seizing our men on Mexican soil.*

"The charge d'affaires turned us over to the military attaché, who told us practically the same thing, even declining to give us a letter of introduction to Mexican officials.

"'Come back in a day or two and maybe I can do something for you,' he told us.

"We returned to the Regis and held a conference. As a result we decided to go to Guadalajara and trust to luck some more. I walked to the hotel desk for the purpose of sending a telegram to Cleveland headquarters and as I did so heard a terrific commotion at the entrance of the hotel. I swung around and saw two men dashing into the street with Cavolo close after them. I recognized Benigno and Coletto in the two who were fleeing.

"They actually had been in the same hotel, having left Guadalajara, and had seen Cavolo and myself together in the lobby.

"I soon caught up with Cavolo and we raced side by side after the others. The chase ended in a large, open square, where I seized Benigno and Cavolo grabbed Coletto. The two fought fiercely for their liberty. Benigno, the larger and older of the two, called out loudly in Spanish, declaring, I later learned, that he was being robbed.

"The result was that, within a few minutes, the public space was filled with a crowd of yelling Mexicans, threatening Cavolo and myself with death.

So close did the crowd gather around us that there was not room to draw our weapons. I doubt that it would have been wise to have done so in any event. There was murder in the Mexicans' hearts.

"Several policemen arrived, but we could not explain to them what we wanted. Benigno and his companion had all the advantage. They could speak Spanish and they told wild stories of being victims of robbery. At length, however, we convinced the police that we wanted to go to the police station and wanted the others to go along.

"At the station we succeeded in getting our men locked up, but we had no assurance they would be held. Benigno was defiant and demanded that I release him immediately. He said I had no authority, which was true, but I wasn't going to let a little matter like that stop me when luck had played so far in my favor.

"Again, Benigno, speaking in Spanish, demanded of the Mexican police that he be released. He turned to me and said that he would show me the biggest battle of my life before he was through with me.

"With our prisoners safely under lock and key for the moment, I returned with Cavolo to George Summerell, the United States charge d'affaires. He had gone. We then got assurance that the Mexican jailer would hold our prisoners at least for the night, and while Cavolo stood guard outside the prison on the chance our men would prevail on the avaricious Mexican jailers to let them go, I went again in search of Summerell and asked him to notify police to hold our prisoners until we were able to return them to America. He said again that he could not help me."

Up until the moment of the arrest, Matowitz didn't know that Benigno was in the company of Charles Coletto, a young, rising hood in the Mayfield Road Mob who, years later, became one of the most prolific killers in the gang. After receiving word of his capture, Stanton promptly had him indicted as a co-conspirator in the case. The newspapers reported that Coletto, "for some time" was suspected of being "a seventh member of the murder band."

Word of the arrests came during the early morning hours of June 3 in the form of a dispatch from the *Associated Press* to the *Plain Dealer*. Reporters called the home of Chief Smith, but he later admitted he was sleeping so soundly the telephone failed to wake him. Reporters then woke Stanton, who sent an officer to the chief's house to inform him of the arrests. Smith admitted it was the first word he had heard of Matowitz since he left for Mexico.[2]

Late Friday morning Smith received a direct dispatch from Matowitz stating, "Benigno and Coletto arrested. Wire me $1,000. Everything fine.

Will wire more information later." Expressing his dissatisfaction with the lack of information coming from his captain, Chief Smith declared, "That's all I've heard from Matowitz. Damn it! He makes his telegrams too short."

On a more positive note, Smith told reporters, "Their whereabouts has been kept a secret ever since they started for Washington. If anyone had known they were headed for Mexico, Benigno's friends in Cleveland would have got in touch with him immediately and the whole thing would have fallen through.

"I want to say this much for Cavolo. It is due to his work that we have rounded up five of the Sly-Fanner murderers. Two have been sentenced, another awaits trial and the two just captured we hope, will be deported from Mexico as undesirables and then extradited to Cleveland. Two more are still at large. I have heard rumors to the effect that they are in Italy."

Smith, like everyone else, believed that even though there wasn't an extradition treaty between the United States and Mexico, they might still surrender the prisoners. He told reporters, "I think Mexico in its present situation can do nothing less than send these men back from where they came. If that's the case, Captain Matowitz and Detective Cavolo will simply accompany the deported men to the point in this country from which they emigrated, and arrest them there." From this point on, however, nothing Matowitz and Cavolo accomplished fell into the category of "simply."

The United States lacked a formal diplomatic relationship with Mexico. The two countries were at war from 1845 to 1848 and a second war nearly came to pass in March 1916 after border raids, carried out by Pancho Villa, were answered by a force led by American General John J. Pershing. From 1913 to 1920 the country was divided by strife and revolution even after the election of Alvaro Obregon as president.[3]

In Cleveland, Detective Mooney uncovered information that revealed Benigno's friends in town were collecting donations to thwart his return for trial. The *News* reported, "A group of quiet-moving men have been circulating through the Italian quarter of Cleveland for several days, seeking, by arguments and threats, to raise enough money to enable Dominic Benigno and Charles Coletto to fight extradition…" The newspaper also reported that a telegram was sent to Mexico City advising the two to "engage the best attorney" that could be found. Mooney discovered that the plan to preempt the return was being overseen by Thomas Benigno. Since detectives had lost his trail in Chicago, Thomas had gone to Mexico and was spreading money around and giving his brother encouragement that he would not be sent back to Cleveland.

As the prisoner had warned Matowitz, it was immediately clear that Benigno was going to fight for his life. In a telegram received in Cleveland late Friday afternoon, Matowitz requested, "Send me word as soon as possible whether Benigno and Coletto are American Citizens." The two were attempting to avoid being returned to the United States by claiming they were not American citizens.

Cassidy and Lieutenant Potts went to the board of elections and discovered from the poll books and naturalization records that Coletto's father was admitted to citizenship on October 12, 1896, in Hamilton County Common Pleas Court in Cincinnati, five years before Charles was born, clearly making him a United States citizen. Proving Benigno was a citizen was a little more difficult. Police began combing marriage records in Philadelphia and Cleveland.

Details of the arrest were read with great interest by Louis Komer, who asked a number of questions about how police found the pair. Before Prosecutor Cassidy and a reporter from the *Plain Dealer*, Komer gave this statement:

> "I can't say I'm sorry they got Benigno. He was the 'brains' of the gang, as you probably already know.
>
> "I met Benigno the day before the robbery in a poolroom. He had the details all planned, he had worked them all out. I told Benigno we would need at least two automobiles and he said, 'I'll take care of that. I'll get the guns, too.'
>
> '[The next morning] He handed revolvers to me and Frank Motto. I'm not sure that he didn't distribute the guns to the whole gang.
>
> "I was in the car with Benigno. Motto and Purpera were in the first car. After I got out of Benigno's car, I can't remember just what he did."

Komer did not identify Coletto as one of the gang members on the bridge that day. He said he thought Coletto might be the "big fellow" who was Benigno's pal around Cleveland. It was not clear whether Komer's description of "big fellow" was meant to indicate size or gang stature. Coletto, at the age of 21, fit neither description.

Another *Associated Press* dispatch from Mexico City on June 5, stated that the Mexican national government had taken "political cognizance of the situation. They [Benigno and Coletto] will be deported to the United States if it can be proved they are anarchists." This latest development came on the heels of unrest, believed to be stirred up by Thomas Benigno, after a threat to blow up the American Embassy in Mexico City by Italian anarchists. It was reported that 100 Mexican police officers, armed with rifles and on horseback, had surrounded the embassy to provide protection.

In another move by Chief Smith, Bertillon Expert George Koestle* was sent to the United States / Mexico border. Koestle had an amazing career as a Cleveland Police officer. The early years of the young man's professional life were not spent as a patrolman, but as a photographer in the employ of one of Cleveland's noted criminal photographers. Born in Cleveland in 1865, Koestle attended local schools and after graduation decided to get into photography and went to work in the commercial studio of E.B. Nock, who was often called on by the Cleveland Police Department when it was decided that a criminal was "important enough" to merit a mug shot.

In 1896, hard times hit Cleveland, as well as the rest of the country. When Koestle's work with the photographer was reduced he found he needed money to support his new family and joined the Cleveland police force. He was on a foot beat for the first year and a half before his talents as a photographer became known. At the time law enforcement used an identification system known as the Bertillon[4] system for the recording of information of criminals. In learning the new system, Koestle found that it was also a learning experience for the criminal too. The first time he took a photograph of an arrestee the man had to be strapped to a chair before he submitted to the procedure.

Koestle was selected to travel to Cincinnati to be trained by Bertillon experts there. When he returned to Cleveland he went to work establishing the Criminal Identification Bureau here and in neighboring cities. During the early years of the bureau approximately 40 mug shots were taken annually. By the time of Koestle's retirement in 1939 local criminals were being photographed at the rate of 6,000 per year. In 1911 the fingerprinting system was introduced to police work and by 1926 replaced the Bertillon method.

During the first dozen years of the 20th Century, Koestle became a confidante of Police Chief Fred Kohler and Captain Thomas C. Martinec. The relationship served him well, at one time leading to rumors of him being named police chief. During the reign of Chief Frank Smith the two men conferred almost on a daily basis.

Due to Koestle's working relationship with the chief, Smith considered it a good move to have someone in or near Mexico that he could communicate with. Authorities believed that once President Obregon gave the order for the prisoners to be returned to the United States they would cross into Texas by one of three routes – Eagle Pass, Laredo or El Paso. The plan called for Koestle to meet and assist his fellow officers. Smith contacted the chief of police in each city and asked for their cooperation when the prisoners arrived. Once the prisoners were arrested and placed in a Texas jail, Detective Mooney would travel to Columbus and have

Governor Davis sign the extradition papers. On June 6, three days after the arrests, Smith received a telegram from Matowitz that was several days old, informing him that, "We may have to take the men out of Mexico by way of Cuba or Guatemala." This new information scuttled the plans to have them meet Koestle at the Texas border.

The lack of communication coming from Matowitz left the police department and the newspapers in the dark as to what was happening south of the border. Stories appeared daily on the efforts to get the prisoners returned to Cleveland, problems with the Mexican government, and the efforts to rally support from United States government officials and politicians. Matowitz was flabbergasted by the lack of effort from government officials in America. He demanded of Summerell, if there was not someone in all of Mexico who would assist them. Summerell gave him the name of Albert Pani, the Mexican Minister of State. In him the captain found an "amicable gentleman" who had a genuine desire to help.

"I am in trouble and I need your assistance," Matowitz told Pani. He then explained the situation.

"You ask a lot, considering the relations, or lack of relations, between our respective governments," Pani replied. "But don't worry, my boy. First permit me to congratulate you on the capture. It was very fortunate and your courage and your good fortune should not go for nothing. Tell me exactly what you want."

"I want my men held in prison until tomorrow at least," Matowitz answered.

"It shall be done," said Pani.

In retrospect, it was apparent that two stories were going on at the same time. One was what the Cleveland newspapers were reporting based on the efforts going on locally and on what little they could gather from Mexico. The other was the yet unreported, but actual events as Matowitz related once the ordeal was concluded. A summary of the Cleveland reporting through June and July was as follows:

June 7 – After Assistant Prosecutor Cassidy traveled to Columbus to speak with the governor, Davis wired Secretary of State Hughes urging him to "use every means in his power" to effect the return of the prisoners.

Since the most recent telegram from Matowitz was three days old, Chief Smith had no idea where his men even were. It was suspected that if they weren't enroute to the border that perhaps they were trying to track down the other suspects in Mexico – Amato and Lonardo.

June 8 – Matowitz and Cavolo were in Vera Cruz "shadowing" the suspects who were told they could leave Mexico and go to a destination of their own choosing. There was a concern that if they went to Italy they would have to be tried there because there was no extradition treaty with the United States.

The Italian foreign minister in Mexico was being urged, if not outright bribed by Thomas Benigno, to put pressure on President Obregon to let the men leave to a place of their own choosing from Vera Cruz, and to refuse any request from the United States for extradition on the grounds that the U.S. State Department had ruled all treaties between the two countries suspended due to lack of recognition.

Believing that Benigno and Coletto may try to leave for Italy by steamship, a check was made with a local steamship consultant[5] who confirmed that no steamships were leaving Vera Cruz bound for Italy.

Cassidy, back from his trip to Columbus, was off to Washington D.C. to confer with Congressman Theodore E. Burton[6] and Secretary of State Hughes to discuss the extradition of the prisoners. Burton had already been told by Under-Secretary of State Henry P. Fletcher, that nothing could be done due to the absence of diplomatic relations.

Alexander C. Brown, of the Cleveland Chamber of Commerce, sent a telegram to President Obregon with this message:

> "The Cleveland Chamber of Commerce, an organization of 4,000 business and professional men, enjoying an intimate and cordial business relationship with the business interests of Mexico, requests the privilege of expressing to your excellency its earnest hope that you will find it consistent to instruct the proper officials of your government to co-operate with Captain Matowitz and Detective Cavolo of the Cleveland police department, now in Mexico City, in arranging for the apprehension upon American soil of Dominic Benigno and Charles Coletto, who are wanted by Cleveland police authorities in connection with the commission of one or more important crimes in this jurisdiction.

June 9 – Conflicting stories were still being cast about regarding the status of the prisoners. Cassidy was on his way to Washington D.C. in search of aid in the process and wondering if he was going to Cuba, assuming that would be a stop once the men were deported by steamer

After arriving at his hotel in the capital city, Cassidy received a message from Koestle, forwarded from Cleveland, that, "Coletto and Benigno probably will be turned over by Mexican authorities today or tomorrow at Laredo, Tex., to the department of justice, who will put them in jail at Laredo and hold subject to requisition by governor of Ohio. I am leaving San Antonio for Laredo and will advise you when they arrive."

June 11 – It was still unclear where Matowitz and his prisoners were. A report surfaced that the captain of a Spanish ship, docked in Vera Cruz, refused to allow Benigno and Coletto on board.

President Obregon in response to the Chamber of Commerce telegram, wired Alexander C. Brown with this message:

> "Your valued message received. The day before yesterday Dominic Benigno and Charles Coletto were apprehended and, due to considering them undesirable aliens, I apply to them Article thirty-three (of the constitution) under which I rule their expulsion from this country."

United States Senator Frank B. Willis of Ohio contacted the Mexican bureau of the U. S. State Department and added his appeal to those of other Ohio representatives.

Cassidy paid a visit to the White House where he called on Presidential Secretary George Christian. The *Plain Dealer* reported, "He explained his mission in Washington, and Mr. Christian showed keen interest. It was cabinet day and the president's calendar was crowded, but Mr. Christian arranged to have Mr. Cassidy meet President Harding and pay his respects."

Cassidy was able to gain an audience with Secretary of State Hughes, who had previous notice of the situation. He assured Cassidy that everything possible was being done.

June 12 – It was apparent that absolutely nothing was accomplished as a wire from Matowitz to Smith stated, "If you can have men who are acquainted with President Obregon wire him, do so. Case still under consideration." Benigno and Coletto were still sitting inside a jail in Mexico City.

June 15 – The Italian consul in Mexico City was acting as an attorney for Benigno and Coletto, advising the men and trying to influence President Obregon.

The *Cleveland News* reported the Benigno "defense fund campaign" was still in full swing and had collected over $10,000. One East End resident told a reporter, "They came to me a few days ago and said, 'We want $200 from you for Dominic and Charlie.' I haven't any sympathy with the effort to free those men, but I gave the money in a hurry. I knew what would happen to me if I didn't."

June 16 – Because the defense fund money posed a danger to the lives of Matowitz and Cavolo, Chief Smith ordered George Koestle to proceed at once to Mexico City to assist the men.

Fred Caley issued a statement that the Cleveland Automobile Club was prepared to raise their own fund to $20,000 to help authorities with the return of the prisoners.

At one point in late June a telegram arrived from Matowitz stating, "Looks like just one chance to keep our hands on them. But this deal will cost $3,000, at least, and we haven't that much money. Benigno and Coletto have just received $1,000 from some mysterious source."

As was the case throughout the adventure, Cleveland officials were upset with Matowitz's short message. Cleveland Automobile Club officials telegrammed back, "Wire more details, at least 100 words. Don't spare expense."

The response to the Matowitz wire was a plan to send Frank Merrick to Mexico City with $5,000 in "substantial American gold." A request was made through the state department to have a passport prepared and forwarded to Laredo, where Merrick would retrieve it. The Cleveland Automobile Club was also preparing to hire Pinkerton detectives to help watch Benigno and Coletto. The next telegram from Matowitz, however, stated arrangements had finally been made for the deportation.

June 29 – Nearly two weeks had passed and no movement in the situation had occurred. Chief Smith was considering sending a new detail of detectives to Mexico City to relieve Matowitz, Koestle and Cavolo. Smith declared, "I intend to keep men there to watch Benigno and Coletto if it takes ten years. We are going to go to the limit in bringing back the men who took part in the most cold-blooded murder in the history of Cleveland."

A "new ray of light" appeared as Chief Smith was given the name of William Vail to contact. Vail, the assistant secretary of the American Chamber of Commerce, was a personal friend of President Obregon.

June 30 – It was perhaps this last contact with Vail that ended the logjam. The next day the *Plain Dealer* received a message from the American Chamber of Commerce in Mexico City informing them that Benigno and Coletto have been ordered deported immediately from Mexico by President Obregon. The message said the detectives and their prisoners will depart Vera Cruz on the steamship *Columbia* the next day. A check of the steamship registers, however, did not list any vessels under that name at Vera Cruz. That afternoon the *Cleveland News* confirmed that no steamship named *Columbia* was due to arrive or leave Vera Cruz in the near future.

July 1 – Dispatches early in the day claimed that Benigno and Coletto, who were given permission by President Obregon[7] to leave the country on any boat they choose, had selected a French vessel. The ship had a scheduled stop in Havana, Cuba. Authorities in Cleveland were in the process of contacting Cuban police officials to have the men arrested when the ship docked there. Then a second dispatch arrived. It was from Matowitz, dated Mexico City by way of Vera Cruz, it read:

> "We are bringing home the bacon under the American flag. Sailing on the United States bound steamer *Monterey*. Expect to reach New York July 14."

July 2 – Even the good news couldn't survive controversy. After the receipt of Matowitz's telegram, a wire was received by the *Plain Dealer*:

> "Two Italian murderers sailing from Vera Cruz today, July 1 on steamship *Monserrat* of Compania Trans Atlantic Espanola for Havana, New York, Cadiz and Barcelona. Arrives Havana Tuesday or Wednesday. Six days quarantine at Havana against Vera Cruz. Two Cleveland detectives on board *Monserrat*. Mexican government, at their request, bought tickets for Cadiz for Italians."

While everyone wanted to believe the earlier message from Matowitz, some were skeptical, due to the fact that some of his wires had come after considerable delay in the past. All the same, authorities were preparing for a showdown in Havana if indeed Benigno and Coletto were aboard the Spanish vessel. State Department personnel were being contacted, as well as Havana government officials, to assist in the arrest of the pair, if necessary.

July 7 – While Cleveland authorities waited patiently for the *Monterey* to arrive in Havana, Frank Merrick of the Cleveland Automobile Club announced that it was "definitely established" that both Angelo Amato and Dominic Lonardo were in Italy. Merrick declared that the club offered to pay the expenses of detectives to go to Italy and conduct a search for the suspects. The club also offered to pay the expenses of any witnesses who will have to attend the trial.

Meanwhile, George Koestle had arrived in Mexico City to assist in the guarding and the return of the prisoners. What follows is an accounting of the officer's sabbatical, after he arrived in Mexico City, as it was related to a *Cleveland News* reporter:

The three called on Col. Miller, United States military attaché in Mexico City, urging him to assist in holding the prisoners, but he shook his head and said he could do nothing.

Nothing remained but for the Cleveland officers to take turn about at guarding their men in the Mexican jail. And from time to time sundry Mexican officials would approach them and make offers of assisting them in taking Benigno and Coletto from the country, for a money consideration. All such offers were turned down.

Also, from time to time, dark-visaged Mexicans, with bland smiles and an exaggerated courtesy for the particular Cleveland officer on guard, would make their way to the cell where the prisoners were confined, shout something in Spanish and then depart.

Such visits always were followed by periods of great cheerfulness on the part of the captives, and it later dawned on the detectives that messages of hope were being sent in from without.

Who the sender of the relayed message was, however, remained a mystery for the time being. A glimpse of Thomas Benigno, brother of the imprisoned Dominic, on the street one day in earnest conversation with a Mexican solved the riddle. It was Dominic's brother who was inspiring hope in the captives.

The third day after Matowitz had locked up his prisoners he received word that President Obregon, in answer to Minister Pani's petition, had ordered Benigno and Coletto deported, and held in duress until placed aboard ship. The fugitives were removed to Belen prison to await departure of a ship which would take them out of the country.

There was a [French] boat in port and the two prisoners, exercising their right to pick their own vessel, said they would go on that. But the captain, learning they were not [French] subjects, refused to take them.

The Spanish liner Monserrat was the next vessel due to sail, with an American ship, the Monterey, following a close second. This was on June 28, and as it was evident the prisoners would be taken on either one or the other of the steamers, Matowitz notified the Mexican police officials that he would take the train that night for Vera Cruz, the port of embarkation. The Mexican police were to deliver the prisoners aboard whatever boat the murder suspects desired to sail on.

It was at this point that the Cleveland officers learned the depth of Mexican cunning.

Matowitz, on going to the depot to buy his ticket, was told there would be no more trains that night. He returned to the jail and told the officers there was no train, but they insisted there was and that he and his fellow officers had better leave right away. They were trying to give him a hint that it would be well for the American policemen to make themselves scarce, prisoners or no prisoners. They even appeared with a truck and offered them the use of that and the protection of three native policemen.

But Matowitz stood pat. He would not leave his prisoners. So they promised to have Benigno and Coletto at the station at 7 p.m. Matowitz, Koestle and Cavolo waited in vain until almost 9 p.m. when Police Chief Lazerene and three of his Mexican officers appeared on the scene with the two prisoners. They came in a truck. Chief Lazerene insisted there would be a train, but after talking to the ticket agent, he became profusely apologetic.

"Meet me at 10 o'clock tomorrow and I will send your men and three officers with you to Vera Cruz," the chief said.

But Matowitz stood pat for immediate action, and by way of emphasizing the fact that he would not become a victim of trickery he told Benigno and Coletto that he would follow them to whatever part of the earth they led him.

"My instructions are not to give up until you are behind the bars in Cleveland," was his emphatic declaration.

At this Benigno and Coletto conferred, spoke to the Mexican officers in Spanish for several minutes and then suddenly declared their willingness to give themselves over into the custody of Matowitz and his companion.

So the trip to Vera Cruz was begun and on the following day, June 29, Benigno and Coletto were formally turned over to the Cleveland officers and placed aboard the steamship Monterey, due to sail July 1 for New York via Havana, Cuba.

Even at Mexico City the cunning of the native officers, probably having a leaning toward the prisoners through the efforts of Thomas Benigno, and his display of money, tried to spirit the captives away. While turning the two over to the Cleveland officers they suggested the men be placed in the Vera Cruz jail.

A few words of Spanish between the prisoners and a Mexican officer, however, were understood by Cavolo. Benigno had been told by the Mexican that he need not worry – that some way would be found to get him away in freedom.

Cavolo conveyed the intelligence to Matowitz and it was decided to put the prisoners aboard the Monterey at once. The captain, Albert Smith, was agreeable, and the prisoners were handcuffed, locked in a stateroom and placed under guard.

Late that night Bertillon Expert Koestle became suspicious that further trickery might be attempted, and he went on guard duty on the other side of the prison-stateroom, which overlooked the dock.

As he took up his post he saw two men crouch down behind several cases. They managed to get away under cover of the high piles of goods on the wharf.

"I am certain Thomas Benigno was still busy," said Koestle, "for while on guard a Mexican private detective came to me and told me Benigno's brother had tried to hire him to effect the escape of the two before that ship sailed."

According to the detective, it was planned for the prisoners to throw themselves into the water, where they would be rescued and carried away in a boat.

The Monterey *sailed the morning of July 1 and made her first stop at Tampico, where she laid over five days, during which many attempts were made to get word to the prisoners.*

On leaving Tampico the boat sailed for Progresso, where it was learned that a cablegram for $500 had reached Vera Cruz for the prisoners a few hours after they had sailed. The cabled money order was from a Cleveland bank, and the money was no doubt part of the immense fund raised in the Forest City to aid the fugitives in eluding capture.

At Havana a man tried to board the Monterey *to see the prisoners, but he was turned back by Havana police, who had been sent to the dock as special guard in response to a radiogram previously sent to the Havana chief by Smith.*

As the *Monterey* neared Havana for the short layover, management officials for the *Plain Dealer* back in Cleveland were preparing to get an exclusive interview with Matowitz when he arrived in the Cuban capital by way of a new Key West-to-Cuba telephone cable, which had only been in operation for six weeks. The lucky reporter who got to conduct the historic interview was Joseph H. Zucker, whom Matowitz was familiar with. It was clear from the first question the captain asked Zucker what was on the minds of all three officers.

"My God, Joe," Matowitz barked into the receiver, "It seems good to hear someone you know. How are all our families?"

Matowitz then gave this account of their departure from Mexico:

"You know the president of Mexico finally ordered Benigno and Coletto deported through Vera Cruz, and had tickets purchased for them on the Monserrat. *This was after they had been given their choice of a vessel sailing from Vera Cruz and had tried to get tickets on a French liner for Italy, but had been refused by the French captain.*

"Well the Monserrat was due to sail July 3. As our orders were to follow them to the end of the world, we had just about made up our minds to go to Spain, too.

"But in the meantime the Monterey came into port and we learned she was going to get away from Havana and New York on the night of July 1.

"So we got busy and pulled a few wires here and there which worked better than the wires the prisoners had been pulling right along, and God knows they had been pulling a lot of 'em.

"I'm not going to tell you everything, but on the night of July 1 we had them on the Monterey as our prisoners for the first time, because up to then they had been held only as undesirables.

"This lack of any formal relation between the United States and the present Mexican government has just played hob with our work. We're all in.

"From the time we first laid hands on them [Benigno and Coletto], we had to watch them day and night ourselves. We were never sure of them, and I won't feel safe till we pull out of this harbor.

In discussing the hardships the men endured, Matowitz confirmed that both Cavolo and Koestle had "a touch of fever" having fallen victim to the tropical heat. "But those fellows never quit on the job," the captain proudly added. "They took their turns on guard, sick or well. But I'll tell you the strain has been almost unbearable. Koestle's hair is turning white."

Zucker then turned the telephone over to Chief Smith.

"Congratulations!" bellowed the chief.

"Thanks," replied Matowitz. "But chief we're broke. Whoever you send down to New York, tell him to bring us some money."

"Don't worry," Smith laughed, "We'll have Fred Caley and probably others from the Automobile Club with us at the pier. They say the sky's the limit. Just bring home those prisoners. Anything else we can do?"

"Tell our people not to worry," the Captain stated. "We got the bacon and are going to hang on to it."

Smith turned the telephone back over to Zucker, who questioned the captain for a few more minutes. The reporter asked him about Koestle's arrival in Mexico City.

"We sure were glad to see him," Matowitz replied. "We'd been doing twelve hour tours of guard duty, and we needed some relief." Matowitz talked about their departure from Vera Cruz:

"Benigno and Coletto were mighty disappointed when they found they couldn't get an Italian ship at Vera Cruz. They tried the French line as their next best bet, and we in our turn were mighty happy when the French captain refused to carry them.

"The Mexican government had finally bought tickets on the Spanish liner Monserrat, *officials declaring they couldn't enjoy their siestas till this matter was off their hands.*

"Talk about the uneasy seat. At Vera Cruz we didn't even have them in jail, although, as Mexican jails go, I don't know that made much difference.

"They were sent to a hotel, and we as a matter of course, became star boarders at the same place. We never let them out of our sight. We played checkers with them by day and stood over them while they slept at night.

[The prisoners were] *"Sulky, most of the time. But occasionally they'd brighten up and get interested in our checker games.*

"Benigno asks constantly, 'How did you find we were in Mexico?'"

Zucker was anxious to hear how the trio managed to get the prisoners aboard the American ship *Monterey*, when they had passage on the Spanish *Monserrat*. Matowitz was not as anxious to tell this story. "Gosh, I'm glad to hear your voice, Joe, but have a heart. That'll keep till we get to Cleveland."

"Was it done at night?" Zucker persisted.

"Oh, well, it was just before the *Monterey* left," the captain stated. "Just hold your horses, Joe. Wait till we get home. We might write a book."

With that Matowitz said, "But say, Joe, you better let me get back to the ship. We leave very soon, and she's whistling now. Don't forget to tell our folks we're all right."

When Matowitz arrived in New York he revealed to *Cleveland Press* reporter Kenneth R. Watson how they got the men on the *Monterey* at Vera Cruz:

"The American boat was sailing in two days. We made arrangements with the captain to take our prisoners on board the night before it sailed. We entertained the prisoners with wine. Darkness helped, and they thought they were being taken on board the Spanish steamer Monserrat *when we took them aboard the American steamer* Monterey.

"We allowed the two prisoners liberty of the decks during the day, but locked them up in their state room at night. At each port we feared an effort to release the prisoners, for Benigno's brother had arrived in Mexico with plenty of money, and had been active in his behalf at Mexico City, boasting that Benigno and Coletto never would be taken back to the United States.

"We were warned of a plan for the two men to jump overboard and be picked up by friends while the steamer was in port at Tampico.

"After that one of us slept with the prisoners while another watched outside."

The *Monterey* left Havana on Sunday and was expected to reach New York on July 14. From Havana to New York the trip was uneventful. The monotony, according to the officers, was terrible. They never once left the area housing the prisoners until the ship reached Pier 15 at Brooklyn. One officer always slept with the prisoners while the other stood guard just outside.

Back in Cleveland, a welcoming committee, including Chief Smith, Harry Parsons, Fred Caley and Frank Merrick, was preparing to leave for New York. On Monday the *Cleveland Press* printed a ludicrous story claiming a plot was in the works to free the prisoners. They reported, "Friends of Benigno and Coletto already are in New York awaiting the arrival of the two suspects from Mexico City…They have criminal gangs organized at all stations en route to Cleveland ready to rush the train." If liberating them from the train didn't work, a jail break was planned for the men as soon as they were placed in the county jail. Fueling this latter rumor was the June 23 escape of Bobby Hunt, James Walsh and a third man from the county jail.

Police had absolutely no incriminating evidence or one eyewitness that could tie Coletto to the murders. Although indicted, he could only be found guilty of choosing the wrong traveling companion. That being said, there was no reason for Coletto to be "rescued" from his captors; meaning that he was more in danger of being "liberated" than he was of being convicted of any crime.

On Thursday afternoon, July 14, the *Monterey* reached the New York City harbor. Benigno in a vain attempt to avoid being brought onto American soil, asked that he be detained at Ellis Island as an alien. The immigration commission denied his request. As the ship made its way from quarantine to the pier in Brooklyn, Matowitz stood near the rail with a green and yellow parrot perched on his shoulder. He later explained that he named the bird, *Manana* (Spanish for tomorrow). "We'd got so used to hearing that word that we just couldn't get along without it after we got aboard the *Monterey*. So, when we touched at Tampico, I went ashore and got this bird.

"Hey, you!" Matowitz called to the bird, "Say 'Manana!'"

With that the parrot screeched, "Manana," over and over.

"Nearly all our troubles in Mexico were due to that word," Matowitz recalled. "But then again, we may owe our lives to it, and our successes in guarding our prisoners."

The next day Matowitz was worried about the bird after it hadn't eaten or repeated its favorite word. "I think it's the Volstead Act," the captain joked. "He misses his mescal in this country."

"Give me the bird," demanded Fred Caley.

"Then what'll I do?" asked Matowitz

"Oh, you can get another next time you go to Mexico," Caley replied.

"Fat chance," responded the captain. "Next time someone goes down there it'll be someone else [who pursues]."

"That goes for us, too," piped in Cavolo and Koestle.

Koestle was still fuming about having to pay $1.85 duty on a dozen packs of cigarettes he purchased in Vera Cruz, which originally cost him only 75 cents.

"If I'd known this I would not have bought 'em," complained the Bertillon expert.

An unsympathetic customs agent responded, "Well, you've got 'em now, haven't you?"

The next morning Benigno and Coletto were arraigned in a Brooklyn courtroom. The two were ordered held as fugitives from justice. Cleveland officials were awaiting the arrival of detective Mooney with the extradition papers. The prisoners, despite the severity of the charges they were facing, remained outwardly calm. The *Cleveland News* reported:

> "Benigno, a handsome chap, tall and well proportioned, has made no statement other than that he was not present at the scene of the double killing.
>
> "His companion. A mere boy, nattily dressed and outwardly cheerful, has maintained constant silence regarding the crime that may mean the death chair for him."

The Cleveland officials suddenly had time to kill when there was a change in the extradition procedure. The paperwork Governor Davis signed was for the sole indictment of Wilfred Sly. According to the law, prisoners could only be tried for the charges they were extradited for. If Benigno, for some reason, was acquitted of the Sly murder, he could not be tried for the killing of George Fanner. Prosecutor Stanton insisted that double extradition papers be prepared "for any emergency that might arise."

While the men awaited Mooney's arrival with the additional paperwork, the police officers, instead of taking a well-deserved rest, busied themselves with investigative work in the Dan Kaber murder, which was currently being tried in Cleveland.

Meanwhile, Caley talked with *Plain Dealer* reporter Joseph Zucker. He explained that the Cleveland Automobile Club was ready to go forward with sending Detectives Cavolo and Mooney to Sicily to find Amato and

Lonardo, as well as Vittorio Pisselli, one of the "hit men" in the Kaber murder case.[8] Caley told Chief Smith, "If the remainder of the gang are in Italy, I want you to send someone to run them down and put them in jail. I know Italy seldom permits extradition but that is an obstacle that we will try to meet when the time comes. At least the Italian authorities will be furnished with the proper evidence which, if the slayers are apprehended, will keep them in prison for life."

Caley also announced that he was proposing to the directors of the club that a contingency fund of $10,000 be set aside for the Cleveland Police Department to help run down criminals "who in any way" use automobiles in their activities. He said Frank Merrick would be charged with building a greater cooperation between the club and the police to see that auto thieves were punished.

The auto club secretary, who was rooming with Smith, told a story about how much the ordeal with Benigno and Coletto was occupying the chief's mind. Caley said he was awakened by Smith in the early morning hours. He said the chief, while still in a deep sleep, was sitting up in bed, fists clenched, and shouted, "I tell you, you should have put 'em in irons!"

Back in Cleveland, the family of Charles Coletto was already preparing to defend him. His father and four brothers, all living at 12010 Paul Avenue, claimed he had an airtight alibi and plenty of witnesses to prove it.

On Saturday night, July 16, two more lives were extinguished in connection with the Sly-Fanner murders. Frank "Little Frankie" Amato and Mike Rosalina, said to be cousins of Angelo Amato and Frank Motto, were killed by police in a shootout outside the Baldwin Reservoir, near Fairmount Boulevard and Baldwin Road. The young men were 28 and 19 respectively. Amato was referred to as the "brains of the reservoir gang." Police suspected they were behind a wave of local robberies that were being pulled to feed the defense fund of the Sly-Fanner killers.

Patrolmen Thomas Fagan and Frank Garrett were working plain clothes duty that night, staking out several roads leading to the reservoir, which had become a rendezvous for street gangs. Around 10:30 p.m. three men showed up, whom the officers thought were suspicious. Fagan and Garrett stopped the trio, identified themselves and began to search the men. Suddenly one of the trio pulled out a weapon and fired a shot past the ear of Fagan. A deadly shootout followed. Rosalina fell dead with a bullet in his brain, Amato took a bullet in the back while running away, and the third man, John Bennis, escaped. Seconds after the shooting stopped, "Little Frankie" returned, staggering toward Fagan and Garrett. The bullet had hit Amato in his shoulder blade and deflected into his lung.

"I'm shot," he said. "You got me, boys. Take me to a hospital." Amato then dropped unconscious at their feet. Taken to Mount Sinai Hospital, "Little Frankie" died twenty minutes later. The bodies of the two cousins lie side by side in the county morgue before they were officially identified. Police quickly captured Bennis,[9] who denied knowing the other two men; that was until Rosalina's heart-broken 17 year-old sister, apparently uneducated in the practice of omerta, identified him the next day. "That is the man my brother associated with. They went out together last night," the young lady declared.

In New York City, on July 18, Benigno and Coletto, now in the Raymond Street Jail in Brooklyn, were taken to the assistant district attorney's office to await the extradition papers from Albany. Detective Cavolo had gone to the state capital to meet Mooney. The two men returned with the proper paperwork and signatures around 5:00 p.m. From there everyone headed to board a "special car" of the New York Central Railroad, and at 6:45 that evening the train was on its way west.

Smith took an unusual, but highly effective precaution in securing the prisoners. He had Benigno and Coletto stripped of their clothes and then placed in a drawing room with two detectives while more stood guard outside the door. If they were going to escape, it would be in the nude.

It was an uneventful train ride from New York City through up-state New York. The prisoners woke up shortly after the train left Buffalo. They washed, shaved and dressed. New white collars topped off their neatly-pressed dark suits.

Before leaving New York City, Chief Smith sent a telegram to the Central headquarters ordering additional men to meet the train at Union Station. Another detail was ordered to board the train at East 105th and accompany the group the last few miles. When the train reached the East 105th Street Station, a police sergeant spotted a "swarthy stranger riding the rods" of the car Benigno and Coletto occupied. The sergeant dragged the man to the platform and ordered him to "beat it!" Bystanders and spectators thought the man was a member of a plot to free the prisoners.

As the train pulled into Union Station the *Cleveland News* gave this description of the goings on there:

> "A crowd of fully two thousand persons, most of them women, thronged the train sheds and the streets near the union station long before the arrival of the train. Fifty detectives, augmented by a score of patrolmen and three flying squadrons, guarded entrances to the station and fought to keep the crowds back."

At the station the prisoners were brought off the train in handcuffs. The people gathered about the entrance of the station were there simply to catch a glimpse of the two prisoners after having followed a month and a half of news coverage on the pair. In addition, a large contingent of friends was on hand to welcome the two back. Calls of, "Hello, Dominic!" and "Have a good time, Charlie?" echoed through the station. Police were forced to push their way out of the station, but there were no incidents and certainly no attempt was made to free the two men.

Benigno and Coletto exited the train and passed through the crowds without a look of concern on their faces. Both scanned the crowd in hopes of seeing a familiar face. But when photographers from the newspapers began snapping their pictures, both pulled their hats down and tried to conceal their faces. They were soon placed in a squad car and were off to police headquarters.

The prisoners were taken to the office of Chief Smith, where they were asked a number of questions. They were then taken to the Bertillon room where they were measured and photographed. Benigno and Coletto then went through the first of two arraignments. The first one took place in Judge Bernon's courtroom, where they were arraigned on the indictment for the murder of Wilfred Sly. Both pleaded not guilty and trial dates were set – September 12 for Benigno and September 26 for Coletto. They were remanded to the county jail without bail. After this arraignment Bernon took a moment to thank the Cleveland Automobile Club and Fred Caley for their efforts in bringing about the capture of the two prisoners. Addressing Frank Merrick, the judge stated, "The club's financing of the expedition to capture the hunted men was of vast public benefit. All that the club has done, and its proposal to maintain a fund of $10,000 to enable police to take up immediate pursuit of criminals, are deserving of the highest commendation."

Ironically, a week after Bernon's remarks praising the Cleveland Automobile Club, a peculiar article appeared in the *News* titled: "Auto Club Gets No Money Back On Benigno Trip." The story pointed out that the club had spent some $5,000 of its own money, nearly $4,000 of it being advanced to Matowitz and Cavolo. Mayor William S. Fitzgerald was quoted, "There was no agreement concerning the money. We understood the club offered the money willingly. The city has no intention of attempting to pay it back." The county commissioners were in sync with the mayor's stand. Commissioner Fred Kohler, the former police chief, stated, "So far we haven't even considered reimbursing the automobile club for the expenses of the trip. We considered the club had financed it without expecting to be repaid in money. The expenses are pretty heavy for us to attempt to pay."

Fred Caley responded that the club had made a very good investment. He reported that the Cleveland Automobile Manufacturers and Dealers had split the costs 50/50 with them.

What makes the article so bizarre is that there was no explanation as to why the matter was brought up. Caley did criticize the city's annual appropriation "for the pursuit of criminals outside the city." The amount was only $1,000. Caley reiterated the club was considering setting aside $10,000 for future similar needs.

More than a year later, on October 22, 1922, despite comments to the contrary, the Cleveland Automobile Club presented an itemized bill to the county commissioners totaling $4,303. Assistant County Prosecutor Edward J. Thobaben[10] explained to the board that they were responsible for money spent on the capture of criminals. The majority of the expenses were for railroad and steamship fares and hotel bills. It wasn't revealed if *Manana*, the parrot purchased by Matowitz, was one of the itemized items.

After the arraignment for the murder of Wilfred Sly, Benigno and Coletto were arraigned a second time, based on warrants charging them with the murder of George Fanner, before Justice of the Peace Charles N. Carter. Held in an anteroom of Prosecutor Stanton's office, Coletto waived examination, but Benigno demanded a hearing. During the arraignment, one of the spectators was George J. Fanner, the father of the victim. When Benigno saw that Carter was ready to proceed, he insisted the hearing be postponed until he could obtain counsel. Carter refused his request and began hearing testimony, which began with Phil Mooney. The detective testified that Benigno was present at the murder scene in his automobile, and had supplied the weapons used in the robbery / killings.

Benigno laughed while the accusations were made against him. At one point Coletto asked, "Why are you people holding me? No one has said that I was there or knew anything about it."

"You fled, didn't you?" Stanton barked out, "Why did you run away if you knew nothing of the affair?"

At this point Coletto merely smiled while Benigno continued his laughter. Again, both men were ordered held without bail. Taken to the county jail, Sheriff Stannard placed the prisoners in separate cells in the "murderer's row" section.[11]

Detectives prepared a line-up for the prisoners to appear in. Benigno sauntered in shirtless and he and Coletto smoked cigarettes as they joined a dozen prisoners and marched before Louis Komer. At this point Benigno's confidant façade began to fade. The hand holding the cigarette trembled as Komer pointed him out as being present at the murder scene.

The sight of Komer also made Coletto nervous, even though the prosecution's key witness had no way of identifying him. Coletto was placed in a second group of prisoners and again Komer didn't point him out as being a participant. There had to be some concern on the part of police and prosecutors as to what to do with Coletto. No witness could put him on the bridge. The only thing police could charge him with was accessory after the fact, because he aided in Benigno's escape and had accompanied him. An attempt to prove that Coletto had any prior knowledge of the crime would be nearly impossible, unless one of the defendants confessed to it.

During the afternoon, attorney Zottarelli, along with Benigno's wife and mother-in-law, arrived at the jail. The lawyer was asked by the women to meet with Benigno to see if he was interested in retaining him. With Zottarelli's record currently at 0 and 2, Benigno was considering other options. The attorney was allowed to meet with the prisoner, but the women were turned away. The sheriff had a standing order that neither friends nor relatives of prisoners held for first-degree murder were permitted at the jail since Motto's last visitor had almost foiled the effort to retrieve the guns hidden in the lumberyard.

Zottarelli had an easier time gaining entry than did attorney John A. Cline, who sought to represent Coletto. Cline, a former Cuyahoga County Prosecutor, was denied access to the prisoner and had to get permission granted by Common Pleas Judge Thomas M. Kennedy.

Authorities were faced with greater problems than prisoners' families and building a case against Coletto. First a letter was received at police headquarters containing a threat to blow up the jail. Then an Italian lawyer revealed he overheard a "Mafia plot" to assassinate Detective Cavolo for his role in the capture of Benigno and Coletto. The News reported that "every man connected" with bringing the two suspects back from Mexico had received death threats. Detectives Mooney and Cavolo seemed to be the main targets. Cavolo was told he would be shot on sight if he ever again entered Little Italy. Meanwhile, a police guard was stationed at the Matowitz home since mid-June.

There remains one more story to be told about the capture of Benigno and Coletto in Mexico City. In January 1923, Henry Dillon Mollohan, a native Ohioan now living and conducting business in Mexico City, arrived in Cleveland to present Assistant County Prosecutor Edward J. Thobaben with a bill for his services. Mollohan insisted he was entitled to a share of the $500 Sly-Fanner reward money that was offered by the county, which he claimed was promised to him by Matowitz.

Mollohan said that after Benigno and Coletto were placed in jail by Mexican authorities, Matowitz was getting nowhere with the extradition effort. He decided to pay a visit to the palace of President Obregon to see where that would lead him. Mollohan's business partner, Joseph Polin was the brother-in-law of Obregon and both men were at the palace that day. Mollohan's story was:

> "I happened to be there playing cards with my business partner and I noticed the Americans. I talked to Matowitz and he told me of his difficulties. He promised to see that I got a share of the reward if I accomplished anything toward getting the men in his hands.
>
> "Polin and I arranged with an international lawyer to draw up extradition papers for Benigno and his companion on the ground that they were undesirable citizens. It took considerable figuring to get the extradition papers signed by both the minister of state and the president, especially since both had previously refused.
>
> "However, the minister went out of town and his assistant signed the papers after which the president's signature was obtained. Then we arrested the two men. I arranged for the Mexican officers and paid them out of my pocket. I also paid $100 of the $200 fee to the lawyer."

The six-foot, three-inch tall Mollohan said once a boat had been arranged for, that he went to the train with the prisoners and personally tied them to their seats because Matowitz, Cavolo and Koestle had no authority to touch them. While tying Benigno's hands, his captive told him, "I may not live to get you for this, but I have a lot of friends who will."

Mollohan said he was paid $700 by the Chamber of Industry and received $300 from the Industrial Association, but was still due $500 from Cuyahoga County. When approached about the matter, Matowitz stated that he agreed to see that Mollohan received a portion of the reward, but only if his actions were instrumental in getting the prisoners out of the country. The Detective Captain challenged Mollohan to prove that his efforts were actually helpful.

In response, Mollohan declared, "Matowitz knows he would never have gotten the men if he had not come to us. He gave me a contract that I would get a third of the rewards." Mollohan's meeting with Thobaben produced little hope for the businessman. The assistant prosecutor informed him that the files with the records of what was paid out in rewards, along with other court documents, were misplaced. In a parting shot before returning home, Mollohan told reporters, "If rewards were easier to collect there would be fewer American fugitives in Mexico."

Chapter Endnotes

1. Harry C. Gahn (April 26, 1880 – November 2, 1962) was a lawyer, city council member, congressman, and public official." – *The Encyclopedia of Cleveland History*. A one-time law partner of Theodore E. Burton, Gahn was a member of Cleveland City Council from 1911 to 1921, serving as council president from 1918 to 1919. During that time he was a member of the Cleveland River & Harbor Commission. He was elected to the U.S. Congress from Ohio's 21st District in 1921 and served one term.

2. The capture of the two men was announced by Stanton. The *Cleveland News*, the first newspaper to report the capture, claimed the arrests took place in Guadalajara. They also added a new version as to how the detectives knew the men were hiding in Mexico. The article stated, "Benigno and Coletto…were in Guadalajara, practically stranded, without funds. They disclosed their hiding place by writing to Cleveland friends for money with which they might escape to South America. The letter was intercepted and turned over to Frank Merrick, special investigator to the automobile club."

3. Mexico was in a state of civil war since February 1913, when the government of Francisco Madero was overrun and Madero executed. The United States extended de facto recognition to Venustiano Caranza (president 1914-1920) in October 1915. In March 1917, Caranza's secretary of war, Alvaro Obregon retired. Obregon had visions of grandeur and began to build a relationship with advisors to President Woodrow Wilson in late 1917. It took several years to build his power base, but by the spring of 1920 he was ready to strike. Caranza was forced out of the capital city and fled to Vera Cruz, where he was assassinated on May 20. Obregon was elected president in September 1920 and took office in December. Obregon worked to build good relationships with the United States, mostly through the sale of Mexican petroleum, but this took place after the Benigno-Coletto incident in the summer of 1921.

4. The Bertillon system was the first scientific method of criminal identification, developed by the French criminologist Alphonse Bertillon (1853–1914). The system, based on the classification of skeletal and other body measurements and characteristics, was officially adopted in France in 1888, and soon after in other countries. Fingerprinting, added later as a supplementary measure, has largely replaced the system. www.infoplease.com

5. Charles A. Seiner, chief clerk of Akers, Folkman & Lawrence.

6. Theodore Elijah Burton (December 20, 1851 – October 28, 1929) "was a recognized authority on river and harbor improvements and economic, monetary, and banking legislation. As a Republican, he served in the U.S. House of Representatives from 1889-91, 1895-1909, and 1921-28 and was U.S. senator from Ohio from 1909-15 and from 1928 until his death." – *The Encyclopedia of Cleveland History*. Burton was appointed by President Theodore Roosevelt as chairman of the Inland Waterways Commission 1907-1908 and of the National Waterways Commission 1908-1912. Burton is buried in Lake View Cemetery.

7. Alvaro Obregon served as President of Mexico until 1924. He ran for re-election in 1928 winning after a bitterly contested election. On July 17, 1928, Obregon was with friends at an open air restaurant when Jose deLeon Toral, a young man, posing as an artist, came up to him and extended his sketch pad. When Obregon reached for it, Toral drew a pistol and shot him four times in the face killing him instantly. An investigation showed the assassin was manipulated into killing Obregon by a nun named Mother Conchita. Toral was tortured and shot and after a trial Mother Conchita and other conspirators were sent to a penal colony. She was released in the 1970s.

8. In late November 1921, Charles Cavolo and Phillip Mooney traveled to Sicily where they tracked Pisselli down and captured him. They were able to get a written confession from him shortly before friends and family hired one of the top attorneys in Italy to represent him. Tried in the Italian courts for the murder of Dan Kaber, Pisselli was sentenced to 30 years of hard labor. The two detectives returned to the United States in mid-January 1922.

9. At the time of this incident John Bennis was already wanted for robbery. He was soon convicted and sentenced to a fifteen-year term in the Ohio Penitentiary. On October 1, 1921, a dance hall security officer from Luna Park identified Bennis as the man who fought with him, took his gun and then shot him back on May 15 on Woodland Avenue near East 110th Street.

10. Edward J. Thobaben became associated with the Cuyahoga County Prosecutor's office with the election of Edward C. Stanton in November

1920. Assigned to the county commissioner's office, his specialty was preparing legislation for work on highways and public works. He was born in Hamilton, Ontario, but spent his adult life in Cleveland. Thobaben was a long-time lawyer and a prominent member of the Masons, where he served in the position of "high priest" of the Cleveland Chapter. He died at the age of 83 on October 7, 1947, at the Ohio Masonic Home in Springfield. He is buried in Woodland Cemetery.

11. By that time Bobby Hunt and James Walsh were recaptured and placed in the same jail wing. A special guard was posted day and night to insure the men wouldn't attempt another escape. Once Benigno and Coletto arrived, a second deputy was added while additional men were posted outside the jail.

12

Execution of Frank Motto

At the height of the activity to return Benigno and Coletto from Mexico, the appeals process for Frank Motto and Sam Purpura continued. On July 1 the court of appeals upheld the conviction of Frank Motto. Zottarelli announced he would carry the appeal to the next level, the Ohio State Supreme Court. In its ruling the court of appeals stated:

> "Taking the whole evidence together from the whole record one can come to no other conclusion than that Motto was one of the ringleaders in this atrocious murder, and that there is an abundance of evidence in this record and throughout this record, which would warrant his conviction of the crime."

The same day, attorney Zottarelli filed a petition in error with the appeals court asking for a new trial for Sam Purpura. Zottarelli claimed, "The court erred in failing to charge the jury that if the evidence permitted, it could find the defendant guilty of second degree murder or manslaughter." In addition, he listed eleven other reasons in requesting a new trial.

Meanwhile, Frank Motto counted down the days in his death row jail cell. On August 9, just twenty days before the scheduled execution was to be carried out, the Ohio Supreme Court sustained the death decree, denying defense counsel permission to take the case before the court of appeals. Zottarelli immediately announced he would file briefs with the United States Supreme Court claiming that Motto was about to lose his life without due process of law. The attorney's contention was that Motto should have been granted a change of venue. In his appeal he claimed, "The jury at Cleveland was biased against our client and we could not get a fair or impartial trial." He also charged misconduct on the part of prosecutors. What constituted the "misconduct" Zottarelli failed to explain.

Motto's death row companion, Sam Purpura, faired a little better. His execution was deferred while his final state appeal was being heard. One week later Governor Davis met with Ohio Attorney General John G. Price and Superintendent of Pardons & Paroles, the Reverend John Rutledge. After a two-hour conference, the governor announced, "There would be no reprieve for either Frank Motto or Sam Purpera." Zottarelli had asked for the reprieve while he carried Motto's case to the U.S. Supreme Court. The announcement "shattered" any chance of Davis ordering clemency.

On Friday, August 26, U.S. Supreme Court Justice Joseph McKenna[1] denied Zottarelli's application for a stay of execution. The attorney filed an application for a writ of certiorari[2] in a desperate attempt to gain a stay. The writ was frivolous, meaning Motto's only hope to remain alive was for Governor Davis to reverse his earlier decision and grant clemency. The only concession Davis made was that he would grant a reprieve only if asked by Stanton to keep Motto alive to testify against the others, but with Komer in hand that request would not be forthcoming.

The 48 hours prior to Motto's execution, scheduled to be carried out after midnight on Monday, August 29, proved to be hectic ones and provided the Sly-Fanner murder case with its biggest mystery.

In court that Saturday, Zottarelli made a final impassioned plea before Judge Allen, asking her for a stay so that he might carry the case, on appeal for a writ of certiorari, to the U.S. Supreme Court, which wasn't available to hear the request over the weekend.

Allen was adamant. The *Plain Dealer* noted in reporting her response that, "there was no more tremor in Judge Allen's voice when she made the decision than on the day, three months ago, when she sentenced Motto to the chair." Judge Allen told counsel, "Motto was tried and sentenced before me. For that reason I should be inclined to lean backward in my efforts to be fair to him. Two higher courts, however, have affirmed his conviction. I feel therefore that I must decline to grant the stay.

"The law gives the authority to grant a reprieve only to the governor of the state. Under the law, the sentence which was imposed in one term of court cannot be suspended by a judge during the subsequent term." With that statement, Allen washed her hands of the matter.

Zottarelli knew it was futile to approach the governor. Davis had failed to react to recent petitions signed by 3,000 persons to change his decision regarding clemency for the prisoner. The petition claimed that the signers didn't believe Motto was on the scene when the shooting occurred and that the "newspapers had succeeded in imposing upon Motto a jury of twelve who had already formed an opinion of his guilt."

Since his incarceration, Motto had spoken little with reporters who sought to interview him. Part of his reason for remaining silent was stories that were printed about him while he was in prison. One story claimed that he "curses and raves" much of the time; another declared "he prays and weeps twelve hours daily." When asked about the conduct of the prisoner, Warden Preston E. Thomas stated, "He has been quiet, respectful and orderly." Laughing, he added, "He's been looking for a chance to break away, but it's my business to see that he doesn't get it."

On Saturday afternoon Motto spoke to a *Plain Dealer* reporter in the back of the prison chapel. He was reflective and thoughtful in the statements he made, most of which were self-serving:

➤ I've thought about the case, but I haven't thought much about myself. I had nothing to do with the killing, but I helped plan the robbery, though Louis Komer was the instigator. He lied when he said I instigated it.

➤ I never got a cent out of the robbery, and it cost me $25. After I read about the killing, Komer came to me and said he was broke, so I handed him $25 of my own money to help him. After that he testified that I had instigated it.

➤ There were seven of us in the original plan, four that I knew, two that I never saw before, and me. I never knew the name of one man. Komer picked Sam Purpura, Dominic Benigno, Angelo Amato and me, and then he brought in a man named Dominic Lonardo and another. I never saw them before, and I don't know the other man's name. All I knew were Komer, Purpura, Benigno and Amato.

➤ [While the murders took place] I was in a poolroom playing pool. I went outside and stole a Cadillac car in front of Stoner's restaurant. Mr. Stoner saw me and could have identified me. I told [attorney] Cartwright about it, but he didn't call Mr. Stoner and he didn't call the big man at the Williamson Building, who could have identified me to support Mr. Stoner's identification, if he were called. (This last comment confirmed his statement to Judge Allen after the verdict in which he claimed: "I did not have all the questions asked me that I wanted by the prosecutor or by my own attorneys.")

Motto claimed that one of the four men he knew was Angelo Amato. When asked if Angelo Amato was a relative, he replied, "No. He has the same name, but he isn't a cousin or anything else – not even a distant relative."

One comment Motto made that was not self-serving was in declaring that Charles Coletto had nothing to do with the robbery or killings. Motto described him as "a good kid" and that Coletto didn't "even know that it was going to be pulled off."

Before concluding the impromptu interview, Motto told the reporter that he was treated fine at the penitentiary. He was looking forward to seeing his wife and family again.

Sunday morning at the Ohio Penitentiary was anything but uneventful. First, two prisoners attempted to escape.[3] The men, one a bank robber the other in for stealing, formed keys out of tin and used them to pick the locks in their cell block. They over-powered a guard, taking his weapon and keys, before binding, blind-folding and gagging him. Their plan was to use the guard's keys to let themselves out of the prison. But once they got to the "big gate" they found that none of the keys unlocked it. They beat a retreat back to their cell block and locked themselves in just minutes before the bound guard was discovered. A search of the cell block uncovered the guard's revolver and keys still in the possession of the prisoners. Both men were immediately placed in solitary confinement. After the escape attempt, Warden Thomas posted extra guards.

A restlessness swept through the prison as Motto's hour of fate moved ever closer. At different times that day, three automobiles filled with men cruised past the penitentiary causing concern that friends of Motto might attempt to spring him. Death threats were directed at Davis resulting in police placing patrolmen at the governor's residences in both Cleveland and Columbus.[4]

Sadly, some 36 hours before the execution, Mrs. Mary A. Sly died of a heart attack. The 84 year-old mother of Wilfred Sly died at the home of her daughter, Maude S. Hoffman on Saturday afternoon. Hoffman told reporters that her mother "was keenly interested in the trials of the men involved in the case and visited the courtroom when Sam Purpera was on trial. Her desire was to live to see that all those connected with the murder were electrocuted." Hoffman said that while her mother's death was attributed to heart disease, it was directly due to the murder of her son. Mary Sly was buried next to her son and husband in Lake View Cemetery.

With less than 24 hours to go before the execution, a bombshell went off. One tidbit that was not released during the Motto interview with the *Plain Dealer* correspondent was that a Cleveland police officer was involved in the planning of the robbery. Although law enforcement officials in Cleveland and Columbus regarded the accusation as "an eleventh-hour attempt" on the part of the prisoner to gain a reprieve, they moved to address it.

George Matowitz rushed to Columbus where he interviewed Motto in the presence of Warden Thomas and a Columbus detective. Motto declared what he knew about the West Side police patrolman was hearsay that came from Komer. He claimed the officer had driven Komer around the area near the robbery site to show him "the lay of the land." Motto gave his interrogators the name of the officer and said he had received ten percent of the take for his role.

Matowitz didn't have far to travel for his next interrogation. He stepped over to the cell of Sam Purpura. The distraught prisoner dropped to his knees and cried out, "Before God, I will tell you the whole truth." The short exchange amounted to Purpura telling the captain he had no knowledge of the involvement of any policeman.

Back in Cleveland, Deputy Inspector Jacob Graul questioned Louis Komer. The prisoner gave his version of underworld honor stating, "The code of the underworld is to save other fellows. Motto knows the code. He realizes he has no chance for his life. Therefore, he says that in hope of saving Dominic Benigno.

"Motto's story is a lie. The first time I ever heard mention of a policeman in connection with the affair was shortly after Benigno was brought here [county jail] from Mexico. I won't say what I heard, or how. It's merely collusion between Motto and Benigno. Frank, without hope for himself, hopes to save Benigno from the chair.

"I'm sorry for Motto, but what's to this life anyhow?" Komer questioned philosophically.

In Columbus, members of the Motto family came for a final visit. Motto's mother, father and wife arrived early, but didn't get to see him until the interrogation session with Matowitz was over. As the visitors were being searched, Mrs. Motto fainted. At first it was believed the strain on her heart had finally claimed her, but she was finally revived. It was the last time she saw her "baby," the youngest of her children.

At one point during the day Motto talked openly with Warden Thomas, reveling in his prowess at stealing automobiles.[5] He recalled the time he once stole four vehicles only to receive a total of $268 for them. Motto had two requests of the warden. Through the prison grapevine he heard tale that some of the condemned men received a higher jolt of electricity than others. He asked Thomas that he be given no "extra shot of juice" when he is placed in the chair.

"We will give you the same as we have given all the others," the warden promised.

"Well, don't give me any more," Motto pleaded.

The second request was that Motto be allowed to see his brother "that he might preach him a sermon upon the futility and tragedy of crime." Joseph Motto was in the reformatory serving a sentence for automobile theft. When the request was denied, Motto asked that Joseph be able to attend his funeral and perhaps draw the conclusion crime doesn't pay from that.

At 5:45 p.m., after final farewells to family members, Motto was taken to the death cell to wait his execution. At 6:00 he ate his final meal – a chicken supper, which he devoured.

Ohio Attorney General Price paid a visit to Motto to confer one last time about the prisoner's allegations regarding the police officer. The information Price received, along with a report from Matowitz, was brought to Governor Davis. At first it was believed there might be a last minute reprieve. After studying the information for more than an hour, the governor ordered the execution to be carried out.

Adding to the strangeness of the day, after the receipt of the governor's order at the prison, noise from "a series of eerie whistles" arose from outside the prison walls. It was reported that the whistling sounds resembled those from the throat of a bobwhite. Warden Thomas, who was resting on his porch, may have been spooked. He went inside and ordered a cordon of police to patrol the outside of the prison until the execution was over.

The warden was well aware that nearly every official who had a role in the trial and the sending of Motto to the electric chair was threatened with death.[6] Heightening the uneasiness was a series of cat "yowls" just before Motto was removed from his cell. The *Cleveland News* reported, "In the stillness of the early morning the sounds crept under the nerves of even hardened penitentiary officials, but an investigation disclosed that it was a cat and nothing else."

During the day, while Motto showed a relative calm demeanor throughout the ordeal, Sam Purpura was beside himself with fear, alone in his cell. When not pacing in his small cell, he prayed or listened to comforting words from family members who came to calm him during this trying day.

Motto, an impeccable dresser, had donned a dark blue suit, a white shirt and white tie. Tan shoes completed the ensemble he wore to the chair. In the group of twenty spectators who were permitted to watch the execution was Benjamin D. Weller of Cleveland, who was the first to offer a reward for the capture of the Sly-Fanner killers. Except for newspaper reporters, he was the only Clevelander present.

C.V. Talbot, a staff correspondent from the *Cleveland News*, was one of those reporters. He filed these comments:

> "The grimness of the occasion was brought home to those who were to witness the death scene as they left the office of the warden. A steady buzzing greeted the ear as the walk through the penitentiary yard began. It grew into a roar as the death house was reached – the whirr of a dynamo just behind the death chair. Past it each man walked as he went into the room.
>
> "And just outside the door of the death house stood the death wagon, its electric lights brightly gleaming while its three attendants

watched for a body – whose they hadn't the interest to inquire. To them it meant only a part of a night's work.

"As Motto turned the corner that led from the death cell into the room of execution he was grasping a crucifix and by his side walked Father Kelly, prison chaplain. Just inside the room Motto kissed the crucifix with a resounding smack.

"Motto entered the death chamber at 1:08 this morning. The chair was ready for him. As he seated himself, prison attendants began fastening the straps and placing the electrodes. Motto moved his legs to assist them and held back his head to hurry the operation.

"No word had been spoken after the condemned man seated himself. The black cap was placed over his face and while the spectators watched the electric current was turned on. The death scene was enacted while a score of witnesses stood by to see the fatal current of 1,950 volts applied, it was only a routine event in the penitentiary, where six more murderers will go to their deaths before another thirty days have passed.

"There was a splutter and the body stiffened in the chair, straining at the straps which bound it. The penitentiary lights dimmed and faded when the current was applied and a low moan welled through the prison, a farewell to a fleeting soul by the 2,300 inmates.

"Then came a scream, half stifled, carrying the fear of a wavering heart. It was from the lips of Sam Purpera, Motto's companion on that December day which spelled death for Sly and Fanner.

"Then the voltage was reduced and for forty seconds, 750 volts passed through the body, but this was again increased to 1,950 while a light smoke drifted upwards wraith-like.

"Motto died game. His end was like his life – hard, merciless. No protest came from his lips. No plea for mercy, no demand for a last minute confession – nothing came from those lips curled in scorn for those who stood by to watch him die.

"Dr. A.J. Shoemaker, assistant prison physician, examined the body, and turning to Warden P.E. Thomas said: 'I pronounce Frank Motto dead.'

"It was the end."

Warden Thomas stated that Motto "had shown less fear of death than any prisoner executed in years…Motto died as he had lived in the penitentiary – a gentleman."

Possessing a somewhat lesser opinion of the man was Marie Sly. Neither widow chose to attend the execution, but Mrs. Sly told a *Cleveland*

Press reporter afterward, "All others who took part in the murders should be made to pay the death penalty."

Purpura, who was lying in an apparent stupor, began to pace his cell as the execution hour neared. When the lights dimmed "his nerve, always weak, broke completely and he screamed," and fell unconscious to the floor. He knew it was only a matter of time until he followed in the same footsteps.

Hours after the execution, Dr. O.M. Kramer, the chief physician at the Ohio Penitentiary for the past eight years, was called to Warden Thomas' office and given the option of resigning or being discharged. Kramer was to officiate at the electrocution of Motto but opted not to, as he had plans to attend a conference, leaving his assistant, Dr. Shoemaker to pronounce the prisoner dead.

The body of Frank Motto was delivered to a Columbus undertaker for preparation before being sent back to Cleveland for burial. One of Motto's wishes was that his brother Joseph be able to attend his funeral so that he would not follow the same path in life. Joseph Motto was in the Mansfield Reformatory, like his brother before him, serving time for stealing an automobile. Despite the efforts of Zottarelli to make the wish of his late client come true, the request was denied; no guard was available to accompany Joseph to Cleveland.

On Tuesday, August 30, the funeral for Frank Motto was held. Hundreds of people crowded the Motto home at 2524 East 33rd Street[7] during the early afternoon, where a brief service was held. The funeral procession consisted of 23 automobiles, which headed for St. Anthony's Church on Central Avenue.[8] Throngs formed along the streets of Big Italy to watch the cortege. Although a large crowd formed outside the church, the sanctuary where the Reverend Humbert Rocchi delivered a brief service, was but half full.

After the service the procession made its way to Calvary Cemetery[9] at 10000 Miles Avenue where Frank Motto was the first of a long list of Italian Prohibition Era gangsters to be laid to rest.

An editorial titled "Ending Murders" appeared in the *Cleveland News*:

> "When a murderer like Frank Motto is put to death men often say that such punishment 'will not stop murders.' That is true. The best that can be expected is to cut down the number of killings. The murderous violence of human nature will not be eradicated, and it will continue to bear its deadly fruit.
>
> "But the kind of murdering that Motto did could be stopped entirely if the penalty which has been visited upon him were absolutely

certain to fall upon all other slayers of his type. There would not be a single payroll or hold-up murder in the United States, for years at a stretch, if it were positively known that every such crime would be followed by the execution of all who were concerned in it.

"For this reason, if Motto's fate were certain to be the doom of every robber who killed, or had any connection with a murder, such assassinations as he participated in would absolutely stop. The cure for that kind of murder would be perfect."

The body of Frank Motto was not even in the grave before the *Cleveland News*, in a front-page headline, demanded to know, "Why Long Delay In Probe Of Officer's 'Plot' In Slaying." The newspaper sensationalized the accusation of a police officer being the "mastermind" of the robbery and even went as far as to compare the incident to the infamous "Becker Scandal," the murder of a New York City gambler in 1912, allegedly ordered by a corrupt police lieutenant.

It was Stanton who blew the lid off the matter after police claimed the allegations were a ploy by Motto to gain a last minute reprieve. The prosecutor revealed that the story of the officer's role in the robbery scheme was brought to his attention just days after the murders and was well-known to his office.

The newspaper wrote:

"Among other things, it is a matter of common gossip in the underworld that twenty-four hours after the killings, Louis Komer, who is now awaiting trial for his part in the case and who was known then only as 'Big Mouth,' was openly bragging in the haunts of those who participated in the robbery that a policeman was implicated in the murder and was to receive 10 per cent of the spoils. He told and retold the story while detectives without any definite clew to the identity of the actual murderers had spread their widely advertised dragnet in search of the bandits."

The attention suddenly shifted back to the Mansfield Reformatory prisoner, in some circles believed to be none other than Biago "Bundy" DePalma, who Stanton had interrogated shortly before word of Sam Purpura's capture in Los Angeles hit the city. The prisoner, whose name was never revealed in the newspapers, did not participate in the crime. His role, it was reported, was to deliver the policeman's share of the loot, $420, to a West Side saloon the day after the slayings. During an interrogation the prisoner denied he had made any such delivery, but named a police officer as one of the plotters of the crime. He later denied making the accusation.

The *News* dropped another surprise when it reported:

"Stanton declares the first information he received concerning the identity of the Sly-Fanner murderers came from the police officer whose name is now being mentioned as the instigator of the plot.

"Stanton's story varies sharply with that whispered about police headquarters as to how the identity of the killers was learned. It is commonly known that Sam Purpera was the first to be identified and that the information that linked him with the crime came from a relative, who, since the Sly-Fanner murders, has successfully evaded trial for the shooting of a man during the hold-up at the Ukrainian-American Banking Company a short time before the double murder."

Stanton claimed that he had called the officer in for an interview and asked him to work on the case. The officer soon told him that Dominic Benigno was a member of the holdup team. Then the officer mentioned the reformatory youth had "collected the loot" and that the payroll money was to be divided. Stanton said the policeman gave him the name of a West Side saloonkeeper, a relative of a public official, who could offer valuable information about the murders. When Stanton called the saloonkeeper in for two interviews, he said he was unable to obtain anything of value. Then Stanton went to the Mansfield Reformatory to interview the youth. Stanton now reported that, "It was evident to me that there was a leak somewhere. This man in prison knew everything I said to the West Side saloonkeeper. He denied he had handled any of the money and then named the police officer as one of the plotters.

"Later I brought this man from Mansfield to my office and there he repudiated his first story and said the policeman had no part in the plot. He said he named him as the instigator merely because he thought the officer had 'squealed' on him."

The interview was not a wash, though. Stanton admitted the Mansfield prisoner gave him the names of four men he claimed were in on the plot – Benigno, Komer, Motto and the relative of Purpura, who was still awaiting trial in the Ukrainian-American Bank shooting. Biago DePalma was later identified as a "squealer" in the Sly-Fanner case and police suspected this may have led to his death by people close to Benigno. Why DePalma ratted out Benigno when the two were alleged to be close associates in the Mayfield Road Mob hierarchy is anyone's guess – if in fact it was true.

By late Monday the officer had not been called to headquarters for questioning. Inspector John Rowlands said the officer would be given the chance to clear his name. The inspector was one of the many police officials who believed Motto had made up the story to save himself from the chair. Rowlands stated, "The officer has not and will not be arrested. He will be questioned, of course, but merely to obtain a police report for the records. The story told by Motto came at too late an hour to carry any weight."

Motto had related the story of the police officer's involvement to Zottarelli weeks before it exploded in the newspapers at the time of his execution. The attorney took the matter to Stanton, but was told by the prosecutor that Motto's story was based on hearsay.

A *Cleveland News* reporter tracked down Dominic Benigno in the jail's barbershop to solicit a comment from him regarding Motto's claims. "How can I know anything about any officer being in on the plot when I wasn't in on it myself?" he replied.

Chapter Endnotes

1. Joseph McKenna "1843-1926, American jurist, Associate Justice of the U.S. Supreme Court (1898-1925), b. Philadelphia. Admitted to the bar in 1865, he practiced law in California and served in the state legislature (1875-76) and the U.S. Congress (1885-92). A federal circuit judge from 1892 to 1897, he was appointed (1897) U.S. Attorney General by President McKinley. He held this office for only a few months before President McKinley appointed him to the Supreme Court. Although he never developed a consistent legal philosophy, McKenna wrote a number of important decisions. Most notable was his opinion in the case of United States v. U.S. Steel Corporation (1920) in which the "rule of reason" principle, asserting that only those combinations that are in unreasonable restraint of trade are illegal, finally triumphed in antitrust cases." – *www. encyclopedia.com*

2. Writ of Certiorari, informally called "Cert Petition," is a document which a losing party files with the Supreme Court asking the Supreme Court to review the decision of a lower court. It includes a list of the parties, a statement of the facts of the case, the legal questions presented for review, and arguments as to why the Court should grant the writ. "Review on writ of certiorari is not a matter of right, but a judicial discretion. A petition for writ of certiorari will be granted only for compelling reasons." Rule 10, Rules of the U.S. Supreme Court. – *www.techlawjournal*

3. The two would-be escapees were Orville Taylor, a member of the "Jiggs" Losteiner gang, that met its Waterloo at the "Battle of Bedford"

bank robbery debacle, and Fred Mussel, a Cleveland robber sent to the Ohio Penitentiary for a robbery in Huron County.

4. Governor Davis and the Cleveland police took the death threats seriously. While mayor of Cleveland, Davis' house was bombed and a threat was made to kidnap his son.

5. On November 4, 1921, more than two months after the execution, Judge Dan B. Cull voided four indictments against Frank Motto. Three of the indictments were for automobile theft; the fourth was for receiving stolen property.

6. Florence E. Allen related in her autobiography, *To Do Justly*, that she was out campaigning for a seat on the Ohio Supreme Court around the time of Motto's execution. She had recently rented the upper floor of a home and was living there with a friend. On one of her return trips, the friend told her, "I keep hearing someone around this house at night." In November 1921, more than two months after the execution, and after Allen's election to the state supreme court, she was preparing to move to Columbus. When she went to the basement of the house to clean out some lockers in preparation for the move, she discovered "outlined on the basement walls a number of black hands."

7. The home no longer exists, and the area is currently occupied by the track and soccer field of Cuyahoga Community College.

8. Dedicated on May 8, 1887, St. Anthony's Church (also known as St. Anthony's of Padua) was the city's first Roman Catholic parish to serve the large Italian ghetto known as "Big Italy." It also was the church of choice for funerals for practically every Italian mobster to die or be murdered during the Prohibition Era.

For the first 17 years, services were held in a frame structure on Ohio Street, which was later renamed Central Avenue. The Italian congregation was too poor to build their own church or afford a school. In 1904, a culmination of the efforts of Father Humbert Rocchi resulted in the construction of a red-brick, Romanesque-style house of worship at the corner of Carnegie Avenue and East 13th Street.

Despite changes in the ethnic make-up of the neighborhood during the late 1920s, the church remained the cultural center for the Italian community. In September 1938, St. Anthony's congregation merged with that of St. Bridget's, located at 2508 East 22nd Street.

Over the next few decades the Italian congregation thinned out, most moving to other parishes further east. The last mass was held on June 11,

1961. Before that summer was over the church was demolished to make way for a new freeway.

9. Calvary Cemetery is the final resting place for most of Cleveland's Italian mobsters. Opened in November 1893, when it became apparent that the city's other Catholic cemeteries were running out of burial space. Calvary now contains over 300,000 residents on 300 acres of land. The cemetery, located at 10000 Miles Avenue, is located on the south-east side of Cleveland.

The Victims

Wilfred C. Sly succeeded his father as president of the W.W. Sly Mfg. Co. On the last day of his life he was looking forward to the New Year's Eve mascarade party he and his wife hosted annually.

George K. Fanner was a second-generation executive at the W.W. Sly Mfg. Co. His efforts to stop the theft of the company payroll led to his death and that of his friend and boss Wilfred Sly.

All photos appear courtesy of the Cleveland Press Collection at Cleveland State University, except where noted otherwise.

Sly Family grave marker at
Lake View Cemetery
(Author's Collection)

Headstone of Wilfred C. Sly
at Lake View Cemetery
(Author's Collection)

Headstone of George K. Fanner
at Riverside Cemetery
(Author's Collection)

William W. Sly, founder of the W.W. Sly Co. and father of Wilfred C. Sly

Headstone of Mary A. Sly at Lake View Cemetery. The mother of Wilfred Sly, she died of a heart attack hours before the first execution of one of her son's slayers was carried out.
(Author's collection)

Ethyl L. Fanner, widow of George K. Fanner

The Killers

Frank Amata, alias Frank Motto, was one of the top men in the Mayfield Road Mob. His need to pay an attorney in advance to handle his appeal on an auto theft conviction would lead to the deaths of Sly and Fanner. *(Ohio Department of Rehabilitation and Correction)*

Headstone of Frank Motto at Calvary Cemetery. Note the correct name. *(Author's Collection)*

Dominic Benigno, the first leader of the Mayfield Road Mob. He made numerous judgement errors leading up to the ill-fated robbery attempt, the most greivous was allowing himself to be there. *(Ohio Department of Rehabilitation and Correction)*

The marker for the Galletti-Benigno family at Calvary Cemetery. There are no individual headstones. The names of family members buried here are engraved on the back of this monument. *(Author's Collection)*

Ignatius "Sam" Purpura. While not blood relatives, Purpura's sister Josephine was married to Frank Galletti, whose sister Mary was the wife of Dominic Benigno. It was perhaps this connection that brought Purpura into the robbery team fold in the absence of Mayfield Road Mob members Frank Milazzo, Nicholas Angelotta, Biagio DePalma (all serving prison time) and Charles Coletto, whose whereabouts the morning of the murders was never divulged. *(Ohio Department of Rehabilitation and Correction)*

Headstone of Sam Purpura, which he shares with a previously deceased brother at Calvary Cemetery. *(Author's Collection)*

Angelo Amato fled the country and headed back to his native Sicily after the murders. He would not be put on trial until the spring of 1935, some 15 years after the killings.

Louis Komer, the only non-Italian on the robbery team, was allowed to confess and become a state's witness. He was not executed, but spent nearly 43 years in prison.

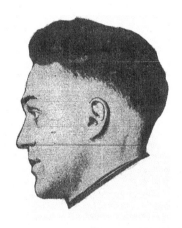

Dominic Lonardo, the younger brother of Cleveland's first Mafia boss "Big Joe" Lonardo. He fled to the West Coast after the murders, where he changed his name to Joseph Piazza and began a new life in San Francisco. Efforts to extradite him failed in 1929 and he was the only gang member not to pay for the crime *(Courtesy of Cleveland Public Library)*

The Police Chiefs

Frederick Kohler, Chief of Police
1903 to 1913. Perhaps Cleveland's most famous Police Chief

Frank W. Smith, Chief of Police
1918 to 1922.

Jacob Graul, Chief of Police
1922 to 1930

The Top Cops

Cornelius Cody. His attempt to bring back Dominic Lonardo from California failed.

Timothy J. Costello. The war-horse of the Cleveland Police Department served 56 years.

Emmett J. Potts rose to the rank of Captain during his 26-year career. His testimony against Frank Motto helped send him to the electric chair.

Charles N. Sterling. His attempt to bring back Sam Purpura from California succeeded.

The story of Charles Cavolo only began with the Sly-Fanner murders. Before the Prohibition Era was over in Cleveland he became a local legend.
(Courtesy of the Cavolo Family)

On the Mexican Excursion

George J. Matowitz. Captain in charge of the Detective Bureau.

George Koestle was the Cleveland Police Department's Bertillion and fingerprint expert. In addition to getting Komer's confession, he helped escort Beningo back from Mexico.

Captain George J. Matowitz and one of his traveling companions
from Mexico, the parrot *Manana*.

The Safety Directors

Thomas Martinec served as Safety Director from 1922 to 1924.

Edwin D. Barry, perhaps Cleveland's most famous Safety Director, served from 1924 to 1932. Barry began a trend that Eliot Ness and Alvin J. Sutton followed in future years in which the Safety Director acted, and was looked upon, as the number one law enforcement official in the city.

The Prosecutors

Frank J. Merrick. As assistant county prosecutor he helped put the Serra Gang auto-theft ring in prison and revealed the early history of the Mayfield Road Mob.

Edward C. Stanton. No other prosecutor in the history of
Cuyahoga County handled such a hornet's nest of cases the likes
of which Eddie Stanton was handed. His work sent three of
the Sly-Fanner killers to the electric chair and another to life in
prison.

James T. Cassidy served as Edward Stanton's Chief Assistant County Prosecutor until 1924 handling some of the most notable court cases of that period.

James C. Connell replaced James Cassidy as Chief Assistant County Prosecutor in 1924 and served under Stanton until he left office. He later served as a common pleas judge and a Federal judge, as this picture depicts.

Ray T. Miller replaced Edward Stanton as Cuyahoga
County prosecutor in 1928. He would later serve as
Mayor of Cleveland, and for twenty years was the leader
of the Cuyahoga County Democratic Party.

The Governor

Harry L. Davis served four terms as Cleveland Mayor and one term as Governor of Ohio. As Governor he had the final say on all the men executed for the Sly-Fanner murders.

Cleveland Mayors & Chief Executives

Mayor William S. Fitzgerald and his political mentor, Harry Davis, the man whom he replaced as Cleveland Mayor. Davis left the mayor's office for the governor's mansion in Columbus

William S. Fitzgerald and his wife, Margaret Chilton Tucker. Fitzgerald maintained that he kept his marriage a secret due to his wife's "exhaustive study of the piano".

William S. Fitzgerald was one of the few Cleveland Mayors never elected to office. As Harry Davis's Law Director, he replaced Davis when he resigned to run for Governor of Ohio.

Frederick Kohler, the former Police Chief, was the last mayor of the 1920s before Cleveland changed to a City Manager form of government. He served from 1922 through 1923.

William R. Hopkins became the first City Manager under the new form of government voted in during the early 1920s. He served in that capacity from 1924 to 1930.

Underworld Figures

Charles Coletto and Frank Milazzo were the top killers in the Mayfield Road Mob. Police believe the pair were responsible for at least 13 murders during the Prohibition years in Cleveland. The absence of the two to help in the payroll robbery no doubt led to the deaths of Sly and Fanner and the subsequent execution of two of the gang's key members.

"Big Joe" Lonardo was the first Mafia Boss of Cleveland. His younger brother Dominic was a participant in the Sly-Fanner murders and survived by fleeing the state. "Big Joe" and two other brothers would be massacred during what became known as the Corn Sugar War in the 1920s

Salvatore ""Sam" Tilocco was at one time a suspect in the Sly-Fanner murders. During the Corn Sugar War, Tilocco was on the opposite side of the Lonardo brothers. He became a murder victim in 1930. *(Courtesy of Cleveland Public Library)*

Return from Mexico

Judge Maurice Bernon sentencing Sam Purpura to death in the electric chair.

Charles Coletto attempts to hide behind Dominic Benigno as the two are being escorted off the ship *Monterey* by two New York City detectives.

Other Stanton Convictions

Bobby Hunt. A cop killer who would testify for the defense at the trial of Dominic Benigno.

George "Jiggs" Losteiner, said to be "the baddest man of Roaring Twenties Cleveland."

Salvatore Cala participated in the brutal slaying of Dan Kaber.

Erminia "Emma" Colavita, another participant in the murder of Dan Kaber. Acquitted in that case, she spent the last 48 years of her life in prison for another murder.

The Judges

Florence Ellinwood Allen set many firsts for women in Ohio and the nation in her legal career. In 1919 she became the first woman assistant county prosecutor in the state and the following year was the first woman elected to the common pleas bench. In 1921 she became the first woman judge in the United States to preside over a capital murder case, becoming the first to sentence a man to die. In 1922 she became the first woman in the United States to be elected to a State Supreme Court. In 1934 she became only the second woman appointed a Federal Judge when she was appointed to the United States Court of Appeals for the Sixth Circuit. In 1958 she became the first woman to serve as Chief Justice of a United States Court of Appeals.

Maurice Bernon oversaw the first trial of Judge Wililam McGannon. In 1921 he handled the murder trial of Sam Purpura

Dan B. Cull oversaw the third trial of Dominic Benigno and sentenced him to die.

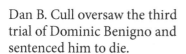

The Defense Attorneys

Mary Grossman set another first for women in Cleveland when she sat on the defense team in a capital murder trial.

Alfred A. Cartwright was a top defense attorney in Cleveland in the 1920s. He defended Mayfield Road Mob members in the Serra auto theft ring and Frank Motto during his murder trial.

William J. Corrigan, a one-time assistant county prosecutor, became one of the top defense attorneys in Cleveland. In 1954 he represented Dr. Sam Sheppard in the sensational murder trial of his wife Marilyn.

Other Players

Fred H. Caley, as secretary of the Cleveland Automobile Club, was the driving force and provided the financing for the pursuit of the Sly-Fanner killers

Louis B. Seltzer, the future editor of the *Cleveland Press*, was a reporter who covered the last days of Sam Purpura before his execution.

Dr. Ardon P. Hammond served as Cuyahoga County Coroner from 1921 to 1928.

Maurice Maschke was a political power in Cleveland as the leader of the Cuyahoga County Republican Party.

Preston E. Thomas, warden of the Ohio Penitentiary from 1913 to 1935.

The "Big Three" of Cleveland law enforcement during the 1920s.
Left to right: Police Chief Jacob Graul, Chief Inspector George
Matowitz and Safety Directory Edwin Barry.

13

The Trials of Dominic Benigno

When the 1921 fall term of the Cuyahoga Common Pleas Court began there were as many important and highly publicized death penalty cases as there were during the spring term. Prosecutor Stanton announced that he and assistants James Cassidy and Harry Parsons would handle all twelve of the first-degree murder cases for the state. Of this total three involved the Sly-Fanner killings (Benigno, Komer and Coletto); four sprung from the Dan Kaber murder (including Salvatore Cala and Emma Colavito); and three from the murder of Cleveland police officer Elmer Sprosty (Bobby Hunt, William Conton and James Walsh).

On Monday morning, September 12, Dominic Benigno's trial got underway with jury selection in the courtroom of Judge Homer G. Powell. One hundred men and women were summoned to provide the jury pool for the case. The prosecution, based on earlier success, was preparing to place as many women as possible on the panel. As in the previous two trials, the state was represented by Edward Stanton, James Cassidy and Harry Parsons. After the failure of Zottarelli and his co-counsels in the earlier cases, Benigno settled on Patrick J. Mulligan, a former assistant county prosecutor, and John J. Babka to represent him.

Benigno entered the courtroom manacled to two deputies. Showered and dressed exquisitely, the defendant smiled and was calm as he was followed to the defense table by Sheriff Stannard. The courthouse and courtroom were well guarded. Benigno was greeted by his young wife Mary and two daughters, Florence, two and Tina, just 18 months old. During the selection process Benigno paid little attention as he enjoyed the entertainment Florence provided as she playfully pranced around the courtroom.

What was hoped to be a two-day jury selection process, dragged on until Friday morning. Each time the 12-member panel was filled defense counsel exercised a peremptory challenge to reduce it again. Despite a first day comment claiming they had no objection to women on the jury, the final panel contained none as Mulligan was able to use his challenges to get all those seated removed. It is interesting to note that while women played an important part in Motto's and Purpura's convictions and death sentences, and that woman on juries around the country were depicted as being "ruthless," the reason most were not accepted by the prosecution in the Benigno trial was the opposition to the death penalty by nearly every woman examined. Throughout the week Judge Powell ordered all prospective jurors kept in the custody of the bailiff. Once selected, the jury remained sequestered for the duration of the trial.

As the week wore on Benigno became more concerned with the selection process. On Friday the *Cleveland News* wrote:

> "Benigno, who up until Thursday had maintained an attitude of gay indifference, was visibly worried Friday. He had the appearance of a trapped animal, helpless, but still seeking a way out. A yellowish pallor overspreads his face, which is deeply creased by wrinkles that zigzag across his forehead and cheeks."

In his opening statement Cassidy told the jury that the state would prove that Benigno selected the men who participated in the robbery and supplied them with weapons. No attempt was made by the state to propose that Benigno was one of the shooters. Cassidy declared the state "would consider the case lost unless the jury returns a death verdict, the same as voted in the Motto and Purpura cases." During Mulligan's opening statement he conceded that Benigno's automobile was used during the crime, but he would prove that his client was not present on the bridge at the time of the killings.

The case against Benigno proceeded in the same manner the earlier cases had, with a trip to the murder scene, followed by testimony from the same witnesses. Additional witnesses testified to Benigno's ownership of the Jordan automobile.

On Monday morning, September 19, four eyewitnesses to the shooting – Mary Blaich, Edith Marklew, Irene Walker and Abbie Barnes – failed to identify Benigno as one of the men they saw the morning of December 31. George Hejna, a truck driver who saw the five men run to the Jordan and chased it for a short distance, testified he was able to get a partial license plate number for police. Then Thomas C. Barrows, the manager of the Hotel Winton garage, testified Benigno brought the Jordan to the garage and parked it at 11:43 that morning.

After lunch on Tuesday the state's key witness took the stand. Louis Komer testified that he first met Frank Motto 24 to 36 hours prior to the robbery, and was told by him that he needed $1,500 to carry his auto theft conviction to the court of appeals. Motto then introduced him to Benigno and the three finalized plans for the robbery. Benigno's role, Komer explained, was to "procure the necessary men, guns and cars."

Komer then testified that Benigno gave Motto and himself the guns that they were to use in the holdup. He said Benigno drove his own car, the Jordan, in which the robbers made their escape. Komer also stated that when he "refrained from shooting the victims" that Dominic Lonardo fired three shots at him.

The cross-examination by Mulligan was a colorful one. The *Plain Dealer* wrote that the confrontation, "resulted in verbal battles during the afternoon, and finally became so heated that Judge Powell several times rebuked the witness for his attitude and demanded that he answer questions." It was brought out during the questioning that back in 1913 Mulligan, then an assistant county prosecutor, had successfully prosecuted a robbery case against Komer.

Defiant on the stand, Komer denied he had planned the payroll robbery on his own, and denied that he had suggested it to anyone else. Komer smiled and laughed out loud at some of counsel's questions. Perspiring under the intense interrogation, Komer frequently wiped his face with a handkerchief.

"Have you been promised anything for testifying in this case?" Mulligan asked.

"I have not been promised anything for testifying," Komer replied. "I am doing it of my own volition. I expect some consideration when my case comes up."

Waiting in the wings to refute Komer's testimony was cop-killer Bobby Hunt. Komer and the prosecution were prepared for this. Just before the state finished its re-direct the next morning, Komer declared that "Hunt had been offered $1,200 to perjure himself in behalf of Benigno." Komer said this was told to him by a fellow prisoner in the county jail, where Hunt and Benigno were in cells near one another.

After completion of Komer's testimony on Wednesday morning, Hunt took the stand as the first defense witness called by Mulligan. He testified that he first met Komer on November 23, 1920. Hunt claimed later on Komer invited him and Frank Marco to where he was rooming on East 19th Street, on the evening of December 30. Further testimony, however, did not disclose that there was any mention of a payroll robbery the next day. The point of Hunt's testimony was to show Komer already had in his possession the gun he testified Benigno gave him the morning of the killings. Marco was brought in from the Mansfield Reformatory for brief testimony to confirm Hunt's statements.

After Hunt's testimony, the defense called Thomas Benigno, Mary Benigno the defendant's wife, and his mother-in-law. They all testified that Benigno was at home the morning of the killings until 11:00 a.m. The Benigno family members were followed by Dominic.

The defendant testified he was asleep on his couch until awakened by his wife at 11:00 a.m. After eating a light lunch, he drove his car to the Hotel Winton garage, on the premise he was going to store it there for the winter. He returned home shortly after the noon hour. Benigno stated that while on his way home he encountered Detectives Albert Soukup and Edward Conroy, not once, but twice, and had conversations with them. Benigno denied he was at the scene of the shooting. He also claimed that his automobile was not used in the killer's escape, contrary to what Mulligan related in his opening statement.

Benigno told the court his trip to Mexico wasn't a flight to avoid arrest, but due to the fact that since his January arrest in connection with the murders, he was "ruined in a business way" and was looking for new opportunities south of the border.

Perhaps here is a good place to interject Frank J. Merrick's recalling of Benigno's role in the crime from the *Plain Dealer* story he wrote in August 1933. Written nearly thirteen years after the crime, Merrick reveals some twists that were not in print prior to this publication:

Accident and mistake lead to the downfall of the majority of crooks. Two mistakes led to the down fall of Benigno and Motto. The Sly-Fanner job had been planned for a week earlier. That payroll was the one before Christmas and included two weeks' pay for each employee, plus bonus and gift money for many – all cash, about $70,000. Benigno and his gang were all set for this job but a mistake on the part of one of the bookkeepers at the First National Bank delayed the making up of the packages of money for more than an hour and the robbers cruised all over the downtown area and West Side looking for the payroll car, finally abandoning the hunt just a few minutes before Sly and Fanner emerged from the bank with the money. Benigno resolved that this choice piece of "business" should not slip through his fingers. He planned to attempt a robbery of the next pay roll of the same company.

It was dangerous to keep the two stolen automobiles to be used on the job and Benigno decided to abandon them and secure others at a later date. Police were hot on the trail of the driver of the first holdup car and he left immediately after the failure of the first attempt. To Motto was given the task of securing two stolen automobiles and having them in hiding a week before the next Sly-Fanner pay day. One was to be high-powered and in excellent running condition. The other was to be an old car of sufficient power to keep up with the small roadster used to transport the money.

Motto did not like the idea of driving a stolen car, even for a day. He was at that time out on bail following conviction [which Merrick had prosecuted] of one auto theft and was to go to jail in a fortnight. In the meantime, he did not want to be caught stealing another car.

With the driver of the robber car unavailable, Motto decided upon a change of the original plans. He knew a tough kid named Sam Purpera, 16 years old and not well known to detectives. Motto told Purpera of the proposed job and Sam agreed to drive the car, providing Motto rode with him. Purpera also agreed to steal the car himself and have it ready. Meanwhile Motto arranged with another member of the gang to steal a high-powered machine.

At the agreed meeting place, Purpera appeared with a car which he had stolen from the late F. H. Goff, president of the Cleveland Trust Co. The other man and car failed to show up. After some wait and with the time for the robbery near, Benigno decided to go along and drive his own car, which was kept nearby. This bold gang leader decided to take part personally in the biggest pay roll robbery of the year, his only precaution being to bend back the first digit on his license plate.

Following the robbery and the killing of two of the city's best citizens, Benigno returned his car to his garage and calmly ordered it washed and stored for the winter.

When Benigno's testimony was completed, the state called Sam Purpura. It was a historic moment as it was the first time in the history of the county that a death row inmate was called as a witness against a defendant accused of the same crime. The *Plain Dealer* reported:

> "Such a throng of spectators was attracted by the announcement that Inspector Sterling asked for additional policemen, while Sheriff Charles B. Stannard assigned every available deputy to guard the court room. All entering the room, including newspaper reporters and attorneys, were searched."

It was Cassidy's plan to call Purpura as a rebuttal witness. Instead he asked leave of the court to reopen the state's case with his direct testimony.

The detail bringing Purpura from Columbus left the penitentiary at 1:50 a.m., arriving in Cleveland at 7:45 Thursday morning. Reporters tried to question the prisoner when he departed the train but were rebuffed by the guards. Purpura presented a pathetic sight in the courthouse as he was ushered in, handcuffed to a penitentiary guard and surrounded by deputies and police officers. He was "pale and gaunt" as he made his way to the front of the court. The *Plain Dealer* gave this description:

"The gray prison uniform hung loosely from his spare frame when he stood, with his right hand raised, to be sworn as a witness. As he ascended the stand he appeared extremely weak. His face was gray and his black eyes protruded over the dark circles beneath.

"One lean hand held his prison cap when Purpera seated himself. Immediately... he began biting his lower lip. He continued to do so for the hour he was on the stand."

Purpura did not look at Benigno, who sat in the same seat he had the day he was condemned to die in the electric chair four months earlier. Benigno, however, eyed every move of the witness keenly as he leaned forward in his chair.

Acknowledging that he was under death sentence for participating in the Sly-Fanner murders, Purpura answered Cassidy's questions repeating his previous stories of how he met Benigno in the dance hall and became a member of the robbery team. As in his previous statements, he claimed he had left the weapon in the automobile and had his back turned to the victims when the shooting began. The *Plain Dealer* reported:

"Benigno, he said, was at the wheel of his own car, and both machines drove to the plant of the W.W. Sly Manufacturing Co. on W. 47th street. Not finding the car in which Sly and Fanner were to go to the bank for the pay roll, they drove back downtown and then, after an hour's wait, found it. They followed it to the West Side, Purpera said. Benigno piloting the car he owned, which carried five men, and Motto driving the second car, containing Motto and Purpera.

"Purpera described the wrecking of the Sly-Fanner automobile on the Nickel Plate Bridge at W. 47th street and his argument with Sly and Fanner as to responsibility for the "accident." He left his pistol in the car, he said, because Sly and Fanner had him covered with their weapons.

"Purpera said he had just reached the running board of Benigno's car, in which Benigno sat at the wheel, when four men began shooting. The four, he testified, were Louis Komer, Amato, Lonardo and Motto..."

For the first time, Purpura claimed that both Komer and Motto were shooters, even though this was at odds with eyewitness testimony. Also, note that the *Plain Dealer* slipped in that there were five men in the Jordan when it arrived, meaning there were seven participants, another declaration contrary to the eyewitness statements.

During cross-examination, Mulligan asked if he had spoken to any member of the police or the prosecutor's staff before his testimony.

Purpura replied that he hadn't and was unaware he was going to be called to testify until he was taken from the penitentiary early that morning. Then this exchange took place:

Mulligan: Have you been promised anything for testifying in this case?

Purpura: No, sir.

Mulligan: Do you hope or expect to have your sentence commuted to life imprisonment for testifying in this case?

Purpura: While there is life there is hope. No, sir; I don't expect anything. I came here to testify voluntarily.

While Purpura was being questioned, Benigno chewed gum incessantly. His family members "appeared extremely nervous" throughout the testimony.

After Purpura left the stand, the prosecution called Detectives Soukup[1] and Conroy as rebuttal witnesses. Both officers testified they had only seen Benigno once on the day of the murders and that was late in the morning. This was followed by the rebuttal testimony of Inspector Sterling and Captain Matowitz, who recalled that four days after the murders, Benigno told them he had taken his car to the garage shortly after 10:00 a.m.

One day after Purpura's testimony, his appeal for a stay of execution was denied. Zottarelli's appeal was based on what the attorney claimed was Judge Bernon erring in his jury instructions, telling the panel they must return either a verdict of guilty of murder in the first-degree or acquittal. The attorney contended other degrees of guilt should have been offered the jury to consider. While a date of execution was not established, rumor had it that if the jury found Benigno guilty both executions might be carried out the same day. Also, that same day the grand jury refused to indict Charles Coletto for the Sly-Fanner killings.

On Friday, September 23, the jury heard final arguments. Harry Parsons began for the state reminding jurors to focus on the testimony of both Komer and Purpura. John Babka, in beginning defense counsel's closing, asked the jury to "exercise extreme caution," claiming evidence offered by the state was not strong enough to send a man to the electric chair.

The second half of the defense's closing argument was worth the price of admission as Patrick Mulligan had nearly everyone in tears. As the attorney tugged the heartstrings of the jury, the defendant for the first time showed emotion by crying at the defense table. His brother, wife and mother-in-law, seated nearby with the children, all shed tears. The attorney's plea even reached the hearts of the two victim's widows. Both wept openly and at one point, Ethyl Fanner collapsed, requiring the assistance of friends to revive her.

In the courtroom that day was Mary Komer, the mother of the "Toledo Kid." She was drawn to tears, too, but for a different reason. Mulligan had characterized her son as a "murderer unworthy of belief."

Cassidy's closing rebuttal again focused on the testimony of the state's two key witnesses, Komer and Purpura, who both positively identified Benigno as the driver of the Jordan getaway car. Because of this the state wanted nothing short of a death penalty verdict.

Judge Powell's jury instructions lasted until 3:30 that afternoon and the case was given to the twelve men of the jury to decide. During the early evening, the jurors broke for dinner and were escorted to a nearby restaurant. After a leisurely meal, they returned to the courthouse to continue their deliberations. Because it was after hours on a Friday night, the elevators weren't running and the panel had to walk up three flights of stairs to get to the jury room on the fourth floor.

On the way up Archie Budd, a 72 year-old member of the panel, collapsed. Advised of the incident Judge Powell summoned two doctors who quickly determined that the exertion of climbing the stairs after a heavy meal caused the elderly juror to suffer a stroke. Budd's son was called and he arranged for an ambulance to pick him up and drive to the courthouse. Members of the jury carried the stricken man back down the three flights of stairs to the ambulance, which took Budd to his home, where he was reported to be in "extremely grave" condition.[2]

Powell ordered the defendant brought to the courtroom, where family members were waiting anxiously for a decision. Benigno, thinking that a verdict was reached, appeared in court nervous and disheveled, his normally immaculate hair mussed. At 10:00 p.m. Powell related the juror's mishap to Benigno and declared a mistrial. He ordered the defendant be granted a new trial, to which Benigno heaved a sigh of relief. The remaining jurors were dismissed and Benigno was led back to the county jail to await a new trial, which by law could begin in twenty days.

It was later reported that the jury had unanimously found Benigno guilty of first-degree murder, but were split, nine to three, over whether to recommend mercy.

Benigno was not the only one to feel temporary relief. Sam Purpura was returned to the death house at the Ohio Penitentiary after being told that Judge Willis Vickery, of the court of appeals, confirmed his execution date would not be assigned because the state might need the condemned man's testimony for the second trial. On the trip back to Columbus, Purpura was joined by Salvatore Cala, who had just been convicted of first-degree murder in the killing of Dan Kaber. Ironically, the jury which found him guilty of the heinous murder recommended mercy for the 32 year-old. Cala was going to Columbus to begin a life sentence, the irony of which could not have been overlooked by the young Purpura.

The second trial of Dominic Benigno was scheduled to begin Tuesday, October 18 before visiting Judge Henry W. Jewell from Delaware, Ohio. While there were no unusual events during the first trial for Benigno, like the ones which had accompanied the Motto trial, Sheriff Stannard still insisted on extra security. Perhaps since Benigno knew he was found guilty by the first panel, he might not want to wait to see what verdict the second jury returned.

The first morning only 33 prospective jurors arrived for roll-call, causing a continuance to be ordered. Deputies were dispatched to locate and bring in five persons who refused to obey the jury summons. By Wednesday, with the selection of eleven jurors, a record for speed in the seating of a first-degree murder jury was anticipated in the county. Five women were included on the panel, but by Friday morning all of the women were removed by peremptory challenges by the defense. Testimony began that day for the 12 male jurors. The examination of witnesses was the same as in the first trail, with few changes.

The trial proceeded, much a repeat of the first one, until it was time for Sam Purpura's testimony. Brought back from his death row cell at the penitentiary, he was accompanied to court this time by Joseph Zottarelli. The attorney told the court that Purpura was his ward and client and as a minor he objected to him being placed on the stand. Judge Jewell overruled his objection. Standing behind his attorney, Purpura let his feelings be known. "I didn't want to come here," he declared.

After the witness was sworn in, Cassidy asked him to give his name. "You know what my name is," Purpura answered defiantly.

Despite orders from Jewell, Purpura refused to answer any of Cassidy's questions. Instead, he asked the prosecutor, "Why don't you let me die in peace?" He was finally taken back to the county jail. Later, during his closing argument, Assistant County Prosecutor Harry Parsons used the excuse that Purpura's refusal to testify against Benigno was because the two men were distant relatives – Purpura's sister was married to Mary Benigno's brother. He failed to explain, however, why this didn't play a role in his testifying against him during the first trial.

While Purpura may have considered his actions on the stand valiant, the Court of Appeals wasted no time in determining his use to society was no longer needed. The day after his non-testimony, Purpura was ordered to be put to death on February 10, 1922.

With the sudden end of the state's case, the defense began calling witnesses on the morning of Wednesday, October 26. The witness list again included Bobby Hunt and Frank Marco. Closing arguments were given Thursday afternoon and once again attorney Mulligan turned the courtroom into a slobbering mass. After the closing statements Mulligan requested of Judge Jewell that in his instructions to the jury he state that the panel could find the defendant guilty of a lesser charge of murder than the first-degree, as had occurred in Motto's case, but not in Purpura's. Judge Jewell, needing time to consider the motion, delayed his jury instructions until Friday morning.

This motion by defense counsel must have left the prosecutors a bit apprehensive, despite their previous victories in the Motto and Purpura trials. They announced that should the jury return with any decision short of a guilty with the death penalty attached, they would place Benigno on trial immediately for the murder of George Fanner.

The next morning Jewell overruled the motion and instructed the jury to return one of three verdicts – guilty in the first degree without mercy, guilty in the first degree with mercy, or acquittal. The case was given to the jury at 10:30 a.m. By late afternoon rumors were swirling through the courthouse that there was little hope the jury could agree on a unanimous verdict. Friday night at 9:30, still deadlocked, the judge ordered them locked down for the night.

On Saturday morning the jury began deliberations at 8:30. At 10:30 Jewell called the jury foreman into the courtroom to inquire of the chances of the panel reaching a decision. The foreman replied, "I believe we can agree." An hour later, however, the foreman let the bailiff know that a unanimous decision could not be reached.

Judge Jewell ordered the jurors back to the courtroom where the foreman informed the court that they were helplessly deadlocked. Before excusing the panel the judge told the jury members they were to refrain from discussing with anyone where they stood in their deliberations. That went unheeded as the first afternoon newspaper revealed that the panel stood eight to four for acquittal. The next day the *News* reported the jury stood eleven to one for acquittal. Whatever the actual count, as it continued to change, it favored Benigno.

As the jury was being released, attorney Mulligan argued that they should be allowed to continue their deliberations. After two trials and no verdict nerves were frayed. An exasperated Cassidy ordered Benigno returned to his "murderer's row" cell in the county jail. Mulligan flew into a rage declaring that the assistant prosecutor had no business ordering his client returned to jail. The two men then went nose to nose in a bitter verbal exchange.

Cassidy announced the state would try Benigno again after the 21-day waiting period. Court officials had already estimated that the two ill-fated trials had cost the county $20,000.

Family dynamics may have played a role in Purpura's refusal to testify during the second trial. It was reported in the weeks following the trial that the reason for Purpura clamming up was because of death threats to his sister, Mrs. Josephine Galletti. For the first time the relationship between Purpura and Benigno became public. If the Benigno family was threatening the life of the young lady they didn't have far to go, she lived at the same 1909 Scovill Avenue address as Mary Benigno. She was married to Mary's brother Frank.

On November 25, Purpura's mother, aunt and his sister Josephine, along with her three year-old daughter, paid a visit to Columbus to see Sam. Shortly after 9:00 a.m. they were escorted to his cell, where a guard stood by watching every movement and listening to every word.

Josephine asked the guard if she could take the child for a drink of water. They were led to an empty cell around the corner from her brother's and the guard returned to his post. Josephine soon rejoined the family.

Moments later a trusty, who worked as a plumber in the death row wing, walked by and called out a greeting to Purpura, to which Sam responded, "Everything is O.K." The words were a signal to indicate that a loaded revolver, hidden inside a newspaper, was deposited in the open cell by Josephine, to be found by the trusty. Now all the trusty had to do was deliver the weapon to Purpura. Instead, the trusty went straight to Warden Thomas' office and surrendered it.

The warden sent a guard to Purpura's cell and Josephine was placed under arrest. Along with her baby, Galletti was transported to police headquarters in Columbus, where she was charged with carrying a concealed weapon.

Other than the reporting of it in the newspapers, the incident was quickly forgotten. It was never determined if Purpura was going to use the gun to commit suicide or in an attempt to gain freedom, which in itself may have been suicide. Using the intertwined family relationship, it's entirely possible that the Benignos bargained that either way Purpura might be killed, thus perhaps gaining Dominic an acquittal in the third trial. It is also possible that the actions of the plumber, in turning the gun over to

Warden Thomas, were agreed to between him and Purpura ahead of time to spare Sam the task of having to kill himself or attempt an ill-conceived escape. There was nothing in Purpura's makeup that caused him to give up hope that he might be spared from the chair and given a life sentence. It was a hope he maintained to the bitter end.

Another possibility is that by delivering the gun Josephine may have gotten off the hook from the death threats. Ten months later, on September 27, 1922, Josephine Galletti pleaded guilty to a charge of carrying a concealed weapon and a sympathetic judge gave her a one-year suspended sentence instead of sending her to the Marysville Reformatory for women.

The third trial of Dominic Benigno began with jury selection on Monday, December 5, in the courtroom of Judge Dan B. Cull.* It was obvious that the defense would try to keep women off the jury again as it exercised peremptory challenges on Tuesday to remove five females. When jury selection was complete it was again an all-male panel.

Testimony began on Thursday with the same slate of witnesses. For their last witness the state again called Sam Purpura. The *Cleveland News* reported, "When he refused to testify at the second trial Purpura declared the life of his sister was threatened because of the evidence he offered against Benigno at the first trial. He said because he himself was on the borderline of death he would not endanger the life of another." The newspaper did not reveal if Purpura had brought this to the attention of the authorities and offered to testify again, or if the prosecutors approached him and he revealed the threat before agreeing to testify a second time. Whatever the case, with his sister now incarcerated and awaiting trial for attempting to smuggle the gun to him in prison, he no longer had reason to fear for her life.

Purpura arrived at the courthouse in the custody of Detective Clarence Banks and a penitentiary guard. Dressed in dark brown clothes and a light gray topcoat, instead of the prison garb he wore at the first two trials, Purpura took the stand. He gave the same damaging testimony he gave at the first trial, much of it substantiating Louis Komer's statements from the previous day, with the exception that he was the lone robber who hadn't fired his weapon. During his time on the stand Purpura kept his eyes cast to the floor, even when told to point to and identify the defendant.

When his testimony was completed, Purpura was led from the courtroom into the corridor where he was met by his mother. Mary Purpura hugged her handcuffed son and cried out, "He didn't kill anyone! He didn't kill anyone! He's my boy, my baby." The guards hustled him back to the county jail.

The case of the defense was the same with Bobby Hunt serving as the key witness. Rumors were rampant that Charles Coletto might take the stand as a witness. Just what Coletto, now out on bond, was to testify about was anyone's guess. He was not called.

During closing arguments Mulligan, as in prior trials, attacked the testimony of Purpura and Komer. If he left the courtroom audience teary-eyed for a third time the newspapers didn't report it. The judge's charge to the jury was the same as Jewell's, giving them three options for a verdict. By 4:30 Tuesday afternoon the case was in the hands of the jury. The only difference seemed to be in the attitude of Dominic Benigno. He appeared much more optimistic when he returned to his cell that afternoon. He exchanged greetings with his fellow prisoners, who called out encouragement to him. Benigno received another boost to his confidence when the jury reported at 10:40 that night that they had not reached a decision.

If Benigno had known the score was against him he might not have seemed so smug. The count before deliberations ended that night was one for acquittal, four for guilty with a recommendation of mercy, and seven wanted to send him to the chair. The next morning a 10:00 a.m. the voting showed that just two jurors were holding out for mercy. An hour later it was unanimous.

At 11:05 the pertinent parties were reassembled in the courtroom. As in the previous trials, neither of the widows was present. As was the case throughout the trial, the defendant's family was on hand, including his two young daughters. The verdict was then read, "Guilty of murder in the first-degree." There was no recommendation of mercy.

Cull immediately pronounced sentence, letting the condemned man know he was to die during the early morning hours of April 27, 1922. As the judge concluded with the words, "And may God have mercy on your soul," Mary Benigno went ballistic.

"He's not guilty! Oh, my God, he's not guilty!" she shrieked as she attacked Cassidy. During the reading of the verdict Mary was the only member of the family allowed inside the railing of the courtroom. From this vantage point she launched herself at the prosecutor and slugged him with her fist.

"I'm going to shoot you, Cassidy," she yelled.

A court bailiff rushed to Cassidy's aid as Mary fought with him. A *Cleveland News* reporter, who had gotten too close, was next. She hit the man in the chest and shouted, "Tell your paper I'm going to kill Cassidy. I'll kill him and go to the chair with my husband."

As Mary screamed her threats, she tore and scratched at her neck and chest until she was cut and bleeding. After Mary Benigno was forcibly removed from the courtroom to an anteroom, she screamed, "I'll shoot the judge. I know how to shoot him and how to kill Cassidy, too. I'll do it!"

While the *Cleveland News* and *Plain Dealer* reported the incident as an outburst by an incensed wife, the *Cleveland Press* sensationalized it as a riot. After Mary and the prosecutor were separated, the newspaper reported, "Then the riot broke out in full sway. The 200 spectators became a crying, fighting, struggling, cursing mass." Somehow the other two dailies missed the intensity of what the *Press* reporter apparently experienced.

Cassidy stated afterwards, "When Mrs. Benigno attempted to seize me by the throat it seemed to arouse the fury of the spectators, many of whom were friends of [the defendant]. Several times the crowd rushed at me. I heard the rail creaking. But the police arrived and settled the disturbance just as it seemed worse."

Later that afternoon, when a reporter visited Mary at her 1909 Scovill Avenue home, he found her with her hair disheveled, her clothing ripped and disarranged and still bleeding from her self-inflicted wounds. She kept repeating, "Dominic did not have a fair trial."

Before watching the emotional episode put on by his wife, Benigno's response to the judge's sentence was a simple, "I thank you." The condemned Mayfield Road Mob leader, as he had done throughout the third trial, remained "calm and coolly defiant." Benigno was led back to his cell in the county jail. Police were sent to help guard both the jail and the prosecutor's office.

Shortly after his removal to the jail late Wednesday morning, Benigno was visited by Mulligan and Babka. After the sentence, and ensuing one-woman melee, Mulligan filed a motion for a new trial. In Benigno's cell, counsel discussed the legal steps being taken on his behalf.

"Do what you can," Benigno replied with an air of indifference. "A man has to die sometime."

Sheriff Stannard couldn't wait to get the condemned prisoner out of his jail. Plans were made to send him to Columbus immediately. During the afternoon, Benigno's wife, mother and mother-in-law were permitted into his cell to say their farewells. He admonished Mary for her actions in the courthouse, but still maintained an air of nonchalance about the whole matter.

Late in the afternoon detective Captain Matowitz arrived with a detail of two flying squads to accompany Benigno to Union Station. Before leaving the jail, the condemned man shouted a farewell to several prisoners, who responded with calls of, "Good luck!" He was directed away from the cell that housed the "Toledo Kid."

Benigno was handcuffed and his feet placed in manacles. At the station he boarded the 6:15 train to Columbus. He smiled and waved goodbye to the detectives left standing on the platform, before sitting down with four deputy sheriffs for the three hour ride.

At Columbus the detail was met by a squad of 30 local policemen and detectives, who escorted them to the penitentiary. Once there, Benigno was stripped of his "fine clothing," including a silk shirt, and given standard prison garb. He was then taken to the death row wing and placed in a cell not far from Sam Purpura.

Chapter Endnotes

1. On February 28, 1922, Albert Soukup, a 12-year member of the detective bureau, was later busted in rank to patrolman by Chief Jacob Graul. Soukup was disciplined for interfering in a federal narcotics investigation by questioning agents about one of two suspects in a drug investigation, whom he was friends with.

2. Archie Budd survived the stroke, but died less than six months later. On the evening of March 6, 1922, Budd passed away at his home after suffering a second stroke. Relatives said he had never fully recovered from the one during the trial. He was buried in Highland Park Cemetery.

14

Changes at the Top

As 1921 came to a close and the one-year anniversary of the Sly-Fanner murders arrived, police and prosecutors could look back at a job well-done. All six gunmen from the shooting were identified; three were found guilty of first-degree murder and sentenced to die, one had already been put to death in the electric chair; and a fourth member was in custody about to be tried.

In November 1921, Mayor Fitzgerald, who had gained the position when Davis ran for governor, was up for election. As a Republican politician Fitzgerald was strictly a party man, never one to use his position as a stepping stone to advance his own interests. While Fitzgerald was always complimented when it came to his physique – 6 feet tall and lean – he was uncomfortable while out "stumping." One observer noted, "Fitzgerald acts on the platform as though he feared someone was going to suddenly kick him from behind." In addition, Fitzgerald didn't have a tough political exterior according to intimates. He was nervous when speaking in public and allowed normal disparaging remarks to get under his skin. It was his first inclination not to run for office in the fall of 1921. Party leader Maurice Maschke, however, decided that as the incumbent he was the best choice. In November, Fitzgerald faced a daunting task as six challengers faced off against him for the office of mayor. His biggest competition was former Cleveland police chief Fred Kohler,* now the popular candidate for mayor. Philip W. Porter, a longtime reporter and editor for the *Plain Dealer* recalled:

> "Mayor Fitzgerald's campaign was a disaster. Republican Boss Maschke had to support him, though he feared the worst, for Fitz would often end an evening of speech-making practically in the bag. A private poll showed that Kohler would beat Fitzgerald, and the shrewd Maschke bet a bundle on Kohler and cleaned up handsomely."

Fitzgerald was defeated by 4,500 votes and in January 1922 vacated city hall. In a political statement years later, Porter summed up the results of the Davis/Fitzgerald years:

"[Davis] turned over city hall to his handsome but inefficient law director, William S. Fitzgerald, and the Fitzgerald administration was so inept that it set the stage for the advent of the city manager charter and the election of Fred Kohler as mayor. The voters were really fed up in 1921, and when they took out their revenge on the pols of both parties they began the greatest period of volatility and instability in Cleveland political history. It lasted twenty-five years, swinging back and forth between hope and disappointment, ideals and cynicism. At least it did until the depression of the 1930s sank the whole country.

On January 1, 1922, Kohler and his new cabinet were ready to take office. As the incoming chief executive of the city, Kohler had one goal in mind, operating the city within its budget, which meant the reduction of hundreds of city employees. Over the next few days Kohler's focus was on reducing the payrolls of every city department. Kohler was determined that he was going to make the city live within its means. To do so he pledged himself to ridding city hall of "all pets, spies, drones and slackers," placed in what amounted to patronage positions by the previous administration.

Kohler had no plans for an inaugural ball. When asked what was planned, he stated, "There are no plans! We want the people to come and shake hands with us, and after they do that they can do as they please, outside of damaging, defacing or wrecking the building."

It was a city hall tradition that the mayor-elect be sworn in by the out-going mayor in the presence of both the retiring and newly appointed city cabinet. When William B. Fitzgerald arrived to perform his last official function as mayor, he looked at the serious faces all around him and then glanced out the window where a fierce gale was swirling.

"A cold day to be out of a job," he quipped.

The swearing-in was quick, followed by the now retired mayor showing Kohler around his new office and turning over the keys to him.

"If there's anything I ever can do to help you, call on me" was Fitzgerald's parting comment.

"If there is anything that I, in my official capacity, can do for you, just let me know," Kohler responded.

No one within earshot doubted the insincerity of either man.

Kohler let reporters know that he was getting down to business. He related his instructions to department heads:

"Prepare in writing and submit to me within the next twenty-four hours a list of every job or every employee you can dispense with and still operate your division. I want the names and addresses of people you think can be let go at once.

"I am asking you to tell me what you think we ought to do in the way of reducing the pay roll in your division. After I get your report, we will take action.

"This cut is necessary because we must get the city's employment and purchasing functions on exactly the same basis as in any big commercial establishment. Furthermore the city hasn't the money to do otherwise."

In addition to the layoffs, Kohler was looking to reduce salaries. He urged the board of control to revise the pay structure under civil service for nearly all classes of workers.

The new mayor was no shrinking violet when it came to performing the hatchet duties himself. While waiting for city council to approve his recommendation for Traction Commissioner, he went to the Hanna Building where the Traction Commissioner's office was located. "I thought it necessary to reduce this organization to a skeleton," Kohler later recalled. Before leaving he personally fired 19 of the 23 employees. By January 7, one week into his term, Kohler had lightened the city hall payroll to the tune of 700 employees, with more cuts expected.

As for the police department, one of the key cabinet changes was the appointing of Thomas C. Martinec* as Director of Public Safety, replacing the embattled Anton B. Sprosty.* Martinec was on the Cleveland police force for twenty-five years, rising to the rank of captain, before leaving to organize a private police force for the massive Otis Steel Company during World War I. An intimate friend of the new mayor, Kohler asked Martinec to take the job.

In turning the reigns of the safety forces over to Martinec, Kohler stated, "Director Martinec is in charge of the safety department. He is going to see that the police and fire departments are good departments and that they keep this town safe and clean. Whatever he says in that department goes."

Issuing his first public statement as the new safety director, Martinec said, "We have no idea of trying to remove Chief Smith. His hands are free to assign the work of the department as he sees fit. All we ask is that he put clean, capable, efficient men in charge of the 'heavy work.'

"We have asked the chief nothing save that he deliver the goods. I have told this to everyone concerned. What shake-ups there are, as far as personnel goes, will be the chief's own business. I haven't suggested the transfer of a single policeman, and I don't intend to."

To prove his point, Martinec was asked about the replacing of Lieutenant Joseph Houser as head of the vice squad. Houser was on sick leave and there was talk of a temporary replacement.

"We would hate above all things to have anyone within or without the police department think there is any 'city hall interference' with the chief's ideas for building up a clean, reliable, and hard-hitting police department. You can't have discipline unless you back your chief up, and this chief is going to be backed up as long as he produces."

Martinec's promise didn't mean, however, that things would remain status quo for Smith. First, Martinec ordered Smith's removal from his office at Central Station to the safety department offices at City Hall. The change was ordered by the safety director at 10:30 on the morning of January 4 and by 1:30 p.m. Smith had a new official residence. Martinec explained the move was made to improve the communication within the department of safety. He pointed out that George Wallace, the city's long-time and most famous fire chief, had his office in the same department.

The changes included other items too. Martinec ordered that all police vehicles were to be used strictly for police business. Smith and his deputy inspectors had use of these cars, along with police chauffeurs on occasion. Smith was ordered to wear his uniform at all times and was given scheduled hours to work.

Two months prior to the fall election, Smith was rumored to be running for the office of mayor. It was quickly pointed out to him by civil service officials that he would have to quit his job as chief if he decided to do so. Smith, who declared that if he ran he "will be elected," questioned the validity of this ruling. Whatever the case, Smith decided not to run.

On January 5, Smith reported for duty at City Hall. He had not been given a private office. Seated in an open area, he was bothered by people coming in from off the street looking for jobs in the new administration. Smith had several conversations with Martinec during the morning and around noon attempted to speak with Kohler, but was unable to get an audience. Smith then waited for the safety director to return from lunch. When he did the chief told him, "Well, I'm through. I'm leaving you; you have my resignation."

Around 4:00 p.m. Martinec addressed the media, telling reporters, "The chief of police resigned to me this afternoon."

Reporters quickly found Smith, as he was preparing to leave, and began firing questions at him.

"I'm through, that's all. I'm not chief now. Nothing more to say."

Smith walked back to the safety director's office and turned over his badge, service revolver and "a bunch of keys." He told Martinec, "That's all that belongs to me, I think. Well, I'm a private citizen now and I'm going right away. I want to wish you all kinds of good luck and prosperity in the police department." With that Smith picked up a satchel containing his personal belongings and left city hall.

Both Kohler and Martinec insisted Smith's resignation came as a "complete surprise" to them. They assured reporters that Smith had left on his own volition and in no way had he been forced out or asked to leave.

Later that night, Smith spilled his guts to reporters stating, "It is chief of police or nothing for me. In the last year I have fought to keep from becoming shackled, and I succeeded. In the last six months I was seldom at city hall. I defy anyone to say that my office was not conducted properly and efficiently.

"It was nothing that was said to me that prompted my action; but what was done. A blind person could have seen that I was being made an office boy or messenger.

"What else could one think when the chief is taken entirely away from police headquarters, without even an office there, when he is told to wear a uniform and given detailed hours?"

Smith complained that his subordinates had more privileges than he did. "Captains and inspectors can travel in uniform or plain clothes as they see fit," he said. "How embarrassing would it be to get an emergency call requiring my immediate attention and then have to stop to put on my uniform? I do not know of any chief in the country required to wear his uniform unless he chooses it for specific occasions such as parades and dress reviews."

That the uniform controversy was a bone of contention with Smith could be seen back in July 1920 when he told an interviewer, "I always insist upon all men wearing the blue, but I come down and spend the first part of the day opening mail and seeing callers and having conferences, and a uniform doesn't seem essential, and then I want to go to lunch with some friends perhaps, and people as a rule are not overly anxious to go out to lunch with a uniform. The boys – the police – all know me, anyhow, so I figure it isn't always necessary. But I do wear it about half the time, and, of course, always at parades…"

In addition to the uniform requirements, the former chief got other issues, which he deemed petty, off his chest.

"I was not even given a private office at City Hall. Today there must have been two dozen job seekers who came to me to ask, 'Can you take care of me? I'm looking for a job.

"My automobile was taken away from me. The reason given was that it must be used only for police business. I always used the car for police business, even if I did use it to take me home from the office and bring me down to it. I did not feel that I was compelled to adhere to an eight-hour basis. Some days it was twenty-four. Fifty per cent of the time that I went home there came a call, as I went into the house, requiring my attention somewhere. I jumped back into the car and went.

"Does it sound reasonable that if something required me to be out all night, as my records will show time and again, I would have to be in the office at a regular hour next day? I've done this many times of my own accord, but it is different when the attempt is to force it on you unjustly."

Smith then explained how he arrived at his decision to resign.

"It's a case of reading the handwriting on the wall. Recent orders received as to how I was to conduct myself led me to go out of town Wednesday night to seek advice. I went to an old friend of mine.

"'I'd go back and quit, or I wouldn't think you the red-blooded man that I take Frank Smith for,' he told me.

"'That is just what I intended to do,' I told him. 'But feeling that two minds are better than one, I decided to see whether you agreed with me.' I added. 'Now I am satisfied I am making no mistake.'"

In his parting comments Smith was asked about his successor.

"I hope my successor will be a chief in fact as well as name, as I would like to have been if I had remained, but which I thought was impossible. I hope he won't be a mere office boy. Unless he has [free rein], it shows either that his superiors have no confidence in him, or that he is not wanted.

"I don't know of a finer fellow than Director Martinec, and I wish him all the success in the world. But I feel he will have to do as he is ordered to. I was sorry I was unable to see Mayor Kohler. I called at his office and asked to see him and was told he was busy and I could see the director. Since he has been mayor – although he is my direct superior – I have had only five minutes with him. I wish him luck, too."

The relationship between Smith and the Fitzgerald administration was stormy at best. At the center of the discord was meddling by the mayor and his people, most notably Safety Director Anton Sprosty. An editorial after the resignation pointed out that despite the interference Smith kept his job. The writer then asked the question, "How could the chief stand for the old administration's serious and supposedly vicious meddling with his work, when he wouldn't let the new administration order him to wear a uniform."

After the afternoon resignation of Frank Smith,* Martinec quickly announced that Jacob Graul,* appointed acting inspector a few weeks back after the surprise resignation of Inspector John Rowlands*, was now the acting chief of police. The media immediately speculated as to who might be the next chief. Graul and Matowitz, both of whom early in their careers advanced on Kohler's watch, were prime candidates for the job. The rumor mill, however, had Bertillon expert George Koestle as the front-runner. The reasoning for this was that Koestle was a long-time friend to both Kohler and Martinec. By chance, he happened to be visiting Kohler, his first opportunity to pay respects to the new mayor, when Smith's resignation was announced. Being an intimate of the two, he was taken into their confidence as they discussed a replacement for Smith. The rumor-mill came to a halt when Graul was named chief.

Just the sound of his name conjures up visions of a Charles Dicken's character – Jacob Graul. That vision, however, was so unlike the real man. Described as methodically thorough and brutally energetic, his high sharp voice, eye for detail, and the crooked smile behind round wire-rimmed glasses hardly made Graul appear as a fictional, hammer-fisted tough cop. Born in 1868 Graul's first career path was as a master plumber. He became a police patrolman on January 5, 1897, walking a beat in the Fifth Precinct. One day the neighborhood tough decided to check out Graul's courage. A free-for-all followed and the thug was knocked cold. Graul then hoisted the punk into a wheelbarrow and carted him off to the station.

Graul was transferred to the Central Station and on August 4, 1903, he was promoted to sergeant. On June 29, 1909, he made lieutenant, and three and a half years later he achieved the rank of captain on December 1, 1912. All these promotions came during the time Police Chief Kohler ran the department. A stickler for details and neatly dressed officers, Kohler couldn't help but be impressed by the young Graul.

On May 1, 1918, Graul was named deputy inspector. Ironically, Graul never became a full inspector, having been in the position of acting inspector for a short while before Chief Smith resigned. After the naming of Graul as interim chief, Martinec announced that the same simple orders given to Smith would now apply to Graul. Kohler believed the department was top-heavy with titles and Graul immediately began a reorganization to address this issue. He announced that Central headquarters would be run by three deputy inspectors – Charles Sterling, Edward H. May and Stephen Murphy – each working an eight-hour shift. The inspector position recently vacated by Rowlands (and temporarily filled by Graul) was abolished.

Inspector Sterling* would not remain in the position long. On February 2, the 26-year veteran asked Graul for an 82-day leave of absence, due to poor health. "The 82 days are due me," he said. They represent the total number of days off that, while head of the Detective Bureau, I worked instead of taking off." If not given the time off Sterling said he would be forced to retire.

With the removal of Sterling as head of the detective bureau, the leadership of that department fell to Detective Captains Matowitz on days and Costello on nights.

The day after being named "acting police chief," Graul was called to the mayor's office. After a meeting with Kohler and Martinec, the three men emerged and the safety director announced that Graul was Cleveland's new Chief of Police.

On January 17 Graul made his most important change in the police department, no doubt at the insistence of Kohler and Martinec, when he dissolved the city's much maligned vice squad and freed up its leader – Lieutenant Cornelius W. Cody.

The Vice Squad, a staple of most police departments across the nation to handle mainly crimes of gambling and prostitution, was established in Cleveland in 1916 when Harry L. Davis first took the mayor's office. Its first rule – known as Order 73, handed down by Safety Director Anton Sprosty – was that no resorts could be raided until an investigation was completed and approved by city hall. The problem with this rule was that too many times the targeted resort was tipped off to the impending raid. Aggravated citizens and businessmen, affected by the illegal activities, complained and the vice bureau came under fire more than any other department over the next six years.

Prior to the formation of the vice squad and Order 73, when Kohler was police chief, plain clothes detectives, working in their own precincts were responsible for the work. The change basically returned "the responsibility for suppression of immorality and gambling" to the hands of the precinct captains.

In announcing the change Graul declared that there were, "Too many leaks in the department. Too many times when the vice squad was sent out on a raid the reported resort had closed up and there was nothing there to raid.

"If the leaks continue, we'll now know where they are. When a captain learns that a raid in his own precinct has failed he will have to know why it failed and where the word of the raid got out.

"This doesn't mean any letup on suppression of vice and gambling. Rather it means more action. Instead of a single vice squad trying to cover the whole city, we will have a whole police department watching for and stamping out commercialized immorality and wide-open gambling. And we'll get results or we'll find some new policemen."

Another important reform the new chief made was to reduce the number of precincts from sixteen to eight. The changes were ordered to go into effect on May 13.

15

The Fight to Save Sam Purpura

The *Plain Dealer* reported, "Not in years has so much interest been aroused in an execution – partly because of the youth of the bandit, partly because of the needless killing in which he was involved and partly because of the strong efforts that were made to save him."

While Dominic Benigno adjusted to his first day of life on death row at the Ohio Penitentiary in Columbus, Assistant Prosecutor Cassidy was not far away. He was in the state courthouse at a hearing before the Ohio Supreme Court on a motion for a new trial for Sam Purpura. The defense team's motion was filed based on "newly discovered evidence," claiming alleged prejudice on the part of two jurors.

Back in Cleveland, Stanton was seeing to the upcoming trial of the "Toledo Kid." Attorney Elden J. Hopple was representing Louis Komer and, like the attorneys for Motto, Purpura and Benigno, was concerned solely with keeping his client out of the electric chair. Under Hopple's direction, the prosecutor's office was being inundated with petitions urging that the defendant be allowed to plead guilty to a murder charge less than first-degree. A sentence of life in prison was then requested in consideration for Komer's testimony in the Motto and Benigno murder trials. Hopple insisted that Komer would be needed as a witness if and when Amato and Lonardo were apprehended.

January 1922 proved to be a busy month – aside from the changes in City Hall and the police department – with a number of peripheral events taking place. Mayfield Road Mob members Nick Angelotta and Frank Milazzo were on the list of inmates to receive a clemency hearing on January 10. The two were convicted and sentenced in December 1920 as members of the "Serra Gang" auto theft ring. Had the two men not accepted their punishment and gone directly to prison, there is little reason to believe they might not have been involved in the robbery of the Sly-Fanner payroll. Catching wind of the clemency hearing, Cleveland Automobile Club attorney Frank Merrick, who successfully prosecuted to pair, and club Secretary Fred Caley sprang into action. Merrick was delegated to represent the club in Mansfield at a hearing of the Board of Pardons and Paroles.

Fred Caley claimed that "a criminal gang" was "exerting every influence" to help get the pair out of prison, despite the fact that the Reverend John Rutledge, now the former chairman of the Board of Pardons & Paroles, had denied that any effort had been made to gain the men's release. Rutledge pointed out that under the law they would automatically come up for consideration for parole one year after entering the reformatory. Undaunted by the facts, Caley replied, "That doesn't lessen their guilt or the menace of their release.

"The release of this pair of thieves would renew the danger of murders of the Sly-Fanner type for which the leader of their gang, Frank Motto, was executed. Stolen automobiles were used then and we're going to put a stop to thefts of this kind if we have to go to the limit."

On January 13 the *Cleveland News* reported that the state securities commissioner was helping Marie Sly and Ethyl Fanner to expand the W.W. Sly Manufacturing Company with the authorization to increase its capital stock by $140,000. S.C. Vessey was now the president of the concern, while George J. Fanner, father of the victim, was vice president. Marie Sly was reported to be secretary and whatever role Ethyl Fanner had in the company, other than as a shareholder, was not reported.

With little fanfare the trial of Louis Komer got underway on Monday, January 16, 1922. It didn't last long. The defense team of Elden J. Hopple and Thomas E. Green joined County Prosecutor Stanton and Komer in the chambers of Common Pleas Judge Thomas D. Price. When they returned to the courtroom, Komer pled guilty to first-degree murder. The judge said he would hear testimony in the case Tuesday before rendering a sentence.

The next day Price questioned eleven witnesses. None of the eyewitnesses called could identify Komer as a participant in the robbery / shooting, despite Bertillon expert George Koestle's reciting of Komer's confession. After Assistant County Prosecutor Parsons addressed the court, discussing Komer's aid in the conviction of Motto and Benigno, the judge passed sentence. Price ordered Komer to serve life imprisonment at hard labor for his role in the murders of Sly and Fanner.

The judge was concerned that if Komer were executed it deprived the state of its key witness against Amato or Lonardo, should they be captured and tried. "Otherwise," Price stated, "I would have no compunction in sending him to the electric chair. Such men are not fit to live. His intelligence makes him one of the worst criminals in Cleveland.

The decision upset the Italian community because Komer was the only non-Italian member of the gang; Motto had already been executed and

Purpura and Benigno were both facing the chair. The Cleveland chapter of the Order of the Sons of Italy, organized by Dr. Giovanni A. Barricelli,[1] the group's Grand Commander, was behind the effort to prevent the executions of Benigno and Purpura. The passions in this case intensified as the murder victim's families and the public's sentiments for them, clashed with the fears and resentment toward the Italian community in Cleveland.

Although Charles Coletto's trial was scheduled to follow Benigno's, the prosecution had yet to obtain any evidence connecting him to the case and the grand jury had refused to indict him. Stanton felt that unless information came out during the Benigno trial to implicate Coletto, the charges of first-degree murder against him might have to be dropped.

In January 1922, prosecutors still had two first-degree murder charges pending against Coletto, who had been released from the county jail shortly after Benigno was convicted. On February 1, Stanton declared in court that he had no credible evidence linking him to the double murder. That being said, Judge Frederick P. Walther had no choice but to dismiss the charges against Coletto.

It took the young gangster just eight days before he was in trouble again. On February 9, 1922, Coletto and four others were indicted by the grand jury for the theft of an automobile from a Cleveland Heights resident. Instead of trying to get the trial delayed like his Mayfield Road Mob predecessors had, Coletto simply threatened the man, who then denied the car had ever been stolen.

Coletto's future involvement with the Mayfield Road Mob would make Cavolo and Matowitz one day wish they had left him in Mexico.

In the midst of all the January happenings, the Ohio Supreme Court refused to review the case of Sam Purpura. The decision was announced on January 10. Purpura's defense counsel was seeking a new trial claiming Judge Bernon had erred by not advising the jury that Purpura could be found guilty of less than first-degree murder. The state's position was that since the murder was committed in the course of a robbery, according to Ohio law, it had to be first-degree murder or nothing.

With all hope seemingly lost, the newspaper sent reporters to the prison during the days prior to the scheduled execution, on February 10, to report on the condemned man's activities and record his comments. The warden, guards and fellow prisoners all had comments for the press. Many of the reports contradicted one another, sometimes even within the same newspaper.

Purpura's cell floor was littered with newspapers, all turned to the sports' page. He continued to read his bible and paced his cell and the corridor outside it, waiting for word from his attorney.

Much of the time he spent sitting on his cot smoking cigarettes, one after another, lighting the next from the stub of the last. A sampling of his comments to reporters were:

> ➢ I read all the Cleveland daily papers. I have been having them sent down here, ever since I've been here
> ➢ It doesn't seem they would kill me – I am so young. That doesn't seem right, for I haven't killed anybody. It makes it hard for me to die.
> ➢ Well, if I have to go, I can go with a clear conscience – as God is my judge, I didn't kill anybody. My head is clear of that.

Near Purpura was Dominic Benigno. If there were any hostile feelings between the two, the newspapers didn't report it. As Purpura paced the corridor the day before his execution, Benigno called out to him, "Cheer up, Sam, a lot of things can happen before midnight." When a reporter asked Purpura what he was going to have for his last supper, Benigno offered, "Why don't you order a bottle of wine, Sam?"

On Thursday, February 9, Purpura spent the morning with his mother, brother and brother-in-law. During the visit Mary Purpura collapsed and was taken to the warden's apartment where she was attended to by Mrs. Thomas. Purpura sent out for two boxes of chocolates, which he ate throughout the day.

While Purpura seemed resigned to his fate, he continually asked guards if there was any word from the governor. They kept telling him that Davis was out of town and was not expected back for several days.

All hope was not lost, however. That morning Zottarelli arrived in Columbus with two letters he hoped to present to Governor Davis. When he arrived at the executive offices he was told, not only was the governor out of the city, but that his whereabouts were unknown – even by his private secretary (Davis was vacationing in Florida). Undaunted, Zottarelli hurried to the Ohio Supreme Courthouse for a final roll of the dice.

The attorney quickly prepared an application for a hearing on his motion for a new trial and attached to it letters from Assistant County Prosecutor Cassidy and Judge Cull. Both letters addressed the concerns of a retrial – not for Purpura, but for Dominic Benigno. In Cassidy's note he stated that Benigno's appeal would not be decided until April and wrote, "I suggest for your serious consideration that a reprieve be granted until May."

The letter from Cull was a little more candid, as the judge expressed the opinion that "Komer's testimony for the state would have had little effect in convicting Benigno if it had not been supported by Purpera's testimony." Cull pointed out that in Benigno's second trial he was nearly acquitted without the testimony of Purpura. "Should a new trial be granted to Benigno," Cull wrote, "It is doubtful if there would be a conviction were the testimony of Purpera unavailable."

Zottarelli had a brief audience with the court, which then retired for thirty minutes to review the letters and discuss the matter. Judge E.S. Mathias suddenly appeared in the court's ante room, where he handed the letters back to a glum faced Zottarelli.

"Thirty days," Mathias said. "That gives you until March 10."

How a thirty-day stay helped when the matter couldn't possibly be resolved in sixty was a decision that could only be explained by the Ohio Supreme Court justices. Zottarelli wasn't about to debate it though, he had obtained a thirty-day extension for his client, who by now had less than twelve hours to live.

Zottarelli raced to the Ohio Penitentiary and hurried down the corridor of death row to tell his client. Purpura, haggard and nervous, was lying in the upper bunk of the cell he shared with Steve Myeski, a condemned killer from Youngstown. The attorney spoke a few excited sentences to Purpura in Italian. The young man turned to the warden's secretary, who had accompanied Zottarelli to the cell, and he confirmed the stay in English, after which a broad smile crossed the condemned man's face. Zottarelli's parting comment was, "You read your bible, young man."

Word quickly spread to the other condemned inmates, who shouted words of encouragement to Purpura; all but Benigno, who took the news in silence. He was concerned about Purpura's testimony if Mulligan were to receive the new trial he was fighting for. One of the points of Benigno's appeal was that the jury was "permitted to separate without being cautioned by the trial judge as to their conduct." The "separation" took place during the first Saturday night of the trial. The jurors were driven to their homes by deputy sheriffs "to obtain fresh underwear in anticipation of regular Saturday night baths at a hotel." The court held this procedure to be proper. Benigno now hoped that the state kept to its new March 10 execution date for his death row neighbor.

Another person unhappy that the stay was granted was State Supreme Court Judge R.M. Wanamaker. Berating his colleagues for their decision, Wanamaker declared, "This species of lawlessness has pretty nearly run riot in Ohio. Courts ought not to give it further encouragement by reprieves on pure technical grounds, or further delays which tend to destroy fair justice in the minds of law-loving and law-abiding people of the state."

"If Purpera's testimony in future contemplated trials was so important, that should have been taken into consideration, and not put off until the last minute."

Other justices concurred that the decision to grant the stay was in the best interests of justice.

The weeks of the stay went by quickly. On March 4, with the new execution date for Purpura just six days away, the Ohio Sons of Italy began a campaign to save the life of the condemned teenager. Dr. Barricelli, after a meeting with the governor, began enlisting other associations throughout the state in collecting signatures on petitions to be sent to Governor Davis.[2]

During the 30-day stay Zottarelli filed a motion for the case to be reheard by the appellate court. Tuesday, March 7, served as the key date in the process. It was the day the Ohio Supreme Court was to hear Zottarelli's latest motion. When the body met they denied the motion and refused to hear the case. While a setback, this was certainly no reason to end the fight. Zottarelli's next move was to seek a writ of certiorari in the U.S. Supreme Court and ask for a stay of execution until the case could be argued. When this motion was denied it left the attorney with two choices. One was through a motion to the U.S. Supreme Court. In his arguments, Zottarelli contended that since Purpura was only 16 years-old at the time the crime was committed, the common pleas court had no jurisdiction to try him, instead, the case should have, by Ohio law, been heard in juvenile court. Zottarelli claimed his client was being denied his Fifth Amendment right that guarantees that a person cannot be deprived of life without due process of law.

The other choice was to seek executive clemency from Governor Davis. While just a month earlier this looked like it was out of the question, during a trip to Sandusky the week before the governor told an audience he was against capital punishment. When this comment raised a lot of eyebrows, days later in Cincinnati he clarified his position declaring the death penalty must be employed as long as the state constitution provided for it.[3] Davis said, "My attitude must not be construed as meaning that I will interfere with the execution of those waiting in the death house now."

This clarification undoubtedly was due to pressure being put on Davis to obtain mercy for Purpura. The governor was being bombarded with requests from all around the state pleading for or demanding a life sentence for the prisoner. The Sons of Italy, 50 lodges strong and with 150,000 members, had 30 lodges working at a fever pitch to save Purpura. One committee was organized in Columbus to call on the governor. A petition signed by 3,500 Clevelanders was presented to Davis by Zottarelli. In Columbus, plans were made by Barricelli and Zottarelli to parade to the governor's office in case the appeal to the Ohio Supreme Court failed.

On Wednesday, the day after Zottarelli's latest plea was rejected, sources in Columbus claimed Davis would not intervene in the execution of Purpura. Still the demand on Davis to act – one way or the other – was tremendous. In addition to the Sons of Italy's efforts to save Purpura's life, Davis was contacted by Charles DeWoody of the newly formed Cleveland Association for Criminal Justice with this request:

> "Are you considering, or thinking of considering, commuting or in any way interfering with the execution of the sentence against Sam Purpera? If so, this association desires to be heard before any action is taken. Please wire answer immediately."

The association informed the governor, in no uncertain terms, that it was "unalterably opposed to any reduction in Purpera's sentence and that it will fight any such steps to the utmost." This and other requests of the association went unanswered.

As the days ticked down to the Friday morning deadline, Purpura spent "practically all his time with his rosary beads and his Testament," Warden Thomas revealed. He was visited by his brother Anthony, but his frail mother had not visited since February 9. Purpura prayed fervently each day that "something" would intervene and save his life. Newspaper reporters again returned to record his last days. Told that he could expect no intervention on the part of the governor, Purpura stated, "If the governor doesn't see fit to interfere, I will hold no malice. If I do go, it will be the fulfillment of God's will, and I am resigned to my fate."

On Wednesday evening, after the renewed requests of Cassidy and Cull, Governor Davis granted a sixty-day reprieve. The decision was based solely on the need for Purpura to be available to testify should Dominic Benigno be granted a retrial. Before granting the stay, Davis sent a telegram to Stanton to confirm Cassidy's position. Stanton wired back:

> "The request for a reprieve until May was sought by my assistant… with the only thought in mind that Purpera's testimony would be necessary to bring about full justice to an accomplice in the Sly-Fanner murders.
>
> "The asking of a reprieve in no way indicates that we are seeking a commutation of Purpera's sentence. I am unalterably opposed to any commutation of sentence. I feel that justice demands that Purpera die in the electric chair."

When informed of the reprieve by Warden Thomas, Purpura responded, "I thank you very much."

The two-month stay was expected to be long enough to cover any and all appeals for which Benigno could file motions. Benigno must have been seething in his cell as Purpura received the news. By this time the two men had stopped talking to each other. Meanwhile, Benigno himself was granted a stay of execution on April 18, nine days before his scheduled trip to the electric chair, when the appellate judges decided they needed more time to review his appeal.

The reprieve by Davis suddenly sparked his interest in the case and he contacted John J. Sullivan, now an appellate judge, and asked that complete details of both Purpura's and Benigno's cases be forwarded to him. The governor let it be known that in asking for the information he hoped to reduce the time limit of the stay if the Benigno case could be disposed of before May 10.

The reprieve, and the motives behind it, prompted Willis Vickery, presiding judge of the appeals court, to review the Benigno case without delay. "We will rush the case through as soon as possible," Vickery declared from his sick bed. All this could hardly have pleased attorney Patrick Mulligan, who had yet to file briefs, or Benigno whose hopes depended not only on a retrial, but a retrial without Purpura alive to testify.

The weeks again raced by and on Friday, May 5, Zottarelli traveled to Washington D.C. with another appeal for a stay of execution, this one citing Purpura's age as the reason. The U.S. Supreme Court was not in session and not scheduled to resume sitting until after the Tuesday morning execution date. The attorney went to the home of Associate Justice William R. Day, who "acts in such Ohio cases when the court is not sitting." Justice Day denied the stay.

The key to Purpura's continued existence was Dominic Benigno's ongoing appeal. The Court of Appeals in Cincinnati had heard the case on April 18, and had yet to render a decision. After Justice Day's decision, Governor Davis, who was spending the weekend at his Cleveland home, felt the need to act. He made a call to Columbus and ordered paperwork be initiated for a second 60-day stay for Purpura.

On Saturday morning the Court of Appeals rendered their decision, refusing a new trial for Benigno. Tracked down by reporters, Patrick Mulligan had yet to hear the news. He stated, "I have not been advised of the court of appeal's decision, but it would undoubtedly be accompanied by a ruling of the court setting the date for Benigno's execution at a time sufficiently advanced to permit me to file a motion in the state supreme court for a leave to file a petition in error." Mulligan was certainly in no hurry to file his motion. Should Purpura be put to death, it would surely help his case – if he could obtain a new trial for his client.

When notified of Mulligan's comments, Prosecutor Stanton considered the lawyer's chances remote, at best. He then announced, "I shall ask for no further reprieve for Purpura because I do not believe it is necessary. The matter of filing the motion in the supreme court is purely a legal prerogative – a course of law which precedent prescribes. In a case involving great public interest or a question of constitutionality it would mean something, possibly, in my opinion. In this case, I maintain, it has no significance."

After Davis was notified of the Court of Appeal's decision he ordered the stay of execution, which had yet to be signed, cancelled.

Also washing his hands of the matter that weekend was Dr. Barricelli. On Saturday he told a *Plain Dealer* reporter, "I could have seen the governor here today, perhaps, but I have conferred with him twice and I can see no good in further consultations. The Sons of Italy are none the less convinced that the execution of Purpera would be an outrage, both because of his extreme youth at the time of the crime and because the evidence did not show he had murder in his heart or even a weapon when he participated in the robbery expedition. The governor knows how the Sons of Italy feel. There's no use to bother him again. Purpera's execution will be a stain on the name of Ohio."

Zottarelli was already planning his next legal maneuver. On Sunday, he called the governor's East 97th Street home and through Mrs. Davis made arrangements to speak with the governor. The attorney was also seeking letters from Cull and Cassidy to request that Purpura be kept alive until the case against Benigno was resolved. The attorney told reporters, "I feel sure that Judge Cull and Assistant Prosecutor Cassidy have not changed their minds and that they will be glad to join in my plea to the governor to let Purpera live until Benigno's case is finally closed."

Zottarelli was incorrect in his assessment, however. Cassidy let it be known that, "True, I helped to get Purpera his third reprieve, but that was because we wanted Purpera alive until the court of appeals passed upon Benigno's motion for a new trial. Since this court has denied that demand Purpera's doom is sealed unless the governor steps in on his own initiative. I am definitely committed not to aid any effort to delay his execution."

When Davis and Zottarelli discussed Purpura's disposition, the attorney was told that nothing would be done on the governor's part unless it was requested by a judge or the prosecutor. As Davis boarded the noon train to Columbus that Monday he promised to make a statement from the statehouse at 4:00 p.m. By that time Purpura had just nine hours to live.

By coincidence, Zottarelli was on the same train heading to see his client. While the two men didn't speak on the way down, they talked for a brief moment when the train arrived at the Columbus station.

Zottarelli went directly to the penitentiary to meet with Purpura. The attorney later recalled the conversation.

"'Tell me the truth,' Purpura asked anxiously.

"I told him of my talk with the governor, and I said I was 'not discouraged' at the way I had been received; that there was still a chance the governor might grant a reprieve.

"'Tell me the truth,' he asked again when I said goodbye to him. 'If there isn't any chance I want to know and I'll make the best of it.'

"I told him I had no more information and left."

Zottarelli[4] had performed his last official duty for his client.

Meanwhile, at the statehouse, when Davis arrived at his office he began reading all the current correspondence he had received on the case. At 4:40, with an anxious crowd of newsmen waiting, Davis made this statement:

> "After very careful consideration and investigation of the case, I do not feel that I am justified, as governor, in interfering with the execution of the verdict and the sentence, found and imposed by the jury and court before which Sam Purpera was tried.
>
> "I have examined and considered the great numbers of letters, petitions and other forms of appeals by which executive clemency has been sought for Purpera.
>
> "I have particularly given the most earnest thought to the impressive personal appeals made by Dr. G. A. Barricelli of Cleveland, representing the Sons of Italy.
>
> "However, I am compelled to consider that every possible opportunity has been given to Purpera and his attorneys to take up his case to the highest court in order that the justice of the action by the lower court might be tested.
>
> "The governor's power is not intended to be set up arbitrarily against the judgments of courts and juries of the system of justice in effect in Ohio."

Future *Cleveland Press* editor Louis B. Seltzer, then a reporter, claimed he was the one who broke the news to Purpura. The condemned man had spent the day with his mother and other family members. Purpura's mother was allowed to stay past the normal visiting hours and was leaving when Seltzer arrived. Purpura, who was smoking cigarettes incessantly, was enjoying a cigar when Seltzer informed him of the decision:

"'Sam,' I said, 'the governor has decided that you will have to die tonight.'

"Purpera's face lost the smile with which he greeted me.

"His face blanched.

"The fingers that were clutched about the heavy cigar clenched, breaking it.

"He opened his mouth to speak.

"Words failed him."

Purpura momentarily composed himself. "Well, all right," he said. "All I've got to say is, God bless them all. I have prayed for the governor, and I have prayed for everybody, and if I die I die innocent. God knows I have never killed anybody, and God knows I have never even shot at anybody.

"That's all I have to say now, boys. My time is getting short, and I must say goodbye to you."

Purpura was mostly concerned for his mother. On her way from the cell it was reported she collapsed and had to be attended to by prison personnel. As she was being escorted through the warden's office she saw a copy of the local newspaper discussing the clemency battle. She suddenly threw her arms up and screamed, "Davis! Davis! Davis!" In tears she was helped out of the prison and driven to the home of a "prominent" Italian family to await the result of the night's events.

Purpura was to be moved to new quarters to await his execution. Since he had entered death row, nearly a year ago (May 21), fifteen prisoners had gone to their death. He was the "dean" of the condemned men, having seniority over the remaining seven inmates, who had nicknamed him "the baby." Despite his argument to the contrary, the prison listed his age as 19, making him the second youngest prisoner to be executed. Before he left death row he shook hands with each man. In facing Benigno, if there was any animosity between the two it was kept inside them.

"Goodbye Sam," was all Benigno said.

"Perhaps I will be back here again tonight," Purpura offered hopefully.

Benigno was hoping otherwise. After Purpura left, Benigno told reporters, "Sam put me here. He knows I'm innocent. Why doesn't he say so and clear me? I forgive him for what he did, but he put me in here to save his own life. I was a block away with the car. I didn't do any shooting. They framed me, he and Komer. The prosecutor knows I wasn't there. Yes, Sam lied – he tried to save himself and got both of us in"

In contrast to the atmosphere that surrounded Frank Motto's execution, there were no threats made to the governor and other officials.

Warden Thomas took no chances though. The *Cleveland News* reported, "An extra band of guards had been thrown in a cordon around the prison to prevent a possible attempt to [free] Purpera. All were armed with heavy repeating rifles and standing two by two at intervals they lent the place the air of an arsenal."

Purpura was taken to an annex quarters above the death chamber. Father L.A. Kelly met and spoke with him briefly. He then left, promising to return. Joseph Forestier, an inmate serving a life sentence, was brought in to keep Purpura company in the absence of the priest.

Throughout the day the warden's wife asked Purpura what he desired for his last meal. Superstitious, Purpura refused to tell her claiming it would bring him bad luck. Mrs. Thomas prepared a final meal on her own – a combination of chicken and spaghetti, and strawberry shortcake for dessert – which Purpura shared with Forestier.

Purpura spent the rest of the night seated in a rocking chair, smoking cigarettes and cigars, speaking in Italian with Forestier, chatting with his guards and attendants, praying with Father Kelly – all the while holding tightly a Bible and his rosary beads. At one point he asked the priest for a pen and paper. He wrote a note for a relative and asked Father Kelly to mail it for him. The content of the note and the recipient were not revealed.

It was unclear if reporters were allowed near the prisoner once he was removed to the annex, but at some time during the late afternoon or evening, Louis Seltzer claimed to have had a brief conversation with Purpura.

"Tell Mrs. Fanner that I am sorry," Purpura requested.

"Why," Seltzer asked, "only Mrs. Fanner? Why not also Mrs. Sly?"

"No," said Purpura, "just tell Mrs. Fanner – Mrs. Fanner. Will you promise to do it personally?"

Up in the holding cell the hours passed quickly. Soon the prison clock tower tolled 1:00 a.m. A delegation of fifteen prison attaches and reporters, sent by their newspapers to cover the event, gathered in Warden Thomas' office. They were escorted outside and along a path to the death house, passing a gray hearse and its driver along the way. Once inside they filed past a wicker coffin and its attendant. The group entered a small room where the only piece of furniture was the death chair, positioned in the middle. As prison personnel prepared themselves, the sound of footsteps could be heard in the hallway. Suddenly Purpura and Father Kelly appeared. Louis Seltzer's account appeared in the *Cleveland Press* the next day:

> "White of face, lips moving without a sound issuing from them, eyes uplifted, the slayer entered.

"He glanced neither to the right nor the left.

"'There.' It was Rev. Kelly's voice, indicating the location of the death chair.

"Purpera looked at it, his lips moved quickly, and he slid into it. His eyes closed as he sat there. For several minutes the attendants fumbled with the leather thongs. They bound his arms and wrists to the arms of the chair. Across his chest they fastened another thong.

"About his legs they fastened more thongs. Onto the calf of the right they clapped an electrode to a small circular spot that had been shaved to provide sure contact.

"Then another attendant, moving the electrode above his head on a swivel, drew it down and pressed it upon a small shaven spot in the center of his head. The electrode was clamped. A black mask was placed over Purpera's face.

"Again the room became silent.

"The chief electrician nodded.

"An attendant stepped soundlessly over to a partitioned off space at the further end of the room.

"He dropped his hand – the signal.

"There arose the gradual increasing noise of the whirling dynamo.

"All eyes were fastened upon the man in the chair.

"The shock came.

"The body jerked upright.

"The fists clenched.

"The whirling of the dynamo continued. Then it stopped abruptly.

"Dr. W.A. Whitman, prison physician, stepped onto the platform.

"He unloosened the strap about his chest.

"The stethoscope was applied.

"Dr. Whitman turned to Warden Thomas.

"'Mr. Warden, I pronounce Samuel Purpera legally dead.'

"The wicker basket was brought in.

"But the room was cleared of everyone by the warden's order as the attendants lifted the dead form from the chair and placed it in the basket."

Unlike the execution of Motto, there was only a brief application of the high energy voltage necessary to complete the task. The switch was thrown at 1:06 a.m. and Dr. Whitman declared the prisoner dead at 1:08.

Purpura's body was removed to an undertaker's parlor in Columbus. Services for the young man were held in that city. On Thursday, May 11, he was taken from the family home on Central Avenue and buried in Calvary Cemetery. Police were on hand to guard against any disturbances.

Chapter Endnotes

1. Dr. Giovanni Alfonso Barricelli (Feb. 22, 1873 – April 16, 1934) was a cardiopulmonary specialist, but was best known as one of the early leaders of the Italian community in Cleveland. After graduation from medical school, he came to Cleveland and began his practice on Woodland Avenue in the Big Italy section of the city. – *The Dictionary of Cleveland Biography*. Dr. Barricelli's home is now an inn and restaurant at the corner of Cornell Road and Murray Hill in the Little Italy section.

2. On March 8, the *Cleveland News* reported that Barricelli was quoted "by a local morning paper as saying Davis told him to go out and enlist the aid of the Italian societies throughout the state." What prompted this quote by Barricelli isn't known, nor why it came into contention. The *News* article continued, "This quotation went unchallenged until Wednesday [March 8], when Dr. Barricelli declared he was misquoted and that the governor never told him to seek the aid of Purpera's brothers [figuratively]." Despite the misquoting, Italian societies throughout the state did just what Barricelli said the governor advised.

3. Governor Harry L Davis' comments on the pardons and execution made in Cincinnati on March 4, 1922:

> "Death sentences will continue to be enforced as heretofore. Any other course would lead to a miscarriage of justice. It will be our purpose to work for the abolition of [the] death sentence as quickly as possible, but until that is accomplished there cannot be any change in the system as now carried out. As long as capital punishment is continued, commutations of sentence to get around it would be a serious abuse of the pardon power because of the record of short periods of imprisonment of life termers."

The governor's characterizing of "short periods" was defined as killers being pardoned and released after just seven or eight years of incarceration.

4. On November 15, 1924, attorney Joseph V. Zottarelli was arrested by U.S. Secret Service and Deputy U.S. marshals as the Cleveland leader of a $5.0 million nationwide counterfeit conspiracy. The attorney and several local men were charged with the sale and transfer of counterfeit U.S. securities - $5 war savings stamps dated 1919. The arrest warrant charged Zottarelli with "possessing, uttering, publishing and passing counterfeit securities" of the five-dollar denomination.

The Cleveland Secret Service operative credited Cleveland Detectives Charles Cavolo and Carl Zicarelli with much of the leg work that uncovered Zottarelli's involvement. The attorney was arrested in his berth aboard a Pennsylvania Railroad car as it arrived in Cleveland from Washington D.C. Zottarelli denied knowing the certificates were counterfeit and said he was paid by many of his clients with them. When arraigned, however, he offered to "find the real principals" if his bail were reduced.

It was nearly two years before Zottarelli and co-conspirators Biago Russo and Nicola Salupo were brought to trial. On October 5, 1926, all three were found guilty in federal court in a case prosecuted by U.S. District Attorney A.E. Bernsteen. Representing the defendants were William J. Corrigan and Walter D. Meals. On October 21 fines and sentences were handed down. Zottarelli was sentenced to nine years in the Atlanta Penitentiary and fined $3,000; Russo received seven years and was fined $2,500; and Salupo got five years and a $1,000 fine. The men were released on $15,000 bonds while appeals were pending. Within weeks Zottarelli was disbarred for life from practicing law in the federal courts.

The appeals process was long. In July 1927, the United States Circuit Court reaffirmed the conviction, and in August 1927, the United States Appeals Court upheld the decision. On December 13, the United States Supreme Court refused to review the case. Zottarelli was to be taken to prison immediately, but was bed-ridden at his Bradford Road home in Cleveland Heights. Zottarelli beat the system by dying on January 4, 1928 at the age of 59.

16

The Last Days of Dominic Benigno

On May 10, less than 36 hours after the execution of Sam Purpura, the Court of Appeals set a date for the execution of Dominic Benigno – June 14. Attorney Patrick Mulligan announced that he would begin the appeal process at once. A month passed and on Friday morning, June 9, the Ohio State Supreme Court denied Mulligan's motion to file a petition in error. The dejected attorney conceded, "The fight is over. There's nothing I can do. It's up to the governor now."

It was rumored that Italian societies throughout the state would take up the cause of Benigno, much like they did for Sam Purpura. But there were precious little time remaining to organize a concerted effort with less than five days to go until the execution. On June 12, the governor's office claimed that not a single appeal for clemency was received by Davis.

On Monday, while family members visited, Benigno talked with reporters. Holding Florence, his three-year-old daughter, and caressing her hair, Benigno said, "I can't say much now. It is too late. My attorney has done all he can to save me, but I was framed and I guess I have to go.

"Sam Purpera was a false witness against me. In the last days he spent here we often heard him in his prayers begging God's forgiveness for testifying falsely against Dominic.

"Sam did that to me.

"But he is gone now and I must forgive him. The worst he could say of me was that I drove the automobile, and God alone knows I didn't."

Whether Benigno really said it or if it was just the way the newspapers printed it, the prisoner wavered on his innocence and level of responsibility. Just before Purpura's execution, *Cleveland Press* reporter Louis Seltzer reported that Benigno claimed all he did was drive the car. At other times he was adamant in denying any participation, whatsoever.

On June 13, Benigno was quite talkative, spewing much bravado as he commented on a number of topics. The day marked the six-month anniversary since he walked into the penitentiary and was placed on death row.

"I gave up hope then," he declared. "I knew I had been framed and that there was no chance for me."

Protesting his innocence, he told reporters he didn't want executive clemency, or his sentence commuted to life in prison. He asked for no reprieve so his case could be reviewed. Instead, he declared, "I want to be free, or I want to be executed.

"I didn't have to come back from Mexico. They didn't put anything over on me. I could have sailed for Italy instead of coming back here. But I had nothing to fear and I came.

"I don't want to spend years and years here, being punished for something I didn't do – maybe spend my whole life here.

"I am innocent. I ought to be freed, but I know I won't be."

While his comments the previous day about Purpura seemed forgiving, on this, the last day of his life, they turned to bitterness against his one-time friend, and toward Louis Komer.

"He lied against me," he said, "and if it had not been for him and for Louis Komer, I wouldn't be here tonight."

One of Benigno's claims regarding Purpura lying about him included a statement that when Benigno arrived at the prison the young man begged his forgiveness. Benigno said that Purpura's cellmate, Steve Myeski, the condemned prisoner from Youngstown, could confirm this. A reporter asked Myeski, "Did Sam ever say anything about Benigno?"

"Only when he was praying," answered Myeski.[1] "Every day in his prayers he'd ask God to forgive him for what he'd done to Benigno. He'd done it to try to save his own life."

The Youngstown prisoner had no reason to lie, and yet Benigno never tried to do anything with this information. It's entirely possible that what they heard was Purpura asking forgiveness not for framing his former friend, but for ratting him out.

"That's all right. I'm glad to see him get away with that stuff if he can. But he must remember God will give us justice. I won't get it here. I didn't get any justice in this world and the world, some day, will know I didn't, except in my first trial. That jury would have freed me, but it was discharged.[2] But I will get justice from God and so will Sam Purpura and Komer.

"I ask not mercy from anyone but God.

"I am glad to die and be away from all this. After all, tomorrow at this time I won't have any worries, and I know I am innocent.

"They won't have to put any special 'cops' around the place for me. I will go to the chair quietly and I can die bravely. Death causes no fear for me."

When the afternoon had passed, Benigno bade farewell to his two daughters, his wife and mother-in-law. Tears were shed by all except the condemned man. His brother, Anthony, was granted permission to remain with him until 9:00 p.m. As Benigno was leaving to go to the annex above the death house, he stopped and wished "good luck" to his fellow death row inmates.

After leaving the penitentiary, Mary Benigno made a last ditch plea, confronting an executive clerk for clemency. She claimed she was making the plea on behalf of her daughters. Mary didn't want them to go through life with the stigma of knowing their father died a murderer in the electric chair.

When asked during the day what he wanted for his last meal, Benigno replied, "Nothing! Nothing, I don't want anything to eat." He later requested, "A bottle of wine and a loaf of good Italian bread." To his surprise, the request was granted.

As midnight approached, Benigno told Father Kelly that he had forgiven Purpura and Komer for what they had done. "I have been given no justice in this world," Benigno told the priest. "I have been framed here, but God will deal justly with me. If it were not for Sam Purpera and Louie Komer I would not be here waiting to die. Sam is dead now and I forgive him what he did to me; and Louie, I forgive him, too. He is here for the rest of his life. I would rather die now than stay here so many years."

Benigno was led to the death chamber where an audience of 25 had gathered. In the crowd were Assistant County Prosecutors Walter I. Krewson[3] and Henry J. Williams (their presence was never explained by the newspaper); William J. Pope, the brother-in-law of George Fanner; and a friend of the Benigno family from Columbus whose purpose there was to let Mary know her husband did not beat the system.

By 12:06 a.m. Benigno was seated in the chair with the electrodes in place and the black mask drawn over his face. His heavy breathing was drowned out by the whirl of the dynamo and a current of 1,900 volts being applied to his body. At 12:08 those gathered were led out and Benigno's body was removed to the gray hearse like Motto's and Purpura's before him.

The next day Benigno's body was laid out for viewing in his Scovill Avenue home. Relatives and friends visited the home throughout the day paying their respects and comforting his widow Mary. On Saturday morning funeral services were conducted from the home before the body was laid to rest in Calvary Cemetery.

There was little fanfare in the newspapers about the execution. No long articles. No comments from the widows. No special reporters sent down to cover the electrocution first hand. Perhaps the public had grown tired of the deaths that surrounded the murders of Wilfred Sly and George Fanner – some deserved, others tragic. Since that fateful New Year's Eve day, in addition to the two innocent businessmen, seven other people were dead, all connected one way or another to the activity on the bridge. Frank Motto, Sam Purpura and Dominic Benigno were convicted and had forfeited their lives in the state's electric chair; Mary Sly had a heart attack, still mourning the death of her son; Frank Amato and Mike Rosalina were killed by police who were investigating their crimes in building a defense fund for Benigno; and Archie Budd, the juror, suffered a stroke during the deliberation period of the first Benigno trial and died six months later. In addition, during the course of the trials, Prosecutor Stanton, Assistant Prosecutor Cassidy and Chief Smith all suffered personal tragedies in their families.[4]

The Mayfield Road Mob had lost its first leader, Dominic Benigno. Former prosecutor and judge, Frank Merrick certainly painted him as that; few had more extensive knowledge. Benigno would be the last member of the infamous gang to pay for his crimes with his life – at least legally.

More than a year after the execution of her husband, Mary Benigno told a newspaper reporter that the night before he was to be put to death, he had one dying wish: "I want you to marry my brother Tom. He'll look after you and the children." Why Mary waited until August 1, 1923 to reveal this dying declaration was never explained. When talking to the reporter, her mood seemed anything but excited. Claiming the wedding date would be in October, she stated, "Maybe the first, maybe the last, I don't know yet. We'll be married in Cleveland. Maybe we'll have a honeymoon. I didn't have one the other time." She went on to say that Thomas had loved her children as if they were his own and that he was a fine man and a good provider.

The next day Mary backed off from her previous statements claiming she was not ready to wed and the whole incident was due to a misunderstanding. She stated that she was "comfortably situated," living with her parents and did not know if she would re-marry or not. Mary and Thomas, however, were married on October 31, 1923, at St. Anthony's by Father Humbert Rocchi.

Thomas Benigno and Mary's brother, Frank Galletti operated a bootleg business out of the family home at 1909 Scovill Avenue. Between 1922 and the spring of 1924 the police arrested the men six times at the address before finally padlocking the place in May. The two men reestablished their operation on the West Side, with Thomas and Mary moving to a nice home on River Edge Road. On August 25, 1928, Federal prohibition agents raided a roadhouse they were operating on Rocky River Drive near Ferncliffe Avenue, where beer and whiskey were being sold. On January 10, 1936, Thomas Benigno died at the age of 37. When one of her daughters was wed in 1954, she was listed in the marriage notice as Mrs. Thomas Benigno and living on Hastings Avenue in the suburb of East Cleveland.

By early 1930 Galletti was back at 1909 Scovill Avenue. The former home of the Benignos and Gallettis was now being used as a pool hall still owned by Lumino Galletti. By now Frank Galletti was out of the bootleg business and had moved into narcotics, where he had earned the reputation of being one of the largest distributors of cocaine to "colored addicts" in the city. On January 9, Galletti was arrested by Federal narcotics agents after selling 12 two-grain capsules of cocaine to a government informer. On March 4, Galletti was sentenced to serve two and a half years in the Atlanta Federal Penitentiary. Nothing more was reported about Frank Galletti. When his father Lumino died in November 1954, the death notice indicated he was living in Italy.

Chapter Endnotes

1. Steve Myeski was executed on June 23, 1922, nine days after Dominic Benigno.

2. Dominic Benigno made mention of this on more than one occasion, but he was mistaken. It wasn't the first jury that almost acquitted him; it was at the second trial, where Sam Purpera refused to testify, that a mistrial was declared. The voting by the jury at the time was reported to have 10 to 2 or 11 to 1 (depending on which account you read) for acquittal.

3. Walter Isaac Krewson served as an assistant county prosecutor under Edward Stanton from 1921 to 1925. A practicing attorney for more than 50 years, Krewson served as the law director of Parma from 1928 to 1931; was a West Side councilman from 1932 to 1942; and served as law director of Wickliffe from 1942 to 1961. Krewson died on March 21, 1983, one day before his 88th birthday, after a long bout with heart disease.

4. On April 16, 1921, Edward Stanton, Sr., the prosecutor's father, died at the age of 80 at his home after a two-week illness; on April 21 Neil J. Smith, the 29 year-old son of Chief Frank Smith, was killed along with two other men when a boiler exploded on a freight train on which he was employed as a fireman near Victor, New York; and on October 1, 1921 Mrs. Bridgett Cassidy, the mother of the assistant prosecutor, died from a stroke.

Part III
Aftermath

17

Louis Komer:
"One of Ohio's Living Dead"

In September 1926, some four years after Louis Komer began serving his life sentence, Dan W. Gallagher, a feature writer for the *Cleveland News*, wrote a series of articles for the newspaper titled "Ohio's Living Dead," a multi-part series on men and women confined in Ohio's prisons and reformatories. The "Toledo Kid" was the subject of Gallagher's ninth piece. The writer encountered a pathetic man who was in constant fear of being killed by his fellow inmates.

Komer knew that inside the prison convicts never forgave a squealer. From the day he arrived, he was a marked man. Twice in those first four years inmates tried to kill him. Once a convict attacked him with a knife and succeeded in cutting his throat. The wound kept Komer in the prison hospital for twenty days. This was followed by another knife attack in the dining hall. One of his would-be-killers was William Smith, a member of the ill-fated November 1926 escape attempt with Bobby Hunt and "Jiggs" Losteiner.[1] Komer told Gallagher, "I do not dare eat with or mingle with the others here. It would mean my life would be forfeited in no time. They are seeking the notoriety that would accrue to them by having killed Komer."

Komer protected himself by continually being thrown in the prison hole, known by inmates as the dungeon. His prison record showed a multitude of rules infractions including, "crookedness, fighting, lying, cheating, disobeying orders," all in the hope of being tossed in the "dungeon," a dark, cold place where Komer felt safe and could have peace of mind. In the forty-nine months Komer was in the penitentiary, he had worked less than five. The rest of the time he remained in his cell or in the "dungeon" fearing for his life.

Gallagher wrote:

> "Komer, now thirty-one, wants Warden Preston E. Thomas to construct a cage below the floor of the chapel and thrust him in it and keep him there. He's ostracized by all as things now stand. He keeps to his cell day in and day out, afraid to emerge. Occasionally threatening

notes, written by prisoners, are tossed into his cell. When this occurs, he 'goes to the dungeon' of his own volition. He begs, implores Warden Thomas that he be put in the punishment cell, so that his foes in the prison cannot wreak vengeance upon him. Last Christmas day, he voluntarily entered the 'dungeon' and remained there for twenty-five days."

The prisoner kept Warden Thomas up-to-date on his perilous existence through frequent letters. In one he revealed:

"WARDEN: Today I was again menaced by a prisoner with an improvised dagger. It is the case of another prisoner who wishes to gain notoriety by killing Komer.

"How will it end? Will I be stabbed to death? Will I kill a prisoner in self-defense and then be tried for my life?

"Will my mind break under the strain and make me a blubbering idiot, fit only for the insane asylum? Or will you isolate me – the balm for which I've craved and importuned you during my upwards of four years in prison."

After reading some of the letters to the warden, it was hardly a surprise to Gallagher when Komer informed him he wanted to become a writer of fictional short stories. He showed the reporter one he had started titled: "The Man Who Feared To Leave His Dungeon."

After his visit, Gallagher commented, "I've seen thousands of convicts in upwards of thirty years newspaper work. And Komer is the most terror-stricken of any I ever came across. He assisted in committing one of the most cowardly dual murders ever enacted. And now, in prison, his cowardice is plainly apparent."

In 1926, police arrested a man on a concealed weapons charge, who they believed might be the mysterious and alleged seventh member of the Sly-Fanner murder gang. Detective Inspector Cornelius Cody went to Prosecutor Stanton and wanted to discuss the possibility of bringing Komer up from Columbus, or transporting the suspect there, to be identified.

"Komer is 'prison crazy.'" Stanton revealed. "Some time ago we had a suspect in the Sly-Fanner murders [Sam Tilocco] and asked Komer to identify him.

"Komer said: 'If you say the man shot Sly and Fanner I'll swear to it.'

"We can't prosecute on such testimony," Stanton concluded.

The prosecutors had purposely let Komer remain alive to identify additional suspects or testify in court if Angelo Amato or Dominic

Lonardo were ever apprehended. Komer's mental condition rendered this impossible.

Komer not only survived the Sly-Fanner murder trials he also survived the worst prison fire in this country's history. On the afternoon of April 21, 1930, the day after Easter, three prisoners, hoping to escape, set fire to oil soaked rags on the roof of the "West Block" of the prison. This diversionary plan was to take place while most of the inmates were in the dining hall. With the men out of their cells and en mass the plotters thought they could escape in the confusion. The rags smoldered too long, however, before bursting into flames. By that time most of the prisoners were locked back in their cells.[2]

Soon the cell block was filled with black smoke and the holocaust was on. The tragedy claimed the lives of over 320 inmates. Most of the victims perished from poisonous fumes that came from green lumber that was being used for construction scaffolding. Others simply burned to death in their cells.

As the years passed, nothing changed for Komer in prison. He was considered the "most loathed man in the Ohio Penitentiary." The one friendship he developed over the years even turned on him. George C. Hubbs, a confidence man from Chicago, led the prisoner to believe he was working on his behalf and talked to him about establishing an annuity that would pay Komer $100 a month for five years. Komer gave Hubbs $1,200, but received nothing in return. He was scammed. In March 1940, a warrant was issued for the arrest of Hubbs charging him with obtaining money under false pretenses.

Chapter Endnotes

1. During the chaos that followed the Ohio Penitentiary fire in 1930, (see next chapter end note), Losteiner was identified as one of the ringleaders of the riots that took place. But this was the last hurrah for the Cleveland bad man. In the years that followed the fire Losteiner's health diminished rapidly. By the time of his death, John Bellamy reports, Losteiner was, "Toothless, sick, nearly blind, and old before his time." On July 27, 1937, the 51-year-old hoodlum died in the Ohio Penitentiary infirmary. He was buried in Calvary Cemetery.

2. The Ohio Penitentiary, which was built to house 1,500 inmates, had over 4,500 at the time of the fire. It was rumored that some prison guards purposely let the cells doors remain closed longer than necessary,

thus leading to a higher number of deaths. The tragedy led to repeal of the Norwood law which governed judicial control over minimum sentences that had contributed to the overcrowding of the prison. In the legislation that followed, new laws established the Ohio Parole Board and set guidelines and parole procedures for state prisons, which by 1932 had released 2,346 prisoners from the Ohio Penitentiary alone.

According to a popular website, for decades, "Many people believed that the otherwise empty cell blocks are haunted by the spirits of the men who died in the fire. They say that if you stand outside in the prison yard, you can hear the roar of phantom flames coming from inside.... and the horrible screams of men burning alive in their cells." Of course that all changed in the 1990s when the prison was torn down. The site where the "West Block" stood is now the arena parking lot where the Columbus Blue Jackets of the National Hockey League play. www.prairieghosts.com

18

Cleveland Police Never Gave Up

After a year and a half the excitement of the Sly-Fanner murders and the ensuing trials subsided. In April 1923, Ethyl Fanner[1] accepted $2,500 in a legal settlement with the county. She filed a petition claiming her husband was "lynched at the hands of a mob." The suit was filed under a law that made Cuyahoga County liable for up to $5,000 if failure could be proved to protect a citizen from mob violence. Keep in mind that the word "mob" referred to an unruly gathering of people and not to the Mafia or organized crime, as it later came to be associated.

Lawmakers didn't have this kind of incident in mind when passing the legislation. Provisions of the law stated, however, "A collection of people assembled for an unlawful purpose and intending to do damage or injury to anyone without authority of law, shall be deemed a mob. An act of violence by a mob upon the body of any person shall constitute a lynching." County commissioners, fearing if the case went to trial they would lose and have to pay $5,000, offered half in settlement.

After the convictions of Motto, Purpura, Benigno and Komer, Detective Cavolo's efforts in the case earned him a special commendation presented to him by Cleveland City Council. Now, some four years later, Cavolo was still running down leads in the Sly-Fanner murders. While most people believed there were only two killers still on the loose, Cavolo was convinced there were three. An informant told him there was a seventh man involved, who was said to have been on the bridge that day. This "seventh man," identified by the informant as Salvatore Tilocco, had fled his Cedar Avenue residence shortly after the killings, leaving behind his wife, and hadn't been home since.

Cavolo had developed a stellar reputation during his nine years as a Cleveland detective. His doggedness helped solve murder cases which were considered unsolvable by other members of the department. In his quest to bring these people to justice, Cavolo many times spent his own time and money running down leads, some that took him out of town.

If there was a criticism of Cavolo it was that he didn't always touch base with his superiors during these pursuits. As the decade wore on Cavolo found himself in trouble with his superiors causing at different times suspension, censorship and loss in rank. In today's jargon, Cavolo would have been considered a maverick. The trust the Italian community – on both sides of the law – placed in him led Cavolo to make some legal decisions entirely on his own. Cavolo's way of operating in today's culture surely would have been the basis for a good television crime drama, or at least a decent cop movie.

It was during his search for Tilocco in January 1925, that Cavolo ruffled feathers for the first time – at least it was reported publicly for the first time. Cavolo had made a half-dozen trips out of town tracking leads on Tilocco. Finally the detective received a letter from a friend in Detroit informing him that Tilocco, using the name "Sam Vecchio," was being held in a Pontiac, Michigan jail for his alleged participation in a bank robbery in nearby Farmington. Authorities there told Cavolo they didn't believe they had a good case against Tilocco and were willing to turn him over to Cleveland detectives. Cavolo got permission from Captain of Detectives Cornelius Cody and his old travel companion Inspector George Matowitz, to go to Pontiac and question the prisoner. He took along detective George Zicarelli.

After meeting with police in Pontiac and speaking to Tilocco, Cavolo left Zicarelli behind and hurried back to Cleveland for a meeting with Prosecutor Stanton to discuss a first-degree murder charge against Tilocco. Cavolo, however, was summoned to police headquarters by Chief Jacob Graul and ordered not to go before the grand jury. The chief and new Safety Director Edwin D. Barry[2*] were incensed because they had not been made aware of Cavolo's actions. Cavolo claimed he was "bawled out" by Barry and Graul in the chief's office. He quoted the safety director as stating, "leave this dead wood alone [referring to the Sly-Fanner case] and work on something new."

Although Cavolo had followed proper procedures in notifying his superiors about the trip, the two officials were upset because they had not been informed – which should have been communicated to them by either Cody or Matowitz. Barry, who never admitted that Cavolo was censored, told reporters, "I had no intention of criticizing Cavolo. I only wanted to know when our officers go out of town and where they go. I don't want to hear from the individual detectives, but the chief should notify me."

Graul made it a little more personal when he spoke to reporters. "Cavolo is a peculiar fellow," the chief stated. "He gets information and then goes into conference with Stanton before he tells us about it. We don't like this and object to it."

In defense of his actions, Cavolo told a reporter, "I don't claim that I am a good detective. I only say this, that I put in more hours, work harder, and if it were not for new cases that had come up I would have had Tilocco and the other two men at liberty in the Sly-Fanner killings in jail long ago. I couldn't devote all my time to this one case."

Cavolo was clearly upset and declared he was going to get out of the detective bureau and go back to being a patrolman. "At least I will have some time to spend with my family when I get away from the bureau," he stated. The Tilocco indictment[3] was not pursued and Cavolo remained in his position at the detective bureau.

Chapter Endnotes

1. On May 27, 1926, Ethyl Fanner married Arthur J. Henry. She was now 37 years old. She died in May 1972, at the age of 83.

2. Edwin Daniel Barry served as Cuyahoga County Sheriff from 1901 to 1905. An intimate of Cuyahoga County Republican Party boss Maurice Maschke, he was suggested to William R. Hopkins, who took office under Cleveland's new City Manager Plan on January 1, 1924, as a good candidate for Director of Public Safety. Barry served in that capacity until February 1932.

3. According to a *Sunday News* article on July 6, 1930, Tilocco's Cleveland police record showed an arrest on January 25, 1924, as a suspect in the Sly-Fanner murders. I checked with the Farmington, Michigan, Police Department, but they were unable to provide me with any information regarding disposition of the bank robbery case there.

19

"Big Angelo" Amato Sightings:

Parts 1 & 2

Angelo Amato, who was arrested and questioned on January 4, 1921, just four days after the Sly-Fanner killings, was released and believed to have high-tailed it out of town, leaving immediately for Italy – and hadn't been seen since, despite rumors he had re-entered the city during May 1921.

Around mid-1925, a dispatch was received in Washington D.C. from the consulate general in Rome – Angelo Amato was located. The dispatch alluded to a letter sent in 1921 from Prosecutor Stanton to the U.S. State Department as the basis for the consul general's efforts to find the fugitive. The Cleveland Automobile Club then hired a "secret agent," to trail Amato and track his movements. The agent reported that Amato "supported himself by gambling." When first discovered, Amato was living in Palermo, Sicily, but soon returned to his hometown of Licata.

The state department put the wheels in motion to affect Amato's arrest and on August 13 he was taken into custody. Word of his arrest was cabled to the Cleveland Automobile Club. A meeting was scheduled for the next day to discuss a strategy. Meeting in Safety Director Barry's office were Fred Caley and Frank Merrick of the automobile club, Chief Graul and a member of Stanton's office. Before the meeting convened, Caley had already made it known that the club was prepared to finance the presentation of depositions and evidence for the pending trial.

The Cleveland Police Department and the county prosecutor's office were ecstatic about the arrest. Barry and Graul were making plans to bring former Detective Phil Mooney out of retirement in anticipation of him traveling to Sicily with Charles Cavolo for the trial. Depositions were obtained from witnesses to the killings and a visit was made to Louis Komer at the Ohio Penitentiary.

Stanton, who was in Detroit in connection with the trial of "Big Jim" Morton,* telephoned his office and ordered Harry Parsons to leave for Washington D.C. immediately to meet with state department attaches and ask for an official introduction to the counselor of the Italian embassy. Parsons was then to obtain information pertaining to procedures that would have to be followed by Stanton for a trial in Italy.

Italy had a policy of refusing to extradite its citizens to countries that practiced capital punishment. A *Cleveland News* headline advised: "Expect Quick Justice in Italy." The newspaper reported that Amato's "present status as an Italian citizen would preclude extraditing him to this country for trial, but in view of the spirit of co-operation between Italy and the United States, betokened in previous murder cases, no difficulty was foreseen in bringing him to trial in Italy, where justice has been proved speedily and adequate."

The newspaper's tone changed the next day when it learned "whether [Amato] has been arrested or placed under constant surveillance of the Italian government is not known. Speedy action is necessary...otherwise Amato might slip through the fingers of authorities, who have shown their disposition to co-operate with this country in bringing him to trial in Italy."

On August 18, a certified copy of the indictment was signed by Ohio Governor Vic Donahey and forwarded to the state department in Washington D.C. The next step was to have the state department formally request that Italy place Amato on trial for the murders. Later that day, Frank Merrick announced that reports Amato was arrested were false, but that he was "under surveillance" by special agents who could arrest him at any time.

The next day U.S. Secretary of State Frank Kellogg cabled a request to Italian authorities requesting that they arrest Amato. The Italian government replied that they needed more information before placing an Italian citizen under arrest. Detective Cavolo was then asked to prepare additional documentation. A warrant was then prepared, sworn to by Cavolo, and sent to Columbus for Donahey's signature. The warrant was then forwarded to Kellogg in Washington D.C.

To the dismay of Cleveland law enforcement, the Amato sighting proved to be false and the stories of Amato quickly disappeared from the headlines. More than two years passed before the next sighting. On August 23, 1927 the newspapers reported that a suspect "believed to be Amato" was under surveillance by authorities in Girgenti, Sicily. An attorney for the Italian consul in Cleveland told Stanton that the "Italian authorities desired further information before taking the man into custody." Stanton again began the process of preparing the "desired information."

Stanton made plans to get a Bertillon picture of Amato, taken when he was once jailed as a suspicious person here, to be shown to Komer. On October 28, Stanton's new chief assistant James Connell, traveled to the Ohio Penitentiary along with, now Detective Sergeant Charles Cavolo and Detective Captain Emmett J. Potts. Komer identified the picture of Amato as one of the triggermen and stated, "I would not be mistaken. Amato was one of the killers."

Cavolo told reporters that according to Italian law, a suspect can be held for up to 18 months without being charged with a crime. He said that Assistant County Prosecutor Maurice J. Meyer was getting ready to sail for Paris to attend an American Legion convention. The year-and-a-half window would give him ample time to reach Italy to assist in the prosecution of Amato. During this time all the documentation – trial transcripts, depositions and affidavits –had to be translated to Italian.

The Cleveland Automobile Club quickly offered its services again, however Stanton turned them down citing that after the capture of Benigno and Coletto in Mexico the club had asked for reimbursement. Despite being declined, the automobile club sent Merrick to Sicily to participate in the manhunt. Merrick reported that he was "hot on Amato's trail" and would have placed him under arrest if it hadn't been necessary to obtain an arrest order, signed by Governor Donahey of Ohio. It was reported that when the request went to the governor, word also reached Amato's underworld friends in Cleveland who immediately cabled him and advised him to "keep clear" of Merrick. Amato was said to have made his escape just prior to the arrest orders arriving from Donahey.

The Sly-Fanner murders lay dormant until February 1, 1928. Then a relative of Wilfred Sly approached Prosecutor Stanton and said he believed a man being held on a concealed weapons charge may have been the mysterious "seventh gunman." Whatever information the relative had on which to base his accusation was never revealed. Stanton met with Detective Chief Cody, who told him the prisoner was investigated for the crime back in 1924 and released. Cody was convinced of his innocence and the suspect was released the next day.

20

Dominic Lonardo Revealed

On the afternoon of October 26, 1928, Joseph Piazza was at home in his $35,000 dwelling at 298 Monterey Blvd in the fashionable St. Francis Wood section of San Francisco, relaxing and talking to a neighbor. Piazza was a respectable and prosperous grape buyer. He purchased grapes from local wholesalers and sold them to retailers all over the state. Piazza was conversing with Dominic DeMarco, who had moved into a home across the street from Piazza at 297 Monterey Blvd. Piazza's wife, Constantina, a young lady from a prominent San Francisco family, was married to Joseph for four years. She was across the street with her two young children – Antoinette, 3 and Madeline, 19 months – talking with DeMarco's wife.

The conversation at the Piazza home was suddenly interrupted by a knock at the door. It was a police lieutenant and three detectives. They arrested Joseph Piazza for the murders of Wilfred Sly and George Fanner. The police were convinced that Piazza was Dominic Lonardo. Taken into custody was Dominic DeMarco, Piazza's neighbor of three weeks, who was a nephew of the Lonardo brothers.

There was a mystery to the apprehension of Dominic Lonardo that has never been cleared up. How was Joe Piazza discovered? The *San Francisco Examiner* stated in the opening paragraph of their coverage that, "they 'put the finger on' Joe Piazza." Who "they" were was never discussed in the article. The mystery deepened when the newspaper stated, "Cleveland detectives suspected the fugitive had come to San Francisco. They enlisted the aid of the San Francisco police…" This certainly indicates that whoever revealed that Lonardo was hiding in the Bay City, confided it to the Cleveland Police Department.

The *San Francisco Chronicle* confirmed that the information originated in Cleveland. "The arrests," the newspaper reported, "followed nearly a month of search by the homicide squad…following information from Cleveland that Lonardo was believed to be in San Francisco.

"A few days ago the police received information that Piazza was the man they were seeking. He was away from home and only returned yesterday, when the arrest was made…"

The arrested pair was hustled off to jail where Lonardo, who had $8,000 in his possession, was held for the double murder, and DeMarco as a suspicious person. Lonardo vehemently protested his innocence, while DeMarco refused to talk. When first notified of the arrests, Cleveland officials thought DeMarco might actually be Angelo Amato. This rumor was dispelled after Stanton provided the San Francisco police with a physical description of Amato. The men's wives were unaware of their arrests until informed by a *Plain Dealer* news correspondent. Both protested their husband's innocence, as Constantina cried hysterically.

The same *Plain Dealer* correspondent was able to interview Lonardo at the San Francisco jail, where he "professed bewilderment at the charges against him." Lonardo, claiming to be Piazza, said that he had once lived in Cleveland, but had relocated to the West Coast around October or November 1919, moving from Los Angeles to San Francisco in 1924. He denied allegations that he had gone to Italy after the murders. Lonardo said he married the daughter of a wealthy family from San Francisco. The maiden name of the woman given by Lonardo was found by police to be false.

A detective lieutenant from the San Francisco Police Department revealed that in September they had raided the Piazza residence (for what, he did not disclose). He claimed that Piazza's real identity was questioned at that time, but because of his wealth and "standing among Italian commission men," the authorities decided not to act until they had something beyond suspicion.

The *Plain Dealer* also reported that for some time rumors were circulating that Louis Komer was going insane and might be unable to testify if Lonardo was ever apprehended. Some in law enforcement believed these rumors were started by friends of Lonardo to help destroy a potential case against him, making it possible for him to return to Cleveland and surrender.

Stanton heard the rumors and responded, "I do not think this insanity report is true, but as soon as we are absolutely certain that the man arrested in San Francisco is Lonardo, I'll get to Columbus and talk with Komer." This seems contrary to comments attributed to Stanton by the newspapers two years earlier regarding Komer's mental condition.

Ohio Penitentiary Warden P. E. Thomas was also questioned about the rumor. "Komer is waiting table for me and my family and you can be sure if there were anything wrong with him he wouldn't be serving me," laughed Thomas.

By Monday Lonardo announced he was fighting extradition to Ohio. He was adamant in claiming he was not Dominic Lonardo and his lawyers demanded that witnesses be sent from Cleveland to identify him. Cleveland police were one step ahead. After notification of Lonardo's arrest, witnesses who had testified at the trials of the previously convicted men were being contacted.

Spearheading the effort to bring Lonardo to justice in this new phase of the murder investigation was Detective Inspector Cornelius W. Cody.* Born in Shrewsbury, Massachusetts in 1882, Cody was known as "Connie" to his boyhood chums. As a young man he was said to be desirous of the "active life" and wanting to live in a larger city. While still a teenager he headed for Worcester, Massachusetts, where he found work as a streetcar operator. He soon tired of this and sought out a larger residence, Buffalo, New York. He found work and a wife in the city at the far end of Lake Erie, as well as a new nickname, "Buffalo Bill."

Six months in Buffalo hadn't sated Cody's appetite for big city living, so he moved to Cleveland. Here Cody found work as a guard at the Cleveland State Hospital.[1] After a two-year stint there Cody applied for and became a patrolman on the Cleveland police force. His first day on duty was February 20, 1907.

Beginning at the Euclid-East 105th Street Precinct, Cody spent the next eleven years as a patrolman, walking beats on the East Side and downtown districts. On February 21, 1918, he was promoted to sergeant. It was at this point Cody decided he was going to make it a career on the force and he went about his work with a renewed passion and enthusiasm. Police brass were quick to take notice and less than 20 months later, on October 1, 1919, Cody was promoted to lieutenant.

In his new position Cody was taken off the streets and placed in the Detective Bureau as head of the vice squad. After the appointment of Jacob Graul as Chief of Police in January 1922, the vice squad was disbanded and their work spread among the precincts.

On June 1, 1923, Cody was promoted to captain. Exactly two and a half years later, on December 1, 1925, Cody was named Chief Inspector of the Detective Bureau and given complete command of the department. One newspaper account described him:

> "Behind his ham-like fists is the power of 230 pounds of bone and muscle. In his heart is unquestioned courage. To those who knew him well, Inspector Cody is known as 'The Skipper.' Those who never knew him would have no difficulty picking him out of any throng as a policeman. 'Skipper' is a powerful man, six-feet tall, a square, determined jaw and a pair of sparkling eyes that look not straight at you, but clear through you."

Cody's reputation within the department reached legendary status on September 13, 1928. Paul Jaworski, who boasted of murdering 26 men, was eating in a Fleet Avenue restaurant with John Vasbinder. The two had broken out of the Allegheny County Jail in Pittsburgh on August 18, 1927. Police Patrolmen George Effinger and Anthony Wieczorek, along with three other officers headed to the restaurant after Jaworski was reported there by a former Pittsburgh resident who was familiar with the hood. Jaworski spotted Effinger and Wieczorek as they entered and immediately started blasting. Wieczorek was hit four times, while Effinger was hit once in the lung. In the exchange of gunfire, a bystander was wounded and Jaworski was hit twice.

Jaworski escaped out the rear door of the restaurant and found shelter in a house on nearby Chambers Avenue. The home was quickly surrounded by 75 angry Cleveland police officers. A crowd of spectators, estimated to be near 600, also gathered round. Jaworski appeared in several rooms as police heaved tear gas bombs through the windows trying to force the killer out. Finally, Cody, with a .38 in each hand, raced into the smoke-filled home and flushed Jaworski into the kitchen, where he was felled by a shotgun blast from another officer.

Wieczorek was taken to St. Alexis' Hospital where he died. Effinger's wound contributed to his death some four and a half years later. He died in St. Alexis' Hospital on March 20, 1933. Jaworski recovered from his wounds and was extradited back to Pennsylvania, where he was executed in January 1929 in the electric chair at Rockview Penitentiary in Bellefonte, Pennsylvania.

Before leaving for the West Coast, Cody visited Komer in prison, taking with him a newspaper photograph of Lonardo from the *San Francisco Chronicle*. Cody told reporters that he had obtained a "satisfactory statement" from the prisoner, but refused to confirm if Komer was able to identify the picture. The *Cleveland News* reported, "Cody's announcement that Lonardo would be returned to Cleveland was taken as evidence, however, that Komer had positively linked him as a member of the gang." The day after Cody departed, both the *News* and the *Plain Dealer* reported that Komer had "failed" to identify Lonardo from the photograph. The newspapers also pointed out that only one of the fifteen witnesses from the bridge recognized Lonardo from the same picture.

Stanton initially stated that he would not go to the West Coast unless the suspect fought extradition. Even though the newspapers reported Stanton was going to San Francisco with the statements collected from witnesses, in the end Inspector Cody went with Detective Clarence Banks, who was making an encore appearance on the coast. Cody had informed his superiors that despite the fact he couldn't get a positive identification of the suspect before leaving, he hoped to "break down" Lonardo's alibi. Perhaps Stanton, knowing that Komer had failed to identify Lonardo's picture, decided a trip out west was futile.

On November 5, without explaining his means of identifying the suspect, Cody sent a telegram to Stanton stating that the suspect was "Lonardo all right." Cody then asked the governor of California to issue an executive order for the return of Lonardo to Cleveland. A week later, Cody wired Stanton, "We must know if you can obtain affidavits [from witnesses]. Without affidavits think California governor will refuse papers. Rush answer."

Of the fifteen witnesses to testify, twelve were located, two had passed away, and the last one had moved to "parts unknown." Despite what was reported earlier, not one of the twelve could identify the man calling himself Joseph Piazza, as one of the killers on the bridge back in 1920.

In addition to talking with the witnesses, detectives were interviewing people in the Big Italy neighborhood in an attempt to prove that Lonardo was actually in Cleveland on the day of the murders. Many feared vengeance from the friends of the Lonardo family if they talked. One man claimed to have seen Lonardo in town that day, but refused to sign an affidavit. Parsons dejectedly announced, "We have given up all hope of getting the man back to Cleveland to stand trial."

By mid-November the extradition hearing was about to begin. Cody and Banks lamented that Sam Purpura had not been kept alive to testify. As they prepared to go before California Governor Clement Calhoun Young, Cody confessed, "It looks like the odds are against us." Things only got worse as Cody found out that Lonardo's attorney had 20 affidavits of his own from alibi witnesses stating that Lonardo was not in Cleveland at the time of the murders, and that he was preparing to file habeas corpus writ for his client in case the decision in the extradition hearings favored the Cleveland police.

Despite the bleak outlook, on Friday, November 16, Governor Young signed the extradition warrant after refusing to hear twelve alibi witnesses testify on Lonardo's behalf. Now Cody had but one obstacle left to getting Lonardo on a return train ride to Cleveland – the habeas corpus hearing, which was scheduled for Monday morning. "Were it not for the hearing on the writ," Cody declared, "we would take our prisoner and leave for Cleveland tonight. We anticipate no trouble." Stanton didn't share Cody's optimism, knowing it might take weeks for the habeas corpus hearing to conclude.

Cody needed to produce "positive evidence" to show the suspect was in Cleveland on the day of the murders or Lonardo would go free. Detective

Edward Conroy, who claimed he had seen Lonardo on Scovill Avenue shortly before the murders, went to the prosecutor's office to swear out the affidavit. The statement was air-mailed to Sacramento, the state capital of California, over the weekend. The court did not find the detective's statement compelling enough to drop the motion, and Cody was given another week, until November 26, to provide additional evidence.

On November 24, while the habeas corpus hearing was still proceeding, Lonardo dropped the argument that he was Piazza, but produced a dozen witnesses to say he was in San Francisco on December 31, 1920. The testimony of one of his witnesses was impeached, however, while discrepancies were found in his own statement as to his whereabouts on that fateful day.

On December 1, a month after Cody left for the West Coast, Lonardo lost his habeas corpus battle in common pleas court, but immediately took the case to the appeals court. On December 3, the California Appellate Court heard arguments and announced it would make its decision in two or three days. Nine days later, the appellate court ruled that the evidence provided by Cody was "too meager," and Dominic Lonardo was set free. Cody sadly wired Chief Graul that he and Banks were leaving for Cleveland in the morning after we're "officially notified that we have lost our man."

Waiting for Cody was an angry William R. Hopkins,[2] Cleveland's City Manager, who was already questioning the logic behind Cody's nearly 45-day absence from the city. Hopkins complained, "Why! They send the chief of detectives out to California and he stays there for a month trying to capture a man with children and a respectable position – and they don't have a definite thing on him.

"That's small town stuff! I don't know what Cody's doing out there, but he's been gone since November 1."

Safety Director Barry defended Cody's sabbatical, which cost the city $1,200, stating that it was an important case. "If we had sent a subordinate on this job, and he failed, we could be criticized for not having done our best. However, we sent our best man and he could not succeed and I don't think we are subject to any criticism."

Prosecutor Stanton saw things in a more positive light claiming Cody had obtained information in California that could lead to a stronger case making extradition possible at a future date. He stated the first-degree murder indictment for Dominic Lonardo would remain on file "to be used at the first opportunity."

Chapter Endnotes

1. Known as the Northern Ohio Lunatic Asylum, the Cleveland State Hospital was a state-supported psychiatric facility for long-term care. It was the second insane asylum in Ohio when it opened in March 1855, in Newburgh (a Cleveland neighborhood located in the southeast section, not to be confused with Newburgh Heights, a suburb of Cuyahoga County) it was often referred to as the Newburgh State Hospital. On September 26, 1872, the work of careless repairmen was said to be the cause of a fire which killed several patients and displaced 500 more. The hospital was rebuilt on Turney Road. The hospital was active in the care of patients until the mid-1970s.

2. William Rowland Hopkins served as Cleveland's first City Manager under a new form of government that was approved by the voters in November 1921, to take effect on January 1, 1924. One of Hopkins' first moves was to appoint former Cuyahoga County Sheriff, Edwin D. Barry as his Director of Public Safety. In January 1930, city council members who selected the city manager removed Hopkins and voted in Daniel E. Morgan. Cleveland Hopkins International Airport is named in honor of the former city official. Hopkins died on February 9, 1961, and is buried in Lake View Cemetery.

21

Coletto Suicide

Throughout the Prohibition years Charles "Chuck" Coletto and Frank "Frankie Burns" Milazzo were alleged to have participated in just about every murder carried out by the Mayfield Road Mob. Both were friends of Benigno and Motto. Within a few years of those two being executed for the Sly-Fanner killings, rumors abounded that Biago DePalma had ratted out his old partners. In addition, DePalma, shortly after the Sly-Fanner murders, was convicted of carrying concealed weapons. With the penitentiary staring him in the face he made a trade with police and prosecutors; he would tell them the whereabouts of Emma Colavito. The "potion killer," who was acquitted in the Dan Kaber murder case, was now the main suspect in the poisoning death of another woman's husband, Marino Costanza. Colavito was wanted for murder, DePalma for carrying a weapon, a crime punishable by not more than three years in jail. Frank Merrick later recalled, "It looked like a great trade. I know personally that DePalma turned up Emma Colavito[1] and later his case was disposed of without his having to serve any sentence." But the "ratting out" process made him a target of his former Mayfield Road Mob associates, who quietly bided their time.

In August 1926, DePalma was the key figure in a window smashing ring that began operating in the final weeks of a union painters and glaziers' strike, which was going on since March 1. Police believed the men were hired as goons by the union bosses to target work done by union employees who had drifted back to work. Investigators were frustrated in their efforts to catch the vandals who employed a number of methods; some threw rocks, others used guns, stink bombs were sometimes tossed, and one group used sling-shots to propel objects through the windows from moving cars. DePalma was arrested and while awaiting trial a death threat was made to Prosecutor Stanton. The prosecutor made light of the threat until one night when a man was waiting in the shadows outside his garage as he returned home with his wife and daughter. Mrs. Stanton scared the figure off, but injured an ankle in the excitement. DePalma eventually pleaded guilty and received a 30-day workhouse sentence.

Two months after DePalma's release, during the early morning hours of Saturday, February 19, 1927, Detective Otto Diskowski noticed DePalma's car parked outside a poolroom on Prospect Avenue. The detective also noticed another car parked close behind. At the wheel was Frank Milazzo. In the back seat sat Charles Coletto. When Diskowski asked why they were there, Milazzo answered "We're waiting for a broad."

After leaving the poolroom, around 2:00 a.m., DePalma and his chauffeur, Harry Maciak, picked up Oscar Stanton, an automobile mechanic. The plan was to drop off DePalma first and then for Stanton to drive Maciak home, retaining the automobile to do some mechanical work. With Maciak driving and the other two men in the back seat, the trio arrived at DePalma's 1274 Scovill Avenue address at 2:30. It was reported that the house was "used as a rendezvous for his after-nightfall activities," while his family dwelling was in Avon, Ohio, a small community west of the city just over the Lorain County line. Maciak stopped the car under a bright streetlight in front of the house. DePalma exited the automobile and headed up the driveway, while Stanton climbed into the front seat.

As DePalma neared the front porch, two gunmen with their collars turned up to hide their faces, stepped from the shadows. With one armed with a shotgun and the other a revolver, the first round of fire sent DePalma to the ground. The killers then approached their dying victim to finish him off. One report stated, "Two gunmen stepped over him and fired repeatedly into the prostrate form." The post mortem report showed DePalma was hit in the face by eight bullets, mostly on the left side – one destroyed his left eye. On his hands and chest were about 40 wounds, indicating that DePalma had held out his hands in an act of self-preservation to stop the shotgun blast. Three pellets penetrated the left ventricle of his heart causing his death. Vengeance, though long in coming, was finally achieved.

On July 26, 1934, the life of Charles Coletto came to an end. Coletto wasn't the victim of two slugs behind the right ear or a shotgun blast to the head or chest. He didn't go down in a blazing gun battle with police. Instead, Coletto was killed by the same hand that had snuffed out, by police counts, nearly a dozen lives – his own.

Sometime before Prohibition was repealed Coletto was stricken with tuberculosis. As his condition worsened, doctors advised him to relocate to a warmer, drier climate. Coletto moved to Arizona. A year of "clean living" in the hot Southwest, however, hadn't improved his condition. Coletto grew despondent and returned to Cleveland just two weeks before his death.

The baby-faced enforcer was rooming in an East Side hotel. On the evening of July 26 he hailed a taxi and was driven to 2391 Noble Road in Cleveland Heights, the home of his brother, Anthony. Around the corner and five houses down at 939 Vineshire Road lived another brother, John, with his wife Agnes. A young woman, living in the upstairs suite of

Anthony's house watched Coletto as he exited the cab and approached the front door. He rang the doorbell several times, but no one in the Coletto household was home. He walked slowly around to the back of the house where he entered the garage.

The young woman, Maria Veranti, didn't know who the man was. She quickly left the house and ran to John Coletto's home, where her mother was visiting with Agnes. Maria told the women about the man ringing the door bell and then entering the garage. Having no idea who the man was they thought he might be trying to steal something from the garage. They ran toward the Noble Road home to find out what he was doing. As the two women approached the garage they heard a single gunshot. Charles Coletto, the ace gunman of the Mayfield Road Mob, had ended his suffering by firing a .45 bullet into the left side of his brain.

The two women froze in their tracks. When they regained their composure, they entered the garage and found the body. Both women ran screaming to a telephone and called Cleveland Heights police. Sergeant Homer Davis was the first to respond. He found the 36 year-old Coletto, described as "wasted and emaciated by the ravages of tuberculosis," with a gaping wound to the head.

The only comment from relatives was, "he kept to himself and we didn't see him as often as we see other members of the family." It was easy to understand why. Even in death Charles Coletto kept to himself. He's buried in Calvary Cemetery in an unmarked grave. It is interesting to note that I have looked for Coletto's grave on a couple of occasions over the years. While I was not able to find it, I found it curious that surrounding the area where he is supposed to be resting are the graves of no less than 14 priests!

After the repeal of Prohibition, Frank Milazzo appears to have steered clear of trouble. The only time he made the newspapers was in December 1939 after he pled guilty to a charge of careless driving, that was reduced from driving while intoxicated. Milazzo, who was described in the article as a "night club proprietor," had hit a car in Garfield Heights two months earlier and was found to be "in the third stage of intoxication." His fine and court costs totaled $12.65.

On May 13, 1959, Milazzo "died suddenly" at the Doanbrooke Hotel where he was living. He was 64 years old. His death notice did not denote any wife or children. He was buried in Lake View Cemetery. While I have been unable to find any information in the newspaper's about Milazzo's death, the term "died suddenly" normally indicates the person took his own life. When I asked for help at Lake View Cemetery, in checking for a cause of death in their burial records, I was told that his death was ruled a "homicide."

Chapter Endnotes

1. In June 1924, Emma Colavito was tried for the murder of Marino Costanzo. The man, described as a drunken, abusive husband, died shortly after Colavito began a two-week stay at his home some four years earlier. Fannie Costanzo, the victim's wife, was acquitted of the murder and claimed it was carried out by Colavito. During the trial Colavito was defended by Max L. Bernsteen, the brother of United States Attorney A.E. Bernsteen, while Assistant County Prosecutor Walter Krewson handled the case for the state. Called as a witness, Fannie Costanzo refused to testify and was jailed for contempt. Colavito was found guilty of first-degree murder with a recommendation of mercy on June 5, 1924. Sentenced to life at Marysville, she found herself in the same prison as Eva Kaber, her old partner in crime. The newspapers reported the two "shunned" each other. Colavito died in the prison in 1972 after spending 48 years there.

22

"Big Angelo" Amato Sighting: Parts 3 and 4

On July 8, 1929, seven months after the failed attempt to bring Dominic Lonardo to justice, Angelo Amato was back in the news. It had been nearly four years since it was announced Amato was found in Sicily. The Italian consulate in Cleveland now claimed Amato was arrested and would be tried in Italy in September, 1929. The Italian government refused requests to extradite Amato to Cleveland to stand trial.

It was reported that Amato would be defended by two of the leading criminal defense lawyers in Italy.[1] In addition, local attorney Salvatore M. LoPresti would act as Amato's Cleveland counsel. On July 15, LoPresti announced, "There will be seven or eight alibi witnesses. I don't know just what the alibi is. I haven't talked to witnesses yet." LoPresti immediately began taking depositions from those witnesses and informed new county prosecutor, Ray T. Miller, so he could examine them.

After eight years as Cuyahoga County prosecutor, tying a record of service held by Alexander Hadden,[2] Edward Stanton decided not to seek a fifth term. Instead, he joined his former chief assistant, James Connell, in the law firm of Stanton & Connell with offices in the new Terminal Tower. During his four terms in office Stanton and his assistants handled 12,976 cases, of which 74% resulted in conviction. Eight men were sent to the electric chair under Stanton's watch.

Stanton strongly supported Arthur H. Day to be his Republican successor, but Ray T. Miller launched a smear campaign attacking long-time Republican County Leader Maurice Maschke, as well as Day and Stanton. One of his allegations was that "gangland figures were favorites" of the Maschke organization. While this was never proven, it is interesting to note that within a year and a half of leaving office Stanton was hired by Mayfield Road Mob boss Frank Milano for legal representation, while Connell successfully represented Angelo "Big Ange" Lonardo and his cousin, Dominic Sospirato in their retrial for the murder of Salvatore "Black Sam" Todaro, the alleged mastermind behind the October 1927 slaying of Cleveland Mafia boss "Big Joe" Lonardo and his brother John, the latter a one-time suspect arrested in the Sly-Fanner murders.

In leaving office Stanton had unkind words for the police department. In a newspaper interview he complained, "A man can't stand up under all this and do it every day. You can go just so far and then you're done. The grind just got too hard.

"The police like to hand you a red hot poker and let you make the best of it. I've handled a few – one in the Sly-Fanner murders.

"The only trouble with the police is that they go out and arrest the person they believe committed the crime, and then they quit. They leave the bulk of the evidence for the prosecutor to get. If he doesn't get it, nobody does. That doesn't mean assistants, either, it means the prosecutor."

In announcing his retirement Edward Stanton* complained about "thick-headed police," "faked confessions," and a "fix me this or that" attitude by Cleveland's top brass.

Stanton and Connell's positions in the prosecutor's office were taken by Miller and Frank Merrick, back for his second tour of duty.

At Angelo Amato's deposition hearings, to be held in LoPresti's office in the Society for Savings Building on Public Square, the attorney wanted to take statements from Cavolo, Cody and Costello. The attorney was informed by Merrick that the officers were not obliged to testify for the defense. Representing the Italian government at these hearings was Louis E. Lanza.

LoPresti's strategy was to challenge the testimony of Louis Komer "on the ground that his mind is unbalanced." The rumor of Komer's insanity was apparently still alive. Psychiatrists would be sent to the penitentiary to examine the prisoner's state of mind. On July 17, five witnesses testified in LoPresti's office that Amato was downtown "buying the baby some clothes," at the time of the double murder.

September came and went and soon the Amato trial was pushed back until February 1930. In January, LoPresti wrote to the clerk of courts in the San Francisco appeals court asking for a copy of the transcripts from the habeas corpus hearings of Dominic Lonardo, held 13 months earlier. In responding to his request, the clerk sent newspaper clippings about the disappearance of Dominic Lonardo on December 14. Christiana reported that her husband had left home with a large sum of money and was wearing a valuable diamond. She was sure he was "taken for a ride." Although he was confident that Lonardo would stay clear of Cleveland, Cody ordered all police officers to "be on the lookout" for him. Although his murder was never confirmed, there is no record of Dominic Lonardo ever surfacing in public again.

The reason the Amato trial was pushed back was because he was still a fugitive, it was yet another false arrest report. This time, however, the Italian government decided to try him in absentia. Salvatore LoPresti traveled to Sicily to represent Amato in August 1930. After the prosecution read the documentation supplied by Cleveland officials, LoPresti was told to put on his case. He told the court there could be no defense without the defendant present. The court was about to sentence Amato to 30 years at hard labor when LoPresti filed a motion attacking the jurisdiction of the Italian court on the grounds that the crime was committed on American soil. He obtained a mistrial decree on the promise that Amato would turn himself in later. What time "later" meant was anyone's guess.

Two months after the trial LoPresti was back in Cleveland where he told a *News* reporter, "I was in Italy recently and saw Amato while I was gone, although I will not say where I saw him. He wants to come back and face the music. He is innocent of the charge and will be acquitted." LoPresti raised some eyebrows with his next statement.

"One of Prosecutor Miller's assistants heard me say Amato would waive extradition and return to Cleveland willingly. But Miller has made no effort to communicate with me," the attorney revealed. "He can be located, if the prosecutor is interested in bringing him back. All I ask is that Amato be promised that no deportation proceedings will be started against him."

By the time "Big Angelo" Amato visited the headlines again, in March 1934, there were major changes in the city's political and law enforcement leadership. George Matowitz* had succeeded Jacob Graul as Chief of Police in the fall of 1930. Frank Merrick* – who in succession was an assistant county prosecutor, lead counsel for the Cleveland Automobile Club, back to assistant county prosecutor and then served a short stint as safety director – was now a municipal court judge. Ray T. Miller had served as Cuyahoga County Prosecutor from 1928 to 1931. In this position he played an important role in eliminating the City Manager form of government. For his part, he was elected mayor in November 1931. After a two-year term he ran for re-election and was defeated by former Cleveland mayor and Ohio governor Harry L. Davis. Out of elected office, Miller served as the long-time leader of the Cuyahoga County Democratic Party. The new Director of Public Safety was Martin I. Lavelle. Working for Lavelle on special assignment was now Lieutenant Charles Cavolo, who had accepted the position when Davis took office. The new Cuyahoga County Prosecutor was Frank T. Cullitan.

On March 2, 1934, the *Cleveland Press* revealed that "an unconfirmed report reaching Cleveland police today" claimed Angelo Amato was arrested in Palermo, Sicily.

With Amato's colorful track record of being sighted and/or arrested, then disappearing, it was certain there to be controversy with this latest report. It didn't take long to occur. On March 6, a *Plain Dealer* reporter asked Charles Cavolo if reports were true about Amato's arrest. The paper reported, "Cavolo said that they were and that he had verified the fact by sending a cablegram to Italy. When the reporter who questioned Cavolo by telephone was asking if he had turned the information over to Police Chief George J. Matowitz, Cavolo hung up and could not be reached again."

The reporter then contacted Matowitz, who claimed he had not been made aware of the arrest. The chief stated, "If Cavolo has such information, I should think he would give it to me. I shall confer with him about it tomorrow. It may be that he had confidential information which he was waiting to confirm."

Also hearing about the arrest was Judge Merrick, who made a unique offer. In an interview he declared, "There is a good case against 'Big Angelo.' Louis Komer...the last time I talked to him was willing to testify against Amato. I think it improbable he has changed his mind." This could be because Amato wanted Komer killed immediately after the robbery/murder.

"Of course, I no longer have any direct interest in the case," Merrick continued, "but as a public official I am interested in seeing justice done. I think it was the most brutal murder of the past generation in Cleveland. If the authorities want to give me the proper authority I shall be glad to go to Italy at my own expense to prosecute the case against Amato."

Prosecutor Cullitan had not received any confirmation of Amato's arrest either. He proclaimed, "When official information of some kind has been given me, I shall make an immediate study of the steps necessary to prosecute the case, and you may be sure that whatever steps are necessary will be taken, if they are in my power." Cullitan declined to comment on the offer of Judge Merrick.

On the day after Cavolo's statements appeared in the morning newspaper, he was called into Chief Matowitz's office. The chief wanted to know why Cavolo hadn't shared his information with the rest of the department. Cavolo told the chief that, "like Will Rogers, all he knew was what he saw in the papers." He claimed he had read the *Cleveland Press* account of the arrest and promptly asked the Italian consulate if they could confirm any information about the case. This story didn't match what the *Cleveland News* was reporting; they claimed Salvatore LoPresti had given the information to Cavolo.

In an interview that appeared in the *Plain Dealer* on March 8, LoPresti revealed, "Angelo is now in jail in Agrigento, after surrendering a month ago [February 6] to police in Palermo. He surrendered about a month after his wife died and already has been arraigned before a magistrate. He would like to come to Cleveland for the trial, but the Italian government doesn't permit extradition in murder cases, and unless the government is willing to waive this technicality Angelo will go to on trial in Italy in May. His attorney is Signor Antonio LoPresti, my uncle."

In late January 1935, the Court of Assizes in Agrigento, Sicily informed Cleveland officials that the trial of Angelo Amato would begin on April 5. The Italian court requested that subpoenas be served on Detectives Cavolo and Banks and Inspector Sterling who, by now, had been dead for seven and a half years. The requests carried the statement that, 'if they did not appear, they will be charged with penalties threatened by Article. 144 of the civil code of penal procedure."

Assistant County Prosecutor Frank D. Celebreeze served the subpoenas on Cavolo and the now retired Clarence Banks. When time for the trial came, Cullitan sent Celebreeze, Cavolo and Chief Matowitz to assist and testify. On April 11, the Italian court found Amato guilty of "implication in the holdup murders" of Wilfred Sly and George Fanner and sentenced him to 30 years at hard labor. The three Clevelanders immediately wired their bosses with the triumphant verdict.

Although Italian amnesty laws reduced Amato's sentence to 23 years, everyone seemed happy with the decision. In a foreign land, it was as much as they could hope for. The *Plain Dealer* reported, "The Italian government's determination to end the reputation of its Mediterranean Islands as a haven for bandits had a great deal to do with Amato's ultimate and permanent surrender."

In November 1935, Amato's Italian counsel was preparing an appeal for Amato. He asked Salvatore LoPresti to prepare documentation to show that Dominic Lonardo was acquitted by a San Francisco court after a review of the same evidence that Amato was convicted of in Sicily. In April 1936, Amato appealed his conviction with to the Italian court and lost.

He was not heard from again for another twenty years. In August 1956, Amato, now 67 years-old and in poor health, tried to gain early freedom from his sentence by appealing his case. In his request for a review he asked that five Clevelanders[3] be questioned as to his whereabouts on the day of the murders, which were now some 35 years old. The Italian courts wired Cleveland authorities with the information and a deputy U.S. marshal located four of the five people. The last was believed to have died a year earlier.

The four witnesses were questioned by the Chief Deputy Clerk of Courts in the Federal Building. The line of questions, selected by Amato, centered around these people encountering Amato on the morning of the murders. The four witnesses seemed to have a remarkable memory for an event which had happened three and a half decades earlier. So remarkable that it leaves one to wonder why these people didn't speak up years earlier when they really could have helped Amato.

When the interviews were completed the transcripts were translated to Italian and sent to the Italian consul for forwarding to Italian authorities. It was the last time Angelo Amato was reported on in the Cleveland newspapers. There is no record here of the result of his appeal, or when he died.

In announcing the verdict in the Angelo Amato trial on April 12, 1935, the *Plain Dealer* reported:

> "His arrest and conviction officially end the record of the crime which police said marked the first evidence of a dangerous modern-style gang in Cleveland. The gang is declared by police to have been the nucleus of all the gangs which thrived during prohibition. Many of its young members are still influential Cleveland gangsters. The gang, later identified as the 'Mayfield Road Mob,' was started by Dominic Benigno."

Chapter Endnotes

1. The attorneys were Antonio Abisso, a senator in the Mussolini Parliament and Nicola Inglese.

2. Elected Cuyahoga County Prosecutor in 1884, Alexander Hadden held the office for three terms until 1893. Hadden later served as a judge on the probate bench from 1905 until his death in April 1926. His son John A. Hadden founded the law firm of Arter & Hadden.

3. The five witnesses were identified by the *Plain Dealer* as: Antonio Amato, 57 (no relation), Gaetano Cellura 71, Angelo DeCaro 68, Anna Pomerson 57, and Giuseppe Totaro 59 (believed to be dead).

23

Last Man Standing:

Komer, Free at Last

There was a time when, according to Ohio law, first-degree murder sentences for convicted men came up for parole consideration at the end of 20 full years and then each five years thereafter. The Pardon & Parole Commission, a three-member panel, voted unanimously to oppose executive clemency for Komer in 1946 and 1951. In 1956 the vote was two to one against clemency. In 1961 the panel voted unanimously for clemency, but Governor Michael V. DiSalle failed to act.

Komer's case was not scheduled to be heard again until 1966, but in mid-1963 he petitioned the Pardon & Parole Commission for a release. By now Komer had spent just over 41 years in prison and was 70 years old.

By the early 1960s, details of the infamous double-murder were forgotten by the newspapers, in fact the *Cleveland News* was sold by its owners to its afternoon competitor the *Cleveland Press,* ending publication.[1] In reporting on the four-decade old case, one account claimed Komer was not on the scene, but had turned state's evidence sending three men to the chair. Several articles added that Angelo Amato was tried in Italy and sentenced to 30 years. They failed to even mention Dominic Lonardo; instead they mistakenly claimed the final suspect, never caught, committed suicide in 1934, obviously referring to Charles Coletto.

In September 1963, the Pardon & Parole Commission recommended commutation of the first-degree murder charge to second-degree murder. The governor's office said the change allowed Governor James A. Rhodes to permit an early parole. On November 12, 1963, the Pardon & Parole Commission granted a parole to Komer and announced he would be released from prison the next month. After 42 years and nine months in prison for his participation in the Sly-Fanner murders, Komer did something that his three ex-companions couldn't – he left the Ohio Penitentiary alive.

Komer moved to California to live with a brother after his release. He died in January 1983 in the Mohave Valley section of Arizona at the age of 91.

Chapter Endnotes

1. In the late 1920s, the *News*, failing to overtake the *Press*, "was pushed to the edge of extinction by circulation and advertising declines during the Depression. In 1932, the heirs of Dan R. Hanna, Sr., transferred control of the paper to the Forest City Publishing Co., which also acquired the stock of the *Plain Dealer*. With 5 members on the board to 2 for the *News*, the *Plain Dealer* was the senior partner of the enterprise, a fact underscored by the subsequent suspension of the *Sunday News* on January 3, 1933.

"Postwar *News* circulation peaked at 148,752 in 1952, but shortly began to decline after a price hike from 5 to 7 cents. In 1959 its circulation stood at 130,368, against 320,271 for the *Press*. On January 23, 1960, Forest City Publishing Co. announced the sale of the *News* to the *Press*, and the last edition appeared that Saturday afternoon. The *Plain Dealer* moved into the *News* plant, which provides its current address." – *The Encyclopedia of Cleveland History.*

The *Cleveland Press* ceased publication, due to the economy and revenue losses caused by lost advertising, on June 17, 1982.

24

A Few Selected Biographies

 # = When this appears before a biography it is to indicate that many of that individual's activities during the Prohibition Era will be detailed in a future publication

Allen, Florence Ellinwood – Only a year after becoming the first woman judge in the United States to preside over a capital murder trial, Allen recorded another first when she was elected to the Ohio Supreme Court (the second woman, Blanche Krupansky, would not be named until 1981). Six years later, in 1928, she was re-elected by a wide margin. When that term was up, President Franklin Roosevelt appointed Allen a judge of the U.S. 6th Circuit Court of Appeals. In this capacity, during the landmark Tennessee Valley Authority case in 1937-1938, she wrote an opinion that was upheld as constitutional by the United States Supreme Court.

Allen was a strong advocate in the movement to outlaw war. She spoke frequently on the subject. In 1923 she was named honorary chairman of the Council for the Prevention of War.

Twice in her career Allen was considered for a seat on the U.S. Supreme Court, however, the honor of being the first woman judge on that panel fell to Sandra Day O'Connor in 1981. Instead, Allen settled for being the first woman to become a chief justice of a federal court when she was named to that position in the 6th Circuit Court in 1958. The next year Allen retired from active bench duty, but retained the title of chief justice and remained available for special assignments.

Judge Allen, who never married, was an author and noted speaker, the latter coming from her years promoting the suffrage movement. She penned *This Constitution of Ours* (1940), *The Treaty as an Instrument of Legislation* (1952), *Challenges to the Citizen* (1960) and her autobiography *To Do Justly* (1965). The latter is today an expensive collector's item. Less than a year after her autobiography was released Florence Allen died on September 12, 1966, at the age of 82. She is buried at Waite Hill Cemetery.

On the day she became a lawyer Allen told an interviewer, "If more women entered into competition for jobs now held exclusively by men, women would show their capability of running the government, and a woman would be nearer the White House."

 # *Barry, Edwin Daniel* - Barry served as Cleveland's Director of Public Safety during the city's most turbulent years – January 1924 to February 1932. Barry began a trend that Eliot Ness and Alvin J. Sutton followed in future years in which the safety director acted, and was looked upon, as the number one law enforcement official in the city.

Barry was born in Cleveland and spent his entire life here. During his early adult life he was a ticket broker and a market clerk. Then in 1897 he was appointed a deputy sheriff. Four years later he ran for Cuyahoga County sheriff and won. He was re-elected two years later and served until 1905.

Barry left public office and became successful in real-estate. Despite the fact he missed life in the public eye, it wasn't until nearly 20 years later that he was back in it. He was appointed Director of Public Safety by William R. Hopkins on January 7, 1924, when the new form of government, the City Manager Plan, went into effect. Barry was suggested to Hopkins by county Republican boss Maurice Maschke. Barry, a neighbor and school chum of the party boss, was a life-long friend of Maschke.

As safety director Barry backed down from no man. He was known as "Roarin' Ed" and his outbursts were legendary. During his years in office Barry battled bootleggers, murderers and gamblers. His pet peeve seemed to be slot machines, which he attacked with a vengeance. Still, Barry had a warm heart and was known for his random acts of kindness, one of which was not to prosecute a man who once tried to stab him as he left a city council meeting. It was reported that Barry "quietly aided hundreds of less fortunate individuals and families."

Barry resigned his office when the Democratic administration of Ray T. Miller was voted in during February 1932. In 1936, Barry was persuaded by friends to run for county sheriff again. Although he won the Republican primary, he lost to the Democratic candidate who was swept into office with the Roosevelt wave. He lost again in another attempt four years later.

Barry died of a heart attack at his Lee Road home in Cleveland Heights on March 12, 1944, at the age of 73. He was buried in Calvary Cemetery.

Baskin, Roland A. – Baskin was born in 1887 in Hillsboro, Ohio. After college he attended Western Reserve University Law School and graduated in 1910. After a brief stint in the county prosecutor's office, Baskin spent the next 50 years becoming a leading authority on municipal law. During this time he served as the solicitor or law director of Bay Village, South Euclid, Brook Park, Berea, Middleburg Heights and Beachwood.

Baskin retired from the law firm of Boer, Mierke, McClelland & Caldwell in 1972. Baskin died at his South Euclid home on August 11, 1979, at the age of 93.

Bernon, Maurice – Born in Cleveland on August 24, 1885, Bernon, the son of David J. and Augusta Bernon, was raised in Cleveland and attended Brownell School and Central High School. After college Bernon attended Western Reserve University Law School and passed the bar exam in 1906. In addition to his political / judicial career, which ran from 1908 to 1924, Bernon began a long association with Cleveland's Jewish welfare associations which continued until his death. He removed himself – reluctantly – from his charitable work only during the years he served as a judge.

In 1924, when he resigned his position as a common pleas judge, Bernon stated, "I was still young and had children growing up. I just felt it was better at my age to go into [private] practice."

Bernon was elected president of the Cleveland Bar Association in 1928. A few months into his term, Governor A.V. Donahey ordered an investigation into alleged voter fraud during the August primary. The investigation resulted in the removal of the Board of Elections, which was seen to be under the thumb of the city Republicans. When the new board was formed, Bernon was appointed president and served in that capacity until 1934. That year, Secretary of State George S. Myers refused to reappoint him. After a fight Bernon withdrew as a candidate and his political career was at an end.

Bernon continued his law practice in the firm of Bernon & Keeley (previously Bernon, Mulligan, Keeley & La Fever) into the late 1930s. At that time he was forced to quit due to a heart ailment. But that hardly slowed him down. He simply went back to his welfare, civic and religious work, operating out of his office in the Union Commerce Building (today the Huntington Bank Building).

Bernon had begun as a trustee of the Jewish Welfare Federation in 1908. He served as a member of the Jewish Children's Bureau for 25 years and was a member of the Bureau of Jewish Education Board. He served as a board member of Mount Sinai Hospital for 26 years and as head of the hospital's nursing school board for 20 years. In 1930 he helped organize the Jewish Welfare Fund, serving as its chairman for five years. In 1939, he helped establish the Jewish Vocational Service, acting as its president for five years.

Bernon was a member of the Euclid Avenue Temple for 30 years, serving as president from 1945 to 1947; he headed its religion school for 20 years.

In 1950, at the age of 65, Bernon claimed his philanthropy work was keeping him alive. He was now vice president of the Jewish Welfare Federation (later the Jewish Community Federation), as well as a member of the national executive and administrative committees of the United Jewish Appeal and the National Council of the American Jewish Joint Distribution Committee.

Bernon's crowning moment in his charitable work came in 1947 when he was awarded the Charles Eisenman Award for service to the community as an "able lawyer, distinguished jurist, religious leader and great humanitarian."

In 1912, Bernon married Minnie Reiss. The couple had two sons. They resided in their Shaker Blvd. residence for most of their 42 years of marriage.

On March 23, 1954, the 68 year-old Bernon made the usual trek to his office at Euclid and East Ninth Street. He was conducting business when he collapsed from a heart attack shortly after the noon hour. Rushed to St. Vincent Charity Hospital, Bernon was pronounced dead. Services were held at his beloved Euclid Avenue Temple at East 82nd and Euclid Avenue, before burial in Mayfield Cemetery, located at the eastern edge of Lake View Cemetery in Cleveland Heights.

Caley, Fred Henry – During the early years of the automobile becoming an essential part of the American way of life, Fred Caley worked harder than any other man in the city of Cleveland to promote all the positive things about driving. His motto was, "Good roads, better streets, and better conditions for the man who owns and drives a car!" They were the words he lived by.

Caley was born in Hudson, Ohio, on June 2, 1873, an only child. He received his education in country schools and graduated from Kent High School before enrolling at Ohio Northern University. Caley taught school to help with his college expenses. After graduation Caley drifted through a number of jobs, not really sure what he wanted to do. He taught school, farmed, was employed in the Goodrich and Goodyear tire factories in Akron, sold real-estate and dabbled in the insurance field.

During the 1896 presidential campaign of William McKinley, Caley got the bug for politics. He became active in Republican politics and in 1900 moved to Columbus, where he accepted a position in state government in the Ohio State Insurance Department. A hard worker and an idea man, he became the first state registrar of automobiles for Ohio. In this capacity he organized the State Automobile Department.

By 1910, automobile clubs were being organized as driving became more popular. Caley was asked to become the manager of Cincinnati's new automobile club. Shortly after accepting the position he was offered the job of secretary of the Cleveland Automobile Club, a job he held for the next quarter century. The Cleveland Automobile Club had approximately 475 members when Caley arrived in 1911; by 1922 there were over 27,000. A biography of Caley summed up his life's work:

"Under his administration as secretary of the Cleveland Club it has become a powerful force fighting for the sane and safe use of the streets and making war upon the reckless, drunken and incompetent persons whose misuse of motor cars is the cause of much loss of life and destruction of property and is the source of peril to all who have to drive or walk in public thoroughfares; also, the club has become a relentless, tireless and efficient prosecutor of motor car thieves, and in innumerable other ways has become a benefactor to the entire community and an inspiration to similar organizations throughout the country."

Caley was noted for his efforts to crack down on criminals who used automobiles in the commission of their crimes. When he was not fighting law-breakers, Caley managed the annual automobile shows, which the city became famous for, drawing visitors from all over the country. In addition, Caley served as director of the Ohio State Automobile Association for seven years, three as president, and was a director of the American Automobile Association (AAA) for many years.

A fiery orator, who always spoke his mind, the six-foot tall, heavily built Caley was not above making a political enemy. At one time Caley had Cleveland's license bureau under the wing of the Cleveland Automobile Club. Some motorists complained they couldn't obtain a license without being given a long speech on the benefits of joining the club. Members could receive their license by mail, while others waited impatiently in long lines.

Caley locked horns with Carl C. Janes, secretary of the Ohio State Automobile Association. During an August 1930 meeting, Caley stormed out in the middle of a Janes' speech. Caley became upset when "that whipper-snapper" twice rebuked him for not paying attention to his speech. Caley then resigned from the association.

As the automobile industry grew, new concerns arose and by the early 1930s Caley was campaigning for more stringent examinations of automobiles before they were licensed and put allowed on the road.

In 1932 a tragedy, some claim ironic in nature, struck the Caley family. In July Caley's wife Harriet was charged with careless driving after she struck and seriously injured a man painting traffic lane markers on Lee Road in Cleveland Heights. The 53 year-old Mrs. Caley was distraught over the incident and the embarrassment it brought to her husband. The court case, before Cleveland Heights Police Judge David J. Miller, was continued four times due to several nervous breakdowns suffered by Harriet. Faced with another hearing, at which time Miller had planned to dismiss the charges due to her condition, Mrs. Caley hanged herself in a room at the Statler Hotel at Euclid Avenue and East 12th Street.

Fred Caley never fully recovered from his wife's tragic suicide. His health began to fail him and in 1936, after 25 years as secretary of the automobile club he had made so successful, Caley resigned. He remarried and moved to Los Angeles. There he developed a heart ailment in September 1944. On April 20, 1945 he died in his sleep at home at the age of 71.

Cassidy, James T. - had quite a colorful career after leaving the prosecutor's office – some of it deplorable, some successful – most of it controversial. In May 1927, he was charged with drunk driving in Lakewood after having a collision with a Green Taxicab driver on Clifton Boulevard. Cassidy was kept overnight in jail, but despite the finding of beer and a half pint of whiskey in the back seat of his car, he was not charged with a liquor violation. A newspaper article reported the cab driver claimed there was a woman, who was in the car with Cassidy at the time of the accident, who disappeared before police arrived.

Cassidy fought a battle with alcoholism until he conquered it in the early 1940s. After getting his life back, he sought to rebuild his career and fulfilled his dream of becoming a judge. In 1943 and 1945 he ran for the municipal court bench and lost. He became embroiled in a political battle with two opponents charging them with establishing temporary residences in Cleveland in order to allow them to run for municipal office. One of his actions was carried all the way to the Supreme Court.

Cassidy's years as judge can be described as roller coaster. Assigned to "Drunk Court," the judge had a warm understanding for defendants brought in on drinking violations. During one month in 1950 the judge handled 2,000 drinking cases. He released 1,765 with costs suspended or no fines. Cassidy's policy of going easy on drunks resulted in a high rate of repeat offenders. One court official estimated that out of a daily docket of 75 drunks, 15 were repeaters. When possible, the judge sent the offenders to the County Jail to receive medical and psychiatric care or to the Warrensville Workhouse on medical sentences. He stated, "Anyone expressing interest in A.A. gets a personal hearing in my chambers."

In July 1965, Cassidy, now 78 years old, suffered a minor heart attack. The judge recovered and on his 80th birthday announced he was running again, but lost his bid for another term. Cassidy wasn't out of work for long. Before the end of the month he was named referee in the small claims court of the Municipal Court.

Cassidy retired from the bench in 1968. After the death of his second wife, he continued to live at his Shaker Boulevard home until late 1971 when he relocated to a rest home. Despite being out of the prosecutor's office for 45 years, old reporters still talked about his days as "a fiery orator and a rapid, merciless prosecutor." Phillip W. Porter, who during the 1920s covered the criminal court beat for the *Plain Dealer*, called Cassidy "one of the greatest trial lawyers I have ever seen."

Cassidy was 86 years old when he died on February 10, 1972, at St. Vincent Charity Hospital.

Cavolo, Charles S. – The popular Cleveland detective, who became famous for his work against the Mafia and the Black Hand was born on March 6, 1891, in the Italian city of Vietri de Potenza, which is located in the southern region of the country, centralized between the coasts of the Tyrrhenian and Adriatic Seas, due east of Naples. At the age of nine he boarded the vessel Bismark, headed for the United States, and arrived in New York City on February 7, 1900.

Cavolo moved to Cleveland in May 1910, and lived at 1930 East 123rd Street in the Little Italy section. He took up work as a lapidist, polishing gems for a local jeweler. Cavolo began seeing Josephine Tanno, the daughter of the jeweler, who resided a few doors down. The two were married on September 19, 1912. Oddly, on the marriage license application it lists his place of birth as New York City. The newlyweds moved to a home on Edgehill Road; the first of three children arrived the next year. In 1916 Cavolo applied for naturalization and became an American citizen.

During the Prohibition Era, Cavolo was one of Cleveland's most recognizable police officers and was in the newspapers often. On November 17, 1926, Cavolo was promoted to Detective Sergeant. The promotion, according to Safety Director Edwin Barry, was in recognition of Cavolo's unceasing efforts to maintain law and order." Cavolo later was promoted to lieutenant. His career, however, was somewhat of a roller coaster ride as the detective was known to sometimes take matters into his own hands, which on more than one occasion drew the ire of his superiors. An incident following a murder in 1927, in which Frank Milazzo was accused of killing Ernest Yorkell, resulted in Cavolo receiving a suspension from the department.

In 1932, Cavolo was made a Knight of the Order of the Crown of Italy by the Italian government for his work involving the Black Hand. In the past 12 years the detective had helped send back killers found in this city.

On the trip to Italy in search of Vittorio Pisselli in 1921, Cavolo was briefed about a feud murder in the village of San Giovani after which the slayer fled to the United States. Two years later, in March 1923, based only on a description of the suspect, Cavolo arrested a man he spotted attending a funeral in Lake View Cemetery. During interrogation the man broke down and confessed the crime.

Three years after Repeal, Cavolo left the detective bureau and joined the automobile bureau. After ten years on the job Cavolo received a unique accolade. The *Plain Dealer* reported, "His work in the bureau...was of such a character as to earn him the commendation in 1946 of J. Edgar Hoover head of the Federal Bureau of Investigation. Hoover praised the bureau for its vigilance, for its system of recovering stolen cars and of preventing such thefts, and for cooperation with other police agencies involving crimes of all natures."

In 1947 Cavolo suffered a stroke that forced him to retire the next year. On April 23, 1958, the former detective died at his Edgehill home in Cleveland Heights of a kidney ailment. He was 67 years old.

 # Cody, Cornelius W. – When Cody retired from the Cleveland Police Department in 1935, after 28 years of active duty, he had overseen more than 600 murder investigations. Cody moved into a new position as head of security of the Cleveland Trust Company, a job he held for the next 18 years. On May 8, 1953, while visiting a niece in Hermitage, New York, the 71 year-old Cody suffered a cerebral hemorrhage and died. Cody and his wife Harriett L. Pettigrew were a year shy of their 50th wedding anniversary. They had no children. Cody was buried in Acacia Masonic Memorial Park cemetery on SOM Center Road.

Corrigan, William J. – For nearly four decades Corrigan was Cleveland's most recognized defense attorney. Called an "actor" or "dramatist," the courtroom was his stage. Once when compared to Clarence Darrow, Corrigan replied, "He was a great lawyer. Why, I'm just a small-time attorney."

Corrigan was born in Cleveland on June 21, 1886. His mother was a native of Canada, her father a newspaper publisher in Manitoba. Corrigan went to school at Holy Name and later earned his Bachelor's Degree in 1911 from St. Ignatius College (John Carroll University). He attended law school at Baldwin-Wallace, where he helped support himself as a police reporter for the *Cleveland News*. Corrigan received his law degree in 1915 and passed the Ohio bar the same year.

In 1917, Corrigan became an assistant county prosecutor working under Samuel Doerfler. He soon found himself handling most of the major cases in the county, the "Jiggs" Losteiner trial the most prominent. In 1920, he was named chief assistant prosecutor, but resigned later that year to begin a private practice. For the next 25 years Corrigan held the title of "organized labor's attorney" as he began a long association with unions of the American Federation of Labor.

Corrigan first served as counsel for the Cleveland Federation of Labor and the Building Trades Council. His work for the International Ladies Garment Workers' Union resulted in an honorary membership to the union in 1951. During a strike at the Federal Knitting Mills in 1937, Corrigan joined members on a Congress of Industrial Organization (CIO) picket line and was arrested. Cleveland Mayor Harold Burton called the incident a publicity stunt, as Corrigan was being considered for the Democratic candidate to oppose Burton in the upcoming mayoral election.

During the land scandals, which took place in Cleveland during the late 1920s, Corrigan represented City Clerk Fred W. Thomas, whose trial ended in an acquittal. Next up for Corrigan was the perjury trial of former councilman William E. Potter in the same matter. Potter, however, was murdered just before his trial was scheduled to begin.

Corrigan was best known for his work in several spectacular murder trials, beginning with Sam Purpura in May 1921. This was quickly followed by the murder trial of Eva Kaber. The evidence, testimony and witnesses left no doubt that Eva was guilty of having her husband, Dan Kaber, killed and Corrigan's sole effort was to save her from the electric chair, which he accomplished.

Over the years Corrigan's cases included:

➤ Joseph Gogan, a wealthy industrialist accused of murdering his wife with rat poison

➤ Associates of notorious racketeer Alex "Shondor" Birns, who were accused of blackmail

➤ Labor extortionists Don Campbell and John McGee

➤ Police Chief George J. Matowitz during an attempt to oust him as Cleveland police chief

➤ Cleveland Syndicate members Morris Kleinman and Louis Rothkopf during their infamous "refusing to refuse" episode before the Kefauver Committee during hearings held in Washington D.C. in 1951

Corrigan's most famous client – bar none – was Dr. Sam Sheppard, who was accused of brutally murdering his wife Marilyn in Cleveland's most celebrated murder, surpassing the sensational case of William Potter in 1931. Sheppard was tried after a media blitz led by *Cleveland Press* editor Louis Seltzer in 1954. Convicted after a ten-week trial, Sheppard was sentenced to life in prison in the Ohio Penitentiary. Corrigan spent the remainder of his life working on appeals. (Several years after Corrigan's death Sheppard was granted a new trial and, represented by F. Lee Bailey, was found not guilty of the murder in 1966.)

Corrigan married Marjorie Wilson on August 21, 1922. Perhaps it depends on whose telling of the story as to how the two met. Wilson was a reporter for the *Cleveland News* and covered several murder trials. One story has Corrigan meeting Wilson during his prosecution of "Jiggs" Losteiner. Another claims he met her while defending Eva Kaber. Whatever the case, the couple was married for nearly 40 years.

In his mid-70s, Corrigan was still working. His son, William Howard Corrigan, had joined the practice, which was conducted out of the Williamson Building, located in Public Square – site of the present day Huntington Bank Building. It was here that the elder Corrigan became ill on July 27, 1961. Taken to St. Alexis Hospital by police, the 75 year-old Corrigan died the next morning. He was buried in Calvary Cemetery.

Costello, Timothy Joseph – served in the Cleveland Police Department for 56 years, longer than any other officer. Costello was born to Irish parents in Olmsted Falls, a suburb on the western side of Cuyahoga County, on July 23, 1878. As a young man Costello, with little formal education, trained as a blacksmith during the day when horses were still the main mode of transportation. After he was befriended by the neighborhood beat patrolman, Costello decided on a career in law enforcement.

As a young patrolman Costello developed a philosophy, which he carried through life, that "The beat man was a neighborhood institution. People respected and confided in him. He knew the joys and sorrows in his district almost as well as the parish priest."

Costello began his career as a beat patrolman covering a district that was known as the "Tenderloin," between Ontario and Muirson (East 12th) Streets along Hamilton Avenue. The area was also called the "segregated or red light" district and was home to a number of houses of prostitution until 1915. Costello recalled in later years, "If a policeman ever got licked while making an arrest or merely walking his rounds, he was in trouble. He could expect a beating at least once daily from then on."

Costello was promoted to sergeant in 1913. In 1918, he was awarded two promotions in one year, first to lieutenant and then to captain. During the 1930s he was promoted to deputy inspector and in 1942 to full inspector.

In addition to being the oldest police officer on the force, Costello was also the oldest in point of service. In 1951, Police Chief Frank Story, who replaced George Matowitz after his death, named Costello his executive assistant and made him assistant chief of police.

Costello died on February 10, 1960, from the flu at the age of 81 in St. John's Hospital. He is buried in St. Mary's Cemetery in Olmsted Falls. Costello was survived by three sons, two of them attorneys, and four daughters, three of them nuns.

Cull, Dan B. – described as one of Cleveland's most distinguished public servants, he was born in Miamisburg, Ohio on November 29, 1881. After attending local schools there, he enrolled in the Dayton Business College, a night school sponsored by the YMCA, in Dayton, Ohio. Cull financed his studies by writing for the *Dayton News*.

Cull moved to Cleveland and began taking night classes at Cleveland Law School. As in Dayton, he supported himself by working as a reporter, this time for the *Plain Dealer* and the *Cleveland Press*. One of his law school tutors was Newton D. Baker, who served two terms as mayor of Cleveland, formed the prestigious law firm Baker & Hostetler, and was appointed Secretary of War by President Woodrow Wilson during World War I. Back in 1907 though, Baker had just been appointed city solicitor by Mayor Tom L. Johnson. The new solicitor brought his prize law student, Dan B. Cull on board as an assistant.

In 1912, Cull was elected to the newly created Municipal Court of Cleveland, becoming a charter member. Cull served as judge there until 1917 when he was elected to the Court of Common Pleas, where he served for eight years. When Cull retired, during the middle of his second term, he cited reasons not uncommon for judges of the time. He stated, "The bench does not provide me the income I need to support a rapidly expanding and growing family." After leaving the bench in September 1925, Cull formed a law partnership with Harold H. Burton.

In the mid-1920s, Cleveland was operating under the City Manager form of government. When Daniel Morgan replaced William Hopkins in January 1930, he appointed Burton as city law director. In 1931, city council voted to dissolve the City Manager plan and return to an elected mayor. Morgan, upset with the decision, resigned and Burton served as acting mayor from November 1931 until an election put Ray T. Miller in the mayor's office in February 1932. During his term as acting mayor

(Burton was elected and served from 1936 to 1940) he appointed Cull to Civil Service Commissioner. He was reappointed twice for six-year terms. Cull served in this capacity until his death.

Cull's other important post was his selection to two terms as president of the Cleveland Association for Criminal Justice, the watchdog group formed as a result of the Cleveland Crime Survey, which was launched in early 1921 after the Sly-Fanner murders.

During the summer of 1949 a cancerous tumor was detected on Cull's lung. The growth was removed at St. Vincent's Charity Hospital and doctors felt there might be a complete recovery. In early August he suffered kidney failure and, despite the best efforts of physicians, Cull died on August 8.

Davis, Harry Lyman – was elected four times as mayor of Cleveland and governor of Ohio once.

Born in the Newburgh section of Cleveland, Davis left school when he was 13 to find work and help support his family. He found a job in the city's massive steel mills and over the next eight years earned his education studying at home and attending night school. Davis desired to go into business on his own and after a three-year stint as solicitor for the Cleveland Telephone Company, he established the Davis Rate Adjustment Company, selling telephone securities to the general public. This was followed by the founding of the Harry L. Davis Company, an insurance concern.

Davis got a taste for Republican politics and in 1909 ran for city treasurer and won. Although he lost in his bid for re-election, his future path was determined. His next political campaign was for mayor of Cleveland in 1913. Run by William S. Fitzgerald, the campaign lost out to Newton D. Baker, but Davis became a household name. During the next mayoral election, in the fall of 1915, Davis beat opponent Peter Witt. Davis was a popular mayor with both the citizenry and the Republican Party. He was re-elected in 1917 and 1919. He stocked city government with patronage jobs which would not be eliminated until Fred Kohler's administration in 1922.

As mayor during the First World War, Davis's greatest contribution was the Mayor's Advisory War Committee, formed on April 7, 1917. The committee consisted of 50 business, civic, and religious leaders – key members included former Ohio Governor Myron T. Herrick and Fred H. Goff. According to *The Encyclopedia of Cleveland History*:

> "The mayor's committee and a network of various subcommittees coordinated, financed, and supervised almost all of the city's war-relief work, including fundraising projects of public and private

institutions. It directed distribution of food and clothing, sponsored Americanization classes for immigrants; organized a speakers' bureau; supervised draft boards; and subsequently supervised rent control. This single cooperative effort designed to increase efficiency of money, time, and effort gained national recognition. During the early months of 1919, the Mayor's Advisory Committee held homecoming celebrations, opened neighborhood centers for returning soldiers, lobbied for veteran's compensation pay, and funded a city employment service."

As the soldiers returned home the committee began to disband in the summer of 1919 and by December operations ceased completely.

On May 1, 1920, Davis resigned just months into his third term to focus on his campaign for Ohio governor. Davis was elected in the great Republican landslide that fall despite, ironically, not carrying the majority of the vote in the city that had elected him to three terms as mayor.

After one term in Columbus, Davis decided not to seek re-election in November 1922, and Vic Donahey took over the governor's mansion. In 1924, Davis decided to give it another shot, but this time he could not unseat Donahey.

When Davis resigned to run for governor, William Fitzgerald completed the third term of the former mayor. Fitzgerald decided to run for a full term in the fall of 1921 and found himself facing former Cleveland police chief Fred Kohler. Also placed on the ballot that fall was a call for a new form of government, the City Manager Plan. Disgruntled Cleveland voters approved the plan and the mayor / ward system of city government disappeared at the conclusion of the newly elected Fred Kohler's term.

Davis was not a fan of the new government and for the next six years fought against it. His proposal amendments were rejected by the voters in 1927, 1928 and 1929. After Davis bowed out of the fight, the voters abolished the City Manager Plan in 1931. At the time the plan was voted out Daniel E. Morgan was the city manager. He resigned and city law director Harold H. Burton served as interim city leader until an election was held in February 1932. Democratic County Prosecutor Ray T. Miller campaigned for the newly reinstated office of mayor and beat Morgan. After a stormy term, the Democratic leader was defeated in the fall of 1933 by Harry Davis who completed his political comeback.

In his fourth term as mayor, Davis had lost the old charm that once served him well. Changes he made, such as forcing city workers to join a "social club" and pay one percent of their salaries as dues, turned many of his former friends and supporters against him. At the end of his term Davis went into political retirement after vacating the chairmanship of the

Republican Party in 1936. The last 14 years of his life were spent working on his insurance business, headquartered in the Terminal Tower, where he was joined by his son.

On May 21, 1950, Davis had just sat down to dinner with his wife and son at his South Moreland Blvd home in Shaker Heights. The former mayor had spent three days at St. Alexis Hospital days earlier for a checkup. Davis said that he felt faint and then suddenly collapsed at the table. A Shaker Heights Fire Department rescue squad rushed to the house, but they were unable to revive Davis. His personal physician soon appeared at the home and pronounced Davis dead, stating that he died of a blood clot. Davis was 72. He was buried in Lake View Cemetery.

Dembe, Joseph – An orphan, Dembe was found on the streets of Chicago when he was eight years old and brought to Cleveland, where he was placed in an orphanage. He grew up devoting his life to legal and community work.

Dembe attended Baldwin-Wallace College and received his law degree from Cleveland Law School. He was admitted to the Ohio Bar in 1914. A Democrat, he was appointed assistant county prosecutor during the term of County Prosecutor Sam Doerfler and served until 1921.

During the next 34 years Dembe was prominent in public life in a variety of roles. He was an assistant immigration officer and conducted citizenship classes, he was active at Hiram House and Bellefaire Jewish Children's home.

Dembe remained active in Democratic politics and ran unsuccessfully for public office several times. He was a precinct committeeman in East Cleveland where he lived. Dembe died at his Coventry Road home on January 5, 1955. He was 65 years old.

Doerfler, Samuel - was born in Cleveland on July 30, 1876. In July 1909, at the age of 33, Doerfler married 21 year-old Lillian Gross, a neighbor of his on East 118th Street. In January 1915, Mrs. Doerfler was having trouble with an ear and was operated on. Doctors reported she never recovered from the shock and died on March 1, 1915.

In November 1916, Doerfler was elected Cuyahoga County prosecutor, beating William B. Woods. As prosecutor one of the cases he handled was the murder of Cleveland Police Officer Elmer Glaefke on September 12, 1917. Three men were arrested for the killing, including Antonio Lombardo, who became head of the Chicago Unione Siciliana before his sensational murder in September 1928. Convicted of the murder was Carmello Licati who, after a few years in the Ohio Penitentiary, was released and deported, only to return to Cleveland. Licati was murdered during a bootlegging war here in 1930.

In June 1918, while Doerfler was living at the Hotel Winton, he married Helen Ruth Lang. The marriage didn't last as the 1930 census listed him as divorced.

Until 1919 it was the duty of the county prosecutor's office to recommend the public defenders who represented "indigent" defendants. The Cleveland Crime Survey reported, "As a rule, very young attorneys or incompetent older men were appointed, because successful lawyers do not seek the business." During Doerfler's term this practice was turned over to the judges after there were "suspicions" that defendants who were represented by two former associates of Doerfler were being shown favoritism by the prosecutor.

In 1927, Doerfler represented Lawrence Lupo after the shooting death of Ralph "Curley" Meyer. The killing was ruled justifiable. During the 1920s his clientele included Mayfield Road Mobsters Alfred "Big Al" Polizzi, Charles Polizzi and Charles Coletto.

Doerfler died in Los Angles, California, on July 26, 1960.

Fitzgerald, William Sinton – was born on October 6, 1880 in Washington D.C., where his father was a civil engineer and the librarian for the United States War Department. Fitzgerald received his early education in the local public schools in the nation's capital. As a young man, he was a superior athlete and played end on his college football team. He was attending college when the Spanish-American War began in Cuba. At the age of 18, he joined the Army and was appointed first lieutenant of volunteer troops at Camp Alger, located near Harrisburg, Pennsylvania. He served as an adjutant of the regiment even though they didn't make it out of camp. In 1903, he earned a Master of Laws degree from George Washington University. What compelled him to move west is unknown, but he came to Cleveland and began the practice of law in 1905.

After nine years at city hall, the last 20 months as mayor, Fitzgerald went back to his law practice in the Williamson Building. One thing Fitzgerald was best remembered for during his brief time in office had nothing to do with politics. When Fitzgerald was inaugurated, "in one of the most impressive ceremonies City Hall had seen," his mother was at his side. In his address he stated with deep affection:

> "Everything good I have done, if any measure of success I have accomplished, is due to my good mother and her wonderful influence. There is nothing so wonderful, so unselfish, as mother love, and happy indeed is the man who possesses a good mother like mine."

Fitzgerald was soon viewed as the city's most eligible bachelor, but living at the New Amsterdam Hotel with his mother and about to turn 40 it looked like he was a confirmed bachelor, not an eligible one. So it came as a shock to Clevelanders on August 27, 1921, the day that Fitzgerald announced his candidacy, that he had married Margaret Chilton Tucker back on January 14, 1920. The couple had met in Washington D.C. while Fitzgerald was there on business, they were married in Chicago and she was now living in New York City. He explained they had decided to keep the marriage a secret because his wife was completing "an exhaustive study of piano."

Fitzgerald brought his wife to Cleveland as the campaign got into full swing. Her appearances with the mayor were regarded as "one of the more dramatic features "of the fall campaign. Not much was known about Mrs. Fitzgerald's background. An article, years later, claimed she was "a former model, movie extra and song writer." Whatever the case, Cleveland was not where Margaret Fitzgerald wanted to be. Wherever she went, William Fitzgerald didn't follow and in 1922 she filed for divorce on the grounds of gross neglect; he counter-filed on similar grounds. It wasn't until this was announced in the newspapers that it came to light that the couple had a child, William S. Fitzgerald, Jr.

In 1923, Fitzgerald served as chairman of the Cuyahoga County Republican Party executive committee. In 1924, Fitzgerald was selected by City Council to serve on the board of the Civil Service Commission. He served six years and was replaced. He was out of the public eye until Harry Davis was elected to a fourth term as Cleveland mayor in 1933. Although Fitzgerald wasn't given as high a position in the administration as he held before, Davis appointed him chairman of the City Board of Zoning Appeals.

In March 1933, Fitzgerald married again, this time to his secretary from his days as mayor, Carolina Graner. This one had the air of secrecy also as the clergyman that united them told a reporter, "it would be a simple ceremony with only a few close friends, if any, in attendance."

The next year Fitzgerald was hospitalized with an undisclosed stomach ailment that required a blood transfusion. In February 1935, Fitzgerald was back in the newspapers when it was reported his former wife was seeking a higher alimony. In the original settlement Margaret Fitzgerald was awarded $75 a month. In 1930, it was increased to $106 a month. Margaret said she now needed more as she and her son were living in a single room in Chicago. Fitzgerald was crying poverty too, claiming his only income, $150 a month, came from his job on the zoning commission. He was unable to practice law due to his health and he was behind in his rent at the Williamson Building.

During the mid-1930s, Fitzgerald became associated with former county prosecutor Edward Stanton in his law practice. The association did not last long.

On October 3, 1937, just days before Fitzgerald was to turn 57 he woke up complaining that he was having trouble breathing. A doctor was called and checked on him. After the doctor left, Fitzgerald smoked a cigarette and then began to complain again. Before the doctor could return Fitzgerald had a fatal heart attack.

His cries of poverty apparently rang true. When Carolina Fitzgerald filed an application with the probate court, the former mayor's assets totaled a mere $41.07 from a checking account.

 # Graul, Jacob – was chief of police from January 1922 to September 1930 – eight and a half of the toughest years of crime the city of Cleveland has ever seen, the heart of the Prohibition Era. By the time he resigned, under pressure from Safety Director Edwin D. Barry and City Manager Daniel E. Morgan, Graul had served 33 years in uniform. His years as chief were marked by strict discipline and obedience to every order given to him by his superiors – sometimes to their own chagrin.

Shortly after Graul's retirement, he moved from his long-time home on East 86th Street to a new dwelling he helped build on Calverton Road in Shaker Heights. It was for the most part a quiet retirement, spent tending to the home and a garden he planted. His only struggle was with the police department after they cut his retirement pay in half during the Depression years. Seeking new adventures, in 1935 Graul ran for Shaker Heights City Council and lost. It was the only time he ran for public office.

In mid-January 1938, Graul was named foreman of the Cuyahoga County Grand Jury, a position another former chief, Frank W. Smith, once held. Graul told intimates that this was something he wanted to do since his retirement. On St. Valentine's Day 1938 the panel had just recessed around 12:45pm. Graul told a fellow juror that he was feeling ill and the man assisted him to an ante-room. There Graul collapsed and fell into a coma. His physician was summoned and the former chief was rushed to Charity Hospital, where he died an hour later without regaining consciousness at the age of 69. His death was caused by a cerebral hemorrhage. Graul was buried in Highland Park Cemetery in Shaker Heights.

Hammond, Dr. Ardon P. – served as Cuyahoga County Coroner through most of Cleveland's Prohibition years.

Hammond was born in 1869 in Castalia, Ohio (near Sandusky). In the late 1880s, he arrived in Cleveland to study at Western Reserve University's School of Pharmacy, receiving his diploma in 1889. Later, he attended the medical school, graduating in 1904. After several years of private practice he was appointed city district physician, serving under Mayors Herman Baehr and Newton D. Baker.

In 1921, he began his first of four terms as Cuyahoga County Coroner. Hammond worked long hours and there was plenty of work to do during that lawless period. Autopsies and coroner's hearings took a toll on the doctor. In addition, Hammond's office was constantly under fire from the Citizens League and the Cuyahoga County Funeral Directors' Association.

By 1927, the constant pressure resulted in Hammond developing heart disease. He began assigning more and more work to other physicians. On March 7, 1928, after deciding he could no longer perform the functions of his office, Hammond resigned. His letter of resignation, which was to be effective April 1, stated he was acting on the advice of doctors in leaving the position. Dr. A.J. Pearse was named acting coroner.

By that time his health had declined so rapidly that he passed away ten days before his resignation was to go into effect. Hammond died at his Kingston Road home in Cleveland Heights on March 21, at the age of 59. Hammond, a long-time Mason, who earned his 32nd degree, was buried in the family cemetery plot in Castalia.

Hopple, Elden J. – was a Cleveland Democratic politician, state senator and representative, attorney, assistant county prosecutor and Ohio utilities commissioner. He began his political career with unsuccessful campaigns for city council and the municipal bench. In 1912, he won a seat in the Ohio State Senate and was re-elected in 1914. From 1917 to 1919 he sat in the Ohio House of Representatives, serving as speaker and minority floor leader. In 1920, Hopple turned down an offer to fill the position of Cuyahoga County prosecutor when Sam Doerfler resigned. Instead, he chose to campaign for the position outright and lost to Edward Stanton.

Hopple remained out of politics until Ray T. Miller was elected county prosecutor and took office in January 1929. Hopple was appointed an assistant county prosecutor, serving until 1931, when Ohio Governor George White appointed him to the Ohio Utilities Commission.

Hopple died after a long illness on October 10, 1941, at his Kildare Road home in Cleveland Heights. He was 61 years old. Hopple was best remembered for his efforts during the 1910s in persuading Ohio Governor James Cox not to veto the bill that created the Metro Parks system in Cuyahoga County.

 # Koestle, George – Two things distinguished Koestle from other police officers – his physique and punctuality. While police officers like George Matowitz, Jacob Graul and Timothy Costello were big and brawny and

could easily handle themselves in a fight, Koestle, in contrast, was of medium height and weight. On more than one occasion the newspapers pointed out that he had the smallest feet in the police department.

In his years of overseeing the Criminal Identification Bureau, Koestle was in his laboratory every morning by 7:30. He reviewed all the records of the criminals brought in during the night and checked them against his burgeoning file system. By 1922, the Cleveland bureau was reputed to be the third largest in the country, trailing only New York and Chicago. He seldom missed a day of work. On October 12, 1936, Koestle made news when he took a day off. By now he was a member of the force for 41 years. The occasion was his 50th wedding anniversary to the former Emma Ettner.

During his years as superintendent of the Bertillon and fingerprinting departments, Koestle earned a national reputation. In 1936 *Finger Print Magazine* published an article about Koestle, where it invited police departments across the country to produce the name of a Bertillon expert with more time on the job. When no names were offered, Koestle was dubbed the "Dean of Fingerprinting." A *Cleveland Press* article stated, "His reputation spread throughout the world and he received congratulations from such far away places as China."

Koestle was an advocate of universal fingerprinting and suggested that every child, as of the age of five, be fingerprinted for future identification purposes. He believed that many people might be saved from "Potter's Field" burials and could be easily identified in cases of amnesia or accidents if this process was allowed.

A city ordinance required police and firemen to retire at the age of 70. Koestle fought the law, but was finally forced to retire on January 1, 1939, at the age of 73. Like many of his police contemporaries, Koestle was a Mason and stayed active in the organization. On March 4, 1941, Koestle died at Lakewood City Hospital after an operation. He was 75 years-old. In his will, as an affirmation of his long belief in the fingerprinting system, Koestle kept a set of his own in the documentation along with a note, "For verification of these fingerprints see the FBI in Washington D.C."

Kohler, Frederick – The life of Fred Kohler is worth a book in itself. He served Cleveland as police chief, county commissioner, mayor and county sheriff – the only person ever to do so.

Kohler was born on May 2, 1864, in Cleveland. He left school during the sixth grade to assist his father at the Kohler Stone Works. After his father's death, Kohler tried to maintain the business, but it soon went under. In 1887, he was appointed superintendent of Woodland Cemetery, at Woodland Avenue and East 66th Street.

In 1889, Kohler joined the Cleveland Police Department. An aggressive and effective officer, he rose through the ranks becoming a captain after eleven years. In 1903, Mayor Tom L. Johnson appointed Kohler chief of police. Known as a strict disciplinarian, Kohler molded the department in his own image, demanding that his officers always be well groomed and neat in their appearance.

In the early 1910s, Kohler, described as "blond, handsome, tall and physically attractive to women," and a married man, began a relationship with the wife of a traveling salesman. When the man filed for divorce a public scandal ensued. In February 1913 the Civil Service Commission removed Kohler as chief on the grounds of neglect of duty and gross immorality.

While most men would have fled town in shame after being exposed in such an incident, Kohler remained vowing to one day ride a horse down Euclid Avenue in triumph. He visited the Hollenden Hotel lobby daily where he rubbed elbows with the city's movers and shakers, and discuss politics and other topics of the day. With their support Kohler ran for public office again. What followed was four straight loses. In 1913, the same year he was dismissed as police chief, he ran for city council and lost; 1914 county sheriff; 1915 clerk of municipal courts; and 1916 as delegate to the Republican National Convention. His perseverance paid off in 1918 when, running as a Republican candidate, he was elected a Cuyahoga County Commissioner, serving two terms. As the only non-Democrat on the three-man commission, Kohler kept himself a news item by "heckling the majority."

Kohler's reputation as a tough police chief served him well during the crime-ridden year of 1921 when he decided to run for mayor that fall. He was not a good public speaker, so Kohler built support by going door to door introducing himself to the Cleveland voters. The tactic worked that November as the citizens of Cleveland put him into office and at the same time abolished the office by voting out the mayor / council form of government. Kohler, for all intents and purposes, was to be the city's last elected mayor. The new City Manager Plan would not go into effect until January 1924 and Kohler fulfilled his promise to ride down Euclid Avenue in triumph.

To say that Kohler's term in office was a colorful one would be a pun. Former *Plain Dealer* reporter Philip W. Porter wrote in *Cleveland: Confused City on a Seesaw*:

> "Then he ordered every fireplug in the city painted orange, had park benches painted orange and black, and repainted all the city property that needed touching up (except the city hall itself) in the

same garish colors, orange and black, which were visible night and day. Kohler said he wanted everyone to know which buildings belonged to the taxpayers."

As mayor, Kohler made good on his campaign promises to live within the city's means. He helped accomplish this by refusing to make park or street repairs. When he left office, at the end of 1923, he reported a $1.0 million surplus in the city treasury.

Kohler then ran for Cuyahoga County sheriff and won. As sheriff, Kohler found himself involved in another scandal. This time it was for spending only half of the money that was allowed him for feeding county prisoners.

After the City Manager Plan was abolished in November 1931 many thought Kohler would rise like a Phoenix from the ashes and "ride again." After some thought, he chose not to run again for mayor. In announcing his decision, he wrote the Board of Education and said, "Life is too short." Kohler was going to spend his last years "in travel and in comfort" and soon left for Florida to spend the winter of 1931.

In June 1932, Kohler was making good on his promise to travel. On board an ocean liner, docked at Plymouth, England, Kohler suffered a stroke. Severely paralyzed, Kohler was transferred on a stretcher to another vessel and returned to Cleveland. Over the next year and a half he showed little improvement and was confined to a wheelchair and cared for by a private nurse.

In late January 1934, he suffered a second stroke and his condition became grave. On the night of January 30, with his family gathered around, Kohler slipped into a coma and died, a few months short of his 70th birthday. He was buried in Lake View Cemetery.

Martinec, Thomas C. - was born in Bohemia in 1868. He came to Cleveland as a child with his parents. At the age of 14 he began work as a tailor's apprentice, but the lure of law enforcement soon gave call. In 1892, he became a member of the Cleveland Police Department as a beat patrolman. Martinec rose through the ranks and was appointed captain during the 1910s. During his 25 years as an officer, Martinec was close friends with Fred Kohler, who served as Cleveland Chief of Police from1903 to 1913.

During World War I, Martinec retired from the department to organize and train a private police force for the Otis Steel Company. He served as chief.

In November 1921, Kohler, then a county commissioner, ran for the office of mayor and was elected over incumbent William S. Fitzgerald.

Kohler quickly named Martinec his director of public safety, replacing Anton B. Sprosty.

Martinec served as safety director for two years, Kohler's term in office. When Kohler was elected Cuyahoga County Sheriff in 1924, he again called on his old friend to serve as his chief deputy.

In addition to his work as a law enforcement official, Martinec was a state fire marshal and was twice (1935 and 1938) named foreman of the Cuyahoga County grand jury. In retirement, the man who had once battled bootleggers managed several liquor stores.

Martinec was a longtime member of the Masons, achieving 32nd Degree status in the organization. For years he served as chairman of the safety committee of the Sirat Grotto.

Martinec's wife Josephine died in January 1940. The couple had two children, Martinec, who lived on Beersford Avenue in East Cleveland, died in Huron Road Hospital at the age of 84 on August 30, 1952. He is buried in Acacia Park Cemetery.

Matowitz, George Julius – On August 7, 1930, Matowitz became "acting chief" when Jacob Graul resigned after a month of deadly activity in the Cleveland underworld. Matowitz would officially be named chief in October.

While Matowitz was looked upon as head of the Cleveland Police Department during his 20 years as chief, the fact is a series of powerful safety directors really called the shots for most of those years, not to mention sometimes meddlesome mayors. During Matowitz's time as chief he answered to Edwin Barry, Eliot Ness and Alvin J. Sutton, all forceful men. It was impossible for Matowitz not to lose a part of himself in trying to appease these power personalities. His success showed through as he remained in the position longer than any other man, enduring a pressure along the way that could easily break a lesser individual.

In the mid-1940s, between the Ness and Sutton years, Matowitz came under fire from Mayor Thomas A. Burke as Cleveland battled an active and corruptive force of gamblers. These men were every bit as ruthless, deadly and seductive a group as the police had dealt with during the Prohibition Era. Burke did not understand the situation completely, or how it compared to other cities the same size as Cleveland. All he knew was he was getting endless complaints and he felt Matowitz wasn't responding to his orders to clean up the gambling and policy rackets that were thriving in Cleveland.

In late September 1945, Matowitz was suspended by Burke and brought up on charges of failure to obey orders and gross neglect of duty. Prosecuting the case before a three-man panel heading the Civil Service Commission, of which Dan B. Cull was the senior member, was Director of

Public Safety Frank D. Celebreeze. After several days of highly publicized testimony, Matowitz, represented oddly enough by William J. Corrigan, was exonerated. The low point in the hearings was when Chief Matowitz found out that one of the men who helped in the gathering of evidence against him was Lieutenant Charles Cavolo.

Defeated but not deterred in his effort to remove Matowitz, in 1951 Burke got the support of city council to submit to the voters a charter amendment to remove the position of chief of police from Civil Service protection. The amendment was passed by the voters that November. Several months before the measure passed, Matowitz fell ill and was bedridden. In September he had abdominal surgery. Burke refused to act against Matowitz due to his long and loyal service to the department. Instead, the mayor wanted the chief to resign on his own and then Burke would ask council to make Matowitz chief emeritus with full salary granted for life.

The point became moot when Matowitz's condition worsened. He was diagnosed with cancer of the esophagus and it had progressed too far to be removed. Doctors and his family kept the bad news from him. On November 28, 1951, suffering from pneumonia, he was taken by ambulance to St. John's Hospital where his son was a doctor. The old chief was in grave condition and last rites were administered shortly after he arrived. Matowitz died the next morning with his two sons at his side. He was 69 years old. Burial was at Holy Cross Cemetery on the West Side.

Merrick, Frank Joseph – On February 23, 1932, Frank Merrick became Cleveland's Director of Public Safety replacing Edwin D. Barry. When Ray T. Miller took office as Cuyahoga County Prosecutor, replacing Edward Stanton, on January 1, 1929, he appointed Merrick as his chief assistant and placed him in charge of the criminal division. A year later, Merrick resigned, stating personal and financial reasons, and formed a private law practice. When Miller was elected mayor in February 1932, he made Merrick his new Director of Public Safety. Merrick had a tumultuous term, butting heads on a number of occasions with Miller, before he resigning in March 1933.

Merrick was not out of the public eye for long. On November 18, 1933, he was elected to fill a vacancy in the Municipal Court. Three years later he was elected judge of the Common Pleas Court, remaining in that position for the next 12 years.

In February 1945, Merrick raised a few eyebrows after it was discovered he was one of the last persons known to have conversed with slot machine baron Nathan "Nate" Weisenberg before he was found murdered in his automobile on a Cleveland Heights street. Merrick issued a long statement to investigators, but the meeting of the two in the Hollenden Hotel the night of the murder was simply a chance encounter.

Merrick remained a power in the local Democratic Party for decades, until 1968 when it was deemed not chic for an elected judge to take part in the direction of affairs of a political party. By that time Merrick had spent the last 30 years as a member of the Democratic County Executive Committee.

In 1953, Merrick was appointed to the Probate Court by former Cleveland mayor, now Ohio Governor Frank J. Lausche. Merrick remained in this position for the next twenty years, becoming the presiding probate judge in Cuyahoga County, before retiring in January 1973, at the age of 77.

Merrick was a baseball fan his entire life, back to the days when the Cleveland Indians were known at the Naps. He managed local sandlot teams on the Class C and D level. Merrick discovered a young first baseman, Cleveland-born Joe Kuhel, who played major league baseball from 1930 to 1947 with the Washington Senators and Chicago White Sox.

Despite his success in the legal profession, Merrick was not so lucky at marriage. He was twice divorced, the first one ending in a nasty public case.

After his retirement from the bench Merrick still took on a client on occasion. Such was the case on July 9, 1977, when Merrick was in U.S. District Court defending a man who was contesting a condemnation order on his Cuyahoga Valley National Park home. That night, Merrick and his wife were in their car going out to dinner when the 82 year-old slumped over. Rushed to St. Luke's Hospital, Merrick was pronounced dead.

Mooney, Philip J. – On March 1, 1925, Mooney retired from the Cleveland Police Department after 27 years of service. He was best remembered for his work on two cases – the Dan Kaber murder and the Sly-Fanner killings.

Mooney immediately began work as head of security for the Halle Bros. Company at their huge department store on Euclid Avenue. In 1929 Mooney was briefly back in the news when he was appointed guardian of the estate of late Cleveland Mafia boss Joseph "Big Joe" Lonardo. The guardianship included supervision over Lonardo's widow, Concietta, and her five children, the oldest of which was Angelo Lonardo, the mob boss's 18 year-old son who was a fugitive at the time, having avenged his father's death by murdering Salvatore "Black Sam" Todaro. Robert P. Mooney, the former detective's son, was an attorney and represented Concietta at her trial for involvement in the Todaro murder.

In 1935, Mooney suffered a stroke that forced him to retire from Halle Bros. He lived the remainder of his life in retirement, spending much of his time in Florida. In early 1944, in ill-health, he suffered a broken hip during a fall. While in City Hospital, he died on March 9, 1944, at the age of 75. Mooney left behind a wife, Mary, two sons and four daughters.

Morton, "Big Jim" – James Franklin, alias "Big Jim" Morton, was arrested on August 31, 1919, for the $65,000 robbery of the West Cleveland Bank at the corner of West 101st Street and Detroit Avenue. The robbery was reported to be the largest in the city's history. During the trial eight witnesses identified Morton as the leader of the bank robbery gang. The case was prosecuted by Stephen M. Young and Morton was defended by Patrick J. Mulligan. Morton's defense was that he was in Chicago, but Ohio law prevented the defendant from obtaining depositions from outside the state, thus scuttling his alibi.

On January 9, 1920, he was sentenced to one to fifteen years in the Ohio Penitentiary. On July 5, 1922, Morton's conviction was overturned on the grounds that the law prohibiting the taking of the out of state depositions was declared unconstitutional. In a second trial, prosecuted by Edward Stanton, Morton was again found guilty on January 19, 1923.

After some backroom dealings, Morton was granted a conditional pardon on August 5, 1925. The condition was that he be handed over to Michigan authorities to be tried for a 1918 bank robbery in Detroit. The deal called for Morton to plead guilty and promise never to return to Ohio. It was said that Michigan was tougher on bank robbers than Ohio, and that the state would be rid of a troublesome prisoner, who would spend even more time in prison in Michigan.

Morton, however, and his crafty attorney pulled a fast one and he pled not guilty. The state's key witness then disappeared. Over a number of months Morton obtained eight continuances. Ohio Governor Donahey, embarrassed by the turn of events, made a secret deal with Michigan Governor Alex J. Grosbeck. On December 14, 1925, after a smiling Morton received his ninth continuance, he was lured into an empty office in the courthouse, where he was hand-cuffed and shackled. He was then driven to the state line where Ohio officials were waiting.

During the Ohio Penitentiary fire in the spring of 1930, while fellow inmate "Jiggs" Losteiner wreaked havoc during the chaos, Morton helped save 40 prisoners. In recognition of his bravery he was paroled the next year.

Morton continued his criminal ways, with the same results. He spent much of the next 18 years in prison. In February 1949, at the age of 65, he was released from Joliet prison and returned to Cleveland. The next year *Cleveland Press* editor Louis Seltzer arranged with friends at the *Saturday Evening Post* for Morton's story to be told.

During the last decade of his life, Morton became a minor celebrity offering bank officials around the country help in deterring bank bandits. In 1952, he helped publicize the movie *My Six Convicts*, which featured actor Charles Bronson (still using the name Buchinski) and appeared on radio programs. Clevelanders remember a production in which Morton was the focus on a WEWS-TV special hosted local news analyst Dorothy Fuldheim.

Morton died on July 16, 1960, in Doctor's Hospital in Cleveland Heights.

Page, Anthony "Tony" – Due to their work in the late 1910s and early 1920s, Phillip Mooney and Tony Page became the most famous detective team in the history of the Cleveland Police Department.

Born in Italy around 1885, Page arrived in Cleveland at the age of five. On October 1, 1910, he was sworn in as a Cleveland police patrolman and was believed to be the first Cleveland police officer of Italian descent. Assigned to traffic patrol, wielding the old fashion semaphore apparatus (this in the years before Clevelander Garrett A. Morgan invented the three-color traffic signal), Page encountered more harrowing experiences at East Ninth Street and Superior Avenue than he would during his years as a detective. Five times he was nearly run down, losing his semaphore in the incident.

While Page and Mooney were credited with working on the department's first "Italian squad," or "Black Hand squad," the duo was most famous for their work on bank robberies. It was not unusual for them to inform reporters, such as cub police reporter Louis Seltzer of the *Cleveland Press*, to meet them at a certain location where they took down the culprits before they could execute their robbery plans.

Mooney retired in 1925 and Page stayed on as a detective until 1933. That year he was assigned deputy bailiff of what was known as "drunk court." Page estimated that during 20-plus years he listened to 100,000 drunks explain their actions to a judge. Page took many of the offenders aside and advised, "Let liquor alone. Drink buttermilk like I do."

Page retired from the police department in 1956 after 45 years on the job. On February 11, 1961, Tony Page died in Woman's Hospital at the age of 76.

 # Potts, Emmett J. – was born in Pittsburgh and brought to Cleveland by his family when he was just a year old. He grew up in the Newburgh section of the city. In early 1912, Potts joined the Cleveland Fire Department. He was a member for thirteen months before he decided to become a police officer.

Potts began a 26-year career with the Cleveland Police Department on April 2, 1913. He was promoted to sergeant in 1918, and the next year made lieutenant.

The words "stormy" and "fiery" were used to describe Potts career in the police department. He rose to the rank of captain in 1925, and for a brief time during the third term of Mayor Harry L. Davis, Potts was appointed assistant chief of police, a position which until then didn't exist.

From 1923 until his retirement in 1939, Potts was embroiled in a number of department controversies, some resulting in his transfer to undesirable locations. Potts, who passed the Ohio Bar in 1923, successfully fought these transfers.

After his retirement, Potts became director of security at Ohio Crankshaft Company. He remained there until 1947 when he retired due to ill-health. Potts died at St. Luke's Hospital on May 8, 1955, at the age of 66. He was buried in Calvary Cemetery.

Rowlands, John W. – attained the position of chief police inspector before a sudden fall from grace. Rowlands joined the police department on January 7, 1892. His promotion up the ranks was steady – sergeant, January 1897; lieutenant, April 1901; and captain, 1903. He served in the latter capacity until February 11, 1918, when he was named inspector.

After the resignation of Police Chief William S. Rowe in late 1917, and the taking of the mayor's office by Harry L. Davis, many expected Rowlands to be named the new chief. Up until that time he was considered the "number 2" cop in the department and was a powerful figure in the city. Despite rumors that Rowlands would be named chief, the job went to Frank W. Smith. Rowlands was later named chief inspector and served as "acting chief" in the days that followed the tragic death of Chief Smith's son, on April 21, 1921.

When former police chief Fred Kohler ran for mayor in 1921, Rowlands launched a vicious attack against his former boss. Kohler's victory that fall spelled the end of Rowland's career in the police department. He retired on December 31, 1921, the day before Kohler took office.

Rowlands served as assistant chief probation officer of the Common Pleas Court until the mid-1920s, he then became ill and was forced to retire. In the early 1930s, he suffered a nervous breakdown and underwent treatments at Bellhurst Sanitarium in Mentor, Ohio.

On January 14, 1935, at the age of 75, Rowlands died at his East 70th Street home. He was buried in Calvary Cemetery.

Smith, Frank W. – despite living for another 35 years, the former chief of police managed to keep a pretty low profile. A resident of East Cleveland, he served as that suburb's police chief for a few months. He later worked as a special investigator before leaving that position to become a chicken rancher in Geauga County. Smith also served as a foreman on both the Federal and County Grand juries. A long-time member of the Masons, he reached 32nd degree status with the organization.

Ill health finally slowed the old police officer down in 1955. By now Smith was bed ridden in his Taylor Road home. He died at the age of 85 on October 30, 1955. Smith, like Cornelius Cody, was buried in Acacia Masonic Memorial Park cemetery on SOM Center Road.

Sprosty, Anton B. – was born on June 12, 1872 in what was Cleveland's "Bohemian settlement," a neighborhood around West 50th Street and Clark Avenue. Sprosty's father, brother and nephew were all Cleveland police officers. The father, John Sprosty, was a detective and served as an interpreter in his duties around the Union Depot.

After high school Sprosty began work with a jeweler on Public Square. He became a watchmaker and an expert diamond appraiser. In 1898, he opened his own jewelry store at East 49th Street and Broadway.

Sprosty became interested in Republican Party politics at an early age. He remained an active member for more than 30 years, of which 15 years were spent as a Ward 13 leader. In 1909, he ran for city councilman from the 13th Ward and was elected, serving one term. During this time he became friends with Harry L. Davis and supported him in his run for mayor in 1916. Davis was elected and Sprosty's loyalty was rewarded when he was named Director of Public Safety.

Sprosty held the office for six years, but they were stormy ones as he battled a Democrat majority in council, his police chiefs and the newspapers. His most controversial move was the issuing of "Order 73," which directed that the vice squad must receive his approval before conducting any raids. Incensed city council members charged that City Hall was interfering with the work of the police department. The order eventually led to the dissolving of the city's vice squad in 1922.

Sprosty was replaced by Thomas Martinec, who was appointed by newly elected mayor Fred Kohler in January 1922. In 1926, Sprosty returned to city council as a representative from the Second District. Re-elected in 1928, the next year he became embroiled in a city land scandal along with real-estate businessman Joseph L. Mack. The scandal involved the widening of Perkins Avenue in which the two had obtained land. Sprosty was charged with having direct financial interest in a city land contract. Two trials followed, but the men were acquitted at both. The incident ended Sprosty's political career.

After leaving office Sprosty was named custodian of the Lake Avenue Courthouse. He remained in that position for the next four years.

In early 1940, Sprosty was suffering from failing health. In early May 1945, he fell and broke an arm at his Maple Heights home. He was taken to a hospital where shock set in and led to his death on May 9. He was 72 years old.

Stannard, Charles B. – The council president and county sheriff was born in Huron, Ohio, in 1876. He moved to Cleveland when he was 19 years-old and found work in the insurance business. He then became interested in city politics and began his association with the Republican Party.

After his loss to Fred Kohler for re-election to county sheriff in 1924, Stannard became a sales agent for the International Harvester Company, moving right back into the Keith Building, where he once rented an insurance office. Ten years later, in 1934, he got the bug to run for sheriff again. He soon backed out in order to support the Republic Party candidate.

The ensuing years were not kind to him. In March 1935, Stannard was drinking when he got into an accident with Thomas Reskovac at Northvale and Mount Vernon Roads in Cleveland Heights. Stannard was driving an International Harvester truck at the time. Reskovac confronted Stannard, who was verbally abusive and tried to drive away. Reskovac jumped on the truck's running board, reached in and turned off the ignition and then took the keys.

Stannard left the scene on foot, going to a phone booth on nearby Lee Road, where he telephoned the Cleveland Heights Police Department and told them he was robbed. When police arrived, the obviously intoxicated former sheriff said he was robbed by five or six men who took his wallet, which contained "important papers." After finding his wrecked vehicle, skeptical police officers took Stannard to the Cleveland Heights Police Station on Mayfield Road for further questioning. Still insisting he was the victim of a robbery, police finally told Stannard to shut up, that they didn't believe his story. Soon Reskovac and his girlfriend, a passenger who witnessed the accident, showed up and told their version of events.

Over the next few weeks a scandal ensued as the trial of the former sheriff was delayed several times and accusations arose in the newspapers that Cleveland Heights officials were trying to "hush" the matter. When a reporter asked Cleveland Heights Police Chief W.G. Barrows what happened, the chief snapped, "Just what is your interest in this case? Do you run a story about every man arrested in Cuyahoga County? What are you trying to do – humiliate this man?"

Even Cleveland Heights Mayor Frank C. Cain was confronted. His response was, "I haven't found out anything yet. I have a lot of other things more important."

On May 1, the case was heard before Cleveland Heights Municipal Judge David J. Miller. Although Stannard pled not guilty, he offered no defense after the city presented its case. Miller found Stannard guilty of being intoxicated on the night of the accident. Before sentence was passed, Stannard's lawyer told the court his client was "a poor man, without means, who is trying to make a living." This despite his employment with International Harvester. Miller fined him $35 and costs. The young woman with Reskovac that night, later filed a lawsuit against Stannard and International Harvester since one of their vehicles was involved in the accident.

On Christmas Day 1950, Stannard and his wife Annette celebrated their golden wedding anniversary at a party thrown by their son. In May 1952, Stannard was reported missing from his home. Family members said he was suffering from bouts of memory loss and had not been well since having surgery on his eyes several weeks earlier. Stannard walked into the Central Police Station and asked for shelter. An alert police officer noticed that his attire didn't fit the other transients and he checked the missing persons' reports and found one was filed on Stannard. The family was notified and a son picked him up.

Until his health began to deteriorate, Stannard was a loyal member of the Masons and achieved the rank of 32nd Degree. He was a past master of the Woodward Lodge and a member of the Oriental Commandery, Al Sirat Shrine and the Knights Templar.

Stannard passed away quietly at his Euclid Heights Blvd. home in Cleveland Heights on January 19, 1953, at the age of 76. He was buried in Acacia Park Cemetery.

Stanton, Edward C. – In the years after leaving as county prosecutor Stanton did not seek public office. The law firm of Stanton & Connell didn't last long as James Connell soon went on his own and not long afterwards was named to the Federal bench. The most notable case the two handled as partners was a voting fraud charge against a number of election booth officials after the November 1928 elections.

Stanton's political involvement was low-key, consisting of serving as a Republican state central committeeman and as a delegate to the national conventions. This latter activity lasted until 1943, when party leaders talked him into challenging incumbent Frank J. Lausche in his bid for a second term as mayor of Cleveland.

Reluctant at first to run, especially after intimate friends advised him not to, Stanton threw himself into the political fight with renewed gusto. Despite the fact that Lausche had all the local newspaper support, and was deemed unbeatable, Stanton ran a spirited campaign.

"I've always had opposition," Stanton declared. "I wouldn't know what to do without it. I do not underestimate Lausche as an opponent, but I know I can lick him."

After Stanton was defeated, he refrained from running again for public office. Instead, he buried himself in his law practice. On July 21, 1960, Stanton was defending Francis V. Downey on a manslaughter charge for the killing of her abusive husband. While carrying out his "customary dash and brilliance," Stanton suffered a stroke. The case was declared a mistrial. Three weeks later, on the afternoon of August 11, Stanton died at the age of 72 in St. Vincent Charity Hospital.

Stanton was married to Kathryn "Kate" Duffy, a childhood sweetheart, who he had met during grade school at St. Malachi. The couple had six children.

Sterling, Charles N. – After his heart attack on the boat ride to Detroit to pick up Louis Komer, Inspector Sterling was the never the same. Despite this debilitating condition and the fact that by 1921 Sterling had 25 years of service in and could have retired on pension, the inspector told people close to him that he intended to "wear the blue" as long as he lived. Shortly after the appointment of Jacob Graul as the chief of police in January 1922, Sterling suffered another bout with the heart disease and took a short leave of absence.

After Edwin D. Barry was named Director of Public Safety in January 1924, Sterling fell out of favor. During one of the reorganizations Sterling was removed from the detective bureau. Seeing the move as a demotion he aired his sentiments publicly. For this he was transferred from the Central Police Station to the "Roaring Third," with orders to "clean it up." During his command there Sterling received information that a number of bootleg "joints" were operating unimpeded in the Fifth Precinct. He sent a report of his findings to the chief's office. Instead of acting on this information or forwarding it to the precinct commander of the Fifth, Graul simply transferred Sterling there with orders to clean it up himself. Sterling considered this move another slap.

In December 1926, Sterling incurred the wrath of Barry after he went to U.S. Attorney A.E. Bernstein to complain about the handling of a liquor case by Municipal Judge David. The result was another transfer, this time to the Woodland – East 37th Precinct. The previous summer Sterling had suffered a serious bout from heart disease. With this latest episode Barry soon saw fit to relieve Sterling of command, which he did on February 20, 1927. Although most considered it a "medical leave," and Sterling's position remained officially open, he never returned to police work.

Sterling spent the remaining months of his life mostly confined to bed at his home on West 108th Street, cared for by his wife Mary. On the morning of October 10, 1927, Sterling was in good spirits as his wife brought him breakfast. Shortly after he began to eat, the 60 year-old Sterling suffered a massive heart attack and died.

Despite their differences, Barry was quick to issue a statement saying, "In Sterling, the city lost a brave and fearless officer. There were few as honest and courageous as he was." Chief Graul declared, "The department has lost one of its finest officers. Inspector Sterling was an intelligent, honest, hard-working officer and his services to this city will be missed."

On October 13, Sterling was laid to rest in Riverside Cemetery after a funeral service from his residence. Pallbearers included George Matowitz and George Koestle. A police honor guard accompanied the body to the grave.

Sterling, an active member of the Masons, left behind two sons who were both dentists. His brother John was a Battalion Chief in the Cleveland Fire Department, while another brother, William, was a construction superintendent for the United States government in the Panama Canal Zone. A sister, Katherine, was married to Deputy County Treasurer Fred Moritz.

Death Notices

Name: Allen, Judge Florence E.
Date: Sep 15 1966
Source: Cleveland Press; Cleveland Necrology File, Reel #089.
Notes: Allen. Judge Florence E. Allen, of Hall, Oh. Sister of Mrs. Ester Gaw and Mrs. Elizabeth Saloane. Memorial services will be held Friday, Sept. 23 at 2:30 P. M. Please Omit flowers, family is suggested that gifts may be made to the Florence Allen Scholarship Fund, College of Law New York University, New York City N. Y. or The Old South Church, Kirtland, Oh.

Name: Amato, Frank
Date: 1921
Source: Cemetery record; Cleveland Necrology File, Reel #002.
Notes: 1895 - 1921. Calvary Cemetery Cleveland, Ohio.

Name: Angelotta, Nick
Date: Mar 17 1946
Source: Source unknown; Cleveland Necrology File, Reel #002.
Notes: Angelotta: Nick, beloved son of the late Mr. and Mrs. Antonio Angelotta; brother of the late Charles and Mrs. Mary Augusta, passed away at Tucson. Ariz. Friends received at S. A. Conti & Son's Funeral Home, 2110 Murray Hill Rd. Funeral Monday from Holy Rosary Church at 9:15 am.

Name: Banks, Clarence C.
Date: Feb 23 1948
Source: Plain Dealer; Cleveland Necrology File, Reel #003.
Notes: Banks, Clarence C., of Clarksfield Oh. passed away Feb. 22; beloved husband of Anna (nee Hartenfeld); father of Randolph and James, both of Cleveland; grandfather and great-grandfather; brother of Chester of California. Friends received at the L. D. Gerber Funeral Home, where services will be held Wednesday, Feb. 25, at 2:30 p. m.

Name: Barricelli, Dr. Giovanni A.
Date: Apr 20 1934
Source: Source unknown; Cleveland Necrology File, Reel #004.
Notes: Barricelli: Dr. Giovanni A.: Beloved husband of Orfea M., father of Gianpiero and brother of Vincenzo. Salvatore, Pasquale and Antonia of

Benevento, Italy, Monday, April 16, 1934, at his residence, 2203 Cornell Road. Funeral from the residence Thursday, April 19, at 9 a. m., and from Holy Rosary Church at 10 a. m. Burial Lake View Cemetery.

Name: Benigno, Dominic
Date: 1922
Source: Cemetery record; Cleveland Necrology File, Reel #006.
Notes: 1896 - 1922. Age 26. Calvary Cemetery Cleveland, Ohio.

Name: Benigno, Thomas
Date: 1936
Source: Cemetery record; Cleveland Necrology File, Reel #006.
Notes: 1899 - 1936. Age 37. Calvary Cemetery Cleveland, Ohio.

Name: Bolles, Arthur J.
Date: Aug 15 1965
Source: Plain Dealer; Cleveland Necrology File, Reel #094.
Notes: Bolles. Arthur J. Bolles, beloved husband of Anne S. (nee Bell), dear father of George J. and the late Hazel, brother of Hazel Robinson, Ruth McRae, Cora Putnam, May Toll and the late Frank, John, Harry and George, late residence, 1456 W. 101st St. Friends received at the Leimkuehler Funeral Home, 6722 Franklin Blvd., After 2 P. M. Saturday. Services at St. Luke Episcopal Church, W. 78th and Lake Ave., Monday at 1:30 p. m.

Name: Budd, Archie
Date: March 6, 1922
Source: Cemetery record; Cleveland Necrology File, Reel #011.
Notes: Budd-Archie, aged 72 years, dearly beloved husband of the late Amelia G. (nee Schneider), father of Mrs. John V. Hoffmann, Mrs. John T. Brown, Albert H. and William R., grandfather of Howard J. Connolly, Lois and Donald Brown, entered into rest peacefully Monday, March 6, at 7:15 p. m. at his residence, 2279 E. 90th street. Services Thursday at 2. Friends invited. 3/6/1922. Highland Park Cemetery Warrensville, Ohio.

Name: Caley, Fred H.
Date: Apr 27 1945
Source: Source unknown; Cleveland Necrology File, Reel #012.
Notes: Caley: Fred H., beloved father of Roland C. of Columbus, O., and Don of Cleveland; grandfather of Mrs. James Brundise and Fred W. Caley of Columbus; April 20. Services from the Carnegie Home of the Millard Son & Raper Co., Carnegie at E. 105th st., Friday, April 27, at 2:30 p. m.

Name: Cassidy, James T.
Date: Feb 13 1972
Source: Plain Dealer; Cleveland Necrology File, Reel #098.
Notes: Cassidy. James T. Cassidy (former Cleveland Municipal Court Judge), beloved husband of the late Emma Smith Cassidy, father of James T., Jr. and brother of Charles A. Former residence, 12701 Shaker Blvd. The family will receive friends at The Mahon-Murphy Funeral Home, 13201 Euclid Ave. Funeral Mass Monday, 9:30 a.m. at Our Lady of Peace Church. Visiting Hours Sunday 3-5 and 7-9 P.M. Interment All Souls Cemetery.

Name: Cavolo, Charles
Date: Apr 20 1958
Source: Cleveland Press; Cleveland Necrology File, Reel #098.
Notes: Cavolo, Charles, beloved husband of Josephine (nee Tanno), dear father of Dominick, Mrs. Anna Dindia, Dr. Charles Cavolo, Jr., and grandfather, brother of Joseph Cavolo (deceased), Rev. Nicholas Cavolo of Italy and Miss Lucietta Cavolo of Italy, passed away Wednesday, Apr. 23. The family will receive friends Thursday and Friday at the residence, 2463 Edgehill Rd., Cleveland Heights, where services will be held Saturday, Apr. 26, at 10:30 a. m., and from St. Ann Church at 11:30 a. m. Interment Calvary Cemetery.

Name: Coletto, Madalena Vaccarello
Date: July 4, 1920
Source: Source unknown; Cleveland Necrology File, Reel #015.
Notes: Coletto-Madalena Vaccarello, wife of Michael, beloved mother of Thomas, Ralph, John, Anthony and Charles, died July 2, at 3:15 p. m., at 12010 Paul av. Funeral Monday, at 9:30 a. m., at Holy Rosary church. Friends invited. Please omit flowers.

Name: Costello, Timothy J.
Date: Feb 12 1960
Source: Cleveland Press; Cleveland Necrology File, Reel #101.
Notes: Costello, Timothy J., beloved husband of the late Mary (nee McAvoy), father of Sister M. Ignatia CSJ Sister M. Timothy, CSA. Sister M. Colette, SCMM. Daniel, Catherine William and Timothy, brother of James, residence, 9815 Nicholas Ave., Wednesday, Feb. 10, 1960. Friends may call at McGorray Bros. Lakewood Home, 14133 Detroit Ave. Funeral mass Saturday, Feb. 13, St. Ignatius Church, at 10 a. m. Interment St. Mary of the Falls Cemetery. Olmsted Falls.

Name: Cull, Dan B. Sr.
Date: Aug 9 1949
Source: Source unknown; Cleveland Necrology File, Reel #017.
Notes: Cull, Dan B. Sr., beloved husband of Margaret M. (nee McMyler) father of Margaret M., Dan B., Jr., Catherine R., Rita A., John P. S. J., William J. Paul M.; brother of Frank X. Mrs. Mary Baker, Anna Cull of Miamisburg, O., and Mrs. Agnes Buecher of Dayton, O., Sunday, Aug. 7. Friends may call at his late residence, 13700 Larchmere Rd. Funeral Wednesday, Aug. 10, Our Lady of Peace Church at 10 a. m.

Name: Dembe, Joseph
Date: Jan 6 1955
Source: Cleveland Press; Cleveland Necrology File, Reel #103.
Notes: Dembe, Joseph, residence, 1587 Coventry Rd., beloved husband of Marguerite, father of Joseph and Harold Dembe and Mrs. Ethyl Grossman of Columbus, O., brother of Louis and Edward Dembe, both of Chicago, Ill., and grandfather. Services at Cleveland Temple Memorial, Euclid at E. 90 St., Friday, Jan. 7, at 1 p. m. Interment Mt. Sinai Cemetery. Kindly omit flowers.

Name: Fanner, George K.
Date: December 31, 1920
Source: Cemetery record; Cleveland Necrology File, Reel #024.
Notes: Fanner-George K., aged 34 years, husband of Ethel (nee Page), son of Mr. and Mrs. George J. Fanner, brother of Mrs. B.L. White, suddenly Friday a. m. Funeral from late residence, 1285 Virginia avenue, Lakewood, Monday, January 3, at 2:30 p. m. 1886 - 1920. Riverside Cemetery Cleveland, Ohio.

Name: Fitzgerald, William S.
Date: Oct 6 1937
Source: Source unknown; Cleveland Necrology File, Reel #025.
Notes: Fitzgerald: William S., beloved husband of Carolina; former major of Cleveland; suddenly, Sunday, Oct. 3; now at W. W. Young-E. L. Baker, Inc., Funeral Home, 8806 Euclid ave., where services will be held Wednesday, Oct. 6, at 2 p. m.

Name: Franke, George L.
Date: Jul 31 1967
Source: Plain Dealer; Cleveland Necrology File, Reel #109.

Notes: Franke. George L. Franke, residence, 2079 Staunton Rd., beloved husband of Sylvia (nee Behrens), brother of Mrs. Lillian Alexander of Chicago, Ill. Services at Cleveland Temple Memorial, Euclid at E. 90th St., Monday, July 31, at 1 p.m. Interment Mayfield Cemetery. Kindly omit flowers. Friends who wish may contribute to Bellefaire.

Name: Graul, Jacob
Date: Feb 17 1938
Source: Cemetery record; Cleveland Necrology File, Reel #031.
Notes: Graul: Jacob, beloved husband of Alma (nee Lenz), and father of Leona G. Lewis, Alfred L. and Walter J., brother of John, George, Lillian and Mrs. E. G. Krauss, passed away suddenly. Monday, Feb. 14, 1938. Now at the Koebler Funeral Home, 1966 E. 82d st. at Euclid ave. Services there Thursday, Feb. 17, at 3 p. m. 2/14/1938. Highland Park Cemetery Warrensville Hts., Ohio.

Name: Hammond, Dr. Ardon P.
Date: Mar 22 1928
Source: Source unknown; Cleveland Necrology File, Reel #034.
Notes: Hammond-Dr. Ardon P., age 59, beloved husband of Florence (nee Moore), brother of Martha E. Stein and the late Jessie E. Crocker. Funeral Saturday, March 24, at 3 p. m., from the late residence, 2582 Kingston Rd., Cleveland Heights. Services conducted by Holyrood Commandery, K. T. Interment Castalia, Ohio. Monday, at 2 p. m.

Name: Henry, Ethel L. (Fanner)
Date: May 17 1972
Source: Cleveland Press; Cleveland Necrology File, Reel #117.
Notes: Henry. Ethel L. Henry (Fanner) (nee Pope), beloved wife of the late Arthur J., dear mother of Mrs. Robert H. Burnell (Marian), grandmother of Mrs. William Larkin (Beverly) of Chicago, Ill., great-grandmother of Keith, Dale, and Sandra Lorkin, residence, 2693 Goldwood Dr., Rocky River. Funeral services will be held at The Saxton-Klanke Funeral Home, 13215 Detroit Ave., Thursday, May 18, at 1:30 P.M. Friends Received Wednesday 2-4 And 7-9 P.M.

Name: Koestle, George
Date: Mar 6 1941
Source: Source unknown; Cleveland Necrology File, Reel #046.
Notes: Koestle: George, husband of the late Emma (nee Ettner), beloved father of Mrs. Wilbur H. Leopold (Della), grandfather of Wilbur A.

Leopold; brother of William, residence, 220 Buckingham rd., Rocky River. Friends may call at William R. & Roy A. Daniels' Funeral Home, 15800 Detroit ave., where services will be held Thursday, March 6 at 3 p. m.

Name: Martinec, Thomas C.
Date: Sep 1- 1952
Source: Cleveland Press; Cleveland Necrology File, Reel #134.
Notes: Martinec, Thomas C., residence, 1891 Beersford Ave., East Cleveland, husband of the late Josephine, beloved father of Mrs. Mildred Summerhill, Thomas B. Martinet and the late Dorothy Prochaska and Bertine Lockwood, grandfather and great-grandfather, passed away Saturday. Friends may call at A. Nosek & Sons Funeral Home, 3282 E. 55th St., where services will be held Tuesday, Sept. 2, at 3 p. m.

Name: Matowitz, George J.
Date: Nov 30 1951
Source: Cleveland Press; Cleveland Necrology File, Reel #134.
Notes: Matowitz, George J., chief of police, City of Cleveland, late residence, 24133 Mastick Rd., beloved husband of May (Becker), father of Dr. Clayton C., Thomas G., and grandfather, brother of James, Irene Kubik, Marguerite, Frank and the late John. Friends received at Corrigan's Funeral Home, Lorain Ave. and W. 148 St. Funeral Saturday, Dec. 1. St. John's Cathedral, at 11:45 a. m. Interment Holy Cross Cemetery.

Name: Mettel, Max C.
Date: Jul 13 1938
Source: Cemetery record; Cleveland Necrology File, Reel #056.
Notes: Mettel: Max, C., beloved husband of Sadie (nee Koehler), father of Mrs. Beatrice Waltz and Clyde Mettel, son of Bertha, brother of Mrs. Walter Isaac, Sunday a. m. at his late residence, 4010 Riveredge rd., until Wednesday morning. Services at the H. A. Leimkuehler Funeral Home, 6722 Franklin blvd., Wednesday, July 13 at 2:30 p. m. Interment Sunset Park. 7/10/1938. Age 55.

Name: Milazzo, Frank J.
Date: May 16 1959
Source: Cleveland Press; Cleveland Necrology File, Reel #135.
Notes: Milazzo, Frank J., beloved son of the late Joseph and Anna, nephew of Mary, cousin of Anthony and John Milazzo, suddenly Wednesday. Friends may call at the Frank R. Conti Funeral Home, 2110 Murray Hill Rd., Visiting Hours Friday 2 To 10 P. M. Funeral services Saturday, May 16, at Holy Rosary Church, 11 a. m.

Name: Mooney, Phillip J.
Date: March 11, 1944
Source: Source unknown; Cleveland Necrology File, Reel #058.
Notes: Mooney-Phillip J. beloved husband of Mary S. (nee Goggin) father of Robert F., John T., Eileen, Coletta McHenry, Agnes Quick, Cecilia Roth and Mary Hayes (deceased) Thursday, March 9. Friends may call at the Flynn-Froelk Co., Funeral Home, 13104 Euclid Ave. Funeral services Monday, March13, St. Thomas Aquinas' Church at 10 a.m. Elk services Sunday, March 12, at 8 p.m. Please omit flowers.

Name: Mulligan, Patrick J.
Date: Jul 5 1962
Source: Plain Dealer; Cleveland Necrology File, Reel #137.
Notes: Mulligan. Patrick J. Mulligan, beloved husband of Elsie M. (nee Dunn), father of Rev. John D., S. M., Thomas P., Mrs. Dorothy Hanrahan, Patrick J. Jr., Eugene E., William C. and Robert P., and grandfather of 26, brother of Magr. Thomas P. Mulligan and Genevieve Mulligan, late residence, 19101 Van Akan Blvd., Shaker Heights. The family will receive friends Thursday 2-5 And 7-10 P. M. at the New Mahon-Murphy Funeral Home, 13201 Euclid Ave. (ample parking in rear). Funeral mass 10 a. m. Friday, St. Dominic's Church. In lieu of flowers, the family suggests contributions may be made to Charity Hospital.

Name: Page, Anthony (Tony)
Date: Feb 13 1961
Source: Plain Dealer; Cleveland Necrology File, Reel #142.
Notes: Beloved husband of Albina (nee Silveroli); dear father of Carmen and Mrs. Fay Lacey; grandfather and great-grandfather; Saturday, Feb. 11. Friends received at the new Mahon-Murphy Funeral Home, 13201 Euclid Ave. Visiting Hours Monday 2-5 And 7-10 P. M. Funeral services Tuesday, Feb. 14, at St. Joseph's Church (14400 St. Clair Ave.), at 10 a. m. Please omit flowers.

Name: Rothkopf, David R.
Date: May 15, 1932
Source: Source unknown, Cleveland Necrology File, Reel #070.
Notes: Rothkopf: David R., son of Mr. and Mrs. Morris Rothkopf, father of Gloria, passed away suddenly Friday morning. Funeral Sunday at 1:45 p.m. from Deutsch's Chapel.

Name: Rowlands, John
Date: Jan 16 1935
Source: Source unknown; Cleveland Necrology File, Reel #070.
Notes: Rowlands: John, former inspector of police, beloved husband of Catherine (nee Sammon), father of Gertrude Vail, Grace Hesselman and the late Frank Rowlands, grandfather of Gertrude Vail Patchett, Bob, Catherine and Grace Mary Vail, great-grandfather of Cora Belle Patchett at his home, 1734 E. 70th St. Funeral Thursday, Jan. 17, at 10 a. m. from St. Agnes' Church, E. St. Louis papers please copy. Kindly omit flowers.

Name: Sly, Marie A.
Date: Oct 10 1961
Source: Plain Dealer; Cleveland Necrology File, Reel #156.
Notes: (Nee Kurtz), beloved wife of the late Wilfred C.; sister of the late William L. Kurtz; Saturday morning, late residence, 15426 Lake Ave. Friends received at the Nickels Funeral Home, 14500 Madison Ave. Services Tuesday, Oct. 10, St. James Church, Detroit and Granger Aves., at 10 a. m.

Name: Sly, Mary A.
Date: August 27, 1921
Source: Source unknown; Cleveland Necrology File, Reel #075.
Notes: Sly-Mary A., widow of the late William Wesley Sly, mother of the late Wilfred Colfax Sly and of Maud Sly Hoffman, at her residence, 1041 Forest Cliff Drive, Lakewood, in her eighty-fifth year, Aug. 27. Funeral Tuesday at late residence, at 2 p. m. and at 3 p. m. Crawford Road Christian Church. Burial at Lake View Cemetery. Services at the church by Memorial Relief corps.

Name: Hoffman, Maude Sly
Date: Dec ?
Source: Cleveland Press; Cleveland Necrology File, Reel #118.
Notes: Hoffman, Maude Sly, wife of the late Edward C., beloved mother of Wilfred C., sister of the late Wilfred C. Sly, residence, 1041 Forest Cliff Dr. Friends may call at the Daniels Funeral Home, 15300 Detroit, where services will be held Wednesday, Dec. 26, at 1:30 p. m.

Name: Sly, W. W.
Date: May 23, 1911
Source: Source unknown; Cleveland Necrology File, Reel #075.
Notes: Sly-W. W., at his home, 1637 Crawford rd. N. E., Monday a. m. Funeral from residence Wednesday at 2 p. m., interment Lakeview cemetery.

Name: Sly, Wilfred C.
Date: December 31, 1920
Source: Cemetery record; Cleveland Necrology File, Reel #075.
Notes: Sly-Wilfred C., beloved husband of Marie Sly (nee Kurtz), died suddenly Friday, December 31, 1920. Funeral Tuesday, January 4, from the late residence, 13474 Lake Avenue, Lakewood, at 2 p. m. 1920. Lakeview Cemetery Cleveland, Ohio.

Name: Smith, Frank W.
Date: Nov 1 1955
Source: Cleveland Press; Cleveland Necrology File, Reel #156.
Notes: Smith, Frank W. (retired Chief of Cleveland Police Department), husband of the late Ethel C., father of Warren C., and grandfather, brother of Blanche Fairchilds, Leora Brown, Emily Hoffman, Gertrude Gardner, A. W. and Jay V. Smith, Oct. 30, residence, 1849 Taylor Rd. The family will receive friends 7-9 P. M. Tuesday at The Edwards Funeral Home, 13145 Euclid Ave., where services will be conducted by Forest City Lodge No. 388, F. and A. M., Wednesday, Nov. 2, at 1 p. m.

Name: Soukup, Albert J.
Date: Aug 6 1942
Source: Cleveland Press; Cleveland Necrology File, Reel #076.
Notes: Soukup, Albert J.--Residence, 3431 E. 147 street Beloved husband of Zdenka, father of Alberta Marie Fogarty and the late Anthony J., grandfather Roger and Joy, brother of Joseph and James, Tuesday. Services at A. Nosek & Sons Funeral Home, 3282 E. 55 Street, Friday, Aug. 7, at 2 p. m.

Name: Sprosty, Anton B.
Date: May 11 1945
Source: Source unknown; Cleveland Necrology File, Reel #077.
Notes: Sprosty: Anton B., beloved husband of Pauline, father of Dr. Clarence A.; Chester C., grandfather; passed away Wednesday. Funeral Saturday, May 12, S. J. Kubu & Son Funeral Home, 3271 E. 55th st., 2 p. m.

Name: Sprosty, Elmer Frank
Date: April 24, 1921
Source: Source unknown; Cleveland Necrology File, Reel #077.
Notes: Sprosty-Elmer Frank, beloved husband of Cecelia Sprosty (nee Flood), age 24 years, beloved son of Josephine and Frank D. Sprosty, and brother of Lawrence, Daniel Alosia and Raymond Sprosty. Funeral Monday, 2 p. m., at late residence, 2148 W. 96th street. Interment West Park Cemetery.

Name: Sprosty, Capt. Frank D.
Date: Jul 3 1936
Source: Source unknown; Cleveland Necrology File, Reel #077.
Notes: Sprosty: Capt. Frank D., Geneva, O., age 64 years, beloved husband of Josephine (nee Hablesreither), brother of Anton and the late Edward, father of Lawrence, Dan, Alois, Ray and the late Elmer. Funeral Friday, July 3, at 2:30 p. m., from Parlors of Kubu & Son, 3271 E. 55th st. Burial West Park Cemetery. Friends invited.

Name: Stannard, Charles B.
Date: Jan 22 1953
Source: Source unknown; Cleveland Necrology File, Reel #158.
Notes: Stannard, Charles B., husband of Annette; father of Neal D. and Paul L., grandfather of Mrs. Marilyn Taylor, Carol, Sandra and Christopher Stannard; Jan. 19. Friends may call at the Fairhill Home of the Millard Son & Raper Co., Fairhill at East Blvd., where Masonic services will be held Thursday, Jan. 22 at 2 p. m.

Name: Stanton, Edward C.
Date: Aug 15 1960
Source: Plain Dealer; Cleveland Necrology File, Reel #158.
Notes: Stanton, Edward C., dearly beloved husband of Kate (nee Duffy); beloved father of Robert L., Mrs. Robert McCoy (Bette Pat), Mrs. Thomas Davies (Donna Marie), Petra Carla. Fridelma Kay, the late Edward C. Jr.; son of the late Edward and Margaret; dear brother of Mrs. Della Roach, Mrs. Mary Fay, Mars, Margaret Crawley, Mrs. Nellie Heater, Nate, Michael and James, all deceased; Thursday, August 11, 1960. Friends received at the late residence, 28905 Osborn Pd., Bay Village. Please omit flowers. Funeral mass at St. Rose Church (W. 114-Detroit). Tuesday, Aug. 16, at 10 a. m. Interment Calvary Cemetery. Arrangements by Berry's Funeral Home.

Name: Sterling, Charles N.
Date: Oct. 13, 1927
Source: Source unknown; Cleveland Necrology File, Reel #077.
Notes: Sterling-Charles N., beloved husband of Mary (nee Ruff), father of Dr. C. J. and Dr. W. J. Sterling, brother of William C., Chief John J. Sterling and Mrs. Fred Moritz. Funeral from late residence, 1288 W. 108th street, Thursday, Oct. 13, at 2 p. m.

Name: Sullivan, John J.
Date: Sep 2 1930

Source: Source unknown; Cleveland Necrology File, Reel #078.
Notes: Sullivan: John J., suddenly, Saturday, Aug. 30, 1930, in his 70th year, beloved husband of Olive Taylor, father of Adaline T. and Mary T. (Mrs. John W. McCaslin). Funeral services at residence, 2835 Drummond Road. Shaker Heights, Tuesday, Sept. 2, at 2:30 p. m.

Name: Thobaben, Edward J.
Date: Oct 8 1947
Source: Plain Dealer; Cleveland Necrology File, Reel #080.
Notes: Thobaben, Edward J., brother of William W. and Mrs. F. H. Schwabie. Friends may call at the Paul T. Long Funeral Home, 12610 Woodland Ave. (first street north of Shaker Square), where Cleveland City Lodge No. 15, F. and A. M. services will be held Thursday, Oct. 9, at 2:30 p. m.

Name: Toner, James R.
Date: Nov 13 1939
Source: Source unknown; Cleveland Necrology File, Reel #081.
Notes: Toner: James R. (Bud), Sunday, Nov. 12, at residence, 13614 Glenside rd., beloved son of Mrs. Veronica and the late Joseph R., brother of Marie Graham. Now at Mack E. Jones Funeral Home, 1812 E. 82 st. Notice of funeral later.

Name: Wachs, Nathan
Date: Jul 23 1957
Source: Source unknown; Cleveland Necrology File, Reel #164.
Notes: Wachs, Nathan, 13829 Cedar Rd. beloved husband of Rose K.; father of Mrs. Beverly Lewis, Mrs. Edward Benis and Richard Wachs; brother of Walter L. Sally Shapero of Detroit and Elizabeth Whitney, also 7 grandchildren. Funeral services at the Deutsch Funeral Home, 1490 Crawford Rd., Tuesday, July 23, at 10 a. m. Interment Mayfield Cemetery. Family at 3905 Grenville Rd., University Heights.

Name: Walther, Frederick P.
Date: Apr 2 1950
Source: Source unknown; Cleveland Necrology File, Reel #083.
Notes: Walther, Frederick P., residence, 2892 Warrington Rd., Shaker Heights; beloved husband of Adelaide; father of Janet and Mrs. Marcia Schanzenbach, and grandfather; Friday. Friends will be received at Bennett-Sharer Funeral Home, 11212 Euclid Ave., where services will be held Monday, April 3, at 2 p. m. Masonic services Sunday evening at 8 p. m.

Name: Weidenmann, Charles
Date: May 28 1952
Source: Cleveland Press; Cleveland Necrology File, Reel #165.
Notes: Weidenmann, Charles, beloved husband of Anna (nee Yassanye), father of Fred and Mrs. Geraldine Mack, brother of John, and grandfather, passed away Monday, May 26, at the residence, Chippewa-on-the-Lake, O. Friends may call at the Busch Funeral Home, 4334 Pearl Rd., where services will be held Thursday, May 29, at 3 p. m.

Name: Zottarelli, Joseph Vincent
Date: Jan 4 1928
Source: Cemetery record; Cleveland Necrology File, Reel #088.
Notes: Zottarelli-Joseph Vincent, beloved husband of Margaret Grace (nee Huntington), beloved father of Grace, Coral, and Helena, at his residence, 3243 Bradford Road, Jan. 4. Funeral private. 1868-1928.

Name: Zucker, Joseph H.
Date: Feb 15 1954
Source: Source unknown; Cleveland Necrology File, Reel #169.
Notes: Zucker, Joseph H., beloved husband of Rebecca Weinberger Zucker father of Henry Zucker, passed away Tuesday, Feb. 9, at Charity Hospital. Brother of Jay H., Al, Rudolph, Charles and Fred. Services at 1 p. m., Thursday, Feb. 11, at Deutsch Funeral Home, 1490 Crawford Rd. Please omit flowers. Contributions may be made to Hadassah Medical Center or the Cleveland Heart Fund.

Bibliography

Books:

Allen, Florence Ellinwood – *To Do Justly* – 1965 – The Press of the Western Reserve University

Bellamy III, John Stark – *They Died Crawling* – 1995; *The Maniac in the Bushes* – 1997; *The Killer in the Attic* – 2002 – Gray and Company, Publishers

Pound, Roscoe and Felix Frankfurter (directors and editors) – *Criminal Justice in Cleveland: Reports of the Cleveland Foundation Survey of the Administration of Criminal Justice in Cleveland, Ohio* – 1922 by the Cleveland Foundation, 1968 reprinted with permission by Patterson Smith Publishing Corporation

Rose, William Ganson – *Cleveland: The Making of a City* – 1950 – The World Publishing Company

Van Tassel, David D. and John J. Grabowski – *The Encyclopedia of Cleveland History* – 1987 – Indiana University Press; *The Dictionary of Cleveland Biography* –1996 – Case Western Reserve University

Veronesi, Gene P. – *Italian Americans: And Their Communities of Cleveland* – 1977 – Cleveland State University

Documents:

In Honore Casorium…In Honor Of Those Who Have Fallen – Stories of the 142 peace officers from the Greater Cleveland area that have died "In the line of duty" – 1992 – The Greater Cleveland Peace Officer Memorial Society

Newspapers:

Cleveland Plain Dealer
Cleveland Press
Cleveland News
Cleveland Sunday News-Leader
Los Angeles Examiner
San Francisco Chronicle
Youngstown Vindicator

Cast of Characters

Allen, Florence E.	Common Pleas Judge
Allison, Roy A.	Cleveland Police Detective
Amato, Angelo	Mayfield Road Mob member, Sly-Fanner killer
Amato, Frank	Killed by Officers Fagan and Garrett
Andrews, John	Former Cleveland City Councilman
Andrews, Theresa	Café owner, widow of a Cleveland City Councilman
Angelotta, Nicholas	Mayfield Road Mob member
Angersola, Fred	Mayfield Road Mob member
Angersola, George	Mayfield Road Mob member
Angersola, John	Mayfield Road Mob member
Austerhaut, Charles	Suspect in Sprosty murder
Babka, John J.	Defense attorney
Baker, Newton D.	Cleveland Mayor
Banks, Clarence E.	Cleveland Police Detective
Barnes, Abbie	Witness to Sly-Fanner slaying
Barnes, Herbert	Witness to Sly-Fanner slaying
Barricelli, Dr. Giovanni A.	Sons of Italy commander
Barrows, Thomas C.	Manager of the Winton Garage
Barrows, W.G.	Cleveland Heights Police Chief
Barry, Edwin D.	Cleveland Safety Director
Baskin, Roland A.	Cuyahoga County Prosecutor
Bellamy II, John Stark	Cleveland author
Bender, George H.	State Senator
Benigno, Anthony	Brother of Dominic
Benigno, Dominic	Mayfield Road Mob leader, Sly-Fanner killer
Benigno, Florence	Daughter of Dominic Benigno
Benigno, Mary	Wife of Dominic Benigno
Benigno, Thomas	Brother of Dominic
Benigno, Tina	Daughter of Dominic Benigno
Bennett, George	Ohio Penitentiary guard
Bennis, John	Accomplice of Amato & Rosalina
Bernon, Maurice	Common Pleas Judge, Defense Attorney

Bettman, Alfred	Involved in Cleveland Crime Survey
Bianca, Robert	Boxer "Bobby White" murdered by DePalma
Blaich, Benjamin	Witness to Sly-Fanner slaying
Blaich, Elizabeth	Witness to Sly-Fanner slaying
Blaich, Henry J.	Witness to Sly-Fanner slaying
Blaich, Mary	Witness to Sly-Fanner slaying
Blossom, Dudley	Cleveland Welfare Director
Bolles. Arthur J.	Deputy at County Jail
Boyd, William	Defense Attorney
Brandt, Gretchen	Crime Spree Murder Victim
Brenner, William	Cleveland Police Detective
Brickel, Charlie	Son of Mary Brickel
Brickel, Mary	Mother of Eva Kaber
Brown, Alexander C.	Cleveland Chamber of Commerce (CK)
Budd, Archie	Benigno juror who suffered stroke
Buonpane, Blasé	Defense Attorney
Burton, Theodore E.	US Senator and Congressman from Ohio
Cala, Salvatore	Murdered Dan Kaber
Caley, Fred H.	Secretary Cleveland Automobile Club
Callahan, Elmer	Ohio Penitentiary guard
Callan, Martin	Cleveland Vice Squad Officer
Carter, Charles N.	Justice of the Peace
Cartwright, Alfred A.	Defense Attorney
Cassidy, Charles	Brother of James Cassidy
Cassidy, James T.	Chief Assistant County Prosecutor
Cavolo, Charles	Cleveland Police Detective – Sergeant & Lieutenant
Celebreeze, Frank D.	Assistant County Prosecutor
Chance, A.R.	Losteiner gang victim
Chapel, William T.	Owner of Youngstown home where Hunt hid
Christian, George	US Presidential Secretary to Harding
Cline, John A.	Defense attorney
Cody, Cornelius W.	Cleveland Police Detective Inspector
Colavito, Emma	Kaber murder figure ratted out by DePalma

Coletto, Agnes	Wife of John
Coletto, Anthony	Brother of Charles
Coletto, Charles	Mayfield Road Mob member
Coletto, John	Brother of Charles
Connell, James C.	Chief Assistant County Prosecutor
Connell, Thomas F.	Father of James Connell
Conroy, Edward	Cleveland Police Detective
Conton, William	Convicted in murder of Sprosty
Corrigan, William J.	Defense Attorney
Corso, John	Cleveland Police Black Hand Squad
Costello, Timothy J.	Cleveland Police Detective Captain
Cox, James M.	Ohio Governor
Crabbe, Charles C.	Ohio Attorney General
Cull, Dan B.	Judge
Cullitan, Frank T.	Cuyahoga County Prosecutor
Davis, Harry L.	Cleveland Mayor and Ohio Governor
Davis, Homer	Cleveland Heights Police Sergeant
Day, Arthur H.	Candidate for county prosecutor
Day, Frank S.	Common Pleas Judge and defense attorney
Day, William R.	Supreme Court Associate Justice
DeMarco, Dominic	Cousin of Dominic Lonardo
Dembe, Joseph	Assistant County Prosecutor
Dempsey, John P.	Municipal Chief Justice
DeWoody, Charles	Cleveland Association for Criminal Justice official
DePalma, Biago "Bundy"	Mayfield Road Mob member
DiSalle, Michael V.	Governor of Ohio
Diskowski, Otto	Cleveland Police Detective
Doerfler, Samuel	County Prosecutor, Defense Attorney
Dombey, Charles M.	Chief Deputy at County Jail
Donahey, Vic	Governor of Ohio
Doran, James W.	Cuyahoga County Detective
Duffy, Thomas	Cleveland Police Lieutenant
Dryer, Ralph	Cleveland Police Officer
Dwyer, Martin	Suspect in Sly-Fanner murders
Effinger, George	Cleveland Police Officer (slain)
Fagan, Thomas	Cleveland Police Officer

Hendricks, Patrick	East Cleveland Police Captain
Hirstius, A.J. "Gus"	Cuyahoga County Sheriff, Republican Party Big Wig
Hoover, Herbert	President of the United States
Hopkins, William R.	Cleveland City Manager
Hopple, Elden J.	Assistant County Prosecutor, Defense attorney
Horrigan, Martin	Cleveland Police Captain
Houser, Joseph	Cleveland Police Lieutenant – head of vice squad
Howells, George A.	Police Judge
Hubbell, Charles	Auto theft victim of Milazzo/Pettinatto
Hubbs, George C.	Chicago confidence man
Hughes, Charles Evans	US Secretary of State
Hunt, Robert "Bobby"	Killer of Officer Sprosty
Ihlenfeld, Arthur	Accused killer of Foote and Wolfe
Jacobs, Joseph	Cleveland Police Detective
Jacobs, P.A.	Cuyahoga County Coroner
Jaworski, Paul	Cop killer
Jewell, Henry W.	Judge
Johnson, Albert	Losteiner gang member
Johnson, Tom L.	Cleveland Mayor
Joyce, John W.	Cleveland Irish Gangster
Kaber, Dan	Murder victim
Kaber, Eva	Wife of Dan Kaber (murderess)
Kaber, Moses	Father of Dan Kaber
Kagy, Harold	Murder victim
Kellogg, Frank	US Secretary of State
Kelly, Father	Ohio Penitentiary Chaplin
Kennedy, Thomas M.	Common Pleas Judge
Kilbane, Anne	Wife of boxer Johnny Kilbane
Kilbane, Johnny	Cleveland boxing champ
Koestle, George	Cleveland Police Bertillon Expert
Kohler, Frederick	Cleveland Police Chief, Mayor and County Sheriff
Komer, Louis "Toledo Kid"	Sly-Fanner killer
Komer, Mary	Mother of Louis Komer
Koran, Frank J.	Cleveland Police Officer (slain)

McGannon, Dr. A.C.	Brother of Judge McGannon
McGannon, Ann	Wife of Judge William McGannon
McGannon, John	Brother of Judge William McGannon
McGannon, Mary	Mother of Judge William McGannon
McGannon, William	Cleveland Judge charged with Kagy murder
McGonigal, William	Cleveland Vice Squad Officer
McKenna, Joseph	US Supreme Cou
Merrick, Frank J.	Assistant County Prosecutor rt Justice
Meals, Walter D.	Defense Attorney, CAC counsel
Mesker, William R.	Bank payroll clerk
Mettel, Max C.	Cleveland Police Detective
Meyer, Maurice J.	Assistant County Prosecutor
Milano, Frank	Mayfield Road Mob Leader
Milazzo, Frank	Mayfield Road Mob member
Miller, Ray T.	Cuyahoga County Prosecutor, Cleveland Mayor
Moffet, Harley H.	Cleveland Police Sergeant
Mooney, Phillip	Cleveland Police Detective
Moore, E.J.	Official of W.W. Sly Mfg Co
Morley, Raymond	Director of Cleveland Foundation
Morton, "Big Jim"	Cleveland Bank Robber
Motto, Frank	Mayfield Road Mob member, Sly-Fanner killer
Motto, Joseph	Brother of Frank Motto
Motto, Mary	Mother of Frank Motto
Moylan, David J.	Police Judge
Mulligan, Patrick J.	Defense attorney, former Assistant County Prosecutor
Murphy, Stephen	Cleveland Police Inspector
Myeski, Steve	Condemned Ohio Penitentiary prisoner
Neely, Mary	Perjurer in McGannon trial
Ness, Eliot	Cleveland Safety Director
Nord, Herman J.	Defense Attorney
Obregon, Alvaro	Mexican President
Page, Anthony "Tony"	Cleveland Police Detective
Pani, Albert	Mexican Minister of State
Parsons, Harold E.	Assistant County Prosecutor

Rowlands, John	Cleveland Police Inspector
Rutledge, Rev. John	Ohio Superintendent of Pardons & Paroles
Sancetta, James	Mayfield Road Mob member
Santoro, Antoinette	Victim of police shooting
Scafide, Dominic	Associate of Benigno
Scavone, Thomas W.	State informant in Serra auto theft ring
Schoemaker, Dr. A.J.	Doctor who pronounced Motto dead
Seltzer, Louis B.	Cleveland Press reporter
Serra, Angelo	Leader of Serra auto theft ring
Shannon, Frank	Suspect in Sprosty murder
Sly, Marie	Wife of Wilfred Sly
Sly, Mary A.	Mother of Wilfred Sly
Sly, Maude (Hoffman)	Sister of Wilfred Sly
Sly, Wilfred C.	Victim in Sly-Fanner murders
Sly, William W.	Father of Wilfred Sly, founder of the WW Sly Mfg Co.
Smith, Albert	Captain of the *Monterey*
Smith, Edgar H.	Suburban Police officer
Smith, Frank O.	Cleveland Police Captain
Smith, Frank W.	Cleveland Police Chief
Smith, Marian	Witness to Sprosty murder
Smith, Neil J.	Son of Frank W. Smith
Smith, Perry	Suburban Police officer
Smith, William	Ohio Penitentiary escapee
Sospirato, Dominic	Cousin of Angelo Lonardo
Soukup, Albert	Cleveland Police Detective
Southwell, George	Head of Dry Maintenance League
Sprosty, Anton B.	Cleveland Safety Director
Sprosty, Cecelia	Wife of Elmer
Sprosty, Elmer	Cleveland Police Officer (slain)
Sprosty, Frank D.	Cleveland Police Captain, father of Elmer
Stannard, Charles B.	Cuyahoga County Sheriff
Stanton, Edward C.	Cuyahoga County Prosecutor 1920-1929
Stanton, Oscar	Automobile mechanic who was with DePalma
Stephens, William D.	Governor of California
Sterling, Charles N.	Cleveland Police Detective Inspector

Index

Note to reader, the Index does not include names or places from the Chapter End Notes; or names and places appearing only in Chapter 24: A Few Selected Biographies. (d) Death notice. (p) Photograph.

staff members, 16-18
trip West for Purpura, 105-108, 110
Stanton, Oscar, 284
Statler Hotel, 32
Stephens, William D., 107
Sterling, Charles N., 201(p), 243, 291,
  336(d)
  Benigno capture, 118, 226, 228
  biography, 326-26
  early years, 7, 47, 71, 93
  heart attack, 123, 125
  Komer arrest, 117, 118, 123
  Motto arraignment and trial, 115,
    118, 122, 125, 129, 130, 132
  Purpura interrogation, 113, 115, 116,
    117, 129
  Purpura trial, 143, 145
  retirement, 243
  Sly-Fanner investigation, 93, 95-98,
    116-18
  trip West for Purpura, 105-106, 107,
    109, 110
Stoners Restaurant, 32, 182
Sullivan, John J., 114, 129, 252,
  336-37(d)
Summerell, George, 155, 159
Svia, Angela, 103-104
Sweeney, Martin L., 54-55, 57

Talbot, C.V., 185
Taylor, Orville, 8, 9
Thirteenth Precinct, 31
Thobaben, Edward J., 174, 175, 176,
  337(d)
Thomas, Preston E., 60, 181, 220(p),
  266
Thompson, Amos Burt, 41
Tilocco, Salvatore, 213(p), 267, 270,
  271-72
Todaro, Salvatore, 287, 318
Toner, James, 47, 337(d)
Toohey, Maude, 87

Ukrainian-American Banking
  Company, 189
Union Station (Depot), 39, 112, 149,
  172, 235
Union Trust Company (Bank), 128,
  139
United States State Department, 160,
  161, 162, 163, 273, 274
United States Supreme Court, 180-81,
  250, 252, 259, 295
University of Chicago, 122

Vail, William, 162
Vasbinder, John, 279
Veneroso, Louis, 51
Veranti, Maria, 285
Vickery, Willis, 230, 252
Villa, Pancho, 156

W.S. Tyler Company, 17
W.W. Sly Mfg. Co., 1-2, 85, 91, 92, 108,
  118, 227, 246
Wachs, Nathan, 45, 55, 56, 337(d)
Walker Manufacturing Company., 6
Walker, Elmer, 89-90
Walker, Irene, 88, 142-43, 223
Wallace, George, 240
Walsh, James, 44, 47-48, 50-52, 54, 55,
  57-59, 169, 222
Walter, Otto, 87
Walther, Frederick P., 54, 56-57, 58-59,
  247, 337(d)
Wanamaker, R.M., 249
Watkins, James, 51
Watson, Kenneth R., 111, 168
Weidenmann, Charles, 124, 149,
  338(d)
Weller, Benjamin D., 96, 185
West Cleveland Bank, 93, 319
West 53rd Street Precinct, 116
West Park Cemetery, 47